The Best of the Best
in contemporary Praise & Worship

Compiled and Edited by Rev. Mike Zehnder
Fellowship Publications
Phoenix, Arizona 85076

THE OTHER SONG BOOK 2

Another best seller from the people who brought you
The Other Song Book - more than 400,000 sold.

The Best of the Best
The Other Songbook 2

Compiled and Edited by Rev. Michael Zehnder
Assistant: Wayne Stoltz
Music Engraving and New Arrangements: Bill Wolaver, David Thibodeaux and the staff of Living Stone Music Co.
Cover Design: Genesis One Design, 6019 California Ave. S.W., Seattle, WA 98136, www.genesisone.com

Pew Edition (6X9 Perfect Bound)　　　　ISBN 1-891062-00-X
Lead Line Edition (6X9 Spiral Bound)　　ISBN 1-891062-03-4
Accompaniment Edition (9X12 Spiral)　　ISBN 1-891062-01-8
Lyrics Presentation CD　　　　　　　　　ISBN 1-891062-02-6
(Other related products under development. See web site for up-to-date information and releases - www.thefellowship.com)

Copyright © 2000 Fellowship Publications. All Rights Reserved.
Fellowship Ministries, P.O. Box 51510, Phoenix, AZ 85076
Phone 480-838-8500　FAX 480-838-9187　www.thefellowship.com

Second Edition. Printed in The United States of America.

All rights reserved. No part of this publication may be produced, stored in a retrieval system, or transmitted, in any form or by any means, electronic, mechanical, photocopying, recording, or otherwise, without the prior written permission of the publisher and/or the copyright holder indicated on each song.

The Publisher gratefully acknowledges permission received from other publishers, organizations and individuals to print text and music contained in this book. Should there be any error in acknowledgments, we would be happy to make corrections at the earliest opportunity.

Possession of a CCLI license does not grant the copying of this music for any and every purpose. Please be aware of what the privileges the license gives as well as what it does not and to which music contained herein it may apply. For more information contact CCLI at 1-800-234-2446 or view their web site at www.ccli.com. The 253+ songwriters and copyright holders of this book are grateful for your integrity in this matter, motivated by love:

"Each of you should look not only to your own interests,
but also to the interests of others." Philippians 2:4

> *"In the last days I will pour out my Spirit on all people.*
> *Your sons and daughters will prophesy..."* Acts 2:17 (Joel 2:28)

An outpouring of prophetic song (songs that proclaim God's Word) was especially strong during the Reformation. Yet compared with today it seems but a trickle. God appears to be "raining down songs" on His Church. Over 85,000 songs are listed by the Christian Copyright Licensing Co., a veritable spiritual fire hydrant of "new song." Praise God for His creating and refining fire!

No doubt you're anxious to sing these wonderful songs, but please take a moment to investigate the "Biblical References" index. So much Scripture is either quoted or obliquely referenced! After completing the indexes it was astounding to note that **every single book of the Bible was included!** The Biblical worship book, Psalms, is particularly quoted in this collection, witnessing to the changelessness of the Lord. A fascinating Bible study could be developed just by observing what God is saying from Scripture through these songs to His Church. Note which passages are quoted most frequently. Are there certain things God wants to emphasize to His bride, the Church, today? Since the Word is living, active, authoritative, inerrant and God is never done reforming and sanctifying His Church, this collection is useful not only for singing but also for devotion and prayer. Worship planners will also find other helpful indexes listed by topic, key and tempo (*see Introduction to the Indexes*).

As for name, **"The Best of the Best"** what better title could be given such a collection? The songs included represent the best in Christian theology (Christocentric, cross-centered, grace-oriented), the best in contemporary Christian music, the best in good keys for voice, guitar, and keyboard, the best in singable/memorable tunes for congregational singing, the best expressions of intimate, heart-felt praise from 54 very diverse copyright holders around the world, the best from seasoned composers, the best from previously unpublished composers, the best in what's brand new and the best in what's tried and true.

Special thanks to Dave Anderson, president of Fellowship Ministries, for envisioning this project and entrusting it to me. Thank you Dave, for commissioning a book to bless the bride of Jesus!

In any compilation, even a book this large, some tough decisions have to be made. How to choose when the field is so huge? Constant prayer breathed up to the throne room during this process was based on Jesus' revelation in John 4:23-24. "Dear Jesus, please break through my sinful flesh with Your Holy Spirit and enable me to select the very songs that will invite and assist Your people to worship you in spirit and in truth."

May Jesus Christ be high and lifted up! Blessed be His Name!

Rev. Michael Zehnder
Compiler and Editor

A Broken Spirit

A broken Spirit... and a contrite heart... you will not despise. (Psalm 51:17)

Don Harris and Martin J. Nystrom

♩ = 52

CHORUS

A broken spirit and a contrite heart, You will not despise, You will not despise; You desire truth in the inward parts, a broken spirit and a contrite heart.

VERSE

Lord, my heart is prone to wander, prone to leave the God I love; Here's my heart, Lord, take and seal it, seal it for your courts above. A broken

©1993 Integrity's Hosanna! Music, c/o Integrity Music, Inc., 1000 Cody Road, Mobile, AL 36695-3425.
All Rights Reserved. International Copyright Secured. Used by Permission.

But you are a shield around me, O Lord; you bestow glory on me and lift up my head. (Psalm 3:3)

A Shield About Me

Donn Thomas and Charles Williams

VERSE

Thou, O Lord, are a shield about me. You're my glory. You're the lifter of my head.

CHORUS

Hallelujah, hallelujah, hallelujah, You're the lifter of my head.

© Copyright 1980 Word Music, Inc. (ASCAP) and Spoone Music (Admin. by Word Music, Inc.) (ASCAP).
All Rights Reserved. International Copyright Secured. Used by Permission.

3 A Simple Word of Grace

Grace and peace be yours in abundance through the knowledge of God and of Jesus our Lord. (2 Peter 1:2)

Brad and Donna Hoefs
Brad Hoefs

Moderately ♩ = 85

1. A simple word of grace is all I need, flowing from a cross, a cross for me. A gentle word of love is all I need, flowing from a cross, a

2. A simple word of hope is all I need, flowing from Your love, Your love for me. A gentle word of peace is all I need, flowing from Your love, Your

3. Teach me, Lord, to share Your simple grace, Your love for me. Teach me, Lord, to live as You have lived, gently flowing from Your

cross for me. Jesus, You have given me all of Your
love for me.
love for me.

grace so tenderly. I lift my hands and praise Your name. Jesus, You have given me all of Your

love on Calvary. I lift my heart into Your

hands.

1.2. G² 3. G
2. A

© Copyright 1996 Brad and Donna Hoefs, Wings of Grace, Inc.
All Rights Reserved. Used by Permission.

I am the Root and Offspring of David, and the bright Morning Star. (Revelation 22:16)

All Hail, King Jesus

Dave Moody

VERSE: All hail, King Jesus, All hail, Emmanuel: King of kings, Lord of lords, Bright Morning Star. And through-

CHORUS: out eternity I'm going to praise Him, And forevermore I will reign with Him.

© Copyright 1974 Dayspring Music, Inc. (BMI).
All Rights Reserved. Made In The U.S.A. International Copyright Secured. Used by Permission.

All Heaven Declares

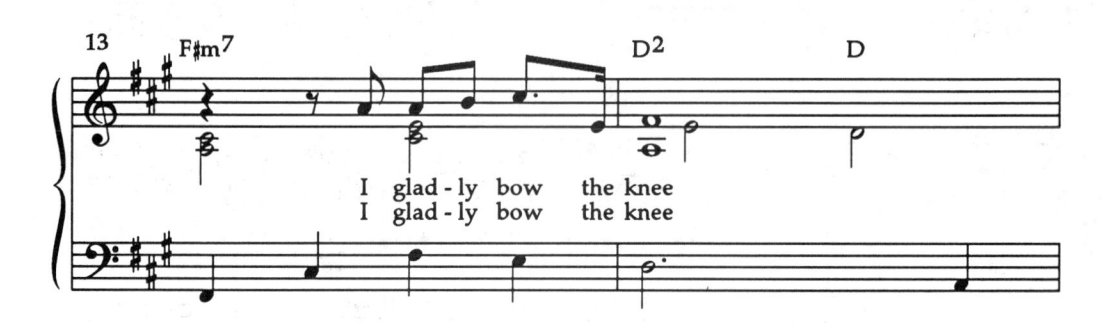

Salvation belongs to our God, who sits on the throne, and to the Lamb. (Revelation 7:10)

Noel and Tricia Richards

Majestically

1. All heav'n declares the glory of the risen Lord. Who can compare with the beauty of the Lord? Forever He will be the Lamb upon the throne. I gladly bow the knee and worship Him alone.

2. I will proclaim the glory of the risen Lord, who once was slain to reconcile man to God. Forever You will be the Lamb upon the throne. I gladly bow the knee and worship You alone.

© Copyright 1987 Kingsway's Thankyou Music/Admin. in North America by EMI Christian Music Publishing.
All Rights Reserved. Used by Permission.

Great and marvelous are your deeds, Lord God Almighty. (Revelation 15:3)

Almighty

Wayne Watson

♩ = 108

CHORUS

Al-might-y, most ho-ly God, faith-ful through the ag - es; Al-might-y, most ho-ly Lord, glo-ri-ous, Al-might-y God. *Fine*

VERSE
1. The beasts of the field, the birds of the air, are si-lent to call out Your name; The earth has no voice, and I have no choice but to mag-ni-fy God un-a-shamed. Let the rocks be kept si-lent for one more day; Let the whole world sing out, let the peo-ple say.

2. Well, time march-es on, with the in-no-cence gone, and a dark-ness has cov-ered the earth; But His Spir-it dwells, He speaks, "it is well," and the hope-less still of-fered new birth. He will break the leash of death, it will have no sting; Let the pris-'ner go free, join the dance and sing.

D.C. al Fine

© Copyright 1990 Word Music, Inc. (ASCAP), 65 Music Square West, Nashville, TN 37203/
Material Music (Admin. by Word Music, Inc.) (ASCAP), 65 Music Square West, Nashville, TN 37203.
All Rights Reserved. Made in the U.S.A. International Copyright Secured. Used by Permission.

7 All Over Again

Grace to all who love our Lord Jesus Christ with an undying love. (Ephesians 6:24)

Mark and Charista Zehnder

Jesus, come, oh come into this place. Jesus, come, I want to see Your face.

Jesus, come, I long for Your embrace. I want to fall in love with You all over again.

CHORUS

All over again,

© Copyright 1996 Mark Zehnder Publishing. All Rights Reserved. Used by Permission.

19
Eb/F (D/E) F (E) Bb2 (A2)
I give You my praise,
21
Bb/D (A/C#) Eb2 (D2)
all o - ver a - gain
23
Eb/F (D/E) F (E) Bb2 (A2)
for all of my days.
25
Bb/D (A/C#) Eb2 (D2)
All o - ver a - gain,
27
Eb/F (D/E) F (E) Bb (A) F/A (E/G#)
with my heart and hands I
29
Gm (F#m) Gm/F (F#m/E) Eb (D) Cm7 (Bm7)
raise to say I love You, Lord,
31
Eb/F (D/E) F (E) 1. Bb (A) Eb/Bb (D/A) F/Bb (E/A)
all o - ver a - gain.
34
2. Bb (A) Bb2/D (A2/C#)
gain. To say I
36
Eb (D) Cm7 (Bm7) Eb/F (D/E) F (E)
love You, Lord, all o - ver a -
38
Bb (A) Eb2/Bb (D/A) Bb (A)
gain.

You are worthy... to receive glory and honor and power. (Revelation 4:11)

All Honor

Chris Falson

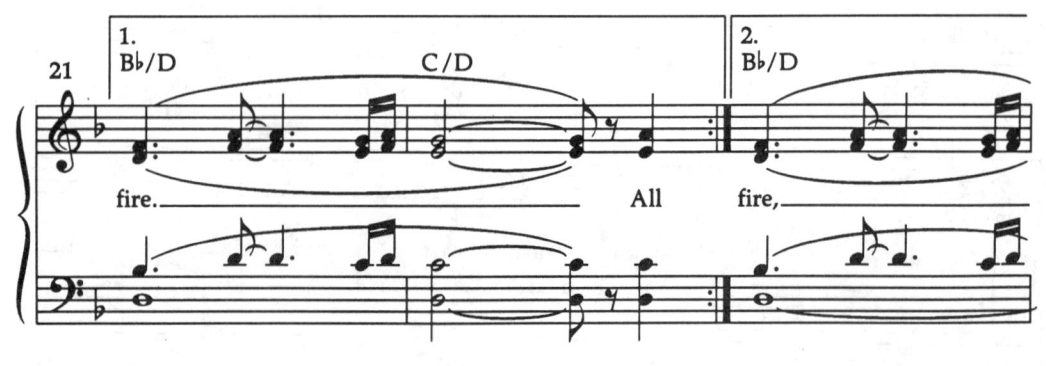

♩ = 58 **VERSE**

All hon-or, all glo-ry, all pow-er to You; all hon-or, all glo-ry, all pow-er to You. Ho-ly

CHORUS

Fa-ther, we wor-ship You, pre-cious Je-sus, our Sav-ior; Ho-ly Spir-it, we wait on You, Ho-ly Spir-it, we wait on You, Ho-ly Spir-it, we wait on You for fire, for fire. All fire,

© Copyright 1990 Maranatha Praise, Inc. (Administered by The Copyright Company, Nashville, TN).
All Rights Reserved. International Copyright Secured. Used by Permission. www.maranathamusic.com

"**Music** is a *gift* and largess of **God**, not a gift of men.

Music drives away the devil and makes people **happy**; it induces one to forget all wrath, unchastity, arrogance, and other vices. After theology I accord to music the **highest** place and the greatest honor.

We note that **David** and all the **saints** used verse, rhymes and songs to express their *godly* thoughts."

Martin Luther, 1541

[This quotation also appears in the pew and lead line editions next to song #13]

For Thou, Lord, art high above all the earth; Thou art exalted far above all gods. (Psalm 97:9)

Above All

Lenny LeBlanc and Paul Baloche

Slow four ♩ = 62

VERSE

A-bove all powers, a-bove all kings, a-bove all nature and all created things; a-bove all wisdom and all the ways of man, You were here before the world began.

A-bove all kingdoms, a-bove all thrones, a-bove all wonders the world has ev-er known; a-bove all wealth and treasures of the earth, there's no way to meas-ure what You're worth.

© Copyright 1999 Integrity's Hosanna! Music/ASCAP and LenSongs Publishing/ASCAP
c/o Integrity Music, Inc., 1000 Cody Road, Mobile, AL 36695-3425.
All Rights Reserved. International Copyright Secured. Used by Permission.

"Therefore God exalted him to the highest place and gave him the name that is above every name, that at the name of Jesus every knee should bow, in heaven and on earth and under the earth, and every tongue confess that Jesus Christ is Lord, to the glory of God the Father."

Philippians 2:9-11

Ancient of Days

His dominion... will not pass away... and his kingdom... will never be destroyed. (Daniel 7:14)

Gary Sadler and Jamie Harvill

With an "island" feel ♩ = 92

VERSE

Bless-ing and hon-or, glo-ry and pow-er be un-to the An-cient of Days; from ev-'ry na-tion, all of cre-a-tion bow be-fore the An-cient of Days.

CHORUS

Ev-'ry tongue in heav-en and earth shall de-clare Your glo-ry, ev-'ry knee shall bow at Your throne in wor-ship; You will be ex-alt-ed, O God, and Your king-dom shall not pass a-way, O An-cient of Days.

3rd time to Coda

1. Dsus D Dsus
2. Dsus D Dsus Your

© Copyright 1992 Integrity's Hosanna! Music/Integrity's Praise! Music
c/o Integrity Music, Inc., 1000 Cody Road, Mobile, AL 36695-3425.
All Rights Reserved. International Copyright Secured. Used by Permission.

"In my vision at night I looked, and there before me was one like a son of man, coming with the clouds of heaven. He approached the **Ancient** of **Days** and was led into his presence. He was given authority, glory and sovereign power; **all peoples**, nations and men of every language **worshiped him**. His dominion is an everlasting dominion that will not pass away, and **his kingdom** is one that **will never** be **destroyed**."

Daniel 7:13-14

But God demonstrated his own love toward us, in that while we were yet sinners, Christ died for us. (Romans 5:8)

11 Amazing Love

Graham Kendrick

♩ = 132 **VERSE**

1. My Lord, what love is this that pays so dearly; That I, the guilty one may go free.
2. And so they watched Him die, despised, rejected; But O the blood He shed flowed for me.
3. And now this love of Christ shall flow like rivers; Come wash your guilt away, live again.

CHORUS

A-mazing love, O what sacrifice, the Son of God, giv'n for me; My debt He pays and my death He dies, that I might live, that I might live.

© Copyright 1989 Make Way Music (adm. by Music Services in the Western Hemisphere) (ASCAP).
All Rights Reserved. Used by Permission.

As the Deer

As the deer pants for streams of water, so my soul pants for you, O God. (Psalm 42:1)

Martin Nystrom

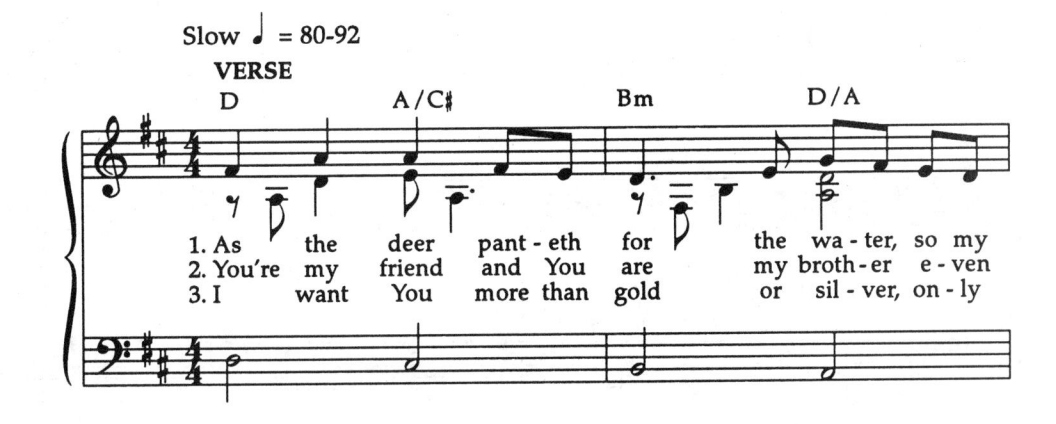

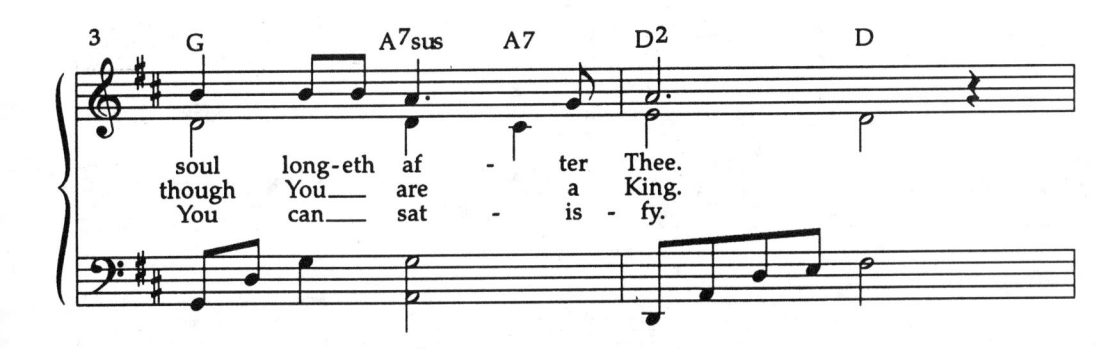

Slow ♩ = 80-92

VERSE

1. As the deer pant-eth for the wa-ter, so my soul long-eth af-ter Thee.
2. You're my friend and You are my broth-er e-ven though You are a King.
3. I want You more than gold or sil-ver, on-ly You can sat-is-fy.

You a-lone are my heart's de-sire, and I long to wor-ship Thee.
I love You more than an-y oth-er, so much more than an-y-thing.
You a-lone are the real joy-giv-er and the ap-ple of my eye.

CHORUS

You a-lone are my strength, my shield; to You a-lone may my spir-it yield. You a-lone are my heart's de-sire and I long to wor-ship Thee.

© Copyright 1984 Maranatha Praise, Inc. (Administered by The Copyright Company, Nashville, TN).
All Rights Reserved. International Copyright Secured. Used by Permission. www.maranathamusic.com

I can do everything through him who gives me strength. (Philippians 4:13)

13 All the Power You Need

Russell Fragar

♩ = 132

VERSE

My God can never fail. He's been proved time and again; trust Him and see He's got all the pow'r you need. He's never early, never late. It takes courage, it takes faith; trust Him and see He's got all the pow'r you need.

CHORUS

He saves, forgives, and heals, takes back what the Devil steals. My debt's been paid in full, and ev'ry day He does miracles.

© Copyright 1996 Russell Fragar/Hillsongs Australia (adm. in U.S. and Canada by Integrity's Hosanna! Music)
c/o Integrity Music, Inc., 1000 Cody Road, Mobile, AL 36695-3425.
All Rights Reserved. International Copyright Secured. Used by Permission.

VERSE
25
G7
I got dreams, turn them in-to plans too big for
28
3rd time to Coda
Em
hu-man hands; trust Him and see He's got
30
C
D7
G7
all the pow'r you need.
33
BRIDGE
G
He's real, He's real; faith's a lot strong-er than
36
what you feel. He's real, He's real;
39
D7(♯5)
D.S. al CODA
I'm be-liev-ing for mir-a-cles.
CODA
41
Em
C
D7
trust Him and see He's got all the pow'r you need.
43
G7
45
Em
C
D7
Trust Him and see He's got all the pow'r you need.
47
G7

14 Arms of Love

The eternal God is your refuge, and underneath are the everlasting arms. (Deut. 33:27)

Craig Musseau

(sing cue 2nd time only)

VERSE
I sing a simple song of love to my Savior, to my Jesus.

I'm grateful for the things You've done, my loving Savior, oh, precious Jesus.

𝄋 My heart is glad that You've called me Your own.

There's no place I'd rather be than in Your

𝄋𝄋 **CHORUS**
arms of love, in Your arms

© Copyright 1991 Mercy/Vineyard Publishing (ASCAP).
All Rights Reserved. Used by Permission.

"How priceless is your

       unfailing love!

Both high and low among men find refuge in the

   shadow of your **wings.**

They feast on the abundance of your house;

you give them drink from your river of delights.

For with you is the **fountain** of **life;**

in your light we see light."

                      Psalm 36:7-9

For as the heavens are high above the earth, so great is his mercy toward those who fear him. (Psalm 103:11)

15 As High As the Heavens

Don Harris and Martin J. Nystrom

♩ = 132

CHORUS

As high as the heav-ens are a-bove the earth,— so great is the Fa-ther's love;— As far as the east is from— the west,— so far has He tak-en our sin— from— us.

VERSE

For His an-ger lasts— on-ly a mo-ment, but His fa-vor lasts— for a life-time; Weep-ing may— re-main— for a night but re-joic-ing comes,— it comes in the morn-ing.

D.C. al Fine

© Copyright 1993 Integrity's Hosanna! Music, c/o Integrity Music, Inc., 1000 Cody Road, Mobile, AL 36695-3425.
All Rights Reserved. International Copyright Secured. Used by Permission.

Greater love has no one than this, that he lay down his life for his friends. (John 15:13)

16 As I Look into Your Eyes

Richard Oddie and John Nolan

Worshipfully ♩ = 120

VERSE
1. Je - sus, I look up - on Your hands, the nail scars in Your feet, then I know I can look in - to Your eyes.
2. Fa - ther, the great - est gift of love was to send Your Son to die for us. He was the per - fect sac - ri - fice.

CHORUS
Draw me clos - er to Your heart; take me deep - er in Your love to the se - cret place of God. You're wor - thy of the high - est praise. Let Your glo - ry fill this place when I see You face to face, as I look in - to Your eyes.

© Copyright 1994 Richard Oddie and John Nolan, Outreach Music/Wholeheart Music.
All Rights Reserved. Used by Permission.

17 At the Cross

God made you alive with Christ. He forgave us all our sins, having canceled the written code...he took it away, nailing it to a cross. (Colossians 2:13-14)

Randy Butler and Terry Butler

♩ = 104-109

Lyrics:
I know a place, a wonderful place where accused and condemned find mercy and grace, where the wrongs we have done and the

© Copyright 1993 Mercy/Vineyard Publishing (ASCAP).
All Rights Reserved. Used by Permission.

18 A/B E
wrongs done to us were
20 Bm11
nailed there with Him,
Last time -Ritard
22 A/B E Fine
there on the cross.
24 E2 D CHORUS
At the cross,
26 A2/C♯ D/G
He (You) died for our sin.
28 E E2 D
At the cross,
3rd time to Coda
30 A2/C♯ D/G
He (You) gave us life again.
1. 2. D.S. al CODA
32 E E E2
At the cross
CODA
35 D/G
gave us life again.
37 E open section-ad lib D.S.S. al Fine

Be exalted, O God, above the heavens; let your glory be over all the earth. (Psalm 57:5)

18 Be Exalted, O God

Brent Chambers

I will give thanks to Thee, O Lord, among the people. I will sing praises to Thee among the nations. For Thy steadfast love is great, is great to the heavens; And Thy faithfulness, Thy faithfulness to the clouds.

CHORUS

Be exalted, O God, above the heavens; Let Thy glory be

© Copyright 1977 and this arr. © 1997 Scripture In Song (a div. of Integrity Music, Inc.) ASCAP, c/o Integrity Music, Inc., 1000 Cody Road, Mobile, AL 36695-3425.
All Rights Reserved. International Copyright Secured. Used by Permission.

Affirmation of Faith

The Apostles' Creed

I believe in God,

the Father Almighty,
Maker of heaven and earth.

And in Jesus Christ,

his only Son, our Lord,

Who was conceived by the Holy Spirit,
born of the virgin Mary,
suffered under Pontius Pilate,
was crucified, died and was buried.
He descended into hell.
The third day he rose again from the dead.
He ascended into heaven
And sits at the right hand of God the Father Almighty.
From thence he will come to judge the living and the dead.

I believe in the Holy Spirit,

the holy Christian Church,*
the communion of saints,
the forgiveness of sins,
the resurrection of the body,
and the life everlasting. Amen.

*The ancient text reads: the holy catholic [universal] Church

[The Apostles' Creed also appears in the pew and lead line editions next to song #225]

My Father will love him, and we will come to him and make our home with him. (John 14:23)

19 Be My Home

Handt Hanson and Paul Murakami

Medium ♩ = 90-108

Be my Savior; be my heart's delight. Be my vision; be my guiding light.

Storms may press against me, threaten to prevail. Be my refuge; be my shelter from the storm. Be my love that keeps me warm. Be my Savior; be my light. Be my home.

© Copyright 1996 Prince of Peace Publishing, Changing Church, Inc.
All Rights Reserved. Used by Permission.

Set your minds on things above, not on earthly things. (Colossians 3:2)

20 Be Thou My Vision

Ancient Irish Hymn — Irish Folk Melody

Capo 1 (D)

Medium ♩ = 76-96

1. Be Thou my Vision, O Lord of my heart;
   Naught be all else to me, save that Thou art—
   Thou my best thought, by day or by night,
   Waking or sleeping, Thy presence my light.

2. Be Thou my Wisdom, and Thou my true Word;
   I ever with Thee and Thou with me, Lord;
   Thou my great Father, I Thy true son,
   Thou in me dwelling, and I with Thee one.

3. Riches I heed not, nor man's empty praise,
   Thou mine inheritance, now and always;
   Thou and Thou only, first in my heart,
   High King of heaven, my Treasure Thou art.

4. High King of heaven, my victory won,
   May I reach heaven's joys, O bright heaven's Sun!
   Heart of my own heart, whatever befall,
   Still be my Vision, O Ruler of all.

© Copyright 1997 Maranatha! Music (Administered by The Copyright Company, Nashville, TN).
All Rights Reserved. International Copyright Secured. Used by Permission. www.maranathamusic.com

---

"Direct me in the path of your commands, for there I find delight. Turn my heart toward your statutes and not toward selfish gain. Turn my eyes away from worthless things; preserve my life according to your word."

Psalm 119:35-37

Satisfy us in the morning with your unfailing love that we may sing for joy and be glad all our days. (Psalm 90:14)

21 Beautiful Savior
(All My Days)

Capo 3 (D)

Stuart Townend

Steadily ♩. = 66

Keyboard: Dm7 / Eb2
Guitar: (Bm7) / (C2)

1. All my days I will
2. I will trust in the
3. long to be where the

F / Bb/D / Eb / Bb
(G) / (G/B) / (C) / (G)

sing this song of glad - ness,
cross of my Re - deem - er;
praise is nev - er end - ing,

Dm7 / Eb2
(Bm7) / (C2)

give my praise to the
I will sing of the
yearn to dwell where the

F / Bb/D / Eb
(G) / (G/B) / (C)

Foun - tain of de - lights; for
blood that nev - er fails, of
glo - ry nev - er fades, where

Cm7 / Ebmaj7 / F
(Am7) / (Cmaj7) / (G)

in my help - less - ness You
sins for - giv - en, of
count - less wor - ship - ers will

Eb / Bb/D / F
(C) / (G/B) / (G)

heard my cry,
con - science cleansed, and
share one song, and

Cm7 / Ebmaj7 / Dm7
(Am7) / (Cmaj7) / (Bm7)

waves of mer - cy poured down on my
death de - feat - ed and life with - out
cries of "wor - thy" will hon - or the

G/B | 1. C
(E/G#) | (A)

life.
end.
Lamb!

2.3. C / C/Bb / **CHORUS** F/A
(A) / (A/G) / (D/F#)

Beau - ti - ful Sav - ior,

© Copyright 1998 Kingsway's Thankyou Music. Administered in the Western Hemisphere by EMI Christian Publishing. All Rights Reserved. Used by Permission.

19 B♭ (G) Wonder - der - ful C (A) Coun - C/E (A/C♯) sel -
21 F (G) our, clothed in Gm (Em) maj - es - ty, Lord of
23 Gm/F (Em/D) his - to - ry, You're the C/E (A/C♯) Way, the Dm7 (Bm7) Truth, the
25 C (A) Life. C/B♭ (A/G) Star of the F/A (D/F♯) Morn - ing,
27 B♭ (G) glo - rious in C (A) ho - C/E (A/C♯) li -
29 F (G) ness, You're the Gm (Em) Ris - en One, heav - en's
31 Gm/F (Em/D) Cham - pi - on, and You C/E (A/C♯) reign, Dm7 (Bm7) You
33 C (A) reign o - ver___ Dm7 (Bm7) all!
35 E♭2 (C2) F (G)
37 1. 3. I D.C. 2.

22 Behold the Lamb

Look, the Lamb of God, who takes away the sin of the world! (John 1:29)

Dottie Rambo

CHORUS ♩ = 84-92

Be - hold the Lamb, be - hold the Lamb, Slain from the foun - da - tion of the world. For sin - ners cru - ci - fied, O ho - ly sac - ri - fice, Be - hold the Lamb of God, be - hold the Lamb.

VERSE

Crown Him, crown Him, wor - thy is the Lamb.

© Copyright 1979 John T. Benson Publishing Co., admin. by Brentwood-Benson Music Publishing, Inc. (ASCAP).
All Rights Reserved. Used by Permission.

"In a loud voice they *sang:*

'Worthy is the Lamb,

who was slain,

to receive power and wealth and wisdom and

strength and honor and glory and praise!'

Then I heard every creature in heaven and on

earth and under the earth and on the sea, and all

that is in them, *singing:*

'To him who sits on the throne and to the

Lamb be praise and honor and

glory and power, for ever and ever!'"

Revelation 5:12-13

Better is one day in your courts than a thousand elsewhere. (Psalm 84:10)

23 Better Is One Day

Matt Redman

With a strong beat ♩ = 90

3rd time to Coda
23
A2
A/C♯
1. Bsus
one day in your courts than thou-sands else-where, than thou-sands
25
E(no3)
2. Bsus
else-where. 2. One else-where.
28
C♯m7
BRIDGE
B
A2
Bsus
My heart and flesh cry out for You, the liv-ing God.
30
C♯m7
B
A2
Bsus
Your Spir-it's wa-ter to my soul.
32
C♯m7
B
A2
I've tast-ed and I've seen. Come once a-gain to me.
34
E/G♯
F♯m7
I will draw near to You, I will draw near to You,
36
Bsus
A2
to You.
39
Bsus
CHORUS
A2
Bsus
E/G♯
Bet-ter is one day, bet-ter is one day, bet-ter is
42
A2
A/C♯
Bsus
2nd time: D.S. al CODA
one day than thou-sands else-where. Bet-ter is
CODA
44
Bsus
A2
else-where.

24 Blessed Assurance

Let us draw near to God with a sincere heart in full assurance of faith. (Hebrews 10:22)

Fanny J. Crosby
Altered and new text by Michael Zehnder

Phoebe P. Knapp
Arr. by Michael Zehnder

VERSE

1. Bless-ed as-sur-ance, Je-sus is mine! O what a fore-taste of glo-ry di-vine! Heir of sal-va-tion, pur-chase of God, Born of His Spir-it, washed in His blood. This is my
2. Per-fect sub-mis-sion— Christ on the cross, For my sal-va-tion He suf-fered loss, Gave up His life and gave up His throne, Pur-chased and won me, made me His own. This is my
3. Know-ing for-give-ness, now I'm at rest, I in my Sav-ior am hap-py and blest; Watch-ing and wait-ing, look-ing a-bove, Filled with His good-ness, trust-ing His love.
4. Vic-t'ry o'er Sa-tan, death, and the grave, O what a joy to know that I'm saved! Claim-ing no mer-it, works of my own, All glo-ry, praise, be to God a-lone!

CHORUS

sto - ry, this is my song, Prais-ing my Sav - ior all the day long; This is my sto - ry, this is my song, Prais-ing my Sav - ior all the day long.

Arr. and new text © Copyright 2000 Michael Zehnder.
All Rights Reserved. Used by Permission.

25 Blessing and Honor

...and to the Lamb, be blessing and honor and glory and dominion forever. (Revelation 5:13)

Jeff Hamlin

CHORUS ♩. = 69

Bless-ing and hon-or, glo-ry and pow'r be un-to the Lamb on the throne; Bless-ing and hon-or, glo-ry and pow'r are Yours both now and for-ev-er, Je-sus, our Sav-ior and Lord.

VERSE

1. You are the sac-ri-fice, dy-ing, You suf-fered Pay-ing the great-est price, re-deem-ing us un-to God, re-deem-ing us un-to God.
2. You are the ris-en King, death could not hold You; Rid-ing in vic-to-ry, Your king-dom will nev-er end, Your king-dom will nev-er end.

D.C. (twice)

© 1987 Integrity's Hosanna! Music c/o Integrity Music, Inc., 1000 Cody Road, Mobile, AL 36695-3425.
All Rights Reserved. International Copyright Secured. Used by Permission.

I appeal to you, brothers...that there may be no divisions among you and that you may be perfectly united in mind and thought. (1 Corinthians 1:10)

26 Blest Be the Tie That Binds

John Fawcett   Johann G. Nägeli

1. Blest be the tie that binds Our hearts in Christian love; The fellowship of kindred minds Is like to that above.
2. Before our Father's throne We pour our ardent prayers; Our fears, our hopes, our aims are one, Our comforts and our cares.
3. When we asunder part, It gives us inward pain; But we shall still be joined in heart, And hope to meet again.

© Copyright 1997 Maranatha! Music (Administered by The Copyright Company, Nashville, TN).
All Rights Reserved. International Copyright Secured. Used by Permission. www.maranathamusic.com

> "Finally, all of you, **live** in **harmony** with one another; be sympathetic, **love** as brothers, be compassionate and humble. Do not repay evil with evil or insult with insult, but with blessing, because to this **you** were **called** so that you may inherit a **blessing**."
>
> 1 Peter 3:8-9

27 Bring Forth the Kingdom

You are the salt of the earth...You are the light of the world. (Matthew 5:13-14)

Marty Haugen

VERSE
Leader:
1. You are salt for the earth, O people:
2. You are a light on the hill, O people:
3. You are a seed of the word, O people:
4. We are a blest and a pilgrim people:

All:
1. salt for the kingdom of God!
2. light for the city of God!
3. bring forth the kingdom of God!
4. bound for the kingdom of God!

Leader:
1. Share the flavor of life, O people:
2. Shine so holy and bright, O people:
3. Seeds of mercy and seeds of justice,
4. Love our journey and love our homeland:

All:
1. life in the kingdom of God!
2. shine for the kingdom of God!
3. grow in the kingdom of God!
4. love is the kingdom of God!

CHORUS

Bring forth the kingdom of mercy,
bring forth the kingdom of peace;
bring forth the kingdom of justice,
bring forth the city of God!

© Copyright 1986 GIA Publications, Inc.
All Rights Reserved. Used by Permission.

28 By Your Blood

We have confidence to enter the Most Holy Place by the blood of Jesus. (Hebrews 10:19)

Capo 1 (G)

♩ = 62

Billy Funk

CHORUS

By Your blood You have saved us, by Your blood You have freed us, by Your blood we can enter in- to Your ho-ly place;— By Your love You for-gave us, by Your pow'r You have raised us, by Your blood, pre-cious blood of the Lamb.

VERSE

Fa-ther God in heav-en, pre-cious Lamb of God, we hum-bly bow be-fore You and cry ho-ly, ho-ly; All of heav-en's sing-ing the song of the re-deemed, giv-ing glo-ry to the Lamb. By Your

D.S. al Fine

© Copyright 1991 Integrity's Praise! Music, c/o Integrity Music, Inc., 1000 Cody Road, Mobile, AL 36695-3425.
All Rights Reserved. International Copyright Secured. Used by Permission.

Love the Lord your God with all your heart and with all your soul and with all your mind and with all your strength. (Mark 12:30)

29 By Your Side

Noel and Tricia Richards

Sweetly ♩ = 91

Lyrics:
By Your side I would stay, In Your arms I would lay. Jesus, lover of my soul, nothing from You I withhold. Lord, I love You and adore You. What more can I say? You cause my love to grow stronger With ev'ry passing day. By Your

© Copyright 1989 Kingsway's Thankyou Music, admin. by EMI Christian Music Publishing. All Rights Reserved. International Copyright Secured. Used by Permission.

30 Cares Chorus

Cast all your cares upon him for he cares for you. (1 Peter 5:7)

Kelly Willard

I cast all my cares up-on You, I lay all of my bur-dens down at Your feet. And an-y-time I don't know what to do, I will cast all my cares up-on You.

"You will keep in perfect peace him whose mind is steadfast, because he trusts in you.

Trust in the LORD *forever,* for the LORD, the LORD, is the Rock eternal."

Isaiah 26:3-4

© Copyright 1978 Maranatha Praise, Inc. (Administered by The Copyright Company, Nashville, TN).
All Rights Reserved. International Copyright Secured. Used by Permission. www.maranathamusic.com

Celebrate Jesus

Rejoice in the Lord always. I will say it again: Rejoice! (Philippians 4:4)

31

Gary Oliver

♩ = 144-152

VERSE

Cel - e - brate Je - sus, cel - e - brate,
Cel - e - brate Je - sus, cel - e - brate.

CHORUS

He is ris - en, He is ris - en, and He lives for - ev - er - more.
He is ris - en, He is ris - en, come on and cel - e - brate the res - ur - rec - tion of our Lord.

© Copyright 1988, arr. © 1992 Integrity's Hosanna! Music, c/o Integrity Music, Inc., 1000 Cody Road, Mobile, AL 36695-3425.
All Rights Reserved. International Copyright Secured. Used by Permission.

I will celebrate before the Lord. (2 Samuel 6:21)

32 Celebrate the Lord of Love

Paul Baloche and Ed Kerr

We are the clay, you are the potter... (Isaiah 64:8)

33 Change My Heart, Oh God

Eddie Espinosa

Medium ♩ = 100

CHORUS

Change my heart, oh God.
Make it ev-er true.
Change my heart, oh God.
Last time to Coda
May I be like You. You are the

VERSE

pot-ter; I am the clay.
Mold me and make me; this is what I pray.
Change my heart, oh God. *D.S. al CODA*

CODA

© Copyright 1982 and this arr. © 1997 Mercy/Vineyard, admin. by Music Services (ASCAP).
All Rights Reserved. International Copyright Secured. Used by Permission.

I have been crucified with Christ and I no longer live, but Christ lives in me. (Galatians 2:20)

34 Christ Above Me

John Chisum and George Searcy

Gently ♩ = 80

CHORUS

Christ above me, Christ beside me, Christ within me ever guiding; Christ behind me, Christ before, Christ, my love, my life, my Lord. *Fine*

VERSE

1. Bread of life from heaven, lover of my soul, Peace of God so ever present, I surrender my control to
2. Mercy ever lasting, tenderness divine, Word of God so ever healing, I surrender heart and mind to

D.C. al Fine

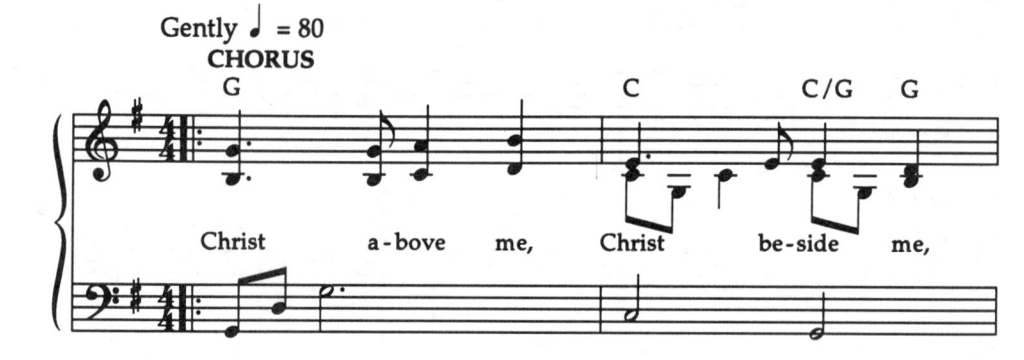

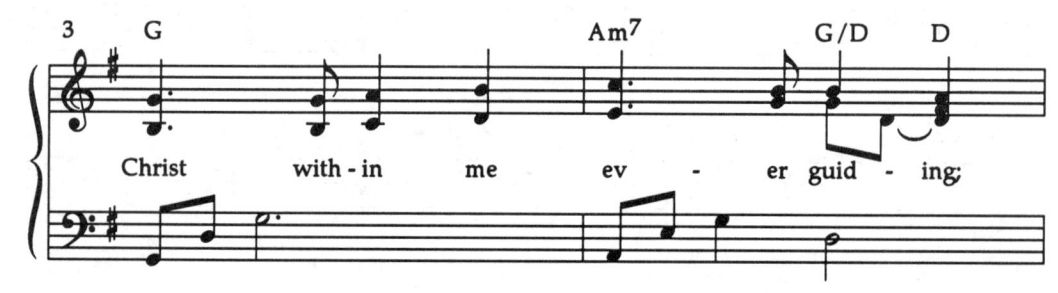

© Copyright 1999 ThreeFold Amen Music/ASCAP and ThreeFold Praise Music/BMI, admin. by ROM Administration. All Rights Reserved. Used by Permission.

One thing I ask of the Lord...to gaze upon the beauty of the Lord and to seek him in his temple. (Psalm 27:4)

35 Come and Behold Him

John Chisum and George Searcy

♩. = 56

VERSE

1. Come and be-hold Him; come, see His glo-ry.
2. Come and be-hold Him; come, see His mer-cy.

Come with an hon-est heart to see all He is.
Come find His ten-der-ness reach-ing to you.

We will dis-cov-er all of His beau-ty. His light will burn a-way all the dark-ness we've known.
Just as a mir-ror shows a re-flec-tion, His Word and Spir-it come, now re-flect-ing His love.

CHORUS

Come and be-hold Him, come and be-hold Him. Come with an hon-est heart to see all He is. Come and be-hold Him; wait now be-fore Him. Come with an hon-est heart to see all He is.

© Copyright 1994 Integrity's Hosanna! Music and Integrity's Praise! Music,
c/o Integrity Music, Inc., 1000 Cody Road, Mobile, AL 36695-3425.
All Rights Reserved. International Copyright Secured. Used by Permission.

36 Come and See

Come and see what God has done, how awesome his works in man's behalf! (Psalm 66:5)

Lenny LeBlanc

1. Come and see the glo-ry of the Lord,
2. Come and give thanks un-to the Lord.

Come, be-hold the Lamb.
Come, be-hold the Lamb.

Come and see the mer-cy of the King,
Come and sing the prais-es of the King,

Bow-ing down be-fore Him.
Bow-ing down be-fore

CHORUS

Him. For He is Lord a-bove the heav-ens, Lord in all the earth. Lord of all the an-gels, Wor-thy to be served.

Al - le - lu - ia, al - le - lu - ia. *Final ending* Lord.

© Copyright 1989 Doulos Publishing (Administered by The Copyright Company, Nashville, TN).
All Rights Reserved. International Copyright Secured. Used by Permission.

They feast on the abundance of your house; you give them drink from your river of delights.
For with you is the fountain of life. (Psalm 36:8-9)

37 Come, Thou Fount

Robert Robinson
John Wyeth

1. Come, Thou Fount of ev-'ry bless-ing, Tune my heart to sing Thy grace; Streams of mer-cy, nev-er ceas-ing, Call for songs of loud-est praise. While the hope of end-less glo-ry Fills my heart with joy and love, Teach me ev-er to a-dore Thee; May I still Thy good-ness prove.

2. Oh, to grace how great a debt-or Dai-ly I'm con-strained to be; Let that grace now like a fet-ter Bind my wan-d'ring heart to Thee: Prone to wan-der, Lord, I feel it; Prone to leave the God I love. Here's my heart, oh, take and seal it, Seal it for Thy courts a-bove.

3. Oh, that day when freed from sin-ning, I shall see Thy love-ly face; Clothed then in the blood-washed lin-en How I'll sing Thy won-drous grace! Come, my Lord, no long-er tar-ry, Take my ran-som'd soul a-way; Send Thine an-gels soon to car-ry Me to realms of end-less day.

Public Domain.

The kingdom of the world has become the kingdom of our Lord and of his Christ, and he will reign for ever and ever. (Revelation 11:15)

38 Crown Him

Sharon Damazio

Capo 1 (G) ♩ = 80

Lyrics:
Crown Him King of kings, crown Him Lord of lords, Wonderful, Counselor, the Mighty God.

CHORUS
Emmanuel, God is with us, and He shall reign, He shall reign, He shall reign forevermore.

© Copyright 1991 Integrity's Hosanna! Music, c/o Integrity Music, Inc., 1000 Cody Road, Mobile, AL 36695-3425.
All Rights Reserved. International Copyright Secured. Used by Permission.

Earnestly I seek you; my soul thirsts for you, my body longs for you. (Psalm 63:1)

39 Come and Fill Me Up

Brian Doerksen

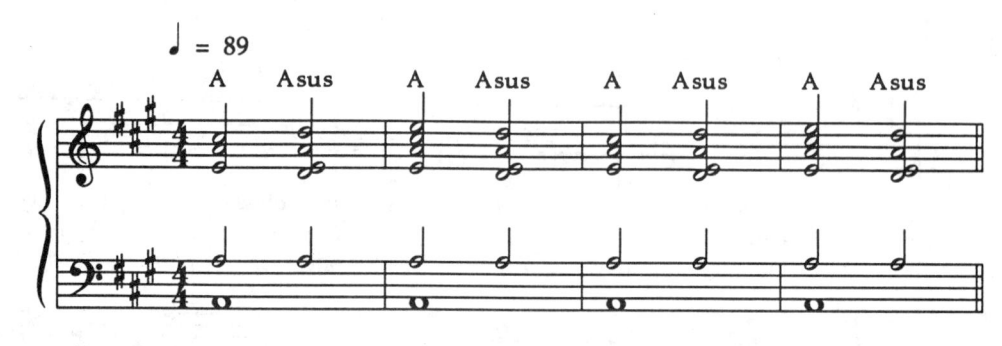

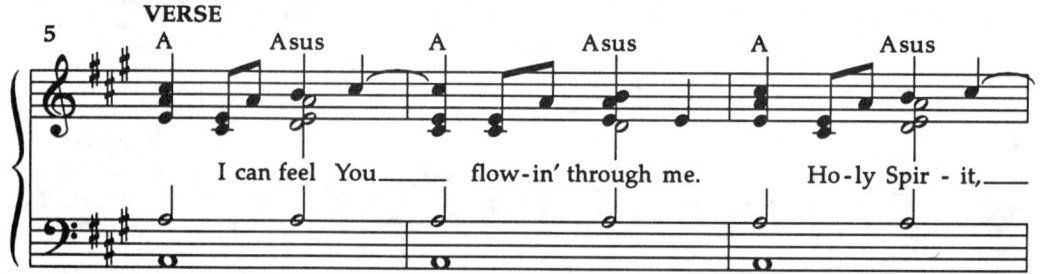

♩ = 89

VERSE
I can feel You flowin' through me. Holy Spirit, come and fill me up, come and fill me up.

Love and mercy

© Copyright 1990 Mercy/Vineyard Publishing (ASCAP).
All Rights Reserved. Used by Permission.

14
A Asus A Asus
fill my sens - es. I am thirst - y
16
A Asus E
for Your pres - ence, Lord;
18
D A Asus A Asus
come and fill me up.
CHORUS
21
Bm7 E
Lord, let Your mer - cy wash a - way
23
A F♯m Bm7
all of my sin. Fill me com-plete-
26
E A F♯m E
- ly with Your love once a-gain.
29
D A D
I need You. I want You. I love Your
32
Esus E D A/C♯
pres - ence. I need You. I want You.
1st time: D.C.
2nd time: D.S.
3rd time: D.S.S.
4th time: Go on
35
D Esus E
I love Your pres - ence.
38
A Asus A Asus A Asus A Asus A

40 Come to the Bread of Life

Blessed are those who are invited to the wedding supper of the Lamb! (Revelation 19:9)

Sean Swanson

With worship

CHORUS

Come to the bread of life. Come, come to the wine. The banquet is prepared and all is ready for the feast.

Last time: Fine

1. (repeat first time only) 2.

VERSE

1. He died so that all of you,
2. Come, all of you,
3. Come

© Copyright 1991 Swansong Music.
All Rights Reserved. Used by Permission.

21
E♭2
we might live.
quench your thirst
young and old,
He
come
23
G♭ G♭2(♯4) G♭ G♭2(♯4) G♭
suf - fered
and be filled
peas - ant
for our
with His
and come
25
B♭m9
sin.
blood.
king.
He was
The
The
27
C♭maj9
lift - ed up
bread that we break
Lord wel-comes all,
as the
is the
be you
29
E♭m9
proph-ets fore-told.
bod - y of Christ,
sin - ner or saint,
and to -
be you
31
1. D♭2 E♭2
On the right hand of God He was
33
F2
seat-ed.
35
2.3. D♭2 E♭2
geth - er we nour - ish our bod - ies and souls.
wea - ry or na - ked or suf-f'ring or a -
37
F2
lone.
1st time: D.S.
2nd time: D.S. al Fine

41 Come to the Table

Truly, truly, I say to you, unless you eat the flesh of the Son of Man and drink his blood, you have no life in yourselves. (John 6:53)

Claire Cloninger and Martin J. Nystrom

♩ = 78

VERSE

Come to the ta-ble of mer-cy, pre-pared with the wine and the bread; All who are hun-gry and thirst-y, come and your souls will be fed.

CHORUS

Come at the Lord's in-vi-ta-tion, re-ceive from His nail-scarred hand; Eat of the bread of sal-va-tion, drink of the blood of the Lamb.

© Copyright 1991 Integrity's Hosanna! Music/ASCAP and Juniper Landing Music (adm. by Word Music) and Word Music (a div. of Word, Inc.)/ASCAP, c/o Integrity Music, Inc., 1000 Cody Road, Mobile, AL 36695-3425. All Rights Reserved. International Copyright Secured. Used by Permission.

"Teach me your way, O Lord, and I will walk in your truth." (Psalm 86:11)

42 Cry of My Heart

Terry Butler

Medium ♩ = 118

CHORUS
It is the cry of my heart to follow You.
It is the cry of my heart to be close to You.
It is the cry of my heart to follow all of the days of my life.

Fine

VERSE
1. Teach me Your holy ways, oh Lord.
   So I can walk in Your truth.
2. Open my eyes so I can see the wonderful things that You do.

The Teach me Your holy ways, oh, Lord. And make me
Open my heart up more and more, And make me
wholly devoted to You.
wholly devoted to You.

D.C. al Fine

© Copyright 1991 and this arr. 1997 Mercy/Vineyard, admin. by Music Services (ASCAP).
All Rights Reserved. International Copyright Secured. Used by Permission.

43 Comfort, Comfort All My People

Comfort, comfort my people...speak tenderly...to her...that her sin has been paid for. (Isaiah 40:1-2)

Robin Mann

♩ = 92-104

CHORUS
Comfort, comfort all my people with the comfort of my Word. Speak it tender to my people: All your sins are taken away.

Last time to Coda

1. Though your tears be rivers running; though your tears be an ocean full; though you cry with the hurt of living: comfort, comfort.

Ev'ry valley shall be lifted, ev'ry mountain shall be low, ev'ry rough place will be smoother, comfort, comfort.

2nd time: D.C. al Coda (or go to optional verses)

CODA
comfort.
comfort!

© Copyright 1975 Robin Mann. All Rights Reserved. Used by Permission.

2. Though your eyes see only darkness, though your eyes can see no light, though your eyes see pain and sorrow: comfort, comfort. Every night will have its morning, every pain will have an end, every burden will be lightened: comfort, comfort.

Optional Verses (3 and 4):
3. Though we build strong walls for prisons, though we feast while others starve, though we fill this world with weapons: comfort, comfort. Every prisoner will be rescued, every hungry mouth be filled, every gun will rust, forgotten: comfort, comfort.

4. Though we fracture God's creation, though we stand so far apart, though we fail to love each other: comfort, comfort. Every wall will crack and crumble, every stranger will be friend, every one embrace another: comfort, comfort.

Emmanuel

They will call him Immanuel — which means, 'God with us.' (Matthew 1:23)

Bob McGee

Lyrics:
Emmanuel, Emmanuel, His name is called Emmanuel; God with us, revealed in us; His name is called Emmanuel. Emmanuel.

© Copyright 1976 C.A. Music (div. of Christian Artists Records, Inc.) (ASCAP).
All Rights Reserved. Used by Permission.

For when you did awesome things...you came down and the mountains trembled before you. (Isaiah 64:3)

45 Did You Feel the Mountains Tremble?

Martin Smith

1. Did you feel the moun-tains trem-ble?___ Did you hear the o-ceans roar when the peo-ple rose to sing of___ Je-sus Christ, the ris-en One?___

2. Did you feel the peo-ple trem-ble?___ Did you hear the sing-ers roar when the lost be-gan to sing of___ Je-sus Christ, the sav-ing one?___

3. Do you feel the dark-ness trem-ble___ when all the saints join in one song, and all the streams flow as one riv-er___ to wash a-way our bro-ken-ness?___

BRIDGE

And we can see that, God, You're mov-ing, a might-y riv-er through the na-tions; and young and old will turn to Je-

And here we see that, God, You're mov-ing; a time of ju-bi-lee is com-ing, when young and old re-turn to Je-

© 1994 Curious? Music UK/Administered in North America by EMI Christian Music Publishing, P.O. Box 5085, Brentwood, TN 37024. All Rights Reserved. International Copyright Secured. Used by Permission.

28 C
Dm7
- sus. Fling wide, you heav-en-ly gates;
- sus.
31 F2
G7
C2
pre-pare the way of the ris-en Lord.
34 Gsus
C2
CHORUS
37 C
F/A
O - pen up the doors, Let the mu -
40
Dm7
- sic play. Let the streets re - sound with
43 C
G
C
sing-ing: songs that bring
46
F/A
Your hope, songs that bring Your joy,
49 Dm7
Last time to Coda
C
danc - ers who dance up-on in-jus-tice.
52 1. G
2. G
D.S. al CODA
CODA
54 C
G
C2
tice.

46 Do This in Remembrance of Me

This cup is the new covenant in my blood; do this, whenever you drink it, in remembrance of me. (1 Cor. 11:25)

Billy Christopher

With meaning

CHORUS

Do this in re-mem-brance of Me. Do this in re-mem-brance of Me. This is My bod-y, this is My blood.

TAG

Do this in re-mem-brance of Me. *Fine*

VERSE

This is My bod-y giv-en for you. Do this in re-mem-brance of Me. This cup's the new cov-en-ant, sealed in My blood.

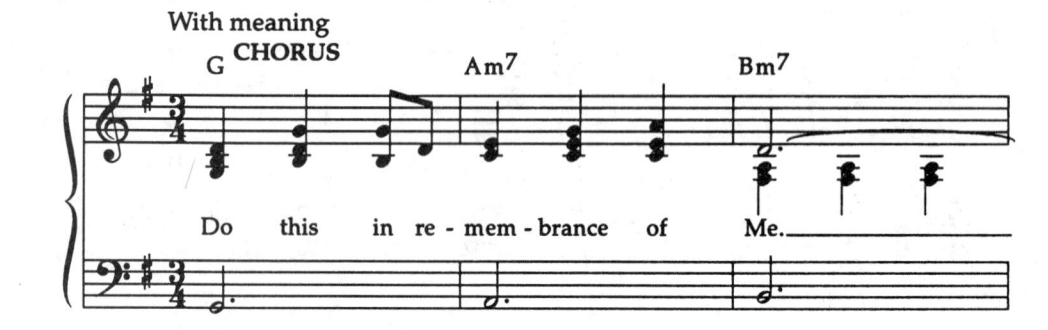

© Copyright 1999 Billy Christopher.
All Rights Reserved. Used by Permission.

> "For I received from the Lord what I also passed on to you: The Lord Jesus, on the night he was betrayed, took bread, and when he had given thanks, he broke it and said, 'This is **my body,** which is for you; do this in remembrance of me.' In the same way, after supper he took the cup, saying, 'This cup is the new covenant in **my blood;** do this, whenever you drink it, in remembrance of me.' For whenever you eat this bread and drink this cup, you **proclaim** the **Lord's death** until he comes."
>
> 1 Corinthians 11:23-26

> "Is not the cup of thanksgiving for which we give thanks a *participation* in the **blood** of Christ? And is not the bread that we break a *participation* in the **body** of Christ? Because there is one loaf, we, who are many, are one body, for we all partake of the one loaf."
>
> 1 Corinthians 10:16-17

I consider everything a loss compared to the surpassing greatness of knowing Christ Jesus my Lord, for whose sake I have lost all things. (Philippians 3:8)

47 Draw Me Close

Kelly Carpenter

Capo 3 (G)

In two ♩=72

Lyrics:
1. Draw me close to You; never let me go.
2. You are my desire; no-one else will do,

'cause I lay it all down again, to hear You say that I'm Your friend.
nothing else could take Your place, to feel the warmth of Your embrace.

Help me find the way; bring me back to You.

© Copyright 1994 Mercy/Vineyard Publishing (ASCAP).
All Rights Reserved. Used by Permission.

22
Eb/F (C/D)
F (D)
CHORUS
25
Bb (C)
F/A (D/F#)
Eb2/Bb (C2/G)
You're all I want;
28
Bb (G)
F/A (D/F#)
You're all I've ev -
31
Eb2/G (C2/E)
F7sus (D7sus)
F (D)
Bb (G)
- er need - ed. You're all
34
F/A (D/F#)
Eb2/Bb (C2/G)
I want;
37
Eb/F (C/D)
F (D)
To Coda
help me know You are near.
39
1. Bb (G)
Repeat to Beginning
42
2. Bb (G)
Eb/F (C/D)
F (D)
D.S. al CODA
CODA
44
Gm (Em)
Gm/F (Em/D)
46
Eb/F (C/D)
F (D)
Bb (G)
Help me know You are here.

Eagles Wings

Those who hope in the Lord will renew their strength. They will soar on wings like eagles... (Isaiah 40:31)

Reuben Morgan

Moderately ♩ = 76

VERSE

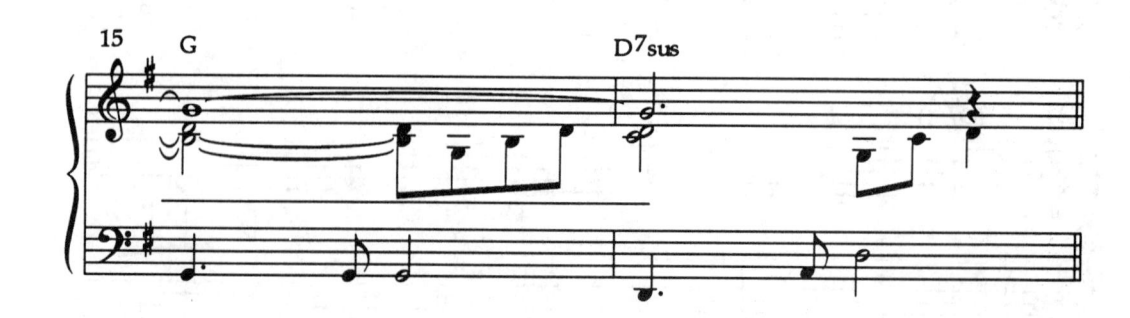

Here I am waiting; abide in me, I pray. Here I am longing for You.

Hide me in Your love; bring me to my knees. May I know Jesus more and more.

© Copyright 1998 Reuben Morgan/Hillsongs Australia (adm. in the U.S. and Canada by Integrity's Hosanna! Music),
c/o Integrity Music, Inc., 1000 Cody Road, Mobile, AL 36695-3425.
All Rights Reserved. International Copyright Secured. Used by Permission.

17
CHORUS
G C G/B Am7
Come, live in me, all my life
19
C/D D
take o - ver.
21
G C G/B Am7
Come, breathe in me, I will rise
23
G/D D
on ea - gles' wings.
25
G C G/B Am7
Come, live in me, all my life
27
C/D D
take o - ver.
29
G C G/B Am7
Come, breathe in me, I will rise
31
G/D D
on ea - gles' wings.
33
G

Enter In

*Since we have confidence to enter the Most Holy Place by the blood of Jesus...
let us draw near to God...in full assurance of faith. (Hebrews 10:19, 22)*

Billy Christopher

Gently

En-ter in - to His pres-ence, en-ter in - to His love. En-ter in - to the pres-ence of the Lord by His blood. En-ter in - to sal - va-tion by the blood of the Lamb. En-ter in - to the throne room of the Great I Am. En-ter in - to His pres-ence and re-ceive by His grace the priv - ilege to wor-ship Him here in this place. En-ter in - to His pres-ence; let us bow be-fore Him, give Him

© Copyright 1999 Billy Christopher.
All Rights Reserved. Used by Permission.

"Therefore, brothers, since we have confidence to enter the Most Holy Place by the **blood** of **Jesus**, by a new and living way opened for us through the curtain, that is, his body, and since we have a great priest over the house of God, let us **draw near** to **God** with a sincere heart in full assurance of faith, having our hearts sprinkled to cleanse us from a guilty conscience and having our bodies washed with pure water. Let us hold unswervingly to the hope we profess, for **he** who promised is **faithful**."

Hebrews 10:19-23

It is good to praise the Lord and make music to your name, O Most High, to proclaim your love...and your faithfulness... (Psalm 89:1-2)

50 Faithful Father

Brian Doerksen

Flowing

1. Father, I can't explain this kind of love, this kind of grace. I know I still break Your heart, and yet You run to welcome me. This is my song of praise to You, for who You are and all that You do. From the moment my life began You have been faithful.

2. Father, I love the way You hold me close and say my name. I know when my life is through, my heart will find its home in You.

© Copyright 1996 Mercy/Vineyard Publishing (ASCAP).
All Rights Reserved. Used by Permission.

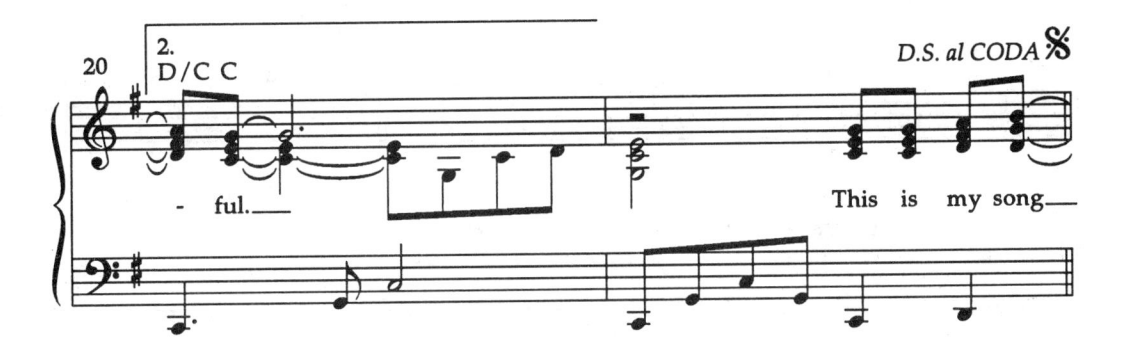

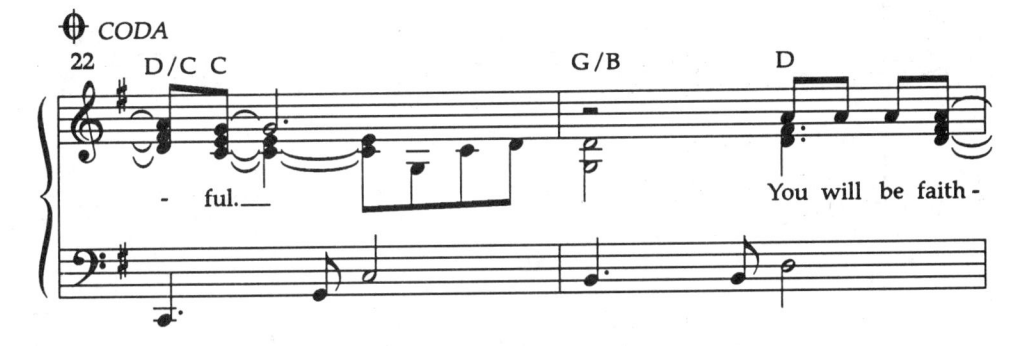

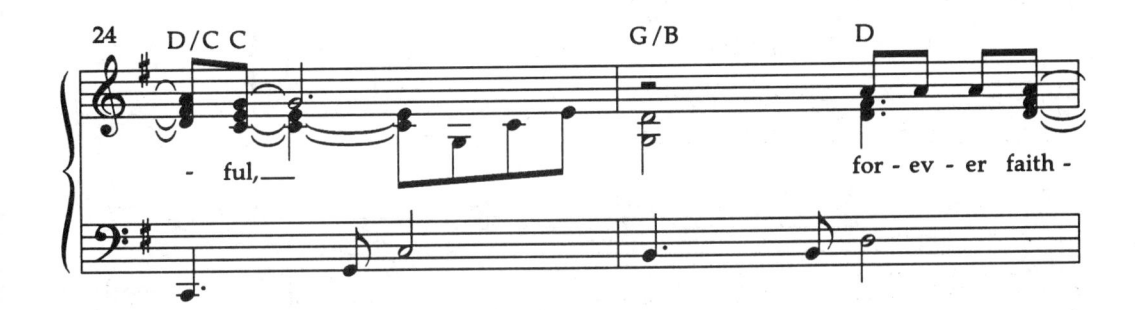

"I will **sing** of the LORD'S

great love forever;

with my mouth I will make

your *faithfulness* known

through all generations. I will declare that your

love stands firm forever, that you established

your *faithfulness* in heaven itself…

O LORD God Almighty, who is like you?

You are mighty, O LORD, and

your *faithfulness*

surrounds you."

Psalm 89:1-2, 8

51 Father Me, Again

You received the Spirit of sonship. And by him we cry, 'Abba, Father.' (Romans 8:15)

Michael Zehnder

Tenderly ♩ = 90

VERSE

Lead me, Lord; guide me, Lord. I'm stepping out, though I don't know how to walk or where to walk. Just hold my hand and don't let go.

CHORUS

Father me, again. Father me, again. Jesus, heal my wounded heart and love me; make me whole again. Father me, again.

© Copyright 2000 Michael Zehnder, P.O. Box 51510, Phoenix, AZ 85076.
All Rights Reserved. Used by Permission.

"I will be a

Father

to you, and you will be my

sons and daughters,

says the Lord Almighty."

2 Corinthians 6:18

"For I am the LORD, your God,

who takes **hold** of

your right hand

and says to you, Do not fear;

I will **help** you."

Isaiah 41:13

Let the little children come to me, and do not hinder them, for the Kingdom of God belongs to such as these. (Luke 18:16)

52 Father Welcomes

Robin Mann

♩ = 115

CHORUS

Father welcomes all His children to His fam'ly through His Son. Father giving His salvation, Life forever has been won.

VERSE

1. Little children, come to me, for my kingdom is of these. Life and love I have to give, Mercy for your sin.
2. In the water, in the Word, in His promise, be assured: Those who are baptized and believe, Shall be born again.
3. Let us daily die to sin; let us daily rise with Him, Walk in the love of Christ our Lord, Live in the peace of God.

D.C. al Fine

© Copyright Kevin Mayhew, Ltd., Buxhall, Stowmarket, Suffolk, IP14 3BW.
Used by Permission.

53 Feed Us Now

Whoever eats my flesh and drinks my blood has eternal life, and I will raise him up at the last day. For my flesh is real food and my blood is real drink. (John 6:54-55)

Robin Mann

Unhurried ♩ = 84-90

1. Feed us now, Bread of life, In this holy meal; Let us know your love anew; We hunger for you.
2. Piece of bread, glass of wine: Lord, this food is good! Love and mercy come to us; Your promise we trust.
3. God is here, O so near; Nearer than our thoughts. Stay with us where-'er we go; Lord, help us to grow.

Feed us now, Bread of life, Come and live within;
Piece of bread, glass of wine; Who can understand
God is here, O so near, In this heaven's meal.

Let your peace be ours today, Lord Jesus we pray.
How His mercy works in these? Yet, Lord, we believe.
May we always feed on you— On bread that is true.

© Copyright 1976 Robin Mann.
All Rights Reserved. Used by Permission.

54 Fear Not
(I Love You This Much)

Do not fear for I am with you; do not be dismayed, for I am your God. (Isaiah 41:10)

Lana Gibbons

1. Fear not, all my children, for I will always stay in all of your tomorrows, and I'm with you today. Fear not, all my children, I'll always be with you in ev'ry moment of your life in ev'rything you do.

(2. Fear) not, all my children, don't ever be dismayed, for all your pain and sorrows, the price has all been paid. Fear not, all my children, courageous ever strong, for I'll not fail you or forsake you all your whole life long.

(3. Fear) not, all my children, I won't leave you alone, I will prepare a mansion, right at my Father's throne. Fear not, all my children, I'll rise up from the dead, I am God's Son; the vict'ry's won, remember what I've said: For

© Copyright 1989 Lana Gibbons.
All Rights Reserved. Used by Permission.

CHORUS
19 G F♯m7
I love you this much my
21 G D/G G D G
arms are o - pened wide, for I love you
24 F♯m G Gmaj7 G6 G E7sus
this much I bled for you and died.
27 A7 G F♯m
For I love you this much there's
30 G D/G G D G F♯m/G G
noth - ing you can do to take a - way the
33 D Bm Em G A
love that I have for ev - 'ry one of
36 1.2. D
you.
2. Fear
3. Fear
38 3. D G
you. To take a - way the
41 D Bm7 Em G
love that I have for ev - 'ry one
44 A D
of you.

Do you truly love me? ...Feed my lambs. (John 21:15)

55 Feed My Lambs

Lana Gibbons

Gently ♩ = 102-108

CHORUS

"Feed My lambs, feed My lambs," that's what Je-sus did say. "Feed My lambs, feed My lambs, feed them My love to-day. Feed them hope, feed them joy. Feed them wis-dom from a-bove. If you love Me, feed My lambs with My love."

Last time to Coda ⊕

VERSE

1. Teach them all that He's done to give them life. Teach them Je-sus in all you do.
2. Show them all that He does to care for them. Show them Je-sus so they can see.
3. Tell them how He's their Friend and holds their hands. Tell them He's there in day and night.
4. Feed them all they will need to grow up strong. Feed them food that our Shep-herd does give.

Copyright © 1992 Lana Gibbons, Marengo, Illinois.
All Rights Reserved. Used by Permission.

> "He tends his flock
>
> like a shepherd:
>
> He gathers the lambs in his arms
>
> and carries them close to his heart;
>
> he gently leads those that have young."
>
> Isaiah 40:11

Lyrics (mm. 28–40):

Teach them how they are loved and how they should live. Teach them Jesus loves me and He loves you.

Show them how they must love and worship His name. Show them how He loves first loved you and me.

Tell them He lights their way and shows what to do. Tell them shine for Him, little Gospel light.

Feed them God's saving grace and wisdom for life. Feed His lambs so in heaven they will live.

"Feed My sheep... If you love Me, feed My lambs with My love."

56   Fill Me

May the God of hope fill you with all joy and peace as you trust in him, so that you may overflow with hope by the power of the Holy Spirit. (Romans 15:13)

Janet L. Janzen

Quietly

VERSE 1

Fill me with Your Spirit and take Him not away. Fill me with Your power to walk in Your way. (fill me) Fill me with Your love; let me love You more today. Fill me, (Lord) Lord Jesus, I pray.

VERSE 2

Guide me with Your light;____ let it shine on my way. Guide me with Your truth;_____ let me

© Copyright 1990 Janet Lindeblad Janzen.
All Rights Reserved. Used by Permission.

> "Who among you fears the LORD
>
> and obeys the word of his servant?
>
> Let him who walks in the dark,
>
> who has no light,
>
> *trust*
>
> in the name of the LORD and
>
> rely on his God."
>
> Isaiah 50:10

57 Find Us Faithful

Remember your leaders...Consider the outcome of their way of life and imitate their faith. (Hebrews 13:7)

Jon Mohr

O may all who come behind us find us faithful; May the fire of our devotion light their way. May the footprints that we leave lead them to believe, And the lives we live inspire them to obey. O may all who come behind us find us faithful.

© Copyright 1987 Birdwing Music/Jonathan Mark Music Music, admin. by Music Services.
All Rights Reserved. Used by Permission.

...Love the Lord your God with all your heart and with all your soul and with all your mind. (Matthew 22:37)

58 First Love

Paul Baloche and Gary Sadler

Moderately ♩ = 80

VERSE

Light the can-dle,___ stir the flame,___ let the sword of___ Your Word___ pierce my heart a-gain;___ Ho-ly Spir-it,___ move in me,___ draw me close to___ Your heart, where

CHORUS

I need___ to be.___ First love, Je-sus,___ my Sav-ior, my one de-sire,___ to love You___ more. First love, Lord, make___ me faith-ful, I want You al-ways___ to be my first love.___

© Copyright 1998 Integrity's Hosanna! Music, c/o Integrity Music, Inc., 1000 Cody Road, Mobile, AL 36695-3425.
All Rights Reserved. International Copyright Secured. Used by Permission.

59 Firm Foundation

He will be the sure foundation for your times, a rich store of salvation and wisdom and knowledge. (Isaiah 33:6)

Nancy Gordon and Jamie Harvill

With confidence ♩ = 112

CHORUS

Je - sus, You're my firm foun - da - tion, I know I can stand se - cure; Je - sus, You're my firm foun - da - tion, I put my hope in Your ho - ly Word, I put my hope in Your ho - ly Word. *Fine*

VERSE

MEN: unison
WOMEN: unison

1. I have a liv - ing hope, I have a fu - ture; God has a plan for me, of this I'm sure.
2. Your Word is faith - ful, might - y in pow - er; God will de - liv - er me, of this I'm sure.

D.C. al Fine

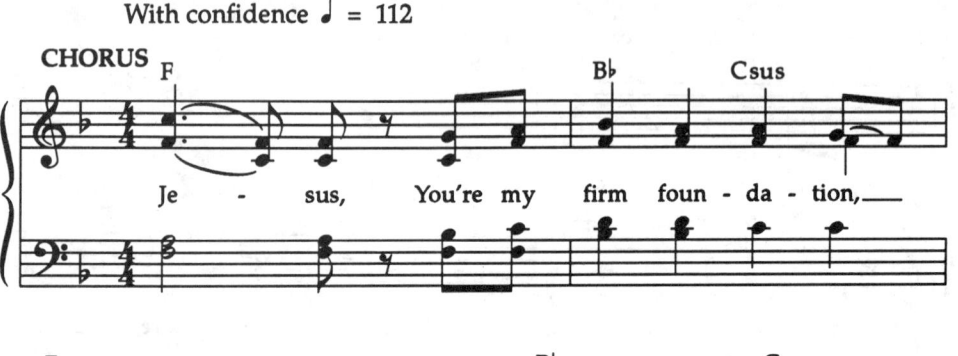

© 1994 Integrity's Hosanna! Music & Integrity's Praise! Music,
c/o Integrity Music, Inc., 1000 Cody Road, Mobile, AL 36695-3425.
All Rights Reserved. International Copyright Secured. Used by Permission.

Now that you have purified yourselves by obeying the truth...love one another deeply from the heart. (1 Peter 1:22)

60 Flowing River

Rita Baloche

VERSE

Pour Your Ho-ly Spir-it up-on me.

Let Your pres-ence fill me up.

Make my life a flow-ing riv-er

of Your ev-er-last-ing love.

CHORUS

Like a liv-ing stream flow-ing from Your might-y o-cean,

pur-i-fy in me

my de-sire and my de-vo-tion.

Make my life a flow-ing riv-er

of Your ev-er-last-ing love.

© Copyright 1998 Integrity's Hosanna! Music, c/o Integrity Music, Inc., 1000 Cody Road, Mobile, AL 36695-3425.
All Rights Reserved. International Copyright Secured. Used by Permission.

61 Foolish Pride

God opposes the proud but gives grace to the humble. (James 4:6)

Michael Zehnder

Tenderly, in a slow two ♩ = 62-68

I thank You, Lord, for loving me in spite of all the dirt in me. I thank You, Lord, for freeing me from all the sin that drags on me. I thank You, Lord, for changing me, Your Word and Spirit shaping me. Now help me, Jesus, let go of my foolish pride. I'm sick with self and sin, foolish pride that keeps You out, not in. Oh Jesus, break down all my pride and open me again.

© Copyright 2000 Michael Zehnder, P.O. Box 51510, Phoenix, AZ 85076.
All Rights Reserved. Used by Permission.

> "Though the LORD is on high, he looks upon the **lowly**, but the **proud** he knows from afar."
>
> Psalm 138:6

> "This is the one I esteem: he who is *humble* and **contrite** in spirit, and **trembles** at my word."
>
> Isaiah 66:2

62 For the Lord Is Good

For the Lord is good and his love endures forever... (Psalm 100:5)

Lynn DeShazo and Gary Sadler

With a beat ♩ = 132

For the Lord is good, and His love endures forever; He's a faithful God to all generations. For the Lord is good, and His mercies will not fail us; they are new each day, O, lift your voice and say, "The Lord is good!"

4th time to Coda

1. For the Lord

2.3.

SOLO (or MEN)

Great is Your faithfulness, O Lord.

© Copyright 1997 Integrity's Hosanna! Music, c/o Integrity Music, Inc., 1000 Cody Road, Mobile, AL 36695-3425.
All Rights Reserved. International Copyright Secured. Used by Permission.

23 CHOIR (or WOMEN) A D/A E/A
Great is Your faith - ful - ness, O Lord
25 SOLO (or MEN) A D/A
Your lov - ing - kind - ness fills our
27 ALL Bm7 E
hearts to o - ver - flow - ing.
29 SOLO (or MEN) A D/A E/A
Songs of re - joic - ing and sweet praise,
31 CHOIR (or WOMEN) F♯m E/F♯ F♯m SOLO (or MEN)
(songs of praise) they fill
33 D2 CHOIR (or WOMEN) ALL
our hearts, (they fill our hearts) they fill
1st time: D.S. 𝄋
2nd time: D.S. al CODA 𝄋
35 E
our days. For the Lord
𝄌 CODA
37 A D2 F♯m Esus E
The Lord is good!
39 A D2 F♯m Esus E
The Lord is good!
41 A D2 F♯m rit. Esus E A
The Lord is good!

63 Friend of Sinners

This man welcomes sinners and eats with them. (Luke 15:2)

Matt Redman

Gently

1. Friend of sin-ners, Lord of truth, I am fall-ing in love with You.
2. Friend of sin-ners, Lord of truth, I am giv-ing my life to You.

Friend of sin-ners, Lord of truth, I have fall-en in love with You. Je-
Friend of sin-ners, Lord of truth, I have giv-en my life to You.

CHORUS

-sus, I love Your name, the name by which we're saved. Je-sus, I love Your name, the name by which we're saved.

© Copyright 1996 Kingsway's Thankyou Music/Administered in North America by
EMI Christian Music Publishing, P.O. Box 5085, Brentwood, TN 37024-5085.
All Rights Reserved. Used by Permission.

64 From My Heart to Yours

Grace to all who love our Lord Jesus Christ with an undying love. (Ephesians 6:24)

Paul Baloche

Moderately ♩ = 80

From my heart to Yours, from my heart to Yours, I lift a love song up to You, I lift a love song up to You, from my heart. From my heart to Yours, from my heart to Yours, I lift a love song up to You, I lift a love song up to You, I love ev'rything about You and ev'rything You do, O Lord, from my heart to Yours.

© Copyright 1998 Integrity's Hosanna! Music, c/o Integrity Music, Inc., 1000 Cody Road, Mobile, AL 36695-3425.
All Rights Reserved. International Copyright Secured. Used by Permission.

65 Give Thanks

Sing and make music in your heart to the Lord, always giving thanks to God the Father for everything. (Ephesians 5:19-20)

Henry Smith

♩ = 88-96 VERSE

Give thanks with a grateful heart, give thanks to the Holy One, Give thanks because He's given Jesus Christ, His Son. Give thanks with a grateful heart, give thanks to the Holy One, Give thanks because He's given Jesus Christ, His Son.

CHORUS

And now let the weak say, "I am strong," let the poor say "I am rich because of what the Lord has done for us." And now let the

© Copyright 1978, Arr. © 1991,1992 Integrity's Hosanna! Music,
c/o Integrity Music, Inc., 1000 Cody Road, Mobile, AL 36695-3425.
All Rights Reserved. International Copyright Secured. Used by Permission.

"If it would help matters along,

I would have

all the bells pealing, and

all the organs playing,

and have *everything* ring

that can make a sound."

Martin Luther, 1526

I will praise you...with all my heart; I will glorify your name forever. (Psalm 86:12)

66 Glorify Thy Name

Donna Adkins

VERSE

1. Fa - ther, we love You, we wor - ship and a - dore You,
2. Je - sus, we love You, we wor - ship and a - dore You,
3. Spir - it, we love You, we wor - ship and a - dore You,

Glo - ri - fy Thy name in all the earth.

CHORUS

Glo - ri - fy Thy name, Glo - ri - fy Thy name, Glo - ri - fy Thy name in all the earth.

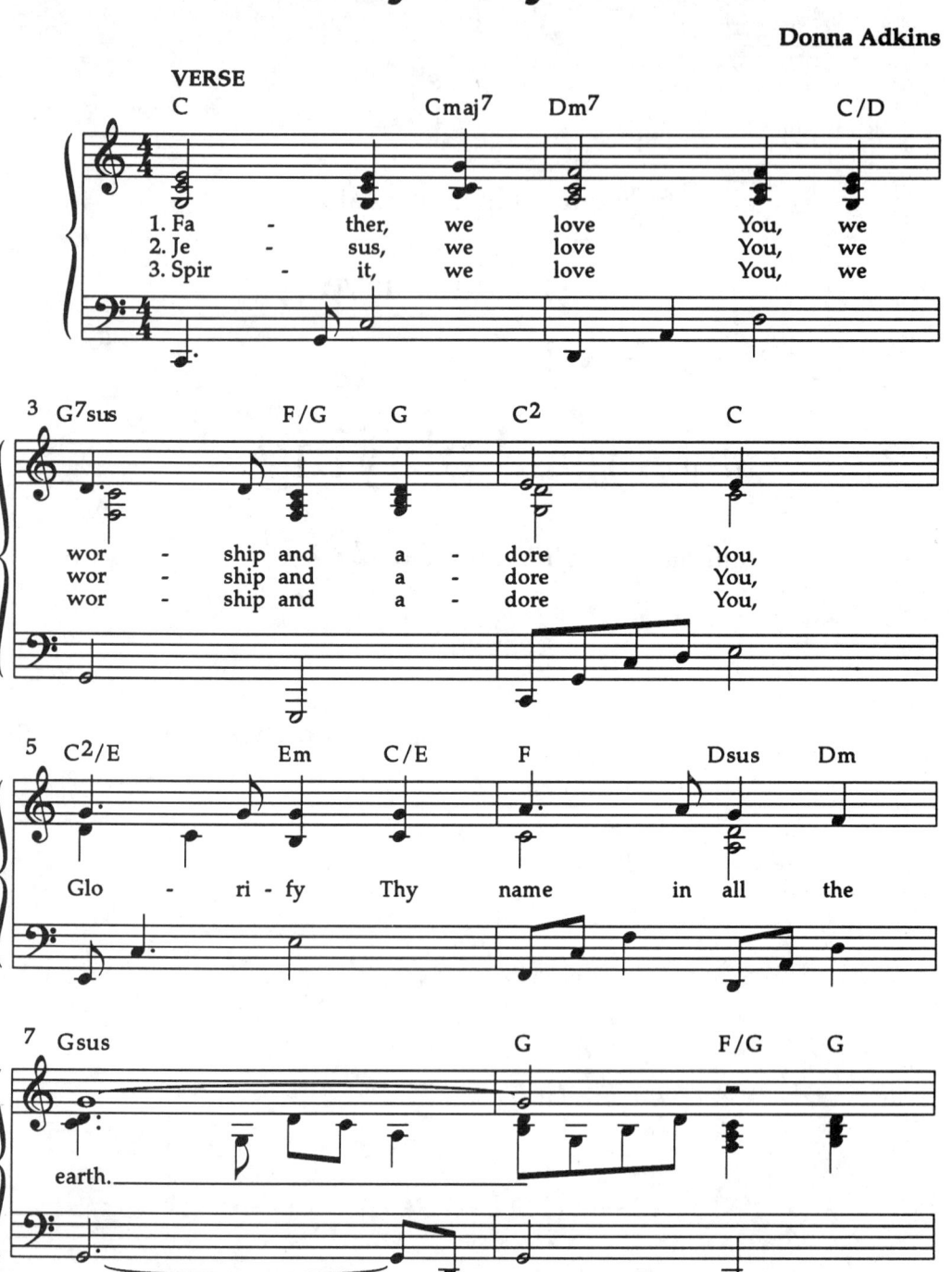

© Copyright 1976 Maranatha! Music (Administered by The Copyright Company, Nashville, TN).
All Rights Reserved. International Copyright Secured. Used by Permission. www.maranathamusic.com

67. Glory

To the only God our Savior be glory, majesty, power and authority through Jesus Christ our Lord. (Jude 25)

Geoff Bullock

With drive ♩ = 126

CHORUS

Glo - ry to the King of kings. Maj - es - ty, pow'r and strength to the Lord of lords.

VERSE (4th time: Fine)

1. Ho - ly One, all cre - a - tion crowns You King of kings. Ho - ly One, King of kings, Lord of lords, ___ Ho - ly ___ One.
2. Je - sus, Lord, with eyes un - veiled, we will see Your throne. Je - sus, Prince of Peace, Son of ___ God, Em - man - u - el.

D.C. al Fine

© 1990 Word Music, Inc. (ASCAP), 65 Music Square West, Nashville, TN 37203/
Maranatha! Music (Admin. by Word Music, Inc.) (ASCAP), 65 Music Square West, Nashville, TN 37203.
All Rights Reserved. International Copyright Secured. Used by Permission. www.maranathamusic.com

68 Glory to the Lamb

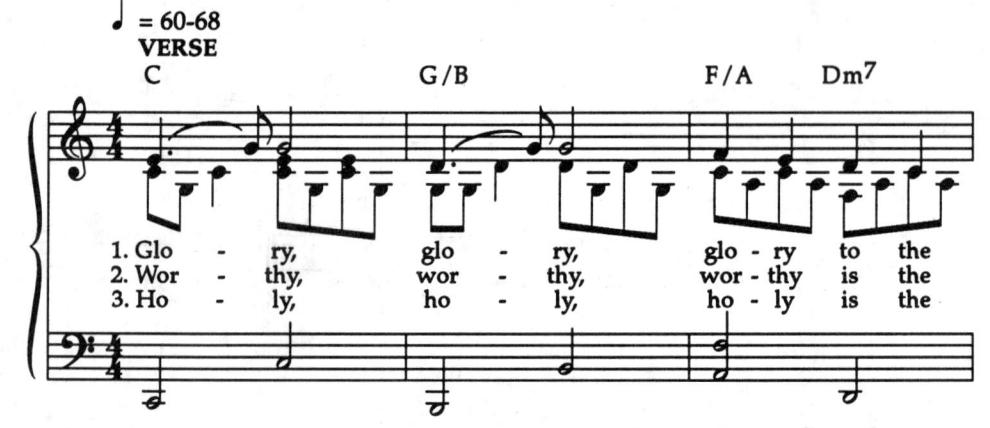

To the Lamb be praise and honor and glory and power forever and ever! (Revelation 5:13)

Larry Dempsey

♩ = 60-68

VERSE

1. Glo - ry, glo - ry, glo - ry to the Lamb.
2. Wor - thy, wor - thy, wor - thy is the Lamb.
3. Ho - ly, ho - ly, ho - ly is the Lamb.

Glo - ry, glo - ry, glo - ry to the Lamb. For He is
Wor - thy, wor - thy, wor - thy is the Lamb.
Ho - ly, ho - ly, ho - ly is the Lamb.

CHORUS (opt. D.S.)

glo - ri - ous and wor - thy to be praised, the Lamb up - on the throne; And un - to Him we lift our voice in praise, the Lamb up - on the throne.

Repeat ending D.C.

Optional chorus repeat D.S. | **Song ending**
throne. For He is throne. *slight rit.*

© Copyright 1983 ZionSong Music, P.O. Box 574044, Orlando, FL 32857.
All Rights Reserved. International Copyright Secured. Used by Permission.

You are a chosen people, a royal priesthood, a holy nation, a people belonging to God. (1 Peter 2:9)

69 Go Out As People of God

Gloria Lien

Driving ♩ = 128

CHORUS

Go out as people of God.

Go out as people of hope,

Go out as people renewed. Your

sins are forgiv'n, You are made whole, Now

walk in the light of God. *Fine*

VERSE

You are the people God made as His own.

Made in His image, no longer alone.

His seal is on us, His Spirit divine,

Called to be people of God. *D.C. al Fine*

© Copyright 2000 Gloria Publishing, 1604 9th St., Wilmar, MN 56201.
All Rights Reserved. Used by Permission.

Go and make disciples of all nations, baptizing them...and teaching them...and surely I am with you always, to the very end of the age. (Matthew 28:19-20)

70 Go, Make Disciples

Handt Hanson

With energy

Go, make dis-ci-ples, bap-tiz-ing them, teach-ing them.

Go, make dis-ci-ples, for I am with you till the end of time.

Go, be the salt of the earth.

Go, be the light for the world.

Go, be a cit-y on a hill, so all can see that you're serv-ing me.

Go, make dis-ci-ples.

© Copyright 1996 Prince of Peace Publishing, Changing Church, Inc.
All Rights Reserved. Used by Permission.

71 God Is Good

Surely God is good to Israel, to those who are pure in heart. (Psalm 73:1)

Graham Kendrick

Capo 1 (Em)
♩ = 140 **CHORUS**

God is good, we sing and shout it,
God is good, we celebrate;
God is good, no more we doubt it,
God is good, we know it's true. *Fine*

VERSE

And when I think of His love for me, my heart fills with praise and I feel like dancing; For in His heart there is room for me, and I run with arms opened wide.

D.C. al Fine

© Copyright 1985 Kingsway's Thankyou Music.
All Rights Reserved. Used by Permission.

72 Go, My Children, with My Blessing

Jaroslav J. Vajda   Old Welsh Melody

The Lord bless you and keep you; The Lord make his face shine upon you and be gracious to you; the Lord turn his face toward you and give you peace. (Numbers 6:24)

Gently ♩ = 90

For use at weddings, verse 5 may be sung in place of verses 2 and 3.

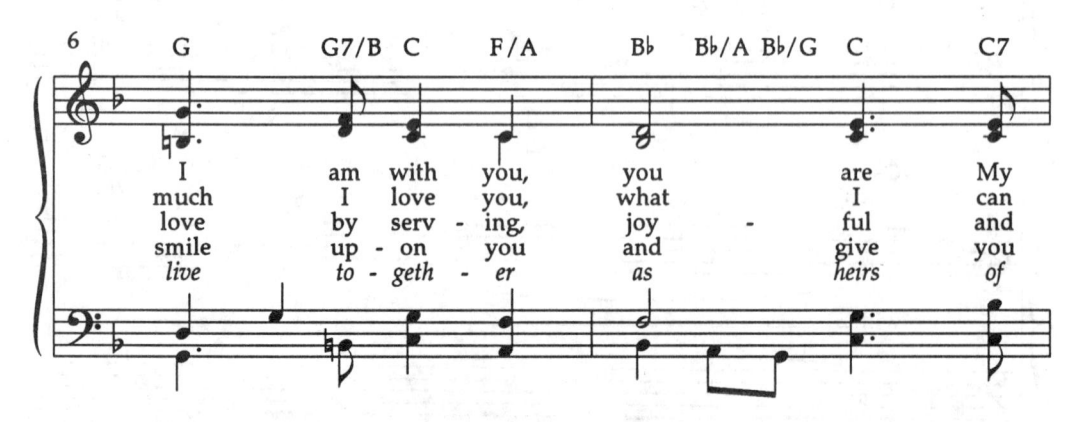

1. Go, My children, with My blessing, never alone; Waking, sleeping, I am with you, you are My own.
2. Go, My children, sins forgiven, at peace and pure. Here you learned how much I love you, what I can cure.
3. Go, My children, fed and nourished, closer to Me. Grow in love and love by serving, joyful and free.
4. I the Lord will bless and keep you and give you peace. Now, My children, live together smile upon you and give you peace.
5. *In this union I have joined you husband and wife. Now, My children, live together as heirs of life:*

In My love's baptismal river I have made you Mine forever.
Here you heard My dear Son's story, Here you touched Him, saw His glory.
Here My Spirit's power filled you, here His tender comfort stilled you.
I the Lord will be your Father, Savior, Comforter and Brother.
Each the other's gladness sharing, Each the other's burdens bearing,

Go, My children, with My blessing, you are My own.
Go, My children, sins forgiven, at peace and pure.
Go, My children, I will keep you and give you peace.
Now, My children, live together as heirs of life.

Music: Public Domain. Text: © Copyright 1983 Jaroslav J. Vajda, 3534 Brookstone South Drive, St. Louis, MO 63129-2900. All Rights Reserved. Used by Permission. This song is NOT covered by CCLI. For permission to reprint, please contact the author as listed above.

His compassions never fail. They are new every morning; great is your faithfulness. (Lamentations 3:22-23)

73 Great Is Thy Faithfulness

Thomas Chisholm
William Runyan

VERSE

1. "Great is Thy faith-ful-ness," O God my Fa-ther,
There is no shad-ow of turn-ing with Thee;
Thou chang-est not, Thy com-pas-sions, they fail not;
As Thou hast been Thou for-ev-er wilt be.

2. Sum-mer and win-ter, and spring-time and har-vest,
Sun, moon and stars in their cours-es a-bove,
Join with all na-ture in man-i-fold wit-ness
To Thy great faith-ful-ness, mer-cy and love.

3. Par-don for sin and a peace that en-dur-eth,
Thy own dear pres-ence to cheer and to guide;
Strength for to-day and bright hope for to-mor-row,
Bless-ings all mine, with ten thou-sand be-side!

CHORUS

"Great is Thy faith-ful-ness! Great is Thy faith-ful-ness!" Morn-ing by morn-ing new mer-cies I see; All I have need-ed Thy hand hath pro-vid-ed "Great is Thy faith-ful-ness," Lord, un-to me!

© Copyright 1923. Renewal 1951 and this arr. © 2000 Hope Publishing Co., Carol Stream, IL 60188.
All Rights Reserved. Used by Permission.

Even though I walk through the valley of the shadow of death, I will fear no evil, for you are with me. (Psalm 23:4)

74 God Is Good All the Time

Don Moen and Paul Overstreet

Country feel ♩ = 116

CHORUS

God is good all the time; He put a song of praise in this heart of mine. God is good all the time; through the dark-est night, His light will shine. God is good, God is good all the time.

VERSE

1. If you're walk-in' through the val-ley, and there are shad-ows all a-round, do not fear; He will
2. We were sin-ners, so un-wor-thy, still for us He chose to die. Filled us with His Ho-ly

© Copyright 1995 Integrity's Hosanna! Music/ASCAP and Scarlet Moon Music/BMI (adm. by Copyright Management), c/o Integrity Music, Inc., 1000 Cody Road, Mobile, AL 36695-3425.
All Rights Reserved. International Copyright Secured. Used by Permission.

18
C♯m
A
guide you. He will keep you safe and
Spir - it, now we can stand and tes - ti -
20
B
F♯m7
sound. 'Cause He has prom - ised to nev - er leave
fy that His love is ev - er - last -
22
B
F♯m7
you nor for - sake you, and His
ing and His mer - cies, they will
24
A Asus4/2 B
Word is true. God is
nev - er end.
3.
E
BRIDGE
C♯m
Though I may not un - der - stand
27
G♯m7
Bm7
F♯m7
all the plans You have for me, my
30
C
G
life is in Your hands, and through the
32
F♯m7(4)
E/G♯
A
A/B
D.S. al CODA
eyes of faith, I can clear - ly see. God is
CODA
34
A
B
good, He's so good. God is
36
A
B
F♯m7
good, He's so good. God is good, He's so
39
B
E
A/E
E
good, all the time.

God Is the Strength of My Heart

God is the strength of my heart and my portion forever. (Psalm 73:26)

75

Eugene Greco

♩ = 106
VERSE

Whom have I in heaven but You? There is nothing on earth I desire (er) beside You; My heart and my strength, many times they fail, But there is one truth that always will prevail.

CHORUS

God is the strength of my heart, God is the strength of my heart; God is the strength

© Copyright 1989, Arr. © 1992 Integrity's Hosanna! Music,
c/o Integrity Music, Inc., 1000 Cody Road, Mobile, AL 36695-3425.
All Rights Reserved. International Copyright Secured. Used by Permission.

"You **hold me** by my right hand.

You *guide* me with your counsel,

and afterward you will

take me into *glory.*

Whom have I in heaven but you?

And earth has nothing I desire besides you.

My flesh and my heart may fail,

but **God** is the **strength** of my

heart and my portion forever."

Psalm 73:23-26

I am making a way in the desert and streams in the wasteland. (Isaiah 43:19)

76 God Will Make a Way

Don Moen

♩ = 108-120

CHORUS

God will make a way where there seems to be no way, He works in ways we can-not see, He will make a way for me; He will be my guide, hold me close-ly to His side, with love and strength for each new day, He will make a way,

© Copyright 1990 Integrity's Hosanna! Music, c/o Integrity Music, Inc., 1000 Cody Road, Mobile, AL 36695-3425.
All Rights Reserved. International Copyright Secured. Used by Permission.

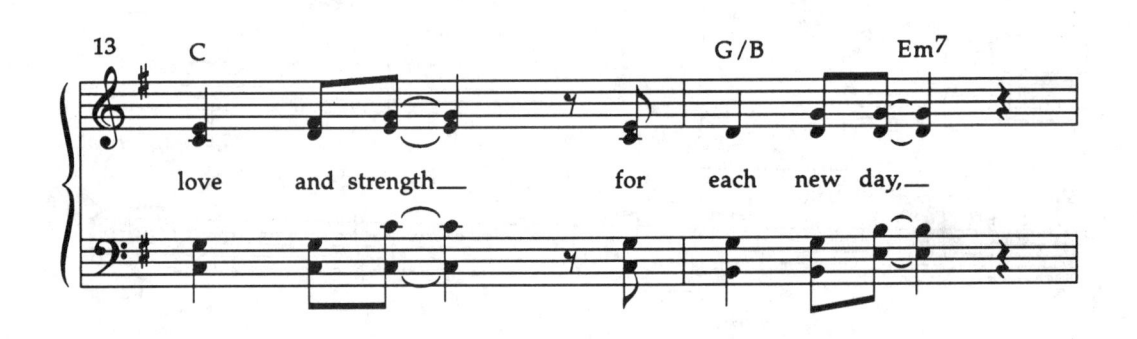

He will make a way.

-ert will I see;

By a

Heav-en and earth will fade but His

VERSE

road-way in the wil-der-ness He'll

Word will still re-main, He will do

lead me, and riv-ers in the des-

some-thing new to-day.

D.C. al Fine

77 Grace Alone

All have sinned and fall short of the glory of God and are justified freely by his grace through the redemption that came by Christ Jesus. (Romans 3:23-24)

Scott Wesley Brown and Jeff Nelson

Moderately, in four ♩ = 70

VERSE

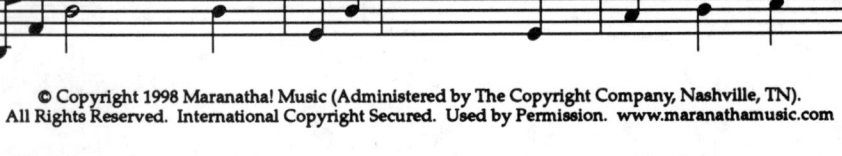

1. Ev-'ry prom-ise we can make, ev-'ry prayer and step of faith, ev-'ry dif-f'rence we will make is on-ly by His grace.
2. Ev-'ry soul we long to reach, ev-'ry heart we hope to teach, ev-'ry-where we share His peace is on-ly by His grace.

Ev-'ry moun-tain we will climb, ev-'ry ray of hope we shine, ev-'ry bless-ing left be-hind
Ev-'ry lov-ing word we say, ev-'ry tear we wipe a-way, ev-'ry sor-row turned to praise

is on-ly by His grace.
is on-ly by His grace.

CHORUS

Grace a-lone which God sup-plies, strength un-

> "For it is by **Grace** you have been saved, through faith—and this *not* from yourselves, it is the **gift** of **God**—*not* by works, so that no one can boast."
>
> Ephesians 2:8-9

Yours, O Lord, is the greatness and the power and the glory and the majesty and the splendor. (1 Chronicles 29:11)

78 Great and Mighty Is He

Todd Pettygrove

♩ = 152

CHORUS

Great and mighty is He, great and mighty is He; Clothed in glory arrayed in splendor, great and mighty is He. Great and mighty is He, great and mighty is He; Clothed in glory arrayed in splendor, great and mighty is He.

VERSE

Let us lift His name up high, celebrate His grace; For He has redeemed our lives, and He reigns on

© Copyright 1987 Integrity's Hosanna! Music, c/o Integrity Music, Inc., 1000 Cody Road, Mobile, AL 36695-3425.
All Rights Reserved. International Copyright Secured. Used by Permission.

"Great and marvelous are your deeds, Lord God Almighty. Just and true are your ways, King of the ages. Who will not fear you, O Lord, and bring glory to your name? For you alone are holy. All nations will come and worship before you, for your righteous acts have been revealed."

Rev. 15:3-4

79 He Is Able

To him who is able to do immeasurably more than all we ask or imagine... (Ephesians 3:20)

Rory Noland and Greg Ferguson

VERSE

He is a-ble, more than a-ble to ac-complish what con-cerns me to-day. He is a-ble, more than a-ble to handle an-y-thing that comes my way. He is a-

CHORUS

-ble, more than a-ble to do much more than I could ev-er dream. He is a-ble, more than a-ble to make me what He wants me to be.

© Copyright 1989 Maranatha Praise, Inc. (Administered by The Copyright Company, Nashville, TN).
All Rights Reserved. International Copyright Secured. Used by Permission. www.maranathamusic.com

80 He Who Began a Good Work in You

He who began a good work in you will carry it on to completion... (Philippians 1:6)

Jon Mohr

♩ = 88 to 96
CHORUS

He who began a good work in you,
He who began a good work in you
will be faith-ful to com-plete it,
He'll be faith-ful to com-plete it;
He who start-ed the work will be faith-ful to com-plete it in you.

Repeat Ending

Song Ending

© Copyright 1987 Birdwing Music/Jonathan Mark Music.
All Rights Reserved. Used by Permission.

81 He Will Come and Save You

Do not fear...The Lord your God is with you, he is mighty to save. (Zephaniah 3:16-17)

Bob Fitts and Gary Sadler

VERSE

1. Say to those who are fearful-hearted, "do not be afraid"; The Lord, your God, is strong with His mighty arms. When you call on His name;
2. Say to those who are broken-hearted, "do not lose your faith"; The Lord, your God, is strong with His loving arms. When you call on His name;

He will come and save. He will come and save.

CHORUS

He will come and save you, He will come and save you; Say to the weary one, "your God will surely come," He will come and save you.

© Copyright 1995 Integrity's Hosanna! Music, c/o Integrity Music, Inc., 1000 Cody Road, Mobile, AL 36695-3425.
All Rights Reserved. International Copyright Secured. Used by Permission.

19
E | A | B | E | E/G#

He will come and save_____ you._____ He will come and

22
A | B | C#m

save_____ you;_____ Lift up your eyes_____

24
A | E/B | B | E/G#

_____ to Him, you will a-rise_____ a-gain, He will come and

26
1. A | Bsus | B | A

save_____ you.

28
2. A | Bsus | B | E

save_____ you._____

30 BRIDGE
C#m | B/D#

He is our ref-uge in the day of trou-ble,

32
E | F#m7

He is our shel-ter in the time of storm;_____

34
E/G# | A | E/G#

He is our tow-er in the day of sor-row, our

36
F#m | Bsus | B | E | D.S.

for-tress in the time of war._____ He will come and

39
3. A | Bsus | B | E | Fine

save_____ you._____

By him we cry 'Abba Father.' The Spirit himself testifies with our spirit that we are God's children. (Romans 8:15-16)

82 Hear Me Say I Love You

Mark Zehnder

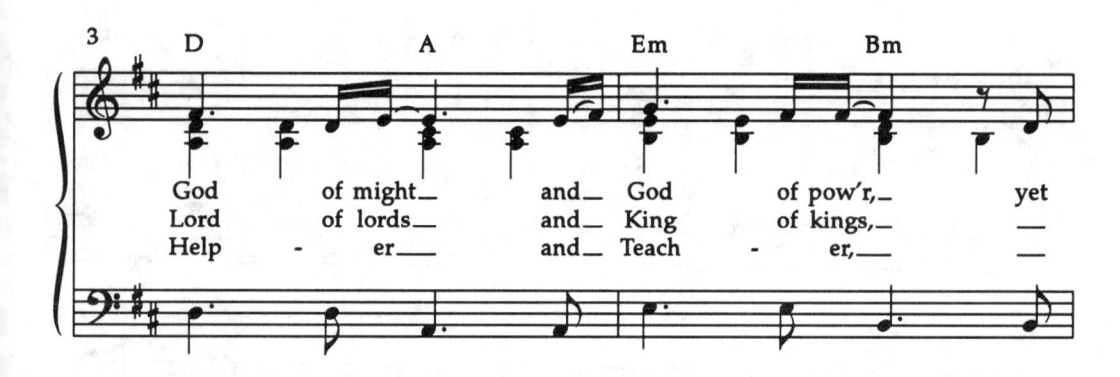

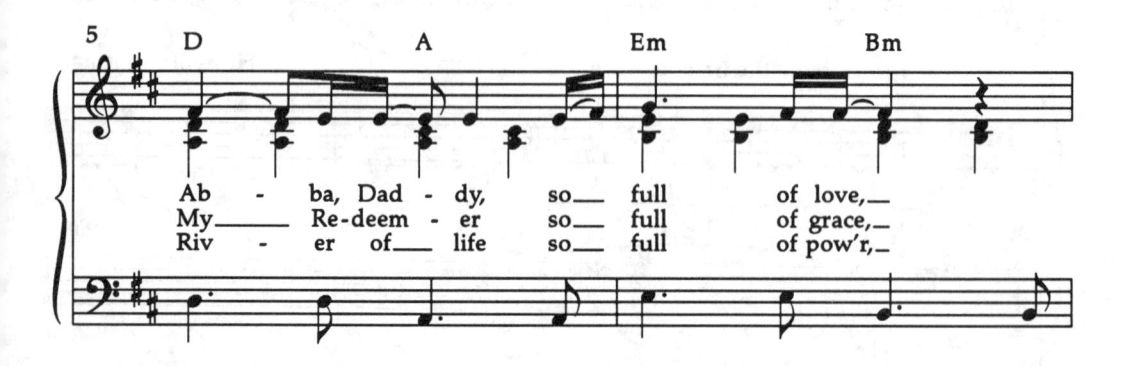

Sincerely

VERSE

1. Fa - ther, my Cre - a - tor,
2. Je - sus, my Sav - ior,
3. Spir - it, my Com - fort - er,

God of might and God of pow'r, yet
Lord of lords and King of kings,
Help - er and Teach - er,

Ab - ba, Dad - dy, so full of love,
My Re - deem - er so full of grace,
Riv - er of life so full of pow'r,

come to me from Your throne a - bove to hear me say:
come to me here in this place to hear me say:
come to me in this ver - y hour to hear me say:

CHORUS

Fa - ther, I love You. Oh
Je - sus, I love You. Oh
Spir - it, I love You. Oh

Fa - ther, I love You. Oh
Je - sus, I love You. Oh
Spir - it, I love You. Oh

Fa - ther, I love You. I love
Je - sus, I love You. I love
Spir - it, I love You. I love

*An excellent arrangement of this song moving through various keys is available through Fellowship Ministries.

© Copyright 2000 Mark Zehnder Publishing.
All Rights Reserved. Used by Permission.

15
1.2. Asus
A
You.
You.
17
3. Asus
A
You.
I love You,
19
BRIDGE
B♭
E♭
Fa - ther. I love You, Son. I love You,
21
B♭
F
E♭/F
Spir - it, the Three in One. You are my
23
B♭
E♭
God. You are my King. You are my
25
B♭
F
E♭/F
Lord, my ev - 'ry-thing. Hal-le - lu -
27
B♭
E♭
jah, hal-le - lu - jah, hal-le - lu -
29
B♭
F
E♭/F
jah, hal-le - lu-jah. A -
31
B♭
E♭
men, a - men, a -
33
B♭
F
E♭/F
B♭
men, a - men, a - men.

The kingdom of God is within you. (Luke 17:21)

83 Heaven Is in My Heart

Graham Kendrick

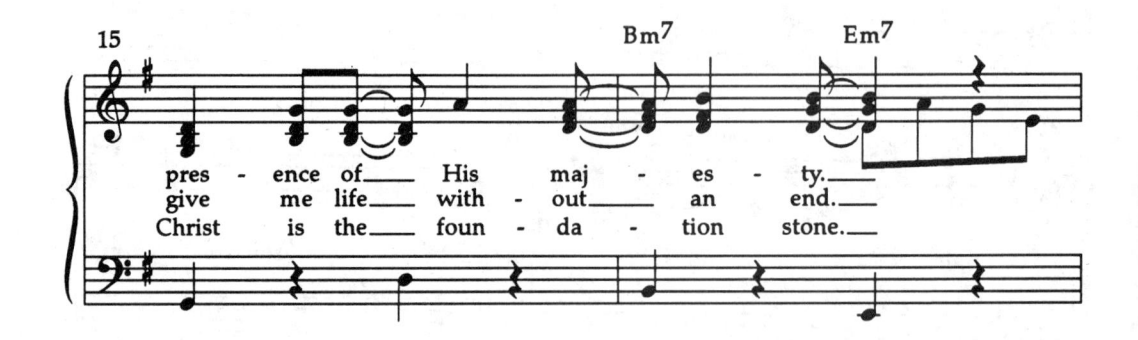

Oh!

Heav-en is in my heart! Oh!

Heav-en is in my heart! *Last time to Coda*

1. The
2. His
3. We

king-dom of our God is here.
pre-cious life on me He spent.
are a tem-ple for His throne.

Heav-en is in my heart! The
Heav-en is in my heart! To
Heav-en is in my heart! And

pres-ence of His maj-es-ty.
give me life with-out an end.
Christ is the foun-da-tion stone.

Heav-en is in my heart! And
Heav-en is in my heart! In
Heav-en is in my heart! He

© Copyright 1991 Make Way Music (admin. by Music Services in the Western Hemisphere) (ASCAP).
All Rights Reserved. Used by Permission.

"I have set the LORD always before me.

Because he is at my right hand,

I will not be shaken.

Therefore my **heart** is **glad** and my

tongue rejoices;

my body also will rest secure,

because you will not abandon me to the

grave, nor will you let your Holy One see

decay. You have made known to me the path

of life; you will

fill me with **joy**

in your presence,

with eternal pleasures at your right hand."

Psalm 16:8-11

If anyone is thirsty, let him come to me and drink. (John 7:37)

84 Healer of My Heart

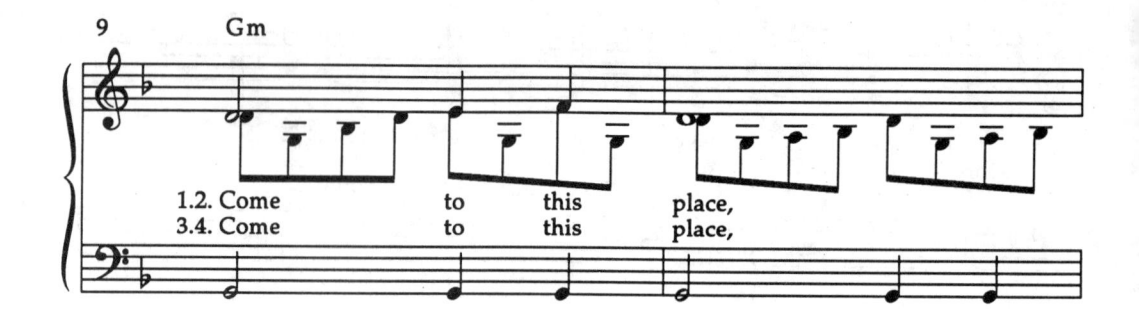

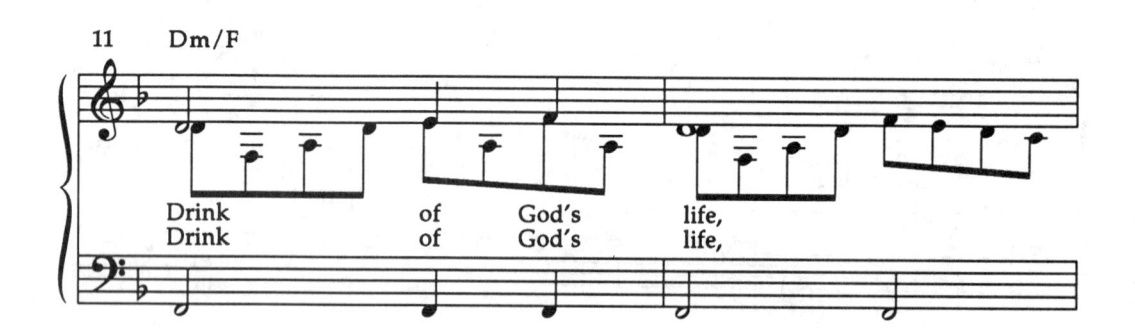

Gloria Lien

Hopefully ♩ = 90

1. Heal-er of my heart, Crip-pled with sin.
2. Par-a-lyzed with doubt, Con-fusion lingers all a-bout, Bent on my knee.
3. Je-sus, God of pow'r, Jesus, all au-thor-i-ty, sins are for-giv'n."
4. Heal-er of my heart, Heal-er of my stub-born ways,

Heal-er of all bro-ken-ness "Your
Wear-y, lost and thirst-y The
Je-sus man of ac-tion,
Place Your seal up-on my head,

old has passed a-way.

1.2. Come to this place,
3.4. Come to this place,

Drink of God's life,
Drink of God's life,

Rest, fill your soul and be made whole.
"Go sin no more and be made whole."

© Copyright 2000 Gloria Publishing, 1604 SE 9th Street, Wilmar, MN 56201, e-mail: cti@willmar.com

Ask of me, and I will surely give the nations as thine inheritance,
and the very ends of the earth as thy possession. (Psalm 2:8)

Here Am I

Bob Kilpatrick

Here I Am, Lord

Here I am...Speak, Lord, for your servant is listening. (1 Samuel 3:8-9)

Daniel Schutte

VERSE

1. "I, the Lord of sea and sky, I have heard my people cry. All who dwell in deep-est sin My hand will save. I, who made the stars of night, I will make their darkness bright. Who will bear My light to them? Whom shall I send?"

2. "I, the Lord of snow and rain, I have borne my people's pain. I have wept for love of them. They turn a-way. I will break their hearts of stone, give them hearts for love a-lone. I will speak My Word to them. Whom shall I send?"

3. "I, the Lord of wind and flame, I will tend the poor and lame. I will set a feast for them. My hand will save. Fin-est bread I will pro-vide till their hearts be sat-is-fied. I will give My life to them. Whom shall I send?"

CHORUS

Here I am, Lord. Is it I, Lord?

© Copyright 1981 by Daniel J. Schutte and New Dawn Music.
All Rights Reserved. Used by Permission.

"Then I heard the voice of the Lord saying,

'*Whom* shall I send?

And who **will *go*** for us?'

And I said,

'**Here** am I. **Send** me!'"

Isaiah 6:8-9

87 Here in This Place

Through Jesus...let us continually offer to God a sacrifice of praise. (Hebrews 13:15)

Julie Schroeder
Bobby L. Schroeder

Worshipfully ♩ = 74

Here in this place we worship You. Here in this place we adore You. We offer praises to You alone, As we bow before Your throne. Here in this place we worship You. Here in this place we adore You. We offer praises to You alone As we bow before Your throne.

1. Here in this
2. Here in this

© Copyright 1999 BLS Ministries.
All Rights Reserved. International Copyright Secured. Used by Permission.

88 Here Is Bread

Whoever eats my flesh and drinks my blood has eternal life. (John 6:54)

Graham Kendrick

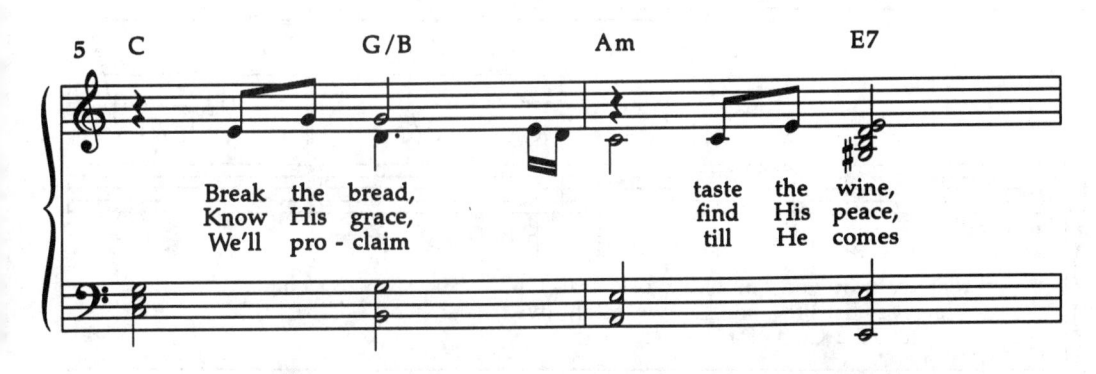

1. Here is bread, here is wine, Christ is with us, He is with us.
2. Here is grace, here is peace, Christ is with us, He is with us.
3. Here we are, joined in one, Christ is with us, He is with us.

Break the bread, taste the wine, Christ is with us here.
Know His grace, find His peace, feast on Jesus here.
We'll proclaim till He comes Jesus crucified.

CHORUS

In this bread there is healing, in this cup is life forever. In this moment by the Spirit, Christ is with us here.

© Copyright 1991 Make Way Music (admin. by Music Services in the Western Hemisphere) (ASCAP). All Rights Reserved. Used by Permission.

Holy, Holy, Holy is the Lord God Almighty. (Revelation 4:8)

89 Holy Is Our God Medley

Brad and Donna Hoefs

*Holy Is Our God**

Ho-ly is our God, whose name we praise for-ev - er.

Glo-ry to the Son, who reigns in maj-es-ty!

Come, Spir-it, come and fill our hearts with wis-dom, that

4th time to Coda

we may long to wor-ship You a - lone.

*Text and Music by Donna Hoefs.

© Copyright 1998 Wings of Grace, Inc.
All Rights Reserved. Used by Permission.

1. Our Fa-ther is the great Cre - a - tor
2. For Je-sus is the Fa-ther's on-ly Son,
3. Oh Spir-it, come and u-nite us

of all we have and all we see.
giv-en in love for ev-'ry-one.
in one com-mu-nion with our Lord.

He made us in His im - age
Lamb of sac-ri-fice, a hum-ble King,
Free us from the chains that bind us,

that we may hon-or and wor-ship Him.
He gave His life so we might live.
for the Com-fort-er has come.

D.S. al CODA

*Text by Reginald Heber / Music by John B. Dykes.

How sweet are your words to my taste, sweeter than honey to my mouth. (Psalm 119:103)

90 Holy and Anointed One

John Barnett

© Copyright 1988 Mercy/Vineyard Publishing (ASCAP).
All Rights Reserved. Used by Permission.

---

*Jesus, You Are My Guide and Wisdom**

art, ev-er-more shalt
Per-sons, bless-ed Trin-i-ty!

be. Je-sus, You are my guide and wis-dom. Je-sus, You are the strength that I need. Je-sus, You are my rea-son for liv-ing. Je-sus, You are all that I need. Je-sus need.

*Text and Music by Brad and Donna Hoefs.

9
G D C Am7 G/D D
1.3. Ho - ly and A - noint - ed One, Je -
2.4. Ris - en and Ex - alt - ed One,
12
1.3. Repeat to CHORUS (to meas. 5)
G C2/E D7/F♯
sus.
2.4. To VERSE
G G/B
sus. Your name is like hon -
VERSE
14
C G G/B
- ey on my lips, Your Spir - it like wa -
16
C G G/B
- ter to my soul. Your Word is a lamp
18
C Em7
un - to my feet, Je - sus, I love
20
Cmaj7
You, I love You.
1. Optional D.S. to CHORUS (to meas. 5)
D C/D
22
2. Optional Repeat to VERSE (to meas. 14)
D G/B
You. Your name is like hon -
3. SONG ENDING
D C/D
You.
24
G Bm7 C G D
Je - sus, Je -
27
C2 C Bm Am G
sus.
rit.

91 Hide Me in Your Holiness

Your life is now hidden with Christ in God. (Colossians 3:3)

Steve Ragsdale

Capo 1 (D)

VERSE

Hide me, Lord, in Your holiness, ev'ry sin I now confess. Praise to You, forgiving Lord, hide me in Your holiness, hide me in Your holiness.

CHORUS

Hide me, hide me, hide me, Lord. Won't You hide me, hide me, hide me in Your holiness, hide me in Your holiness.

© Copyright 1986 Maranatha Praise, Inc. (Administered by The Copyright Company, Nashville, TN).
All Rights Reserved. International Copyright Secured. Used by Permission. www.maranathamusic.com

92. Holy, Holy, Holy Is the Lord of Hosts

Holy, Holy, Holy is the Lord Almighty, the whole earth is full of his glory. (Isaiah 6:3)

Nolene Prince

Ho-ly, ho-ly, ho-ly is the Lord of hosts;

Ho-ly, ho-ly, ho-ly is the Lord of hosts. The whole earth is full of His glo-ry, The whole earth is full of His glo-ry, The whole earth is full of His glo-ry; Ho-ly is the Lord.

© Copyright 1976 Nolene Prince (Administered by Resource Christian Music Pty., Ltd., c/o The Copyright Company, Nashville, TN). All Rights Reserved. International Copyright Secured. Used by Permission.

"He first makes us to know his holy name, and so keeps us from polluting it and engages us to *honor* it. The heathen, those that never knew it, or would not own it, shall know that 'I am the Lord, the Holy One in Israel.'"

Matthew Henry, 1662-1714

93 Holy, Holy

Holy, Holy, Holy is the Lord God Almighty who was, and is, and is to come. (Revelation 4:8)

Nathan Fellingham

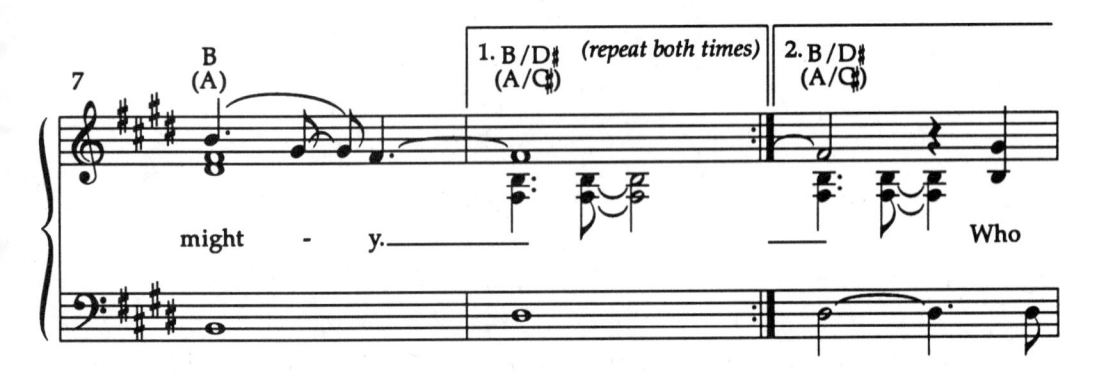

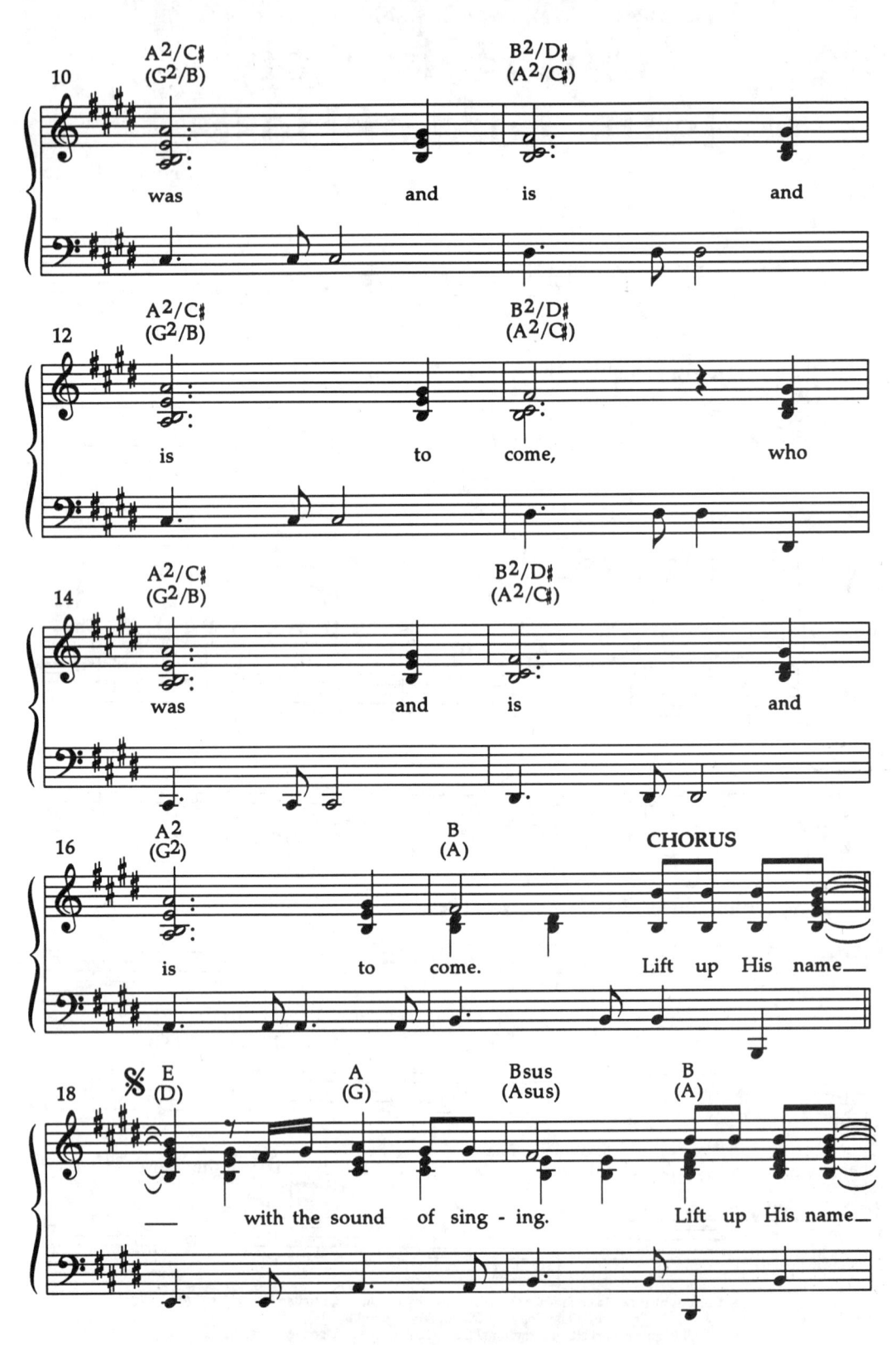

"Each of the four living creatures had six wings and was covered with eyes all around, even under his wings.

Day and night they never stop saying:

'Holy, holy, holy *is the Lord God Almighty,*

who was, and is, and is to come.'

Whenever the living creatures give glory, honor and thanks to him who sits on the throne and who lives for ever and ever, the twenty-four elders fall down before him who sits on the throne, and worship him who lives for ever and ever. They lay their crowns before the throne and say:

'You are worthy, our Lord and God, to receive glory and honor and power, for you created all things, and by your will they were created and have their being.'"

Revelation 4:8-11

94 Holy Lamb of God

Worthy is the Lamb, who was slain, to receive power and wealth and wisdom and strength and honor and glory and praise! (Revelation 5:12)

Bob Fitts

♩ = 80-100

VERSE

Ho-ly Lamb of God we ex-alt Your name,
Ho-ly Lamb of God we ex-alt Your name,
Ho-ly Lamb of God we de-clare Your praise;
Ho-ly Lamb of God we ex-alt Your name,
Ho-ly Lamb of God we ex-alt Your name,
Ho-ly Lamb of God we de-clare Your praise.

CHORUS

Praise Him, praise Him! Praise His name!

© Copyright 1986 Scripture In Song (a div. of Integrity Music, Inc.)/ASCAP.
All Rights Reserved. Used by Permission.

95 Hosanna

Hosanna! Blessed is he who comes in the name of the Lord. (Mark 11:9)

Carl Tuttle

♩ = 112-120

1. Ho-san-na, ho-san-na, Ho-san-na in the high-est; Ho-san-na, ho-san-na, Ho-san-na in the high-est. Lord, we lift up Your name, With hearts full of praise; Be ex-alt-ed, O Lord, my God, Ho-san-na in the high-est.

2. Glo-ry, glo-ry, Glory to the King of kings; Glo-ry, glo-ry, Glory to the King of kings.

Optional Extended Ending (opt.-repeat as desired)

est. Ho-san-na in the high-est. Ho-san-na in the high-est.

© Copyright 1985 Mercy/Vineyard Publishing (ASCAP).
All Rights Reserved. Used by Permission.

96 How Could You Love Me So Much?

God so loved the world that he gave his only begotten Son, that whoever believes in Him should not perish, but have everlasting life. (John 3:16)

Mark Zehnder

♩ = 76

Intro: Piano Vamp

VERSE

1. Oh Lord, my God, I stand a-mazed, as I be-hold Your match-less grace; I see You smil-ing down up-on this child, and see that my gain be-came Your loss. To know that in Your heart of hearts, I am the ap-ple of Your eye, I mar-vel at Your love for me, Oh Lord, to think Your love would make You die!

2. And now I'm free from guilt and shame, by Your shed blood up-on the cross; To think Your love would take You, Lord, that far, so With all my heart and all my soul, with all my strength, I wor-ship You. With ev-'ry-thing I have with-in me Lord, Lov-ing You is all I want to do!

© Copyright 1997 Mark Zehnder Publishing
All Rights Reserved. Used by Permission.

CHORUS
F F/A B♭2
Oh, how could You love me so much, that You
Gm7 Gm7/F Csus C B♭/C C F F/A
gave Your life for me? Oh, how could You
B♭2 Gm7 Gm7/F
love me so much that You shed Your blood to
E♭ 1. Csus rit. C 2. C/D rit. D
set me free? free?
G G/B C2
Oh, how could You, love me so much, that You
Am7 C/G Dsus D G G/B
gave Your life for me? Oh, how could You
C2 Am7 Am7/G
love me so much, that You shed Your blood to
F Dsus rit. D G
set me free? Set me free!
Optional Tag Ending
G C/G G C/G
free! You set me free! You set me
G C/G rit. G
free! You set me free!

God...gave him the name that is above every name. (Philippians 2:9)

97 How Shall I Call You?

Robin Mann

Gently ♩. = 58

VERSE

1. How shall I call You? Maker of heaven, poet of sunset and painter of sky. Father almighty, who's running to find us, giving His Son who must suffer and die:
2. How shall I call you? Lover of children, shepherd and teacher and brother and friend, healer of blind man and healer of leper; you are beginning and middle and end:
3. How shall I call you? Spirit of comfort, cloud in the day-time and fire in the night, guide as we wander, protector in danger, list-'ner and helper and giver of sight.
4. How shall I call you? Master and servant, Lord of the seasons and Lord of the years; faithful and constant in loving and mercy, giver of laughter and taker of tears:

CHORUS

Glory to the Father, the Son and the Spirit, let's sing it again and again. Glory to the Father, the Son and the Spirit, let's sing it again and again.

© Copyright 1977 Robin Mann.
All Rights Reserved. Used by Permission.

For you have been bought with a price. (1 Corinthians 6:20)

98   I Am Not My Own

Martin J. Nystrom

♩ = 83

I am not my own,— I was bought with a price,— I was pur-chased with the pre-cious blood of Je-sus Christ;— All my debts were paid— by His sac-ri-fice,— hal-le-lu-jah to the Lamb— Who re-deems my life.—

© Copyright 1991 Integrity's Hosanna! Music, c/o Integrity Music, Inc., 1000 Cody Road, Mobile, AL 36695-3425.
All Rights Reserved. International Copyright Secured. Used by Permission.

"I believe that Jesus Christ, true God, begotten of the Father from eternity, and also true man, born of the Virgin Mary, is my Lord, who has redeemed me, a lost and condemned creature, *purchased* and won me from all sins, from death, and from the power of the devil; not with gold or silver, but with His holy, precious blood and with His innocent suffering and death, that I may be His own, and live under Him in His kingdom, and serve Him in everlasting righteousness, innocence, and blessedness, even as He is risen from the dead, lives and reigns to all eternity. This is most certainly true."

Martin Luther, 1529

99 I Am the Bread of Life

I am the living bread...If anyone eats of this bread, he will live forever. (John 6:51)

John Michael Talbot

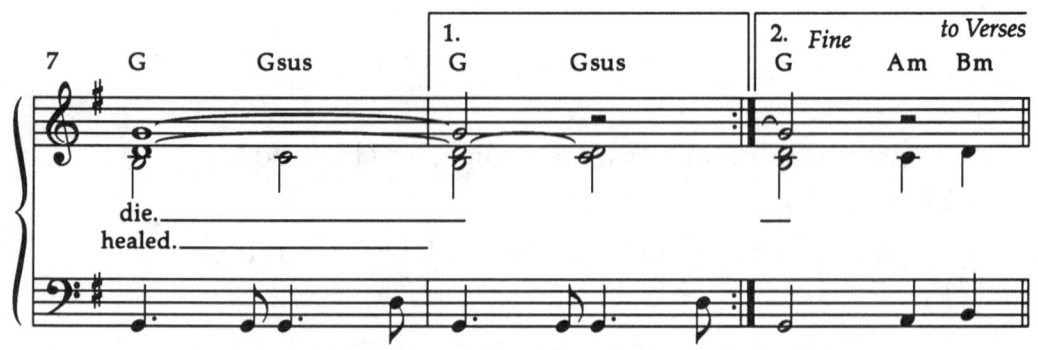

CHORUS

I am the Bread of Life.
I am God's love revealed.

All who eat this Bread will never die.
I am broken that you might be healed.

VERSE

1. All who eat of this heavenly Bread,
2. No one who comes to Me shall ever hunger again.

All who drink this cup of the covenant
No one who believes shall ever thirst.

you will live forever for I will raise you up.
All that the Father draws shall come to Me and I will give them rest.

© Copyright 1982 Birdwing Music/BMG Songs, Inc.
All Rights Reserved. International Copyright Secured. Used by Permission.

I am the resurrection and the life. He who believes in me will live even though he dies. (John 11:25)

100 I Am the Bread of Life

Suzanne Toolan

Capo 1 (G)

VERSE

1. ___ I am the Bread of life. ___ You who come to Me shall not ___ hun-ger; and who be-lieve in Me shall not thirst. ___ No one can come to Me ___ un-less the ___ Fa-ther beck-ons.
2. The bread that ___ I will give ___ is My flesh for the life of the world, ___ and if you eat ___ of this bread, ___ you shall live for ___ ev-er, you shall ___ live for ___ ev-er.
3. Un-less ___ you eat ___ of the flesh of the Son of ___ Man and ___ drink of His blood, and drink ___ of His blood, you shall ___ not have life with-in ___ you.
4. ___ I am the Res-ur-rec-tion, ___ I ___ am the ___ life. ___ If you be-lieve ___ in Me, ___ e-ven though you die, ___ you shall ___ live for ___ ev-er.
5. Yes, Lord, ___ I be-lieve ___ that You ___ are the ___ Christ, ___ the ___ Son of ___ God, ___ Who has ___ come ___ in-to the ___ world.

CHORUS *Harmony:*

"And I will raise ___ you up, ___ and I will raise ___ you up, ___ and I will raise ___ you up-on the last ___ day."

© Copyright 1993 GIA Publications, Inc.
All Rights Reserved. Used by Permission.

101 I Believe in Jesus

Christ died for our sins...was buried...was raised. (1 Cor. 15:3-4)

Marc Nelson

VERSE

1. I believe in Je-sus,
2. And I believe in You, Lord.

I believe He is the Son of God.
I believe You are the Son of God.

I believe He died and rose a-gain,
I believe You died and rose a-gain,

I believe He paid for us all.
I believe You paid for us all.

CHORUS

And I be-lieve that He's here now,
And I be-lieve that You're here now,

Stand-ing in our midst.

Here with the pow-er to heal now,

And the grace to for-give. give.

© Copyright 1987 and this arr. © 1997 Mercy/Vineyard (ASCAP), admin. by Music Services.
All Rights Reserved. International Copyright Secured. Used by Permission.

102 I Exalt Thee

For you, O Lord, are the most High over the earth; you are exalted far above all gods. (Psalm 97:9)

Pete Sanchez, Jr.

♩ = 80 to 96

VERSE
For Thou, O Lord art high above all the earth. Thou art exalted far above all gods. For Thou, O Lord art high above all gods.

CHORUS
I exalt Thee, I exalt Thee, I exalt Thee, O Lord.

I ex- bove all gods.

Repeat Ending D.C. — Lord.
Song Ending — Lord.

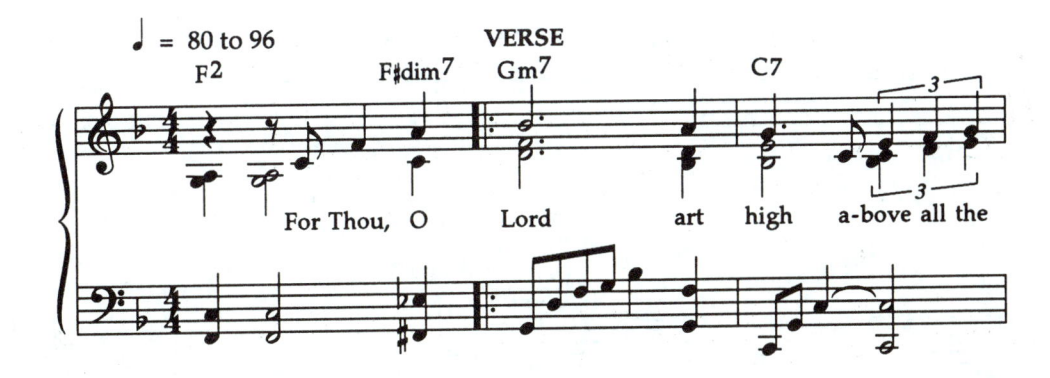

© Copyright 1977 Pete Sanchez, Jr. (ASCAP), Administered by Gabriel Music, Inc.,
P.O. Box 840999, Houston, TX 77284-0999 U.S.A.
All Rights Reserved. Used by Permission.

I Could Sing of Your Love Forever

I will sing of the Lord's great love forever. (Psalm 89:1)

Martin Smith

Capo 3 (D)

VERSE

O-ver the moun-tains and the sea Your riv-er runs with love for me, and I will o-pen up my heart, and let the Heal-er set me free.

I'm hap-py to be in the truth, and I will dai-ly lift my hands, for I will al-ways sing of when Your love came down.

CHORUS

I could sing of Your love for-ev-er,

I could sing of Your love for-ev-er.

I could sing of Your love for-ev-er,

I could sing of Your love for-ev-er.

Last time to Coda

© Copyright 1994 Curious? Music U.K./Administered in North America by EMI Christian Music Publishing/P.O. Box 5085, Brentwood, TN 37024-5085
All Rights Reserved. Used by Permission.

"Whoever sings, prays twice."

St. Augustine 354-430

104 I Give You My Heart

Earth has nothing I desire besides you. (Psalm 73:25)

Reuben Morgan

VERSE

This is my de-sire, to hon-or You. Lord, with all my heart I wor-ship You. All I have with-in me, I give You praise. All that I a-dore is in You.

CHORUS

Lord, I give You my heart. I give You my soul. I live for You a-lone.

© Copyright 1995 Reuben Morgan/Hillsongs Australia, admin. by Integrity's Hosanna! Music, 1000 Cody Road, Mobile, AL 36695-3425. All Rights Reserved. International Copyright Secured. Used by Permission.

"I truly desire that all Christians would *love* and regard as worthy the lovely **gift** of **music**, which is a precious, worthy, and costly treasure **given** mankind by **God**. The riches of music are so excellent and so precious that words fail me whenever I attempt to discuss and describe them…next to the Word of God, the noble **art** of **music** is the **greatest treasure** in this world. It controls our thoughts, minds, hearts, and spirits…

Our dear fathers and prophets did not desire without reason that music be always used in the churches. Hence we have so many songs and psalms. This precious gift has been given to man alone that he might thereby remind himself of the fact that God has created man for the express purpose of **praising** & extolling **God**."

Martin Luther, 1538

[This quotation also appears in the pew and lead line editions next to song #244]

I want to know Christ and the power of his resurrection. (Philippians 3:10)

105 I Live to Know You

Darlene Zschech

Moderately ♩ = 106

1. Stand-ing in Your pres-ence, Lord, my heart and life are changed, just to love You and to live to see Your beau-ty and Your grace. Heav-en and earth
2. You've called me; I will fol-low Your will for me, I'm sure. Let Your heart beat be my heart's cry. Let me live to serve Your call.

CHORUS

cry out Your name. Na-tions rise up and see Your face. And Your king-dom is es-tab-lished as I live to know You more. Now I will nev-er be the same. Spir-it of God, my life You've changed, and I'll for ev-er sing Your praise. I live to

© Copyright 1996 Darlene Zschech/Hillsongs Australia, admin. by
Integrity's Hosanna! Music, 1000 Cody Road, Mobile, AL 36695-3425.
All Rights Reserved. International Copyright Secured. Used by Permission.

"But whatever was to my profit I now consider loss for the sake of Christ. What is more, I consider everything a loss compared to the surpassing **greatness** of knowing Christ Jesus my Lord, for whose sake I have lost all things. I consider them rubbish, that I may gain Christ and be found in him, not having a righteousness of my own that comes from the law, but that which is through faith in Christ—the righteousness that comes from God and is by faith. I want to *know* Christ and the power of his resurrection and the fellowship of sharing in his sufferings, becoming like him in his death, and so, somehow, to attain to the resurrection from the dead."

Philippians 3:7-11

106 I Love to Be in Your Presence

In thy presence is fulness of joy. (Psalm 16:11)

Paul Baloche and Ed Kerr

Lyrics:

CHORUS
I love to be in Your presence, with Your people singing praises; I love to stand and rejoice, lift my hands and raise my voice.

VERSE
You set my feet to dancing, You fill my heart with song; You give me reason to rejoice.

Lift my hands, lift my hands, lift my hands and raise my voice.

© Copyright 1992 Integrity's Hosanna! Music, c/o Integrity Music, Inc., 1000 Cody Road, Mobile, AL 36695-3425.
All Rights Reserved. International Copyright Secured. Used by Permission.

107 I Love You, Lord

The Lord delights in those...who put their hope in his unfailing love. (Psalm 147:11)

Laurie Klein

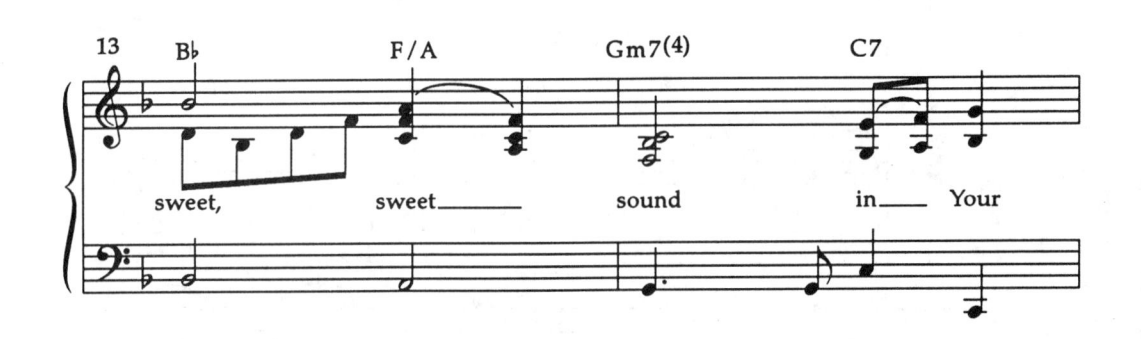

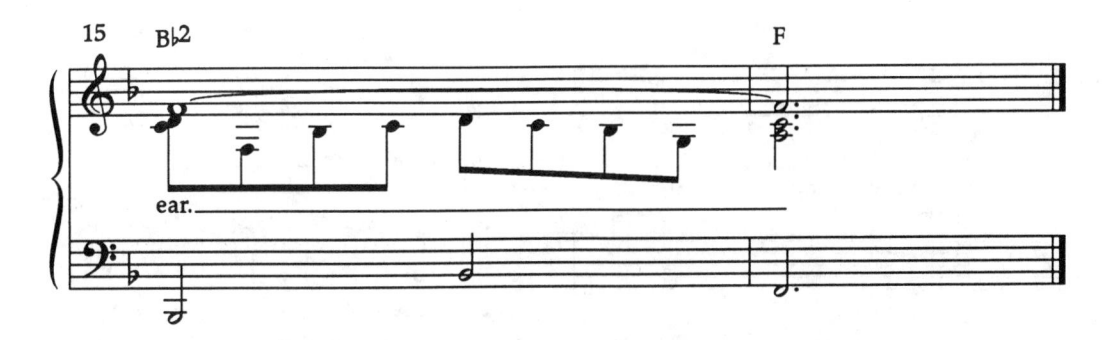

I love You, Lord, and I lift my voice to worship You, O my soul rejoice. Take joy my King in what You hear, may it be a sweet, sweet sound in Your ear.

© Copyright 1978 House of Mercy Music (Administered by Maranatha! Music c/o The Copyright Company, Nashville, TN).
All Rights Reserved. International Copyright Secured. Used by Permission. www.maranathamusic.com

Offer your bodies as living sacrifices, holy and pleasing to God. (Romans 12:1)

108 I Offer My Life

Claire Cloninger and Don Moen

♩ = 76

VERSE

1. All that I am, all that I have, I lay them down before You, O Lord; All my regrets, all my acclaim, the joy and the pain, I'm making them Yours.
2. Things in the past, things yet unseen, wishes and dreams that are yet to come true; All of my hopes, all of my plans, my heart and my hands are lifted to You.

CHORUS

Lord, I offer my life to You, ev'rything I've been through, use it for Your glory; Lord, I offer my days to You, lifting my praise to You as a pleasing sacrifice, Lord, I offer You my life.

© Copyright 1994 Word Music, Inc. (ASCAP) 65 Music Square West, Nashville, TN 37203/
Juniper Landing Music (Admin. by Word Music, Inc.) (ASCAP) 65 Music Square West, Nashville, TN 37203/
Integrity's Hosanna! Music (ASCAP), c/o Integrity Music, Inc., 1000 Cody Road, Mobile, AL 36695-3425.
All Rights Reserved. Made in the U.S.A. International Copyright Secured. Used by Permission.

"If anyone would come after me, he must *deny* himself and take up his cross daily and *follow* me."

Luke 9:23

109 I Need You

Lord have mercy on me; heal me, for I have sinned against you. (Psalm 41:4)

Rick Founds

Lord, look upon my need. I need You, I need You. Lord, have mercy now on me. Forgive me, O Lord, forgive me and I will be clean.

O Lord, You are familiar with my ways; there is nothing hid from You. O Lord, You know the number of my days. I want to live my life for You.

D.C. al CODA

CODA

clean.

© Copyright 1989 Maranatha Praise, Inc. (Administered by The Copyright Company, Nashville, TN). All Rights Reserved. International Copyright Secured. Used by Permission. www.maranathamusic.com

To this you were called...that you should follow in his steps. (1 Peter 2:21)

110 I Want to Be More Like You

Clint Brown

Capo 1 (D)

Worshipfully ♩ = 100

Keyboard: E♭2
Guitar: (D2)

Lyrics:
I want to be more like You.
I want to be more like You.
I want to be a vessel You work through.
I want to be more like You.
I want to be more like You.

© Copyright 1990 Integrity's Hosanna! Music, c/o Integrity Music, Inc., 1000 Cody Road, Mobile, AL 36695-3425,
arr. © 1991 Van Ness Press, distributed by Genevox Music Group.
All Rights Reserved. International Copyright Secured. Used by Permission.

111 I See the Lord

...I saw the Lord seated on a throne, high and exalted, and the train of his robe filled the temple. (Isaiah 6:1)

Paul Baloche

Worshipfully ♩ = 112

VERSE

I see the Lord, and He is seat-ed on the throne;____ the train of His robe is fill-ing the heav-ens.____ I see the Lord, and He is shin-ing like____ the sun,____ His eyes full of fire,____ His voice like the wa-ters. Sur-round-ing His throne are thou-sands, sing-ing:

CHORUS

"Ho-ly, ho-ly, ho-ly is the Lord God Al-might-

© Copyright 1998 Integrity's Hosanna! Music, c/o Integrity Music, Inc., 1000 Cody Road, Mobile, AL 36695-3425.
All Rights Reserved. International Copyright Secured. Used by Permission.

"We did not follow cleverly invented stories when we told you about the power and coming of our Lord Jesus Christ, but we were *eyewitnesses* of his majesty. For he received honor and glory from God the Father when the voice came to him from the Majestic Glory, saying,

'This is my Son, whom I love; with him I am well pleased.'

We ourselves heard this voice that came from heaven when we were with him on the sacred mountain. And we have the word of the prophets made more certain, and you will do well to pay attention to it, as to a light shining in a dark place, until the day dawns and the morning star rises in your hearts."

2 Peter 1:16-19

Holy, holy, holy is the Lord Almighty; the whole earth is full of his glory. (Isaiah 6:3)

112 I See the Lord

Chris Falson

Majestically ♩ = 102

113 I Want Jesus to Walk with Me

The Lord is close to the brokenhearted and saves those who are crushed in spirit. (Psalm 34:18)

African American spiritual
Harmonization: J. Jefferson Cleveland and Verolga Nix

Heartfelt ♩ = 112

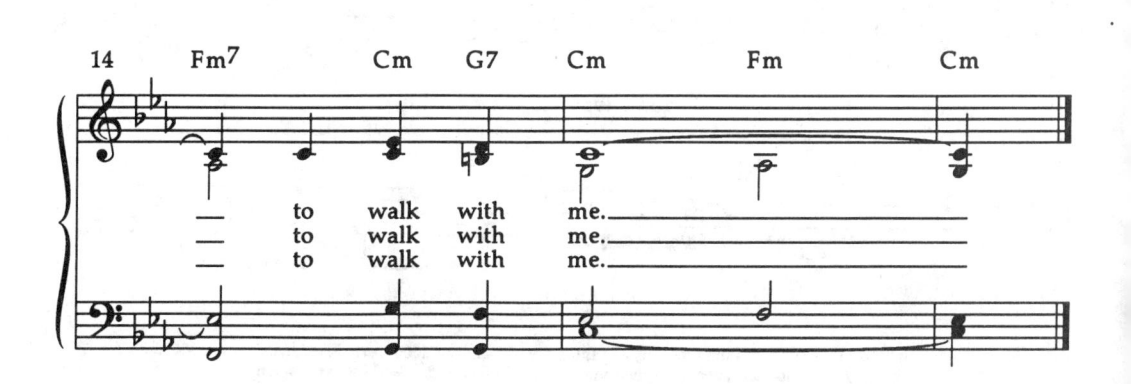

1. I want Jesus to walk with me;
2. In my trials, Lord, walk with me;
3. When I'm in trouble, Lord, walk with me;

I want Jesus to walk with me;
In my trials, Lord, walk with me;
When I'm in trouble, Lord, walk with me;

All along my pilgrim journey,
When my heart is almost breaking,
When my head is bowed in sorrow,

Lord, I want Jesus to walk with me.
Lord, I want Jesus to walk with me.
Lord, I want Jesus to walk with me.

© Copyright 1981 Abingdon Press (Administered by The Copyright Company, Nashville, TN).
All Rights Reserved. International Copyright Secured. Used by Permission.

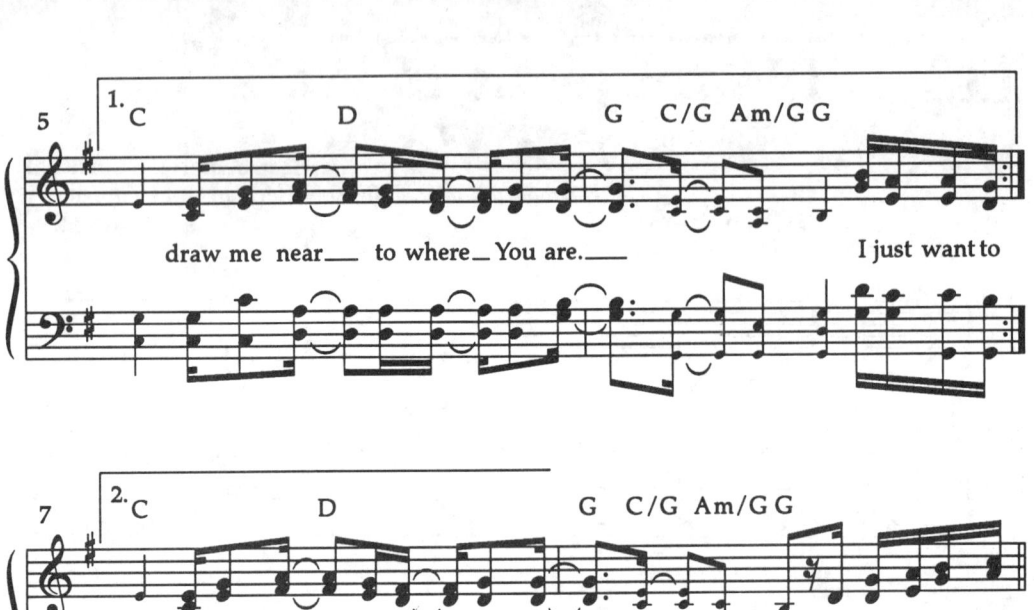

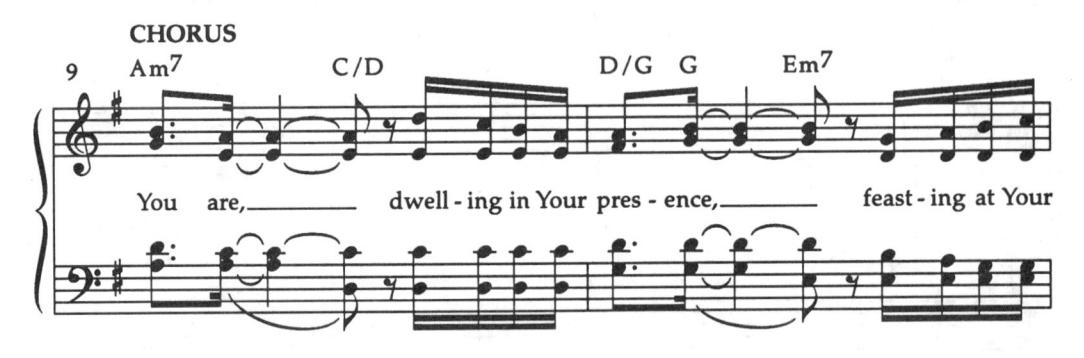

You will fill me with joy in your presence. (Psalm 16:11)

114 I Want to Be Where You Are

Don Moen

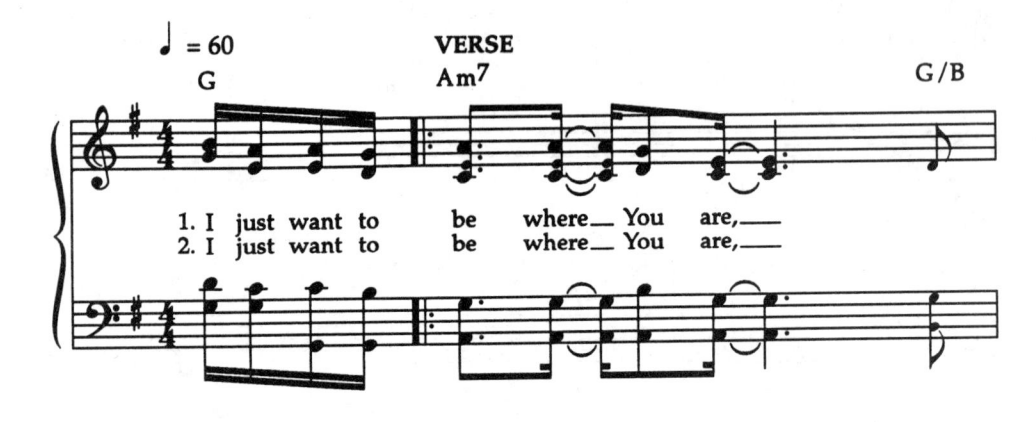

♩ = 60 VERSE

1. I just want to be where You are,
2. I just want to be where You are,

dwell - ing dai - ly in Your
in Your dwell - ing place for -

pres - ence; I don't want to wor - ship from a - far,
ev - er; take me to the place where You are,

draw me near to where You are. I just want to

I just want to be with You. I want to be where

CHORUS

You are, dwell - ing in Your pres - ence, feast - ing at Your

ta - ble, sur - round - ed by Your glo - ry; In Your

© Copyright 1989 Integrity's Hosanna! Music, c/o Integrity Music, Inc., 1000 Cody Road, Mobile, AL 36695-3425.
All Rights Reserved. International Copyright Secured. Used by Permission.

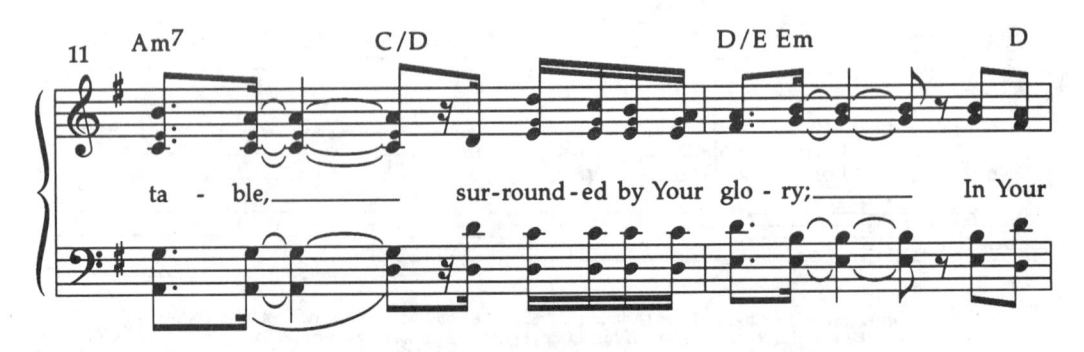

"You have made known to me the path of life; you will fill me with joy in your presence, with eternal pleasures at your right hand."

Psalm 16:11

115 I Want to Walk as a Child of the Light

Whoever follows me will never walk in darkness but will have the light of life. (John 8:12)

Kathleen Thomerson

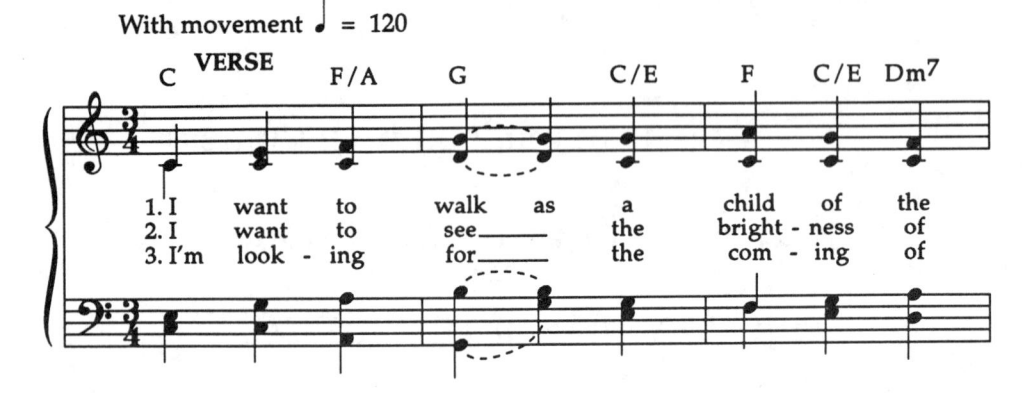

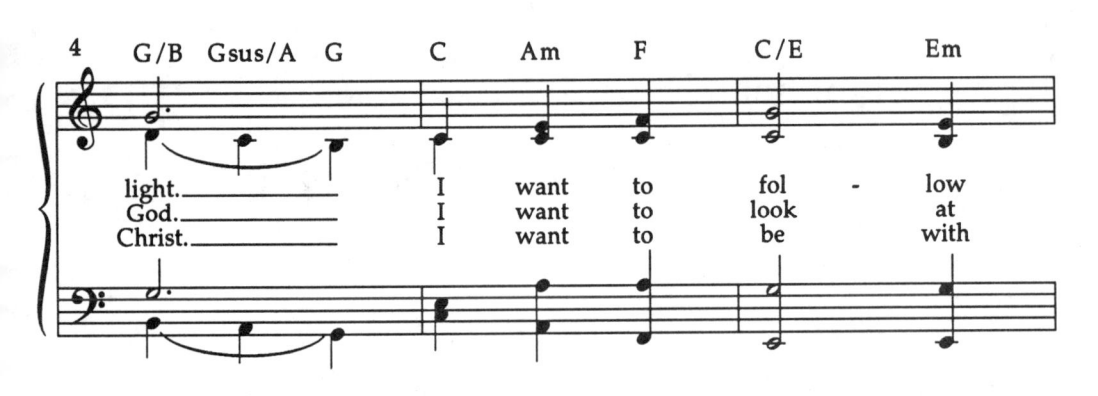

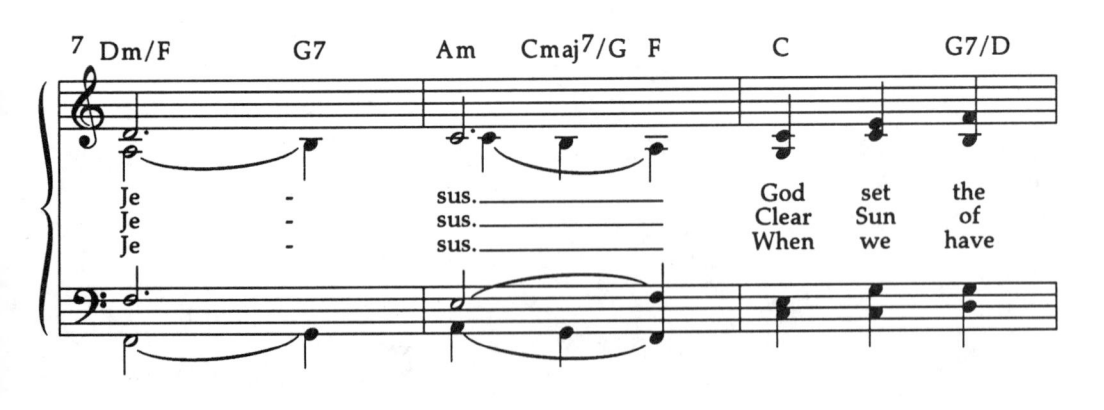

With movement ♩ = 120

1. I want to walk as a child of the light. I want to follow Jesus. God set the
2. I want to see the brightness of God. I want to look at Jesus. Clear Sun of
3. I'm looking for the coming of Christ. I want to be with Jesus. When we have

stars to give light to the world. The star of my life is Jesus.
Righteousness, shine on my path, and show me the way to the Father.
run with patience the race, we shall know the joy of Jesus.

CHORUS

In Him there is no darkness at

© Copyright 1970 Celebration (Administered by The Copyright Company, Nashville, TN).
All Rights Reserved. International Copyright Secured. Used by Permission.

Lyrics (under music):

all. The night and the day are both a-like. The Lamb is the light of the cit-y of God.

TAG
Shine in my heart, Lord Je-sus.

"This is the message we have heard from him and declare to you:

God is light;

in him there is no darkness at all. If we claim to have fellowship with him yet walk in the darkness, we lie and do not live by the truth. But if we

walk in the light,

as he is in the light, we have fellowship with one another, and the blood of Jesus, his Son, purifies us from all sin."

1 John 1:5-8

My frame was not hidden from you when I was made in the secret place...your eyes saw my unformed body. (Psalm 139:15-16)
He has given us new birth into a living hope (1 Peter 1:3)

116 I Was There to Hear Your Borning Cry

John Ylvisaker
Arr. by Henry Wiens

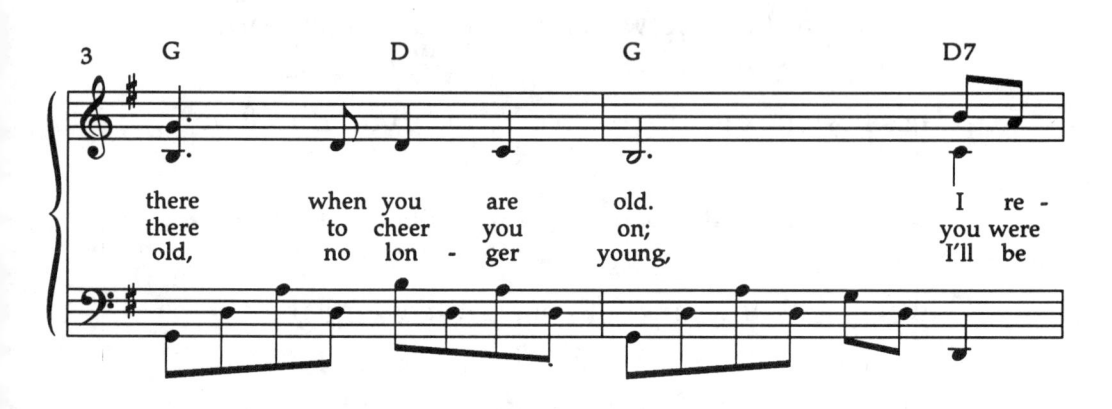

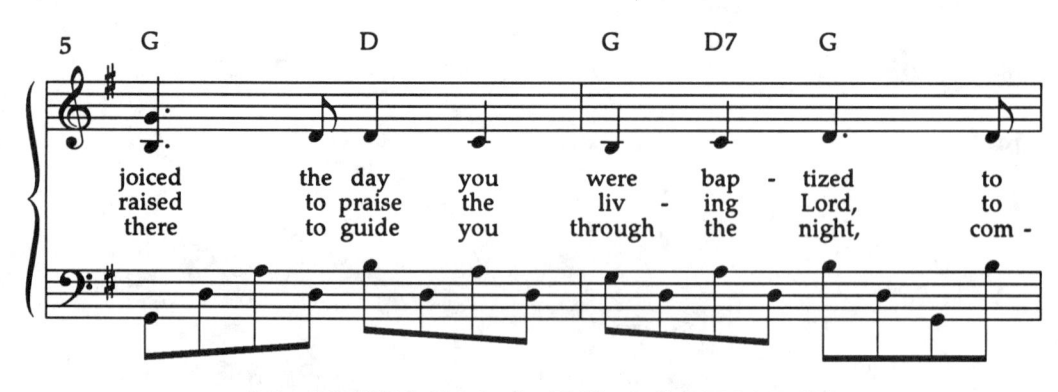

1. "I was there to hear your born-ing cry, I'll be there when you are old. I re-joiced the day you were bap-tized to see your life un-fold. I was there when you were but a child, with a faith to suit you well; in a blaze of light you wan-dered off to find where de-mons dwell."

2. "When you heard the won-der of the Word I was there to cheer you on; you were raised to praise the liv-ing Lord, to whom you now be-long. If you find some-one to share your time and you join your hearts as one, I'll be there to make your vers-es rhyme from dusk till ris-ing sun."

3. "In the mid-dle a-ges of your life, not too old, no lon-ger young, I'll be there to guide you through the night, com-plete what I've be-gun. When the eve-ning gent-ly clos-es in and you shut your wea-ry eyes, I'll be there as I have al-ways been, with just one more sur-prise."

3rd time to stanza 4

© Copyright 1985 John Ylvisaker, Box 321, Waverly, IA 50677, 319-352-0765.
No reprints allowed without express permission from the copyright holder as listed above.

4. "I was there to hear your borning cry, I'll be there when you are old. I rejoiced the day you were baptized to see your life unfold."

"For you created my *inmost being;* you knit me together *in my mother's womb.*"

Psalm 139:13

"Jesus answered, "I tell you the truth, no one can enter the kingdom of God unless he is born of water and the Spirit. Flesh gives birth to flesh, but the Spirit gives birth to spirit. You should not be surprised at my saying, '*You must be born again.*'"

John 3:5-7

I will praise you as long as I live, and in your name I will lift up my hands. (Psalm 64:4)

117   I Will Celebrate

Rita Baloche

With a solid beat ♩ = 172

I will celebrate, sing unto the Lord; Sing to the Lord a new song.

I will celebrate, sing unto the Lord; Sing to the Lord a new song. *Fine*

With my heart rejoicing within, With my mind focused on Him; With my hands raised to the heavens, All I am, worshiping Him.

D.C. al Fine

© Copyright 1990 Maranatha Praise, Inc. (Administered by The Copyright Company, Nashville, TN).
All Rights Reserved. International Copyright Secured. Used by Permission. www.maranathamusic.com

I love you, O Lord. (Psalm 18:1)

118 In Moments Like These

David Graham

♩ = 76-88

VERSE

In moments like these, I sing out a song, I sing out a love song to Jesus. In moments like these I lift up my hands, I lift up my hands to the Lord.

CHORUS

Singing I love You, Lord, singing I love You, Lord; Singing I love You, Lord, I love You.

Repeat Ending D.C.

Song Ending

You. You.

© Copyright 1980 C.A. Music (a div. of Christian Artists Records, Inc.) (ASCAP).
All Rights Reserved. Used by Permission.

119   I Will Praise Him

...and the blood of Jesus his Son cleanses us from all sin. (1 John 1:7)

Margaret J. Harris

Slow ♩ = 44

I will praise Him, I will praise Him, praise the Lamb for sin-ners slain; Give Him glo-ry, all ye peo-ple, for His blood has washed a-way each stain, for His blood has washed a-way each stain.

Public domain
This arr.© Copyright 1991 Integrity's Hosanna! Music, c/o Integrity Music, Inc., 1000 Cody Road, Mobile, AL 36695-3425.
All Rights Reserved. International Copyright Secured. Used by Permission.

120   I Will Celebrate

He put a new song in my mouth, a hymn of praise to our God. (Psalm 40:3)

Linda Duvall

♩ = 120-126

I will cel-e-brate, sing un-to the Lord, I will sing to Him a new song. I will praise Him, I will sing to Him a new song.

© Copyright 1982 Grace Fellowship (Administered by Maranatha! Music c/o The Copyright Company, Nashville, TN)
Maranatha Praise, Inc. (Administered by The Copyright Company, Nashville, TN).
All Rights Reserved. International Copyright Secured. Used by Permission. www.maranathamusic.com

9 Am D Gmaj7
I will praise Him,
11 C B7 Em
I will sing to Him a new song.
13 Em Am
Hal - le - lu - jah, hal - le - lu - jah, hal - le - lu - jah, hal - le - lu - jah,
15 F♯m7(4) B7 1. Em 2. Em
hal - le-lu, hal-le - lu - jah. lu - jah.
18 Em Am D Gmaj7
I will praise Him,
20 C B7 Em Am
I will sing to Him a new song. I will
23 D Gmaj7 C B7 Em
praise Him, I will sing to Him a new song.
Repeat Ending
D.C.
26 C B7 Em
I will sing to Him a new song.
Song Ending
28 C B7 Em
I will sing to Him a new song.
30 Bsus B Em
I will sing to Him a new song!

121 I Will Change Your Name

You will be called by a new name that the mouth of the Lord will bestow. (Isaiah 62:2)

D. J. Butler

♩ = 96-112

1. I will change your name,
   You shall no longer be called wounded, outcast,
   lonely or afraid.
2. I will change your name,
   Your new name shall be confidence, joyfulness,
   overcoming one,
   Faithfulness, friend of God, one who seeks My face.

© 1987 Mercy/Vineyard Publishing (ASCAP).
All Rights Reserved. International Copyright Secured. Used by Permission.

May I never boast except in the cross of our Lord Jesus Christ. (Galatians 6:14)

122 I Will Glory in the Cross

Kirk and Deby Dearman

Worshipfully ♩ = 50

I will glory in the cross where my
(opt. lyric) (Hal-le - lu - jah for the cross)
Je - sus was cru - ci - fied. Through His
blood I stand for-giv - en, cleansed from
sin and jus - ti - fied. I will
(Hal - le -
glory in the cross.
lu - jah for the cross.) I will
ev - er lift it high as a
ban - ner for sal - va - tion, as the
stan - dard for my life. I will life.
(Hal - le) -

© Copyright 1999 ThreeFold Amen Music/ASCAP, c/o ROM Administration and
Expressions of Praise/ASCAP, c/o Music Services.
All Rights Reserved. Used by Permission.

I'm Forever Grateful

I will give you thanks forever. (Psalm 30:12)

Mark Altrogge

With movement ♩ = 82-90

VERSE

You did not wait for me to draw near to You, But you clothed Yourself with frail humanity; You did not wait for me to cry out to You, But You let me hear Your voice calling

CHORUS

me. And I'm forever grateful to You, I'm forever grateful for the cross; I'm forever grateful to You, that You came to seek and save the lost.

© Copyright 1986 People of Destiny International
(Administered by Copycare USA, c/o The Copyright Company, Nashville, TN).
All Rights Reserved. International Copyright Secured. Used by Permission.

For in the day of trouble he will keep me safe in his dwelling; he will hide me in the shelter of his tabernacle. (Psalm 27:5)

124   In the Heart of God

Frank Janzow

Cheerfully ♩ = 120

1. There is a place where we can go when trouble and stress start mounting. There is a refuge fit for the soul deep in the heart of God, deep in the heart of God.

2. There is a perfect hide-a-way where nothing can come intruding. There is a shelter high and safe deep in the heart of God, deep in the heart of God.

CHORUS

Set your burdens down a-while and lean on a strength much greater than you. Let your spirit like a child go rest in the source of love. Lay your heart in the heart of God. Lay your heart in the heart of God, in the heart of God.

© Copyright 1993 Sun Day Publications, W266 53867 Donald Dr., Waukesha WI 53189.
All Rights Reserved. Used by Permission.

I want to know Christ...I press on toward the goal to win the prize. (Philippians 3:10,14)

In the Secret

Andy Park

"I wait for the LORD, my soul waits,

and in his word I put my hope.

My soul *waits* for the Lord

more than watchmen wait for the morning,

more than watchmen wait for the morning."

Psalm 130:5-6

126 Isn't He?

He will be called Wonderful Counselor, Mighty God, Everlasting Father, Prince of Peace. (Isaiah 9:6)

John Wimber

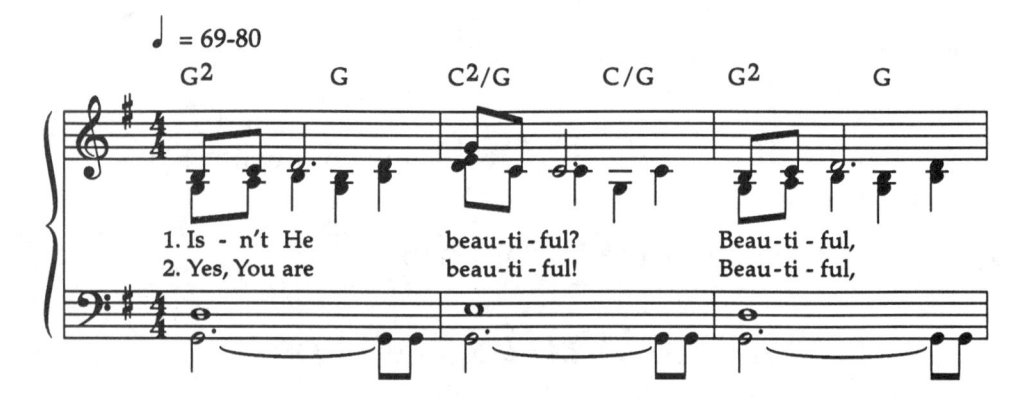

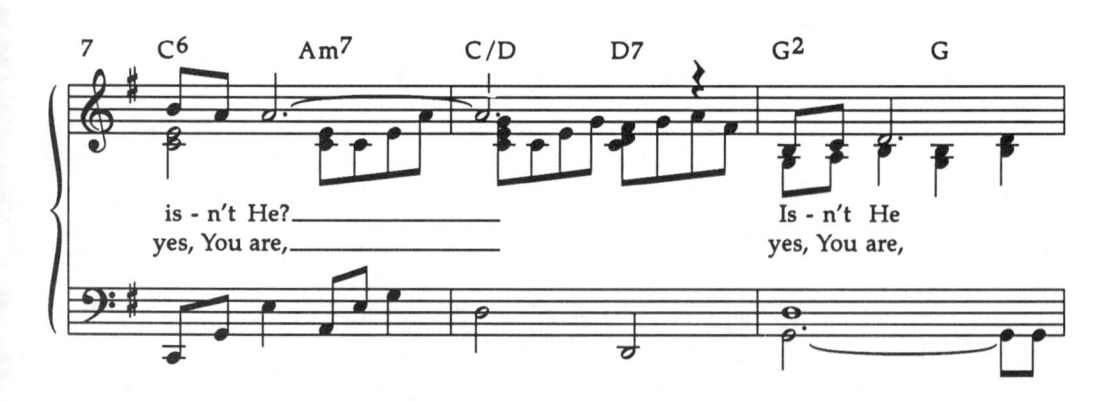

♩ = 69-80

1. Is-n't He beau-ti-ful? Beau-ti-ful, is-n't He? Prince of Peace, Son of God, is-n't He? Is-n't He
2. Yes, You are beau-ti-ful! Beau-ti-ful, yes, You are! Prince of Peace, Son of God, yes, You are, yes, You are,

won-der-ful? Won-der-ful, is-n't He? Coun-sel-or, Al-might-y God. Is-n't He, is-n't He, is-n't He?
won-der-ful! Won-der-ful, yes, You are Coun-sel-or, Al-might-y God. Yes, You are, yes, You are, yes, You are!

Repeat Ending D.C. | Song Ending

© Copyright 1980 Mercy/Vineyard Publishing (ASCAP). All Rights Reserved. Used by Permission.

127 It's Your Blood

The blood of Jesus, his Son, purifies us from all sin. (1 John 1:7)

Michael Christ

Capo 1 (A)

1. It's Your blood that cleanses me, It's Your blood that gives me life, It's Your blood that took my place in redeeming sacrifice, washes me whiter than the snow, than the snow, my Jesus, God's precious sacrifice.

2. It's the blood of the Lamb, It's the blood of the Lamb, It's the blood of the Lamb that can cleanse the deepest stain,

© 1985 Mercy/Vineyard Publishing (ASCAP).
All Rights Reserved. International Copyright Secured. Used by Permission.

128 It's All About You

'For my thoughts are not your thoughts, neither are your ways my ways,' declares the Lord. (Isaiah 55:8)

Paul Oakley

With feeling

CHORUS

It's all a-bout You, Je-sus, and all this is for You, for Your glo-ry and Your fame. It's not a-bout me, as if You should do things my way; You a-lone are God, and I sur-ren-der to Your ways.

Je-sus, lov-er of my soul, all con-sum-ing fire is in Your gaze. Je-sus, I want You to know

© Copyright 1995 Kingsway's Thankyou Music/Administered in North America by EMI Christian Music Publishing/P.O. Box 5085, Brentwood, TN 37024-5085
All Rights Reserved. Used by Permission.

> "Oh, the depth of the riches of the wisdom and knowledge of God! How unsearchable his judgments, and his paths beyond tracing out! 'Who has known the mind of the Lord? Or who has been his counselor?' 'Who has ever given to God, that God should repay him?'
>
> For *from* him and *through* him and *to* him are all things.
>
> To **him** be the glory forever! **Amen.**"
>
> Romans 11:33-36

He is not here, for he has risen, just as he said. (Matthew 28:6)

129 Jesus Is Alive

Ron Kenoly

"Christ **redeemed** us from the curse of the law by becoming a curse for us, for it is written:

'Cursed is everyone who is hung on a tree.'

He redeemed us in order that the blessing given to Abraham might come to the Gentiles through Christ Jesus, so that by faith we might receive the promise of the Spirit."

Galatians 3:13-14

He lifted me...out of the mud and mire; he set my feet on a rock and gave me a firm place to stand. (Psalm 40:2)

130 Jesus, Lover of My Soul

John Ezzy, Daniel Grul and Stephen McPherson

♩ = 76

VERSE

Je-sus, lov-er of my soul,
Je-sus, I will nev-er let You go;
You've tak-en me from the mir-y clay,
You've set my feet up-on the rock and now I know.

CHORUS

I love You, I need You,
though my world will fall, I'll nev-er let You go;
My Sav-ior, my clos-est Friend,
1. I will wor-ship You un-til the ver-y end.
2. I will wor-ship You un-til the ver-y end. *Fine*

© Copyright 1992 John Ezzy, Daniel Grul, Stephen McPherson/Hillsongs Australia
(adm. in U.S. and Canada by Integrity's Hosanna! Music), c/o Integrity Music, Inc., 1000 Cody Road, Mobile, AL 36695-3425.
All Rights Reserved. International Copyright Secured. Used by Permission.

Come near to God and he will come near to you. (James 4:8)

131 Jesus, Draw Me Close

Rick Founds

Intimately ♩ = 74

Je - sus, draw___ me close;___

Clos - er, Lord,___ to You.___

Let the world___ a - round___ me fade a -

way.

Je - sus, draw___ me close;___

Clos - er, Lord,___ to You.___ For

I de - sire___ to wor - ship and o - bey.

© Copyright 1990 Maranatha Praise, Inc. (Administered by The Copyright Company, Nashville, TN).
All Rights Reserved. International Copyright Secured. Used by Permission. www.maranathamusic.com

132 Jesus, Jesus

But you are a shield around me, O Lord; you bestow glory on me and lift up my head. (Psalm 3:3)

Geoff Bullock

Capo 1 (D)   ♩ = 112
VERSE 1

1. Je-sus, Je-sus, one touch of Your Hand, I am healed and I am whole; Je-sus, Je-sus, one glimpse of Your face brings fire to my soul.

CHORUS

And Je-sus, I come, be-hold-ing Your face, I am changed from glo-ry to glo-ry; And now I see,

© Copyright 1996 Word Music, Inc. (ASCAP), 65 Music Square West, Nashville, TN 37203/
Maranatha! Music (Admin. by Word Music, Inc.) (ASCAP), 65 Music Square West, Nashville, TN 37203.
All Rights Reserved. Made in the U.S.A. International Copyright Secured. Used by Permission. www.maranathamusic.com

26
Ab/C (G/B)
Bbm7/Db (Am7/C)
Ab/C (G/B)
and now I know, one
29
Bb (A)
Fm7 (Em7)
touch of Your life, brings glo - ry to my soul.
31
Eb (D)
Ab/Eb (G/D)
Fm/Eb (Em/D)
Eb (D)
Ab/Eb (G/D)
Fm/Eb (Em/D)
33
VERSE 2
Eb (D)
Ab/Eb (G/D)
Fm/Eb (Em/D)
Eb (D)
2. Je - sus, Je -
36
Ab/Eb (G/D)
Fm/Eb (Em/D)
Bb (A)
sus, from dark - ness to light my
38
Fm7 (Em7)
Eb (D)
Ab/Eb (G/D)
Fm/Eb (Em/D)
Eb (D)
Ab/Eb (G/D)
Fm/Eb (Em/D)
life o - ver - flows;
41
Eb (D)
Ab/Eb (G/D)
Fm/Eb (Em/D)
Eb (D)
Je - sus, Je -
44
Ab/Eb (G/D)
Fm/Eb (Em/D)
Bb (A)
Fm7 (Em7)
sus, Your mer - cy and grace like a riv - er flow - ing down.
47
Eb (D)
Ab/Eb (G/D)
Fm/Eb (Em/D)
1. Eb (D)
Ab/Eb (G/D)
Eb/G (D/F#)
2. Eb (D)
Ab/Eb (G/D)
Fm/Eb (Em/D)
And
repeat & fade as desired
50
Eb (D)
Ab/Eb (G/D)
Fm/Eb (Em/D)
Eb (D)
Ab/Eb (G/D)
Fm/Eb (Em/D)
Je - sus, Je - sus!

I am the Alpha and the Omega...who is, and who was, and who is to come, the Almighty. (Revelation 1:8)

133   Jesus, Lamb of God

Mark Zehnder

Worshipfully
VERSE

Je - sus, Lamb of God, seat - ed on the throne of pow - er, we wor - ship You with hon - or and bless - ing, sing - ing:

© Copyright 1996 Mark Zehnder Publishing.
All Rights Reserved. Used by Permission.

CHORUS

Ho - ly, ho - ly God, who was, and is, and is to come.

Ho - ly, ho - ly God, who was, and is, and is to come.

3rd time to Coda

So we say:

God exalted him...and gave him the name that is above every name. (Philippians 2:9)

134 Jesus, Name Above All Names

Naida Hearn

Jesus, name above all names, beautiful Savior, glorious Lord. Emmanuel, God is with us, blessed Redeemer, living Word.

BRIDGE

Come, Lord, come now from heaven to earth. Oh, may Your kingdom come. Oh, may Your will be done. Oh, let Your kingdom come. Oh, let Your will be done forevermore.

D.S. al CODA

CODA

come.

© Copyright 1974 and this arr. © 1997 Scripture In Song (a div. of Integrity Music) ASCAP,
c/o Integrity Music, Inc., 1000 Cody Road, Mobile, AL 36695-3425.
All Rights Reserved. International Copyright Secured. Used by Permission.

135 Jesus, Your Name

Jesus is the Christ, the Son of God ...by believing you may have life in his name. (John 20:31)

Morris Chapman and Claire Cloninger

1. Je-sus, Your name is pow-er,
2. Je-sus, Your name is heal-ing,
3. Je-sus, Your name is ho-ly,

Je-sus, Your name is might.
Je-sus, Your name gives sight.
Je-sus, Your name brings light.

Je-sus, Your name will break ev-'ry strong-hold;
Je-sus, Your name will free ev-'ry cap-tive;
Je-sus, Your name a-bove ev-'ry oth-er,

Je-sus, Your name is life.
Je-sus, Your name is life.
Je-sus, Your name is life.

© 1990 Word Music, Inc. (ASCAP), 65 Music Square West, Nashville, TN 37203/ Maranatha! Music (ASCAP), c/o The Copyright Group, Inc., 40 Music Square East, Nashville, TN 37203. All Rights Reserved. International Copyright Secured. Used by Permission. www.maranathamusic.com

136 Jesus, We Celebrate Your Victory

Thanks be to God! He gives us the victory through our Lord Jesus Christ. (1 Cor. 15:57)

John Gibson

Lively

𝄋 CHORUS

Je-sus, we cel-e-brate Your vic-to-ry;

Je-sus, we rev-el in Your love.

Je-sus,

© Copyright 1987 Kingsway's Thankyou Music/Administered in North America by EMI Christian Music Publishing/P.O. Box 5085, Brentwood, TN 37024-5085 All Rights Reserved. Used by Permission.

TAG
13
G D Em D G D Em
we re-joice, You've set us free; Je - sus, Your death
16
Last time to Coda
To continue
D G
has brought us life.
VERSE
19
C D G D/F♯ Em
1. It was for free - dom that Christ has set us free,
2. His Spir - it in us re - leas - es us from fear,
22
C D
no long - er to be sub - ject to a
The way to Him is o - pen with
25
C D C
yoke of slav - er - y; so we're re - joic -
bold - ness we draw near. And in His pres -
28
D G D/F♯ Em
- ing in God's vic - to - ry, our
- ence our prob - lems dis - ap - pear; Our
31
C Am Gmaj7/B C Em D
D.S. al CODA
hearts re - spond - ing to His love.
hearts re - spond - ing to His love.
CODA
35
C/G Am7/G G
life.

The Lord will comfort Zion...Joy and gladness will be found in her, thanksgiving and the sound of singing. (Isaiah 51:3)

137 Joy and Thanksgiving

Sean Swanson

Joyous Latin feel ♩ = 200

CHORUS

Joy and thanks-giv-ing in all our liv-ing. Why? Be-cause of our Sav-ior, Je-sus Christ. Joy and thanks-giv-ing in all our liv-ing. Why? Be-cause of our Sav-ior, Je-sus Christ.

VERSE *Optional repeat (1st time)*

1. Praise Him with the in-stru-ments; praise Him with the dance. Let the name of Je-sus be a-dored. Raise the roy-al ban-
2. Shout it from the moun-tains to the val-leys down be-low. Je-sus, He has come to set us free. The wa-ters of this foun-

Last time to Coda ⊕

© Copyright 1998 Swansong Music.
All Rights Reserved. Used by Permission.

"Though you have not seen him,

you love him;

and even though you do not see him now, you

believe in him and are

filled with an inexpressible and

glorious joy,

for you are receiving the goal of your faith, the

salvation of your souls."

1 Peter 1:8-9

I consider everything a loss compared to the surpassing greatness of knowing Christ Jesus my Lord, for whose sake I have lost all things. (Philippians 3:8)

Knowing You

Graham Kendrick

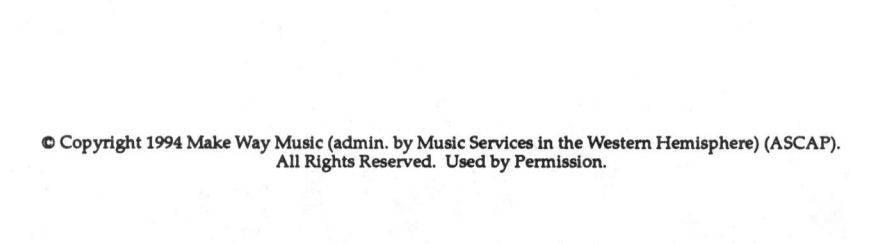

VERSE

1. All I once held dear, built my life up-on, all this world re-veres and wars to own. All I once thought gain I have count-ed loss, spent and worth-less now com-pared to this.

(2. Now my) heart's de-sire is to know You more, to be found in You, and known as Yours. To pos-sess by faith what I could not earn, all sur-pass-ing gift of right-eous-ness.

(3. Oh, to) know the pow'r of Your ris-en life and to know You in Your suf-fer-ings. To be-come like You in Your death, my Lord, so with You to live and nev-er die.

CHORUS

Know-ing You, Je-sus, know-ing You, there is no great-er thing. You're my all, You're the best, You're my joy, my right-eous-ness, and I love You, Lord.

1. 2. Now my
3. Oh, to

Love You, Lord.

© Copyright 1994 Make Way Music (admin. by Music Services in the Western Hemisphere) (ASCAP).
All Rights Reserved. Used by Permission.

139. Lamb of God

They have washed their robes and made them white in the blood of the Lamb. (Revelation 7:14)

Twila Paris

♩ = 60-65

VERSE

1. Your only Son no sin to hide, But You have sent Him from Your side To walk upon this guilty sod, And to become the Lamb of God.

2. Your gift of love they crucified, They laughed and scorned Him as He died, The humble King they named a fraud, And sacrificed the Lamb of God.

(D.C.) 3. I was so lost I should have died, But You have brought me to Your side To be led by Your staff and rod, And to be called a lamb of God.

CHORUS

O Lamb of God, sweet Lamb of God, I love the holy Lamb of God. O wash me in His precious blood, My Jesus Christ, the Lamb of God.

© Copyright 1985 StraightWay Music/Mountain Spring Music.
All Rights Reserved. Used by Permission.

For the message of the cross is foolishness to those who are perishing, but to us who are being saved it is the power of God. (1 Cor. 1:18)

140 Lead Me to the Cross

Graham Kendrick and Steve Thompson

1. How can I be free from sin?
3. How can I know peace with-in?
5. How can I live day by day?

lead me to the cross of Je-sus;
lead me to the cross of Je-sus;
lead me to the cross of Je-sus;

from the guilt, the pow'r, the pain,
sing a song of joy a-gain,
fol-low-ing His nar-row way,

lead me to the cross of Je-sus. *Fine*

2. There's no oth-er way, no price that I could pay,
4. Flow-ing from a-bove, all-for-giv-ing love,

sim-ply to the cross I cling.
from the Fa-ther's heart to me.

This is all I need, this is all I plead,
What a gift of grace, His own right-eous-ness,

that His blood was shed for me.
cloth-ing me in pu-ri-ty.

D.C.

© Copyright 1991 Make Way Music (admin. by Music Services in the Western Hemisphere) (ASCAP).
All Rights Reserved. Used by Permission.

May I never boast except in the cross of our Lord Jesus Christ. (Galatians 6:14)

141 Let It Be Said of Us

Steve Fry

VERSE

Let it be said of us that the Lord was our passion, That with gladness we bore ev'ry cross we were given; That we fought the good fight, that we finished the course Knowing within us the pow'r of the risen Lord. Let the

CHORUS

cross be our glory and the Lord be our song, By mercy made holy, by the Spirit made strong. Let the cross be our glory and the Lord be our song 'Til the likeness of Jesus be through us made known. Let the cross be our glory and the Lord be our song.

© Copyright 1994 MARANATHA PRAISE, Inc. (Admin. by The Copyright Company, Nashville, TN)/Word Music, Inc.
All Rights Reserved. International Copyright Secured. Used by Permission. www.maranathamusic.com

142 Let the Flame Burn Brighter
(We'll Walk)

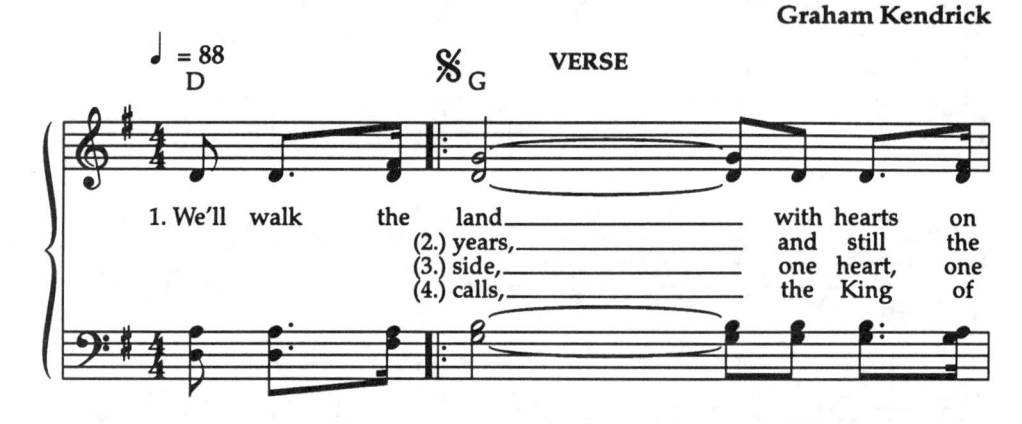

You shine like stars in the universe as you hold out the word of life. (Philippians 2:15-16)

Graham Kendrick

♩ = 88

1. We'll walk the land with hearts on fire, and ev'ry step will be a prayer; Hope is rising, new day dawning, sound of singing fills the air.
2. Two thousand years, and still the flame is burning bright across the land; Hearts are waiting, longing, aching for awak'ning once again.
3. One heart, one side, though many streams, we'll flow as one; Till Christ's compassion floods the nations, and all creation sees Him come.
4. Our Captain calls, the King of kings and Lord of lords, faithful and true; So let our answer resound like thunder, "Jesus, Master, we're with You!"

CHORUS
Let the flame burn brighter in the heart of the darkness, turning night to glorious

© Copyright 1989 Make Way Music (admin. by Music Services in the Western Hemisphere) (ASCAP). All Rights Reserved. Used by Permission.

14 D Am
day; Let the song grow loud - er, as our love grows
16 Em 2nd time to Coda D C2
strong - er, let it shine,
18 Em7 D G C
let it shine!
20 Em7 D G/A D D.S. al CODA
3. And, side by
CODA
22 D C2 Em7 Am7 C D C/D
shine! Let the flame burn
24 G
bright - er in the heart of the dark - ness, turn-ing
26 C D Am
night to glo-rious day; Let the song grow loud - er, as our love grows
29 Em D C2 Em7 D
strong - er, let it shine, let it
32 G C Em7 D G C
shine! let it shine!
35 Em7 Am7 Cmaj7 D C/D G

Whosoever believes in me...streams of living water will flow from within him. (John 7:38)

143 Let the River Flow

Darrell Evans

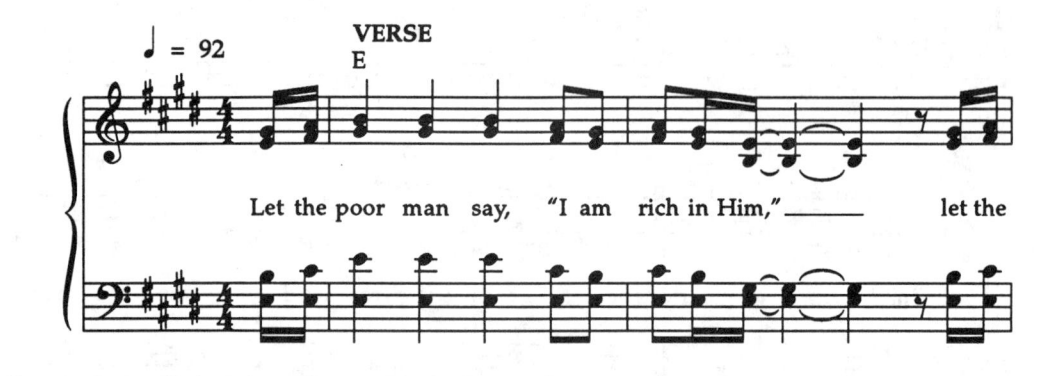

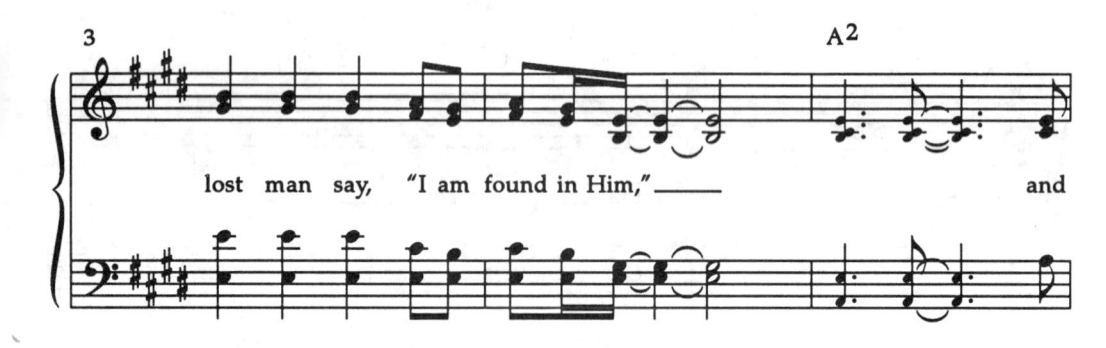

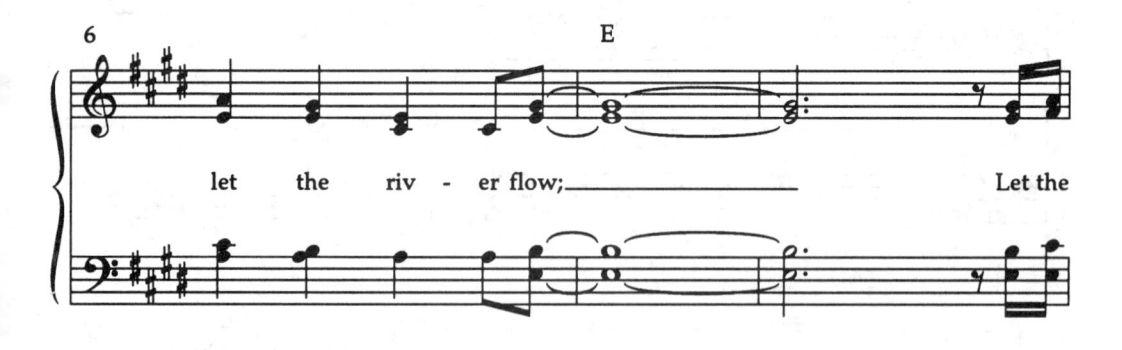

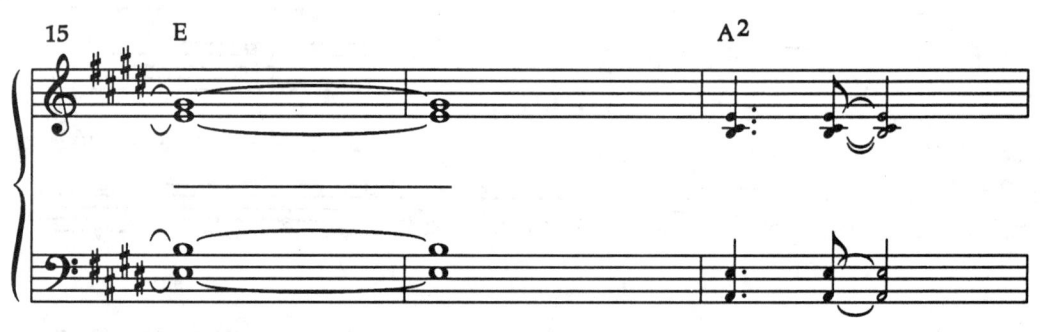

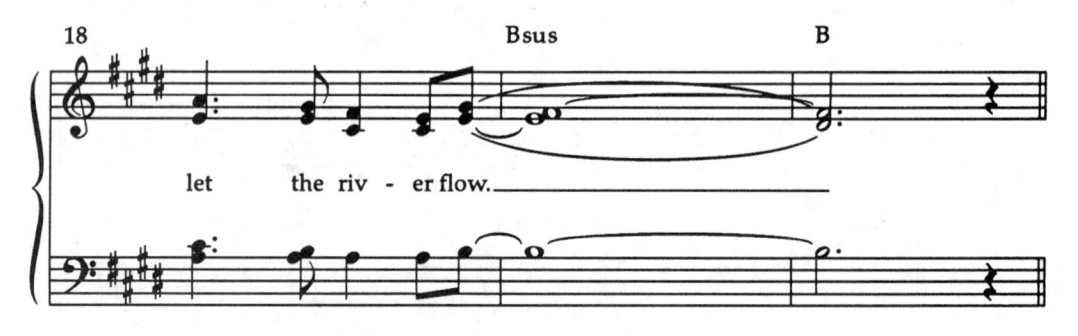

♩ = 92

Let the poor man say, "I am rich in Him," let the lost man say, "I am found in Him," and let the river flow; Let the blind man say, "I can see again," let the dead man say, "I am born again," and let the river flow, and let the river flow, let the river flow.

© Copyright 1995 Mercy/Vineyard Publishing (ASCAP), admin. by Music Services, 209 Chapelwood Drive, Franklin, TN 37064.
All Rights Reserved. International Copyright Secured. Used by Permission.

CHORUS
21 E Bsus B A
Let the riv-er flow, let the riv - er flow;
24 B E Bsus B
Ho - ly Spir-it, come,
27 A B E
move in pow - er. Let the riv-er flow,.
30 Bsus B A B
let the riv - er flow;
33 E Bsus B A
Ho - ly Spir-it, come, move in
36 B F♯m7
pow - er. Let the riv - er flow,
38 A
let the riv - er flow,
40 E
let the riv - er flow.

He himself is our peace who has made the two one and has destroyed the barrier, the dividing wall of hostility. (Ephesians 2:14)

144 Let the Walls Fall Down

Bill Batstone, John Barbour, and Anne Barbour

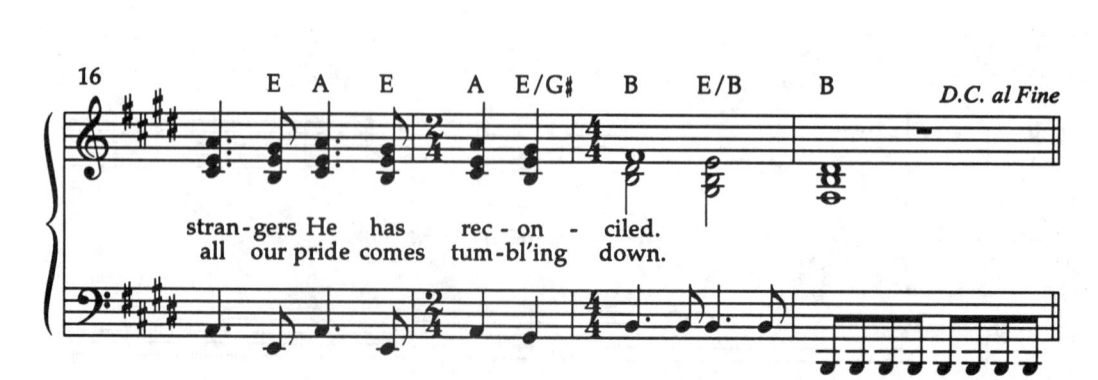

CHORUS

Let the walls fall down,
let the walls fall down,
let the walls fall down;
By His love let the walls fall down. *Fine*

VERSE

1. One by one, we're drawn together,
   One by one, to Jesus' side.
   One in Him, we'll live forever,
   strangers He has reconciled.

2. In His love, no walls between us,
   In His love, a common ground.
   Kneeling at the cross of Jesus
   all our pride comes tumbling down.

D.C. al Fine

© Copyright 1993 Maranatha Praise, Inc. (Administered by The Copyright Company, Nashville, TN).
All Rights Reserved. International Copyright Secured. Used by Permission. www.maranathamusic.com

I have made you a light for the Gentiles, that you may bring salvation to the ends of the earth. (Acts 13:47)

145   Light One Candle

Natalie Sleeth

VERSE

1. Light one can-dle for hope, one bright can-dle for hope, He brings hope to ev-'ry heart, He
2. Light one can-dle for peace, one bright can-dle for peace, He brings peace to ev-'ry heart, He
3. Light one can-dle for love, one bright can-dle for love, He brings love to ev-'ry heart, He

3rd time to Coda

1. comes! He comes!
2. comes! He

CHORUS

comes! Light one can-dle for joy, one bright can-dle for joy, Ev-'ry na-tion will find sal-va-tion in Beth-l'em's ba-by boy.

D.C. al Coda

CODA

comes! He comes! He brings love to ev-'ry heart, He comes! He comes!

TAG

© Copyright 1976 by Hinshaw Music, Inc.
All Rights Reserved. Used by Permission.

146 Light the Candle

The people living in darkness have seen a great light. (Matthew 4:16)

Maureen Griepentrog

♩ = 96

CHORUS

Light the candle as a symbol of the Light that leads the way; For each candle is a symbol of the hope that's ours today. As we
2nd time: (peace)
strike the match and light the wick, come, Spirit, shine bright. Grant that all may see from the darkness Your Gift, Your Truth, Your Light.

BRIDGE

Emmanuel, Son of the Father,

© Copyright 1999 Treble C Music, P.O. Box 1754, Glen Burnie, MD 21061.
All Rights Reserved. Used by Permission.

"Arise, shine,

for your light has come,

and the glory of the LORD rises upon you.

See, darkness covers the earth and thick darkness is over the peoples, but the LORD rises upon you and his glory appears over you.

Nations will

come to your light,

and kings to the brightness of your dawn."

Isaiah 60:1-3

147 Lift Him Up

I will exalt you my God the King; I will praise your name forever and ever. (Psalm 145:1)

Billy Funk

♩ = 88

VERSE

1. I will come in-to Your pres-ence, Lord, with a sac-ri-fice of praise; With a song I will ex-alt You, Lord, bless-ed be Your ho-ly name.
2. I will give You all the glo-ry, You de-liv-ered me from shame; I'm cre-at-ed in Your right-eous-ness, bless-ed be Your ho-ly name.

CHORUS

Lift Him up, His name be lift-ed high-er, lift Him up, ex-alt His ho-ly name; Lift Him up, His name be lift-ed high-er, ex-alt His ho-ly name.

© Copyright 1992 Integrity's Praise! Music, c/o Integrity Music, Inc., 1000 Cody Road, Mobile, AL 36695-3425.
All Rights Reserved. International Copyright Secured. Used by Permission.

148 Living Stones

You also, like living stones, are being built into a spiritual house to be a holy priesthood. (1 Peter 2:5)

Michael A. Schmid

Fast four ♩ = 120

VERSE

1. Jesus Christ is our Cornerstone. He's the Rock; He's the solid foundation.
2. Each of us is a living stone, precious stones in the building of Jesus.
3. Jesus, You are our Cornerstone. You're the Rock; You're the solid foundation.
4. Each of us is a living stone. We're alive in the love of Jesus.

We are building on Jesus alone, building up as the people of God.
In this house we don't stand all alone; we are one. We're the people of God.
We are building on Your love alone. Build us up as the people of God.
We are trusting in Jesus alone; we are His. We're the people of God.

CHORUS

Living stones, we are living, living stones. Built on Christ, living stones, holy people of God, building on the firm foundation. Living

4th time to Coda

of Christ.

D.S. al CODA

CODA

of Christ.

© Copyright 1999 Michael A. Schmid.
All Rights Reserved. Used by Permission.

I counsel you to buy from me gold refined in the fire, so you can become rich; and white clothes to wear, so you can cover your shameful nakedness; and salve to put on your eyes, so you can see. (Revelation 3:18)

149   Light the Fire Again

Brian Doerksen

In four, with a beat ♩ = 100

1. Don't let our love go cold. I'm
2. You know my heart, my deeds. I'm

calling out, "Light the fire again."
calling out, "Light the fire again."

Don't let our vision die. I'm
I need Your discipline. I'm

calling out, "Light the fire again."
calling out, "Light the fire again."

I am here to buy gold refined in the fire.

Naked and poor, wretch-ed and blind I come. Clothe me in white.

© Copyright 1994 Mercy/Vineyard Publishing (ASCAP), c/o Music Services, 209 Capelwood Drive, Franklin TN 37064.
All Rights Reserved. Used by Permission.

"I know your deeds, that you are neither cold nor hot. I wish you were either one or the other! So, because

you are lukewarm

—neither hot nor cold—

I am about to spit you out of my mouth.

You say, 'I am rich; I have acquired wealth and do not need a thing.' But you do not realize that you are wretched, pitiful, poor, blind and naked. I counsel you to

buy from me gold

refined in the fire, so you can become rich; and white clothes to wear, so you can cover your shameful nakedness; and salve to put on your eyes, so you can see."

Revelation 3:15-18

150 Lord Most High

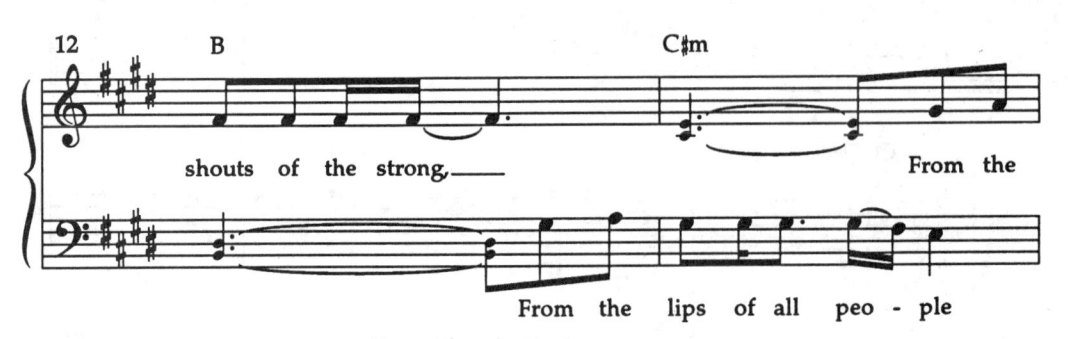

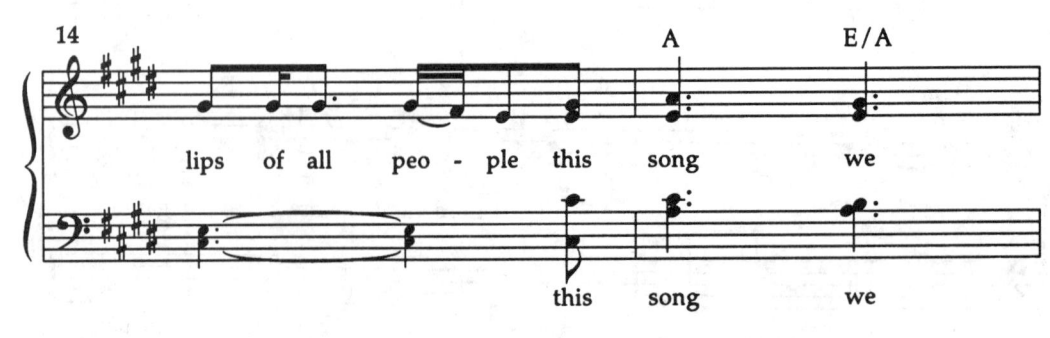

Sing...his praise from the ends of the earth. (Isaiah 42:10)

Don Harris and Gary Sadler

With a lilt ♪ = 145

VERSE

From the ends of the earth,
From the depths of the sea,
From the heights of the heavens Your name be praised;
From the hearts of the weak,
From the shouts of the strong,
From the lips of all people this song we

© 1996 Integrity's Hosanna! Music, c/o Integrity Music, Inc., 1000 Cody Road, Mobile, AL 36695-3425.
All Rights Reserved. International Copyright Secured. Used by Permission.

CHORUS
16 A B E E/G♯
raise, Lord. Through - out the
raise, Lord.
18 Emaj7/A A E/B B7sus E E/G♯
end - less ag - es You will be
20 Emaj7/A A E/B B7sus C♯m A
crowned with prais - es, Lord Most
22 Bsus B E E/G♯
High; Ex - alt - ed in
24 Emaj7/A A E/B B7sus E E/G♯
ev - 'ry na - tion, Sov - 'reign of
26 Emaj7/A A E/B B7sus C♯m A
all cre - a - tion, Lord Most
28 Bsus B E/G♯ 1. A E/A
High, be mag - ni - fied.
30 A 2. A E/A
fied.
From the
32 A Bsus B E

151 Lord, I Lift Your Name on High

Christ died for our sins...was buried...was raised. (1 Cor. 15:3-4)

Rick Founds

VERSE

Lord, I lift Your name on high;

Lord, I love to sing Your praises.

I'm so glad You're in my life;

I'm so glad You came to save us.

CHORUS

You came from heaven to earth to show the way,

From the earth to the cross my debt to pay;

From the cross to the grave, from the grave to the sky;

Lord, I lift Your name on high.

© Copyright 1989 Maranatha Praise, Inc. (Administered by The Copyright Company, Nashville, TN).
All Rights Reserved. International Copyright Secured. Used by Permission. www.maranathamusic.com

For I am convinced that [nothing] in all creation will be able to separate us from the love of God that is in Christ Jesus our Lord. (Romans 8:38-39)

152 Lord, You Love Me

Billy Christopher

Steadily ♩ = 120

Lord, You love me. Lord, You love me, and nothing in this world can change the love You have for me. Lord, You love me.

© Copyright 1999 Billy Christopher.
All Rights Reserved. Used by Permission.

Additional verses:

2. Lord, I love You...
3. Lord, I need You...
4. Lord, I want You...
5. Lord, I praise You...
6. Lord, You love me...

153 Love You So Much

I will praise you O Lord, with all my heart. (Psalm 9:1)

Russell Fragar

Steadily ♩ = 72

VERSE

Hear these prais-es from a grate-ful heart; each time I think of You, the prais-es start. Love You so much, Je-sus. Love You so much. Lord I love You, my soul sings; in Your pres-ence, car-ried on Your wings. Love You so much, Je-sus. Love You so much. How my

CHORUS

soul longs for You, longs to wor-ship You for-ev-er in Your

© Copyright 1996 Russell Fragar/Hillsongs Australia (adm. in the U.S. and Canada by Integrity's Hosanna! Music),
c/o Integrity Music, Inc., 1000 Cody Road, Mobile, AL 36695-3425.
All Rights Reserved. International Copyright Secured. Used by Permission.

21 G A/G Gmaj7 F♯7sus F♯7 Bm7
pow - er and maj - es - ty.
24 A/B Bm
Lift my hands, lift my
26 F♯m7 G D
heart, lift my voice to-wards the heav-ens, for
3rd time to Coda
29 G A/G Gmaj7 F♯7sus F♯7 1. Bm7
You are my sun and shield.
32 Em7 G/A 2. Bm7 A/B D.S. al CODA
shield. How my
CODA
35 Bm7 Em7 G/A
shield.
37 D
Hear these prais - es from a grate - ful heart;
39 Gmaj7
each time I think of You, the prais - es start. Love You
41 F♯m/A Em/A F♯m/A Em/A 1.2. Em/D D
so much, Je - sus. Love You so much.
44 3. Em/D D
Love You so much.

Yours, O Lord, is the greatness and the power and the glory and the majesty and the splendor. (1 Chronicles 29:11)

154 Majesty

Jack W. Hayford

CHORUS

Maj - es - ty, wor-ship His maj - es - ty. Unto Jesus be all glory, honor, and praise. Maj - es - ty, kingdom authority Flow from His throne unto His own; His anthem raise.

VERSE

So exalt, lift up on high the name of Jesus. Magnify, come glorify Christ Jesus, the King.

© Copyright 1981 Rocksmith Music, c/o Trust Music Management, Inc.
P.O. Box 22274 Carmel, CA 93922.
All Rights Reserved. Used by Permission.

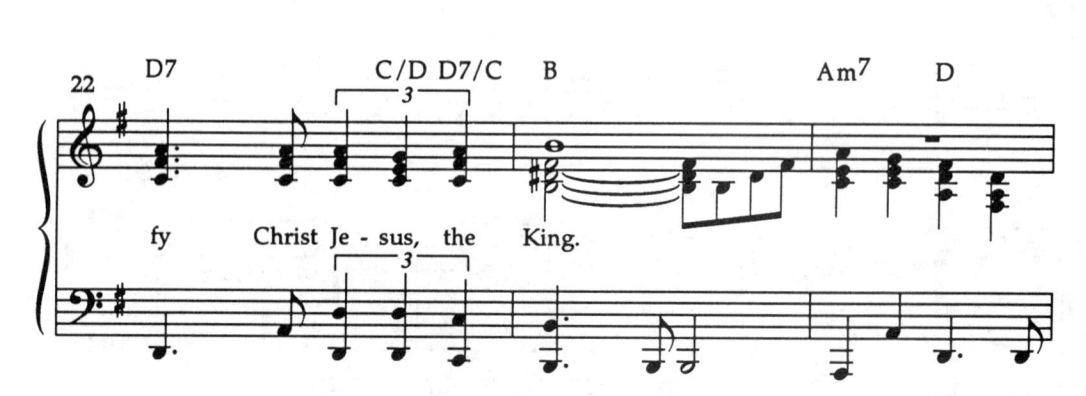

155 Make Me a Servant

Your attitude should be the same as that of Jesus Christ who...made himself nothing, taking the very nature of a servant. (Philippians 2:5, 7)

Kelly Willard

Make me a servant, humble and meek. Lord, let me lift up those who are weak. And may the prayer of my heart always be: Make me a servant, make me a servant, make me a servant today.

© Copyright 1982 Willing Heart Music (Administered by Maranatha! Music, c/o The Copyright Company, Nashville, TN)
Maranatha! Music (Administered by The Copyright Company, Nashville, TN).
All Rights Reserved. International Copyright Secured. Used by Permission. www.maranathamusic.com

Surely I am with you always, to the very end of the age. (Matthew 28:20)

156 May the Feet of God Walk with You

Aub Podlich
Robin Mann

Capo 1 (D)

♩ = 106

May the feet of God walk with you, and his hand hold you tight.
May the eye of God rest on you, and his ear hear your cry.
May the smile of God be for you, and his breath give you life.
May the Child of God grow in you, and his love bring you home.

Text: © Copyright 1983 Aub Podlich. Music: © Copyright 1983 Robert Mann.
All Rights Reserved. International Copyright Secured. Used by Permission.

Who, being in very nature God, did not consider equality with God something to be grasped,
but made himself nothing, taking the very nature of a servant. (Philippians 2:6-7)

157 Meekness and Majesty
(This Is Your God)

Graham Kendrick

Worshipfully ♩ = 96

1. Meekness and majesty, manhood and Deity, in perfect harmony, the Man who is God. Lord of eternity, dwells in humanity; Kneels in humility and washes our feet. O what a mystery, meekness and majesty; Bow down and worship, for this is your God.

2. Father's pure radiance, perfect in innocence; Yet learns obedience to death on a cross. Suff'ring to give us life, conqu'ring through sacrifice; And as they crucify prays, "Father, forgive."

3. Wisdom unsearchable, God, the invisible; Love indestructible in frailty appears. Lord of infinity, stooping so tenderly; Lifts our humanity to the heights of His throne.

© Copyright 1986 Kingsway's ThankYou Music.
All Rights Reserved. International Copyright Secured. Used by Permission.

…ghtier than the thunder of the great waters, mightier than the breakers of the sea — the Lord on high is mighty. (Psalm 93:4)

158 Mighty Is Our God

Eugene Greco, Gerrit Gustafson and Don Moen

159 More Love, More Power

Love the Lord your God with all your heart and with all your soul and with all your mind and with all your strength. (Mark 12:30)

Jude Del Hierro

♩ = 69

CHORUS

More love, more power, more of You in my life; More love, more power, more of You in my life.

And I will worship You with all of my heart, and I will worship You with all of my mind; And I will worship You with all of my strength, you are my Lord, you are my Lord, You are my Lord.

Optional: These chords may be omitted.

© Copyright 1987 Mercy/Vineyard Publishing (ASCAP).
All Rights Reserved. Used by Permission.

160 More of You

My soul yearns for you in the night, in the morning my spirit longs for you. (Isaiah 26:9)

Don Harris and Martin J. Nystrom

♩ = 84

VERSE

Jesus I am thirsty, won't You come and fill me? Earthly things have left me dry, only You can satisfy, all I want is more of You.

CHORUS

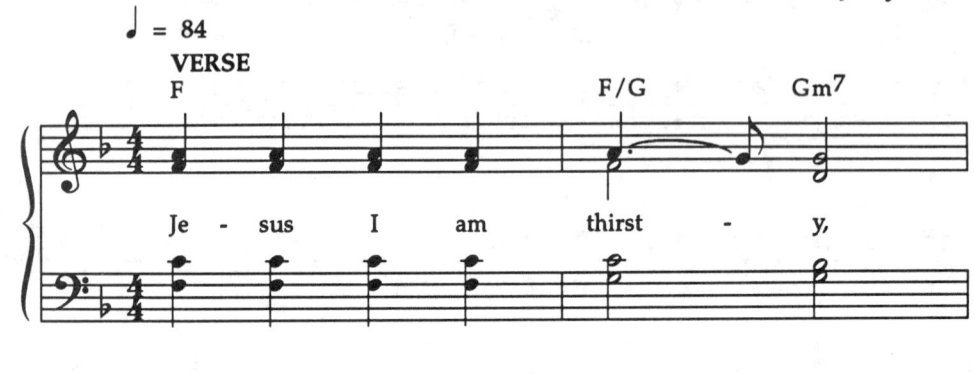

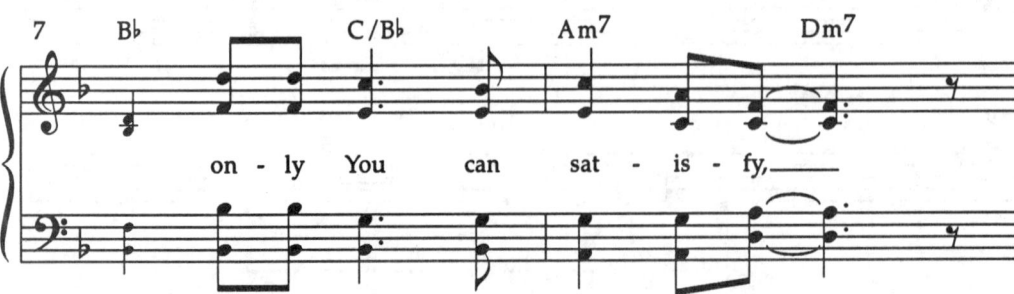

All I want is more of You, all I want is more of You; Nothing I desire, Lord but more of You.

© Copyright 1999 Integrity Hosanna's Music, c/o Integrity Music, Inc., 1000 Cody Road, Mobile, AL 36695-3425.
All Rights Reserved. International Copyright Secured. Used by Permission.

"O God, you are my God, earnestly **I seek** you; my soul **thirsts** for you, my body **longs** for you, in a dry and weary land where there is no water."

Psalm 63:1

It was not with perishable things such as silver or gold that you were redeemed... but with the precious blood of Christ. (1 Peter 1:18-19)

161 More Precious Than Silver

Lynn DeShazo

162 My Faith Looks Up to Thee

Let us then approach the throne of grace with confidence, so that we may receive mercy and find grace to help us in our time of need. (Hebrews 4:16)

Ray Palmer
Lowell Mason
Arranged by Bill Wolaver

1. My faith looks up to Thee, Thou Lamb of Calvary, Savior divine! Now hear me while I pray, Take all my guilt away, O let me from this day Be wholly Thine!
2. May Thy rich grace impart Strength to my fainting heart, My zeal inspire; As Thou hast died for me, O may my love to Thee Pure, warm, and changeless be, A living fire!
3. While life's dark maze I tread And griefs around me spread, Be Thou my guide; Bid darkness turn to day, Wipe sorrow's tears away, Nor let me ever stray From Thee aside.
4. When ends life's passing dream, When death's cold, threatening stream Shall o'er me roll, Blest Savior, then, in love, Fear and distrust remove; O lift me safe above, A ransomed soul!

Arr. © Copyright 2000 Eb and Flo Music (admin. by Music Services) (ASCAP).
All Rights Reserved. Used by Permission.

163 Mourning into Dancing

You turned my wailing into dancing; you removed my sackcloth and clothed me with joy. (Psalm 30:11)

Tommy Walker

CHORUS

You've turned my mourn-ing in-to danc-ing a-gain, you've lift-ed my sor-rows; and I can't stay si-lent, I must sing, for your joy has come.

Fine

VERSE

Where there once was on-ly hurt, you gave your heal-ing hand; where there once was on-ly pain, you brought com-fort like a friend. And I feel the sweet-ness of your love pierc-ing my dark-ness; and I see the bright and morn-ing sun as it ush-ers in your joy-ful glad-ness.

D.C. al Fine

© Copyright 1991 Integrity's Hosanna! Music, c/o Integrity Music, Inc., 1000 Cody Road, Mobile, AL 36695-3425.
All Rights Reserved. International Copyright Secured. Used by Permission.

For a more challenging piano part, see Hosanna Integrity Songbook 10:855.

Let us draw near to God with a sincere heart in full assurance of faith, having our hearts sprinkled to cleanse us from a guilty conscience and having our bodies washed with pure water. (Hebrews 10:22)

164 My Dwelling Place

John Hartley

Steadily ♩ = 102-112

1. This song of love to You, oh Lord, You've shown Your cross so dear. Yet through the pain and silent cries, You whispered life to me.
2. From shore to shore and deep within the secrets of my heart, Such guilt weighed down was washed away; what mercy You impart.

CHORUS
Oh Lamb of God, oh anointed One, in You I trust. In You alone my dwelling place shall be.

© Copyright 1999 worshiptogether.com Songs.
Administered by EMI Christian Music Publishing. P.O. Box 5085, Brentwood, TN 37024-5085.
All Rights Reserved. Used by Permission.

165 My Life Is In You, Lord

Your life is now hidden with Christ...who is your life. (Colossians 3:3-4)

Daniel Gardner

♩ = 144-152

My life is in You, Lord, my strength is in You, Lord, my hope is in You, Lord, in You, it's in You; My life is in You, Lord, my strength is in You, Lord, my hope is in You, Lord, in You, it's in You. My

4th time to CODA

1.3. You. 2. I will praise You with all of my life, I will praise You with all of my strength; With

© Copyright 1986, Arr. © 1992 Integrity's Hosanna! Music,
c/o Integrity Music, Inc., 1000 Cody Road, Mobile, AL 36695-3425.
All Rights Reserved. International Copyright Secured. Used by Permission.

> "Christ above me, Christ beside me,
>
> Christ within me, ever guiding;
>
> Christ behind me, Christ before,
>
> Christ, my love, my life, my Lord."
>
> — John Chisum and George Searcy

I am the resurrection and the life. He who believes in me will live, even though he dies. (John 11:25)

166 My Redeemer Lives

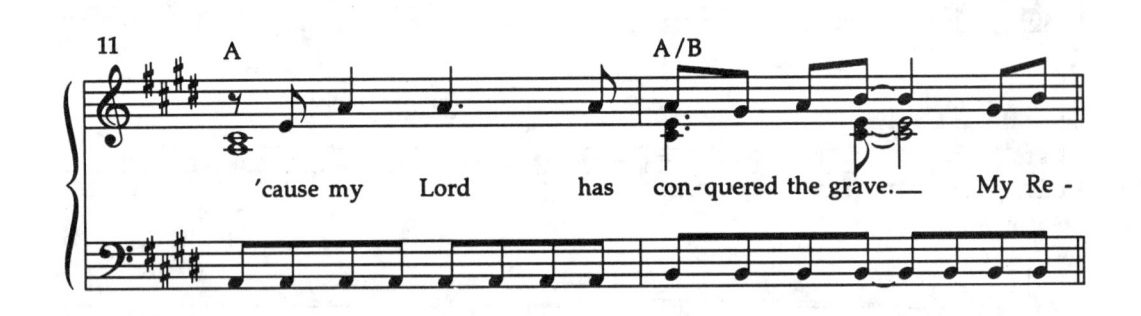

Reuben Morgan

With a beat ♩ = 140

I know He rescued my soul;
My shame He's taken away;
His blood has covered my sins. I believe,
my pain is healed in His name. I believe.

I'll raise the banner, 'cause my Lord has conquered the grave. My Redeemer lives, my Redeemer lives. (My Re-)

Last time to Coda

© Copyright 1998 Reuben Morgan/Hillsongs Australia,
admin. by Integrity's Hosanna! Music, Inc., 1000 Cody Road, Mobile, AL 36695-3425.
All Rights Reserved. International Copyright Secured. Used by Permission.

17 E7 A
19 E7
D.S. al CODA
CODA
21 B D
You lift my bur-
23 A/C♯
- dens; I'll rise with You.
25 E/B
I'm danc-ing on this moun-
27 F♯m7 E/G♯
- tain top to see Your king - dom come.
29 Bsus B
My Re -
31 E A
deem - er lives, my Re -
33 C♯m7 1.-5. B
deem - er lives. My Re -
35 6. B E

I know that my Redeemer lives and that in the end he will stand upon the earth and after my skin has been destroyed, yet in my flesh I will see God. (Job 19:25-26)

167 My Redeemer Lives

John Willison

Majestically ♩ = 74-78

VERSE

1. For I know my Redeem-er lives, and in the end He will stand on the earth. For I know my Redeem-er lives, and in the end He will reign on the earth. Though my flesh— it be destroyed, yet with my eyes I will see God.

2. heart it yearns with-in me for the day when Jesus re- Oh my heart it yearns with-in me for the day when Jesus shall reign.

CHORUS

For I know that my Redeem-er lives, and I will stand with Him on that day. For I know that my Redeem-

© Copyright 1993 Mercy/Vineyard Publishing (ASCAP).
All Rights Reserved. International Copyright Secured. Used by Permission.

"I know that my Redeemer lives,

and that in the end

he will stand upon the earth.

And after my skin has been destroyed, yet in my

flesh I will see God; I myself will see him

with my own eyes—I, and not another.

How my heart yearns within me!"

Job 19:25-27

I love you, O Lord. (Psalm 18:1)

168 My Jesus, I Love Thee

William R. Featherston
Adoniram J. Gordon

1. My Jesus, I love Thee; I know Thou art mine. For Thee all the follies of sin I resign. My gracious Redeemer, my Savior art Thou; If ever I loved Thee, my Jesus, 'tis now.

2. I love Thee because Thou hast first loved me And purchased my pardon on Calvary's tree. I love Thee for wearing the thorns on Thy brow: If ever I loved Thee, my Jesus, 'tis now.

© Copyright 1997 Maranatha! Music (Administered by The Copyright Company, Nashville, TN).
All Rights Reserved. International Copyright Secured. Used by Permission. www.maranathamusic.com

169 Nothing but the Blood of Jesus

Without the shedding of blood there is no forgiveness. (Hebrews 9:22)

Robert Lowry

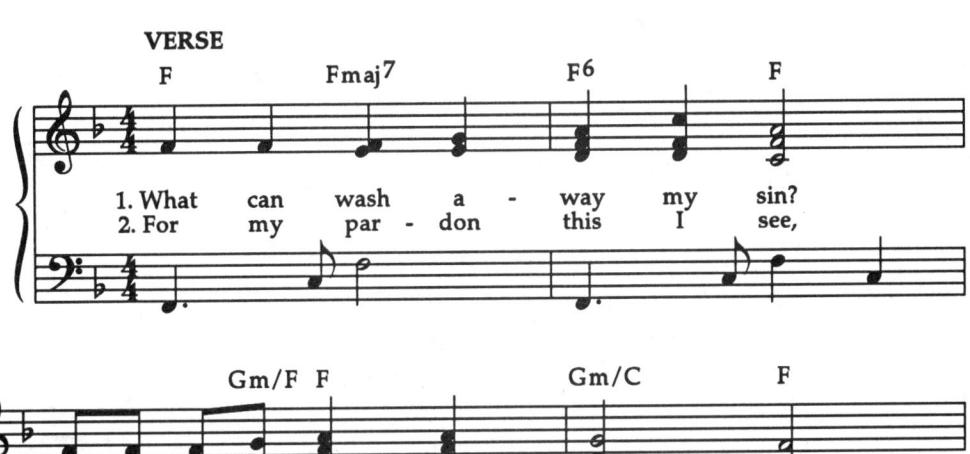

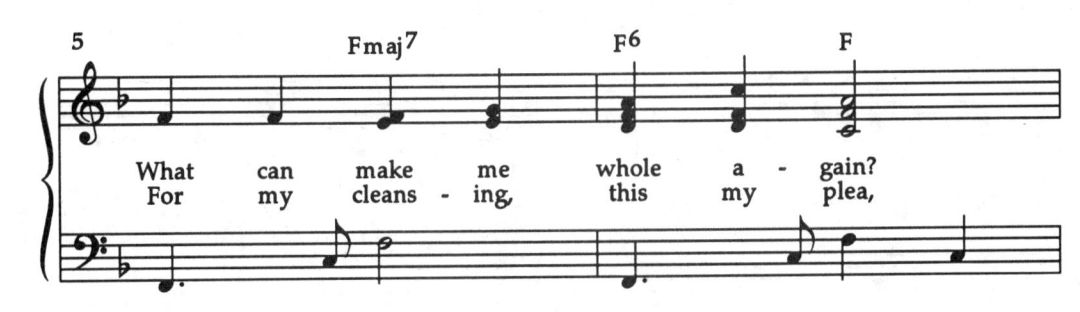

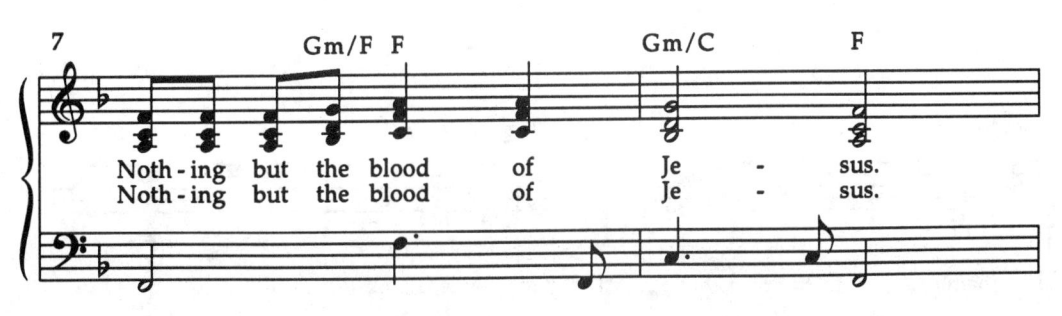

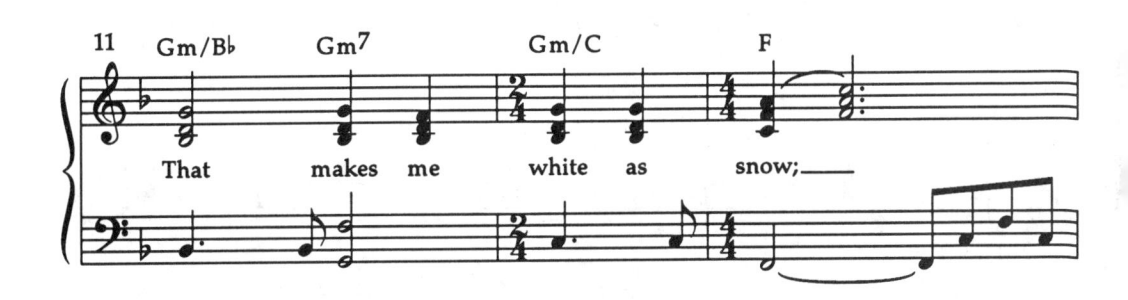

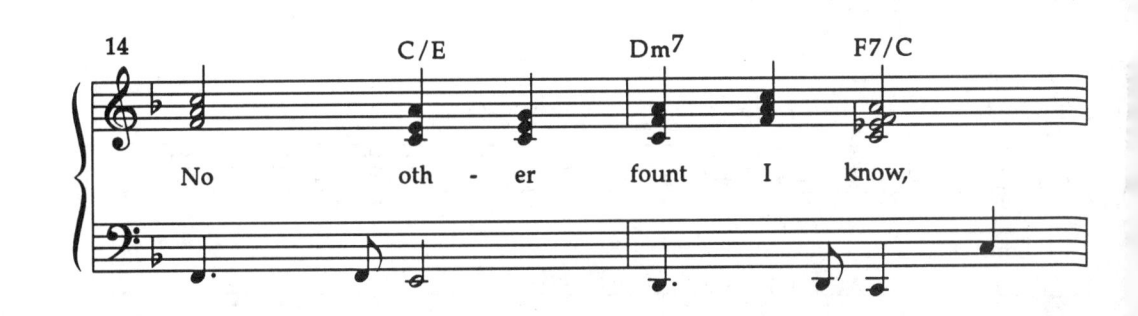

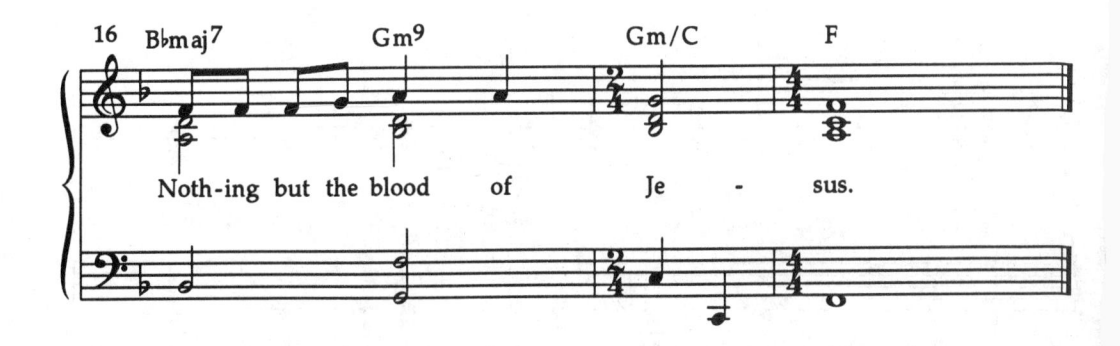

VERSE

1. What can wash away my sin?
   Nothing but the blood of Jesus;
   What can make me whole again?
   Nothing but the blood of Jesus.

2. For my pardon this I see,
   Nothing but the blood of Jesus;
   For my cleansing, this my plea,
   Nothing but the blood of Jesus.

CHORUS

Oh! precious is the flow
That makes me white as snow;
No other fount I know,
Nothing but the blood of Jesus.

© Copyright 1997 Maranatha! Music (Administered by The Copyright Company, Nashville, TN).
All Rights Reserved. International Copyright Secured. Used by Permission. www.maranathamusic.com

170 No Other Name

God exalted him to the highest place and gave him the name that is above every name. (Philippians 2:9)

Robert Gay

No oth-er name but the name of Je-sus, No oth-er name but the name of the Lord; No oth-er name but the name of Je-sus is wor-thy of glo-ry, And wor-thy of hon-or, And wor-thy of pow-er and all praise. No oth-er praise. His name is ex-alt-ed far a-bove the earth, His name is high a-bove the heav-ens: His

© Copyright 1988, Arr. © 1992 Integrity's Hosanna! Music, c/o Integrity Music, Inc., 1000 Cody Road, Mobile, AL 36695-3425.
All Rights Reserved. International Copyright Secured. Used by Permission.

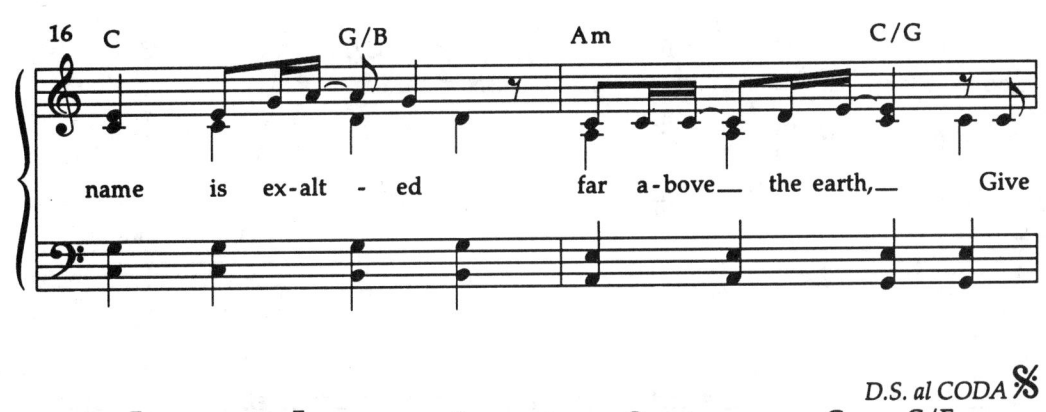

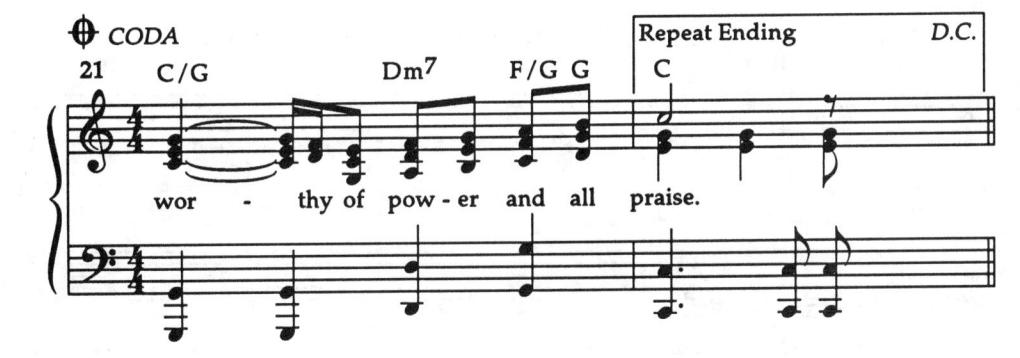

> "Salvation is found in no one else, for there is no **other** name under heaven given to men by which we must be saved."
>
> Acts 4:12

171 Nobody Fills My Heart Like Jesus

You have filled my heart with greater joy than when their grain and new wine abound. (Psalm 4:7)

Dennis Jernigan

Joyfully ♩ = 88 (1st time)
♩ = 140 (2nd & 3rd times)

VERSE

1.2. I'd like to say, Lord, from the start,
(3.) when I am weak, my Lord, You're strong,

thank You for break-ing through my heart.
lov-ing me e-ven when I'm wrong.

Thank You for tear-ing ev-'ry chain a-
Lord, You are my sal-va-tion and my

part.
song.

When I was lost You made a way;
Ev-er-y day I'll make the choice, just

You turned the dark-est night to day.
lis-ten-ing, fol-low-ing Your voice.

You are my joy and Lord, I'd like to
Be-ing with You, I can't help but re-

say
joice!

that
For

CHORUS

no-bod-y fills my heart like Je-sus.

© Copyright 1993 Shepherd's Heart Music, Inc. (Admin. by Dayspring Music, Inc.) (BMI),
65 Music Square West, Nashville, TN 37203.
All Rights Reserved. Made in the U.S.A. International Copyright Secured. Used by Permission.

19 F C/E Dm F C/E C F C/E F B♭
No-bod-y thrills me like You do! Oh, no-bod-y fills my heart
22 B♭/D C C/E Dm Am7 C2 C/E
like Je-sus. No-bod-y, Lord, but You, no-bod-y.
25 F C/E F B♭ B♭/D C C/E
No-bod-y fills my heart like Je-sus.
27 F C/E Dm F C/E C
No-bod-y thrills me like You do! Oh,
29 F C/E F B♭ B♭/D C C/E
no-bod-y fills my heart like Je-sus.
Last time to Coda
31 Dm Am7 C
No-bod-y, Lord, but You, no-bod-y but You.
34 1.2. F C/F F Fsus4/2 C/F F C F C/F F Gm/F
D.S. al CODA
37 C/F F C 3. F C/F F Fsus4/2 C/F F
2.
3. Well,
Oh,
CODA
40 F C/F F Fsus4/2 C/F F C
42 F C/F F Gm/F

Were not all ten cleansed? Where are the other nine? Was no one found to return and give praise to God except this foreigner? (Luke 17:18-19)

172 O Magnify the Lord

Janet L. Janzen

Calypso Rhythm, with energy ♩ = 132-138

VERSE
1.3. Ten were sick,__ but when they found__ Je-sus healed__ them, on-ly one turned a-round,__ bowed him-self__ down to the ground,__ and gave praise__ to the Lord.
2. When I called,__ He heard my prayer,__ but I for-got__ that He was e-ven there.__ Help me, Spir-it, to be a-ware__ and give praise__ to the Lord.

CHORUS
O mag-ni-fy the Lord with me;__ ex-alt His name__ con-tin-u-al-ly!__ He has come__ to set the cap-tives free.__ Give praise__ to the Lord.

Give praise__ to the Lord. Give praise__ to the Lord. Give praise__ to the Lord.

© Copyright 1990 Janet Lindeblad Janzen.
All Rights Reserved. Used by Permission.

173. O the Deep, Deep Love of Jesus

I pray that you...may have power...to grasp how wide and long and high and deep is the love of Christ. (Ephesians 3:17-18)

Samuel T. Francis / Thomas J. Williams

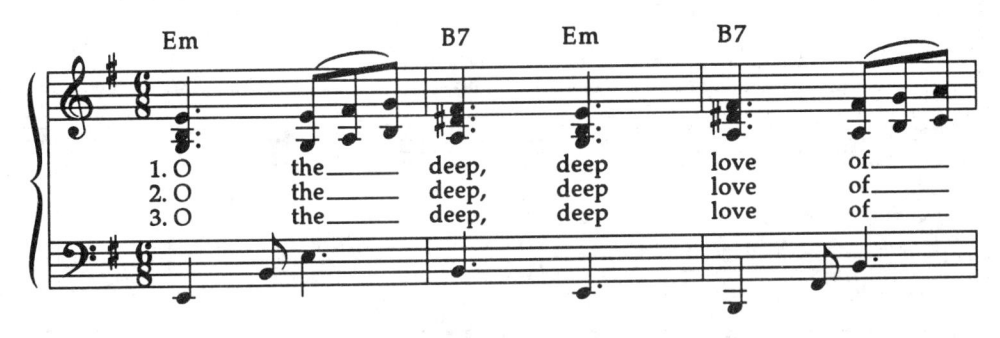

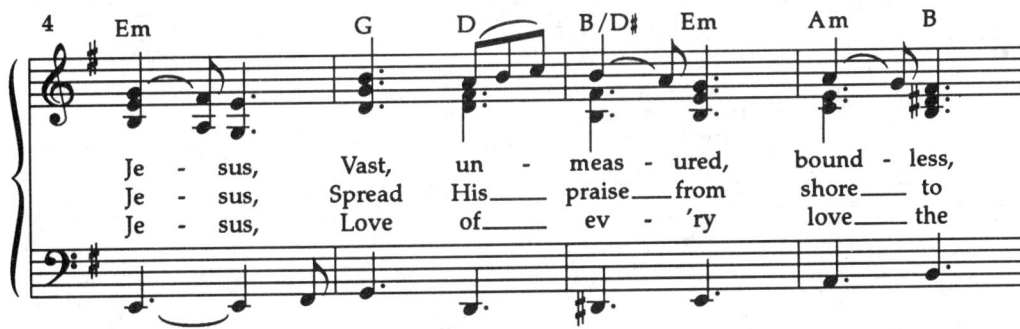

1. O the deep, deep love of Jesus, Vast, unmeasured, boundless, free! Rolling as a mighty ocean In its fullness over me, Underneath me, all around me, Is the current of Thy love; Leading onward, leading homeward, To Thy glorious rest above.

2. O the deep, deep love of Jesus, Spread His praise from shore to shore! How He loveth, ever loveth, Changeth never, nevermore; How He watches o'er His loved ones, Died to call them all His own; How for them He intercedeth, Watcheth o'er them from the throne.

3. O the deep, deep love of Jesus, Love of ev'ry love the best; 'Tis an ocean vast of blessing, 'Tis a haven sweet of rest. O the deep, deep love of Jesus, 'Tis a heav'n of heav'ns to me; And it lifts me up to glory, For it lifts me up to Thee.

Public Domain.

And being found in appearance as a man, he humbled himself and became obedient to death — even death on a cross. (Philippians 2:8)

174 Once Again
(Jesus Christ)

Matt Redman

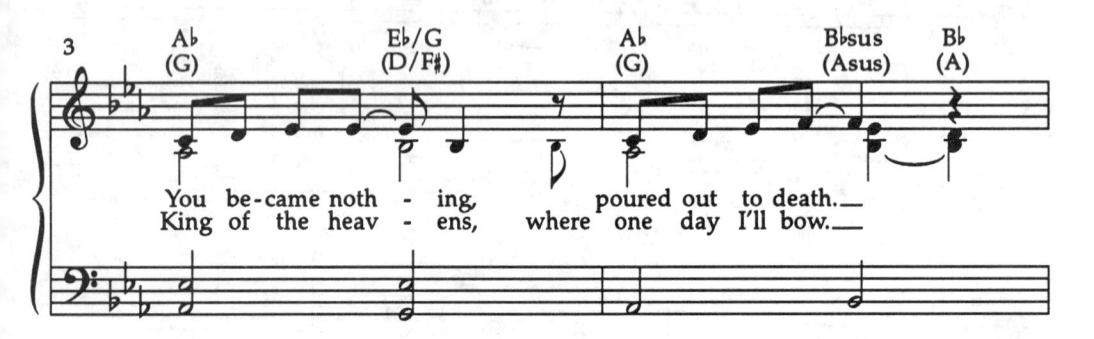

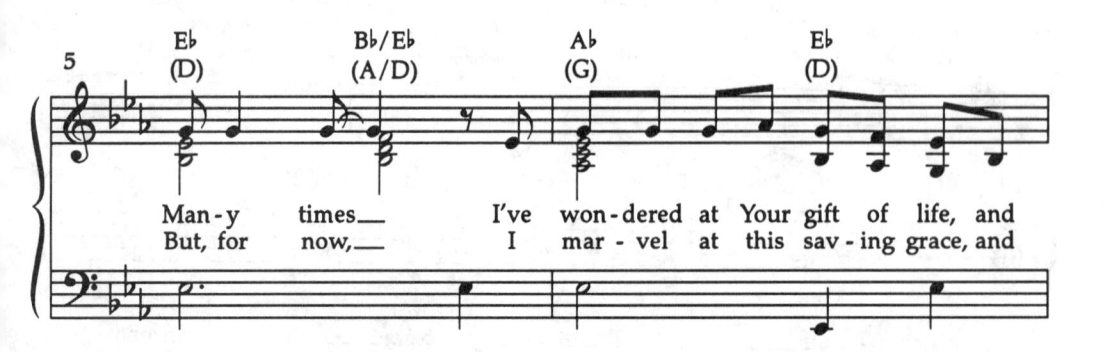

Capo 1 (D)

Thoughtfully, not too fast

VERSE

1.2. Je - sus Christ,___ I think up - on Your sac - ri - fice;
3. Now You are___ ex - alt - ed to the high - est place,

You be - came noth - ing, poured out to death.___
King of the heav - ens, where one day I'll bow.___

Man - y times___ I've won - dered at Your gift of life, and
But, for now,___ I mar - vel at this sav - ing grace, and

I'm in that place___ once a - gain.___
I'm full of praise___ once a - gain.___

I'm in that place___ once a - gain.___
I'm full of praise___ once a - gain.___

CHORUS

Once a - gain I look up - on the cross where You died.___ I'm

hum - bled by Your mer - cy and I'm bro - ken in - side.___

© Copyright 1995 Kingsway's Thankyou Music/Administered in North America by
EMI Christian Music Publishing/P.O. Box 5085, Brentwood, TN 37024-5085
All Rights Reserved. Used by Permission.

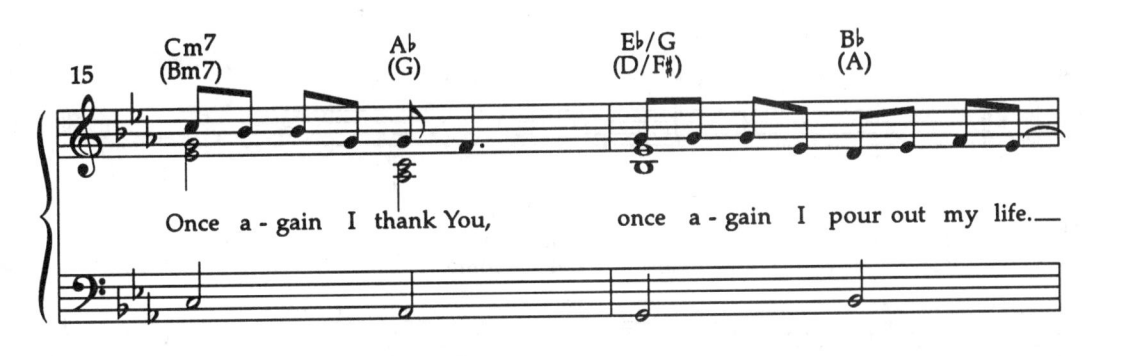

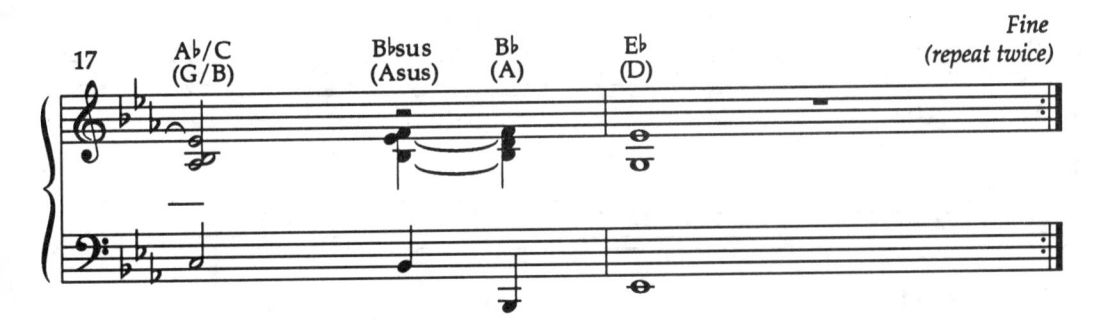

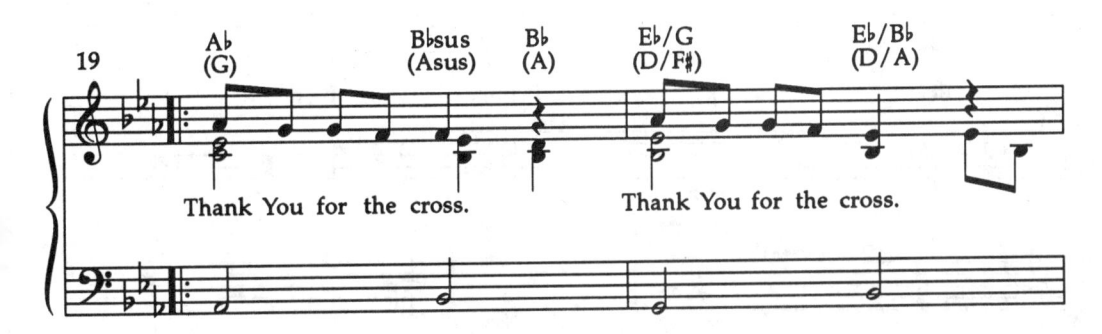

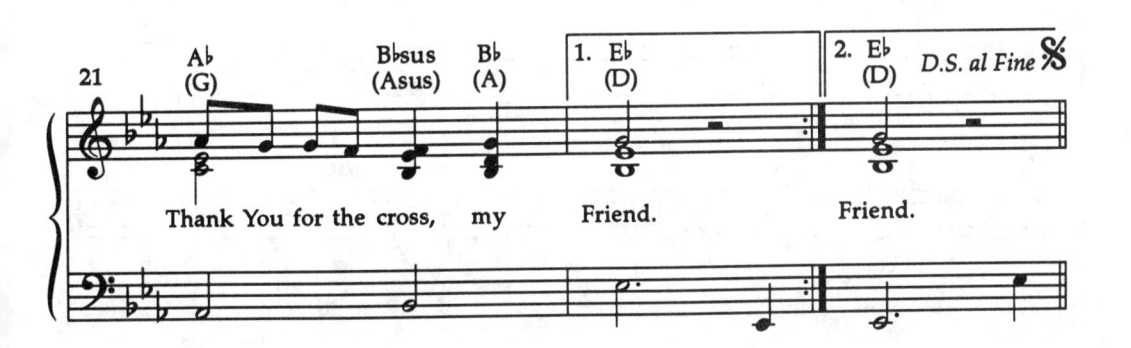

175 Only by the Blood of the Lamb

It was not with perishable things...that you were redeemed...but with the precious blood of Christ, a lamb without blemish or defect. (1 Peter 1:18-19)

Jeff Nelson and Rosemary Foster

On - ly by the blood of the Lamb, only by the blood of the Lamb; We've o - ver - come, in His grace we now stand, On - ly by the blood of the Lamb. On - ly by the blood of the Lamb.

Once a - gain I thank You, once a - gain I pour out my life. *Fine (repeat twice)* Thank You for the cross. Thank You for the cross. Thank You for the cross, my Friend. Friend. *D.S. al Fine*

© Copyright 1992 Rosemary Foster Music (Administered by Maranatha! Music c/o The Copyright Company, Nashville, TN)
Maranatha! Music (Administered by The Copyright Company, Nashville, TN)/Heartservice Music.
All Rights Reserved. International Copyright Secured. Used by Permission. www.maranathamusic.com

Those who hope in the Lord will renew their strength. They will soar on wings like eagles; they will run and not grow weary, they will walk and not be faint. (Isaiah 40:31)

176 On Eagle's Wings

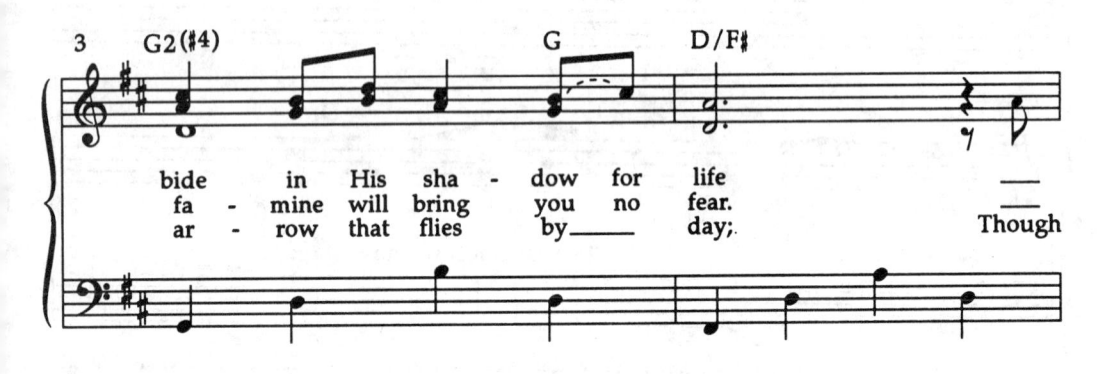

Michael Joncas

Tenderly ♩ = 82-90

1. You who dwell in the shel-ter of the Lord, who a-
(2.) snare of the fowl-er will nev-er cap-ture you, And
3. You need not fear the ter-ror of the night, Not the

bide in His sha-dow for life
fa-mine will bring you no fear.
ar-row that flies by day; Though

Say to the Lord, "My re-fuge, my
Un-der His wings your re-fuge, His
thou-sands fall a-bout you,

© Copyright 1979 by New Dawn Music, 10802 North 23rd Avenue, Phoenix, Arizona 85029.
All Rights Reserved. Used with Permission.

CHORUS

Rock in whom I trust."
faith-ful-ness your shield. And He will
Near you, it shall not come.

raise you up on ea-gle's wings,

Bear you on the breath of dawn,

Make you to shine like the sun, And

hold you in the palm of His hand. 2. The

D.C. (twice)

177 # Only You

Satisfy us in the morning with your unfailing love, that we may sing for joy and be glad all our days. (Psalm 90:14)

Andy Park

VERSE

1. No one but You Lord can come satisfy the longing in my heart.
2. Father I love You, can come satisfy the longing in my heart.

Nothing I do Lord can take the place of drawing near to You. Only
Fill me, o-ver-whelm me, un-til I know Your love deep in my heart.

CHORUS

You can fill my deepest longing, only
You can breathe in me new life, only
You can fill my heart with laughter, only
You can answer my heart's cry.

© Copyright 1988 Mercy/Vineyard Publishing (ASCAP).
All Rights Reserved. Used by Permission.

178 Only by Grace

Since we have confidence to enter the Most Holy Place by the blood of Jesus...let us draw near to God with a sincere heart in full assurance of faith. (Hebrews 10:19-22)

Gerrit Gustafson

CHORUS

On-ly by grace can we en-ter;
on-ly by grace can we stand,
not by our hu-man en-deav-or,
but by the blood of the Lamb.
In-to Your pres-ence You call us; You call us to come.
In-to Your pres-ence You draw us, and now by Your grace we come.
Now by Your grace we come.

Fine

© Copyright 1990 Integrity's Hosanna! Music, c/o Integrity Music, Inc., 1000 Cody Road, Mobile, AL 36695-3425.
All Rights Reserved. International Copyright Secured. Used by Permission.

"For all have sinned and fall short of the glory of God, and are justified freely by **his grace** through the redemption that came by Christ Jesus."

Romans 3:23-24

And the blood of Jesus, His Son, purifies us from all sin. (1 John 1:7)

179   Only the Blood

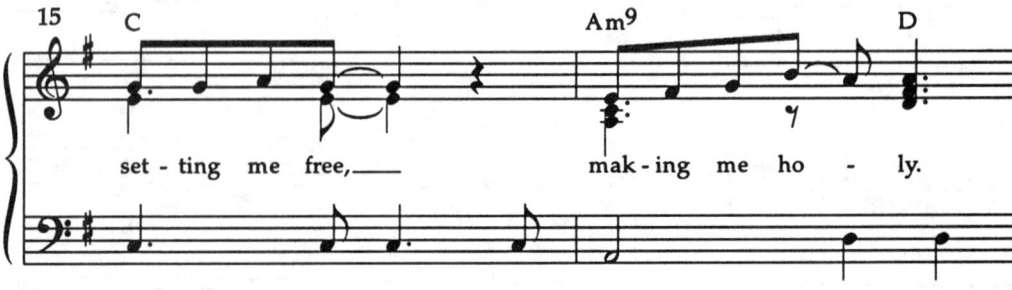

Brian Doerksen

♩ = 84

VERSE

Ho-li-ness is Your life in me,
Mak-ing me clean through Your blood.
Ho-li-ness is Your fire in me,
Purg-ing my heart like a flood.

BRIDGE

I know You are per-fect in ho-li-ness.
Your life in me, set-ting me free, mak-ing me ho-ly.

© Copyright 1990 Mercy/Vineyard Publishing (ASCAP).
All Rights Reserved. International Copyright Secured. Used by Permission.

CHORUS
17 G C2
On - ly the blood of Je - sus
19 G D C
cov - ers all of my sin,
21 G C2
On - ly the life of Je - sus
23 G C D
re - news me from with - in.
25 Em7 C
Your blood is e - nough,
27 Am9 C/D D
Your mer - cy com - plete.
29 Em7 C
Your work of a - tone - ment,
31 F D/F# G C2
D.S. al Fine
paid for my debts, mak - ing me ho - ly.
34 G C2 D
On - ly the blood of Je -
36 G
Fine
sus.

180 Open the Eyes of My Heart

Paul Baloche

I pray also that the eyes of your heart may be enlightened...that you may know the hope to which he has called you... (Ephesians 1:18)

With feeling ♩ = 112

CHORUS

O-pen the eyes of my heart, Lord, o-pen the eyes of my heart; I want to see You, I want to see You.

VERSE

To see You high and lift-ed up, shin-ing in the light of Your glo-ry. Pour out Your pow'r and love as we sing, "Ho-ly, ho-ly, ho-ly."

(optional repeat to beginning)

© Copyright 1997 Integrity's Hosanna! Music, c/o Integrity Music, Inc., 1000 Cody Road, Mobile, AL 36695-3425.
All Rights Reserved. International Copyright Secured. Used by Permission.

"The man without the Spirit does not accept the things that come from the *Spirit* of God, for they are foolishness to him, and he cannot understand them, because they are *spiritually* discerned."

1 Corinthians 2:14

My soul finds rest in God alone...He alone is my rock and my salvation; He is my fortress, I will never be shaken. (Psalm 62:1-2)

181 Our Confidence Is in the Lord

Noel Richards and Tricia Richards

Our con-fi-dence is in the Lord, the source of our sal-va-tion. Rest is found in God a-lone, the au-thor of cre-a-tion. We will not fear the e-vil day, be-cause we have a ref-uge. In ev-'ry cir-cum-stance we say our hope is built on Je-sus. God is our for-tress; we will nev-er be shak-en. God is our for-tress; we will nev-er be shak-en. God is our for-tress; we will

© Copyright 1989 Kingsway's Thankyou Music, admin. EMI Christian Music Publishing.
All Rights Reserved. International Copyright Secured. Used by Permission.

"Though devils all the world should fill,

All eager to devour us,

We tremble not, we **fear *no* ill**,

They shall not overpow'r us.

This world's prince may still

Scowl fierce as he will,

He **can harm** us **none**,

He's judged; the deed is done;

One little word can fell him."

Martin Luther, 1529

Praise the Lord from the heavens...all his angels...you great sea creatures and all ocean depths...you mountains... kings of the earth and all nations...Let them praise the name of the Lord. (Psalm 148:11-13)

182 Praise Adonai

Paul Baloche

Moderately

VERSE

Who is like Him, the Li-on and the Lamb, seat-ed on the throne? Moun-tains bow down, ev-'ry o-cean roars to the Lord of Hosts.

CHORUS

Praise Adonai from the ris-ing of the sun 'til the end of ev-'ry day. Praise Adonai, all the na-tions of the earth; all the an-gels and the saints sing

3rd time to Coda

© Copyright 1999 Integrity's Hosanna! Music, c/o Integrity Music, Inc., 1000 Cody Road, Mobile, AL 36695-3425.
All Rights Reserved. International Copyright Secured. Used by Permission.

183 Peace Be Yours

*Peace I leave with you, my peace I give you, I do not give to you as the world gives.
Do not let your hearts be troubled and do not be afraid. (John 14:27)*

Blair A'Hearn

1. Peace be yours. May the Lord be with you
2. Peace be yours as you scatter from here.
3. Seek your strength where the Lord does abide
4. Always know He has conquered the one

as we gather now and your whole life through,
Anywhere you go, God is always near,
when the greatest evil is at your side.
who defies your life in God's only Son.

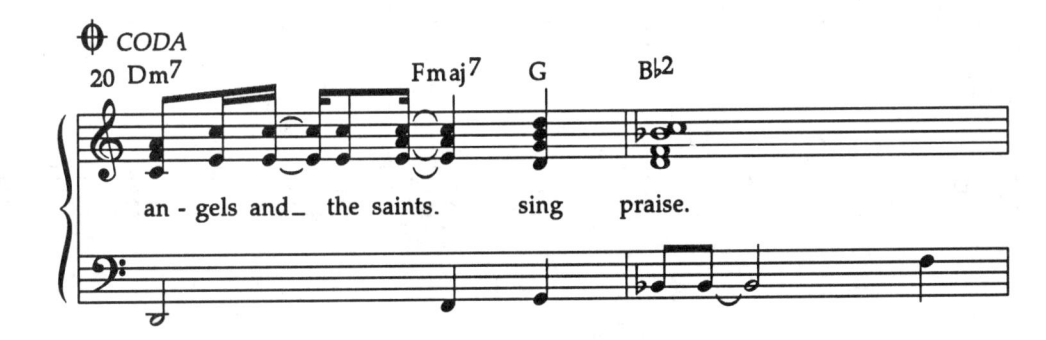

blessing and mercy and wholeness, too.
loving and calming your deepest fear.
In Word and Sacrament, Christ resides.
Yours is the struggle that Christ has won.

May God's peace be yours.

angels and the saints sing

angels and the saints sing praise.

© Copyright 1997 Blair A'Hearn.
All Rights Reserved. Used by Permission.

Let us purify ourselves from everything that contaminates body and spirit, perfecting holiness out of reverence for God. (2 Cor. 7:1)

184 Purify My Heart

Jeff Nelson

CHORUS

Pu-ri-fy my heart, Touch me with Your cleans-ing fire. Take me to the cross; Your ho-li-ness is my de-sire. Breathe Your life in me, Kin-dle a love that flows from Your throne. Oh, pu-ri-fy my heart, Pu-ri-fy my heart.

© Copyright 1992 Heartservice Music (admin. by Music Services)/Maranatha! Music.
All Rights Reserved. Used by Permission. www.maranathamusic.com

Come to me, all you who are weary and burdened and I will give you rest. (Matthew 11:28)

185 Rest

Gracia Grindal

Douglas Norquist

Moderately

VERSE

1. I will rest in the prom-ise of God to be with me, I will rest in the knowl-edge God cares. Though the world and its trou-bles con-fuse and dis-turb me, I will rest in the Lord in my prayers.

2. For God came to the earth in the form of a ser-vant When the Word be-came flesh in our Lord. And He lived and He died on the cross to re-deem me, And He rose to make good on His Word.

3. I will sing of the prom-ise of God to be with me, I will sing with the heav-en-ly throng. For the mer-cies of God come to me with-out num-ber, O-ver-whelm me and fill me with song.

CHORUS

For the mer-cies of God are like show-ers in spring-time. Re-fresh-ing as rain in my soul. They are more than the stars or the sands of the o-ceans, They re-new me, God's love makes me whole.

Text: © 1986 Gracia Grindal. Music © 1992 Douglas Norquist.
All Rights Reserved. Used by Permission.

Go into all the world and preach the good news to all creation. (Mark 16:15)

186 Raise Up an Army

Steve and Vikki Cook

♩ = 104

CHORUS

Raise up an ar-my, O God, a-wake Your peo-ple through-out the earth; Raise up an ar-my, O God, to pro-claim Your king-dom, to de-clare Your Word, to re-veal Your glo-ry, O God.

VERSE

1. Our hope, our heart, our vi-sion, to see in ev-'ry land, Your cho-sen peo-ple com-ing forth; Ful-fill-ing Your ho-ly mis-sion, u-nit-ed as we stand,

2. O God, our glo-rious Ma-ker, we mar-vel at Your grace, that You would use us in Your plan; Re-joic-ing at Your fa-vor, de-light-ing in Your ways,

© Copyright 1987 PDI Music (Administered by Copycare U.S.A. c/o The Copyright Company, Nashville, TN)
All Rights Reserved. International Copyright Secured. Used by Permission.

"Onward, Christian soldiers,

marching as to war,

With the cross of Jesus going on before.

Christ, the *royal* **master** leads against the foe;

Forward into battle see his banners go!

Onward, Christian Soldiers, marching as to war,

With the cross of Jesus going on before.

Like a mighty army

moves the Church of God;

Brothers, we are treading where the saints have trod.

We are not divided, all **one body** we,

One in hope and doctrine, one in charity.

Onward, Christian Soldiers, marching as to war,

With the cross of Jesus going on before."

Sabine Baring-Gould, 1834-1924

Greater love has no one than this, that he lay down his life for his friends. (John 15:13)

187 Redeemer, Savior, Friend

Darrell Evans and Chris Springer

Slow four ♩ = 63

VERSE

1. I know You had me on Your mind when You
climbed up on that hill, for You
saw me with e-ter-nal eyes while
I was yet in sin, Re-

(2.) stripe up-on Your bat-tered back, ev-'ry
thorn that pierced Your brow, ev-'ry
nail drove deep through guilt-less hands said that
Your love knows no end, Re-

(3.) grace You pour up-on my life will re-
turn to You in praise, and I'll
glad-ly lay down all my crowns for the
name by which I'm saved, Re-

deem-er, Sav-ior, Friend.
deem-er, Sav-ior, Friend.
deem-er, Sav-ior, Friend.

2. Ev-'ry

CHORUS

Re-deem-er, re-deem my heart a-gain.
Sav-ior, come and shel-ter me from sin. You're fa-

© Copyright 1999 Integrity's Hosanna! Music, c/o Integrity Music, Inc., 1000 Cody Road, Mobile, AL 36695-3425.
All Rights Reserved. International Copyright Secured. Used by Permission.

"You see, at just the right time, when we were still *powerless*, Christ died for the ungodly. Very rarely will anyone die for a righteous man, though for a good man someone might possibly dare to die. But God demonstrates his own love for us in this: While we were **still sinners**, Christ died for us."

Romans 5:6-8

188 Remember Me

...the Lord Jesus on the night he was betrayed took bread; and when he had given thanks, he broke it, and said, 'This is my body, which is for you; do this in remembrance of me.' (1 Corinthians 11:23,24)

Gerrit Gustafson and Martin J. Nystrom

VERSE 1

Optional: Pastor or Praise Team

On the night You were betrayed You took the bread; After giving thanks, You broke it and

CHORUS 1

said, "This is My body, broken for you, and as you eat it, remember Me; This is My body, broken for you, and as you eat it, remember Me."

VERSE 2

On the night You were betrayed You held the cup; After giving thanks, You lifted it up.

CHORUS 2

"This is My blood, poured out for

*Note: This song could be used in place of the spoken "Words of Institution" as indicated.

© Copyright 1991 Integrity's Hosanna! Music, c/o Integrity Music, Inc., 1000 Cody Road, Mobile, AL 36695-3425.
All Rights Reserved. International Copyright Secured. Used by Permission.

18. you, and as you drink it, re-mem-ber
   F | Bb2/F | F | Dm7

20. Me; This is My blood, poured out for
   Gm7 | Bb/C | F | Bb2/F

22. you, and as you drink it, re-mem-ber
   F | Bb2/F | Dm7 | Gm7 Bb/C C

VERSE 3 *Optional: All*

24. Me." So, we thank You for the wine and for the bread;
   F Bbmaj7 C2 | Dm | G2/B

26. For we see the life You gave and the
   C2 | C | Dm | G/B

28. blood You shed. And we re-
   Bb/C | C | Bb/C

CHORUS 3

30. mem-ber Your won-drous love, You gave Your
   F | Bb2/F | F | Bb2/F

32. bod-y, You shed Your blood; And we re-
   F | Dm7 | Gm7 | Bb/C

34. mem-ber Your won-drous love, You gave Your
   F | Bb2/F | F | Bb2/F

36. bod-y, You shed Your blood.
   Dm7 | Gm7 | Bb/C C | F

Create in me a pure heart, O God and renew a steadfast spirit within me. (Psalm 51:10)

189 Renew Me

Lana Gibbons

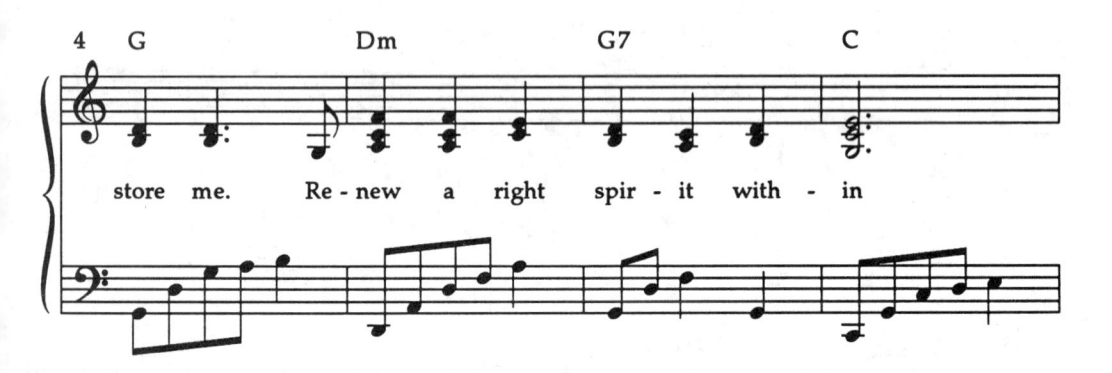

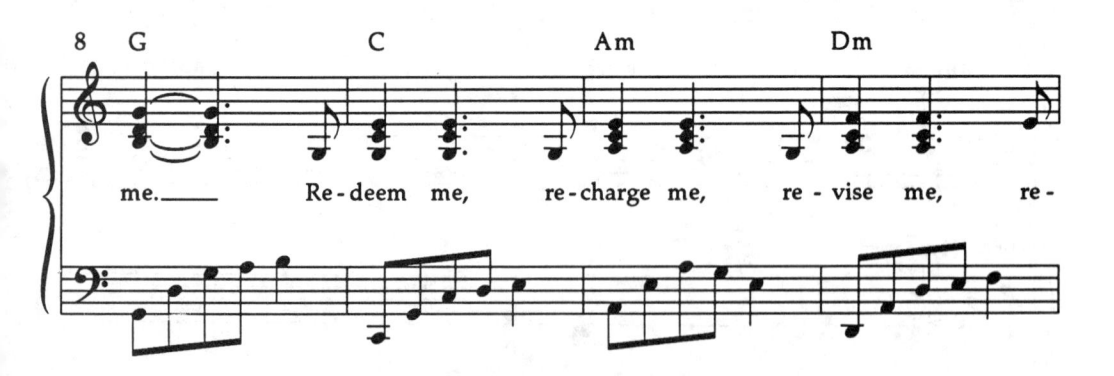

CHORUS

Renew me, re-pair me, re-fresh me, re-store me. Renew a right spir-it with-in me. Re-deem me, re-charge me, re-vise me, re-vive me. Cre-ate in me a clean heart.

VERSE

1. For You a-lone are my strength, my song. Your love re-deems me, makes right of my wrong.
2. For You a-lone can re-store my soul, Your love re-pairs me, turns brok-en to whole.
3. For You a-lone can give me pow'r to start, Your love is kind-ling a pure-ness of heart.
4. For You a-lone are a pre-cious gift, Your love re-news me, You give me a lift.

5th time to Coda

© Copyright 1999 Lana Gibbons, Marengo, Illinois.
All Rights Reserved. Used by Permission.

"Create in me a pure heart, O God,

and renew a steadfast spirit

within me. Do not cast me from your

presence or take your Holy Spirit from me.

Restore to me the joy of your salvation

and grant me a willing spirit, to sustain me."

Psalm 51:10-12

...One more powerful than I will come... he will baptize you with the Holy Spirit and with fire. (Luke 3:16)

190   Revival Fire, Fall

Paul Baloche

♩ = 92

VERSE
WORSHIP LEADER / CONGREGATION / W.L.

1. As we lift up Your name, as we lift up Your name, let Your fire fall, let Your fire fall; Send Your wind and Your rain, send Your wind and Your rain, on Your wings of love, on Your wings of love.

2. As we lift up Your name, as we lift up Your name, let Your kingdom come, let Your kingdom come; Have Your way in this place, have Your way in this place, let Your will be done, let Your will be done.

ALL
Pour out from Heaven Your passion and presence, bring down Your burning desire.

CHORUS
Revival fire, fall, revival fire, fall; Fall on us here in the pow'r of Your Spirit,

© Copyright 1996 Integrity's Hosanna! Music, c/o Integrity Music, Inc., 1000 Cody Road, Mobile, AL 36695-3425.
All Rights Reserved. International Copyright Secured. Used by Permission.

"After two days he will revive us; on the third day he will restore us, that we may live in his presence. Let us acknowledge the LORD; let us press on to acknowledge him. As surely as the sun rises, he will appear; he will come to us like the winter rains, like the spring rains that water the earth."

Hosea 6:2-3

There is no Rock like our God. (1 Samuel 2:2)

191 Rock of Ages

Rita Baloche

19
D
A
es, Je - sus is the Rock.
21
E
F♯m7
D
Rock of Ag - es,
24
A
E
Je - sus is the Rock. Rock of Ag -
26
F♯m7
D
es,
28
A
E
Je - sus is the Rock.
30
G2
D2
Last time to Coda
There is no rock, there is no god like ours.
32
A
Asus
A
Asus
D.S. al CODA
CODA
34
A
Asus
A
Asus
36
A
Asus
A

192 Romans 16:19

Be wise about what is good, and innocent about what is evil. The God of peace will soon crush Satan under your feet. (Romans 16:19,20)

Dale Garratt, John Mark Childers,
Ramon Pink, and Graham Burt

♩ = 132

Ro-mans six-teen: nine-teen says,— Ro-mans six-teen: nine-teen says,— "Be ex-cel-lent— at what is good,— be in-no-cent— of e-vil; Be ex-cel-lent— at what is good,— be in-no-cent— of e-vil. And the God of peace will soon crush Satan, yes, God will crush him un-der-neath— your feet; And the God of peace will soon crush Satan, yes, God will crush him un-der-neath— your feet."

© Copyright 1991 Scripture In Song, a div. of Integrity Music, Inc., 1000 Cody Road, Mobile, AL 36695-3425.
All Rights Reserved. International Copyright Secured. Used by Permission.

193 Rock of My Salvation

*The Lord is my rock, my fortress and my deliverer...my rock in whom I take refuge...
my shield and the horn of my salvation, my stronghold. (Psalm 62:2)*

Teresa Muller

CHORUS

You are the Rock of my salvation, You are the strength of my life. You are my hope and my inspiration, Lord, unto You will I cry.

VERSE

I believe in You, believe in You, for Your faithful love to me. You have been my help in time of need; Lord, unto You will I cleave.

You are the Rock of my salvation, You are the strength of my life.

© Copyright 1982 Maranatha! Music (Administered by The Copyright Company, Nashville, TN).
All Rights Reserved. International Copyright Secured. Used by Permission. www.maranathamusic.com

Peace I leave with you; my peace I give you...Do not let your hearts be troubled and do not be afraid. (John 14:27)

194 Savior, Again to Your Dear Name

John Ellerton

Edward J. Hopkins
Arr. by Joseph Barlowe

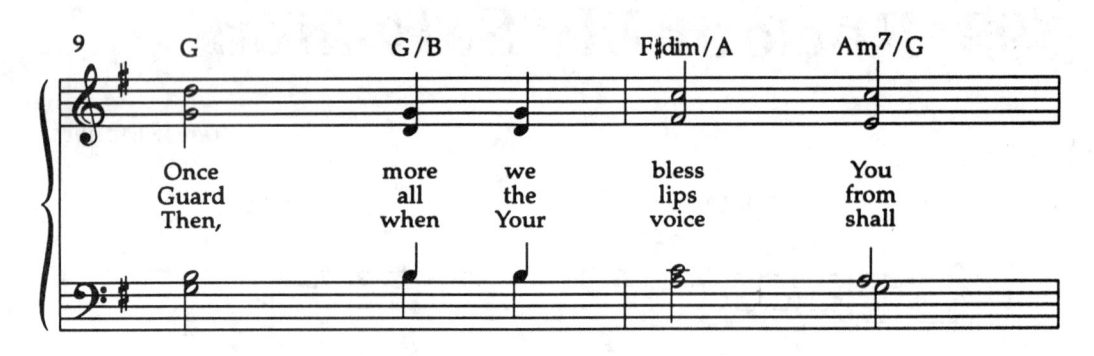

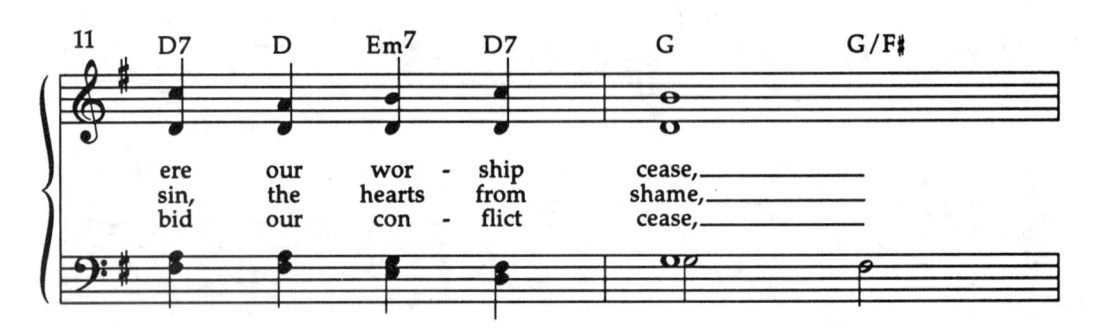

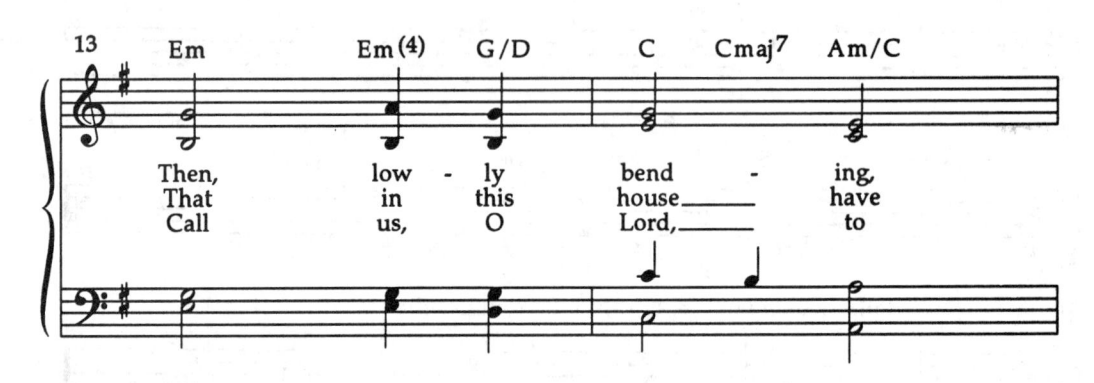

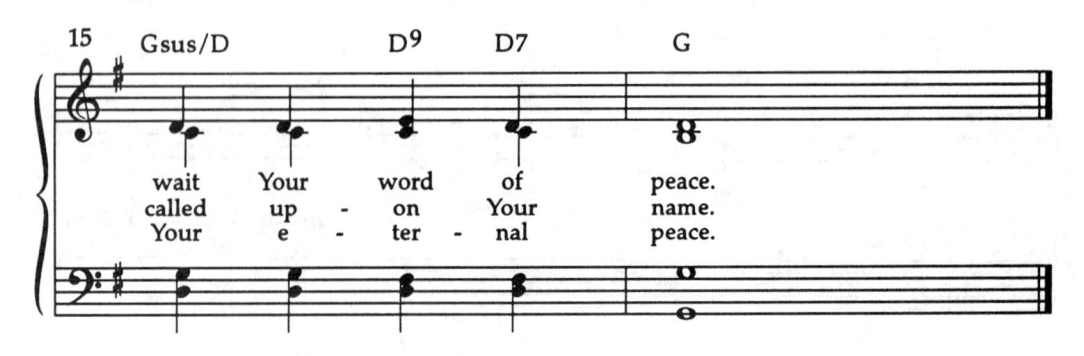

1. Savior, again to Your dear name we raise
With one accord our parting hymn of praise;
Then, ere our worship cease,
Once more we bless You
Then, lowly bending,
wait Your word of peace.

2. Grant us Your peace upon our homeward way;
With You began, with You shall end the day;
Guard all the lips from sin, the hearts from shame,
That in this house have called upon Your name.

3. Grant us Your peace upthrough our earthly life,
Our balm in sorrow and our stay in strife;
Then, when Your voice shall bid our conflict cease,
Call us, O Lord, to Your eternal peace.

© Copyright 1986 Word Music, Inc. (ASCAP), 65 Music Square West, Nashville, TN 37203.
All Rights Reserved. Made in the U.S.A. International Copyright Secured. Used by Permission.

195 Sing Unto the Lord

Sing to the Lord a new song; sing to the Lord, all the earth. (Psalm 96:1)

Author Unknown

♩ = 125

CHORUS

Sing un-to the Lord a new song, sing un-to the Lord all the earth.

Sing un-to the Lord a new song, sing un-to the Lord all the earth.

VERSE

For God is great and great-ly to be praised. God is great and great-ly to be praised!

D.C. al Fine

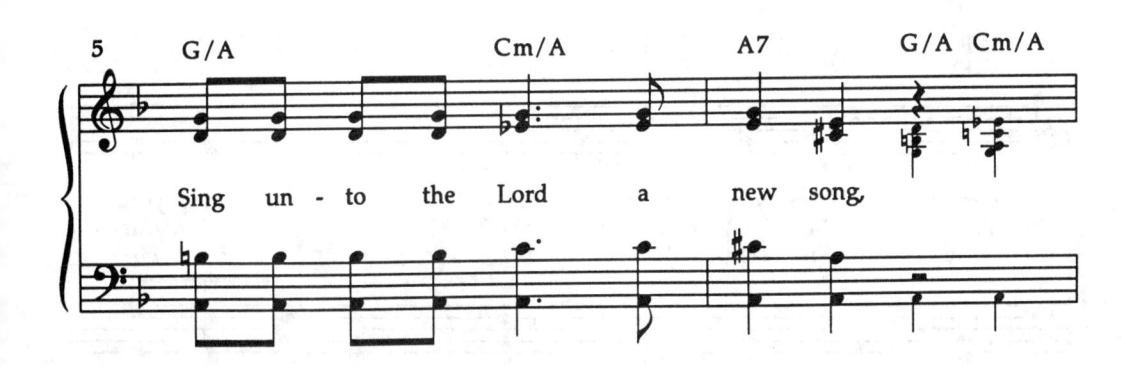

This arr. © Copyright 1987 Integrity's Hosanna! Music, c/o Integrity Music, Inc., 1000 Cody Road, Mobile, AL 36695-3425. All Rights Reserved. International Copyright Secured. Used by Permission.

He saved us through the washing of rebirth and renewal by the Holy Spirit. (Titus 3:5)

196 See This Wonder in the Making

Jaroslav J. Vajda
Old Swedish Tune

1. See this wonder in the making: God Himself this child is taking As a lamb safe in His keeping, His to be, awake or sleeping.
2. Miracle each time it happens As the door to heaven opens And the Father beams, "Beloved, Heir of gifts a king would covet!"
3. Far more tender than a mother, Far more caring than a father, God, into Your arms we place *him/her*, With your love and peace embrace *him/her*.
4. Here we bring a child of nature; Home we take a newborn creature, Now God's precious son or daughter, Born again by Word and water.

Music: Public Domain. Text: © Copyright 1984 Jaroslav J. Vajda, 3534 Brookstone South Drive, St. Louis, MO 63129-2900. All Rights Reserved. Used by Permission.
This song is NOT covered by CCLI. For permission to reprint, please contact the author as listed above.

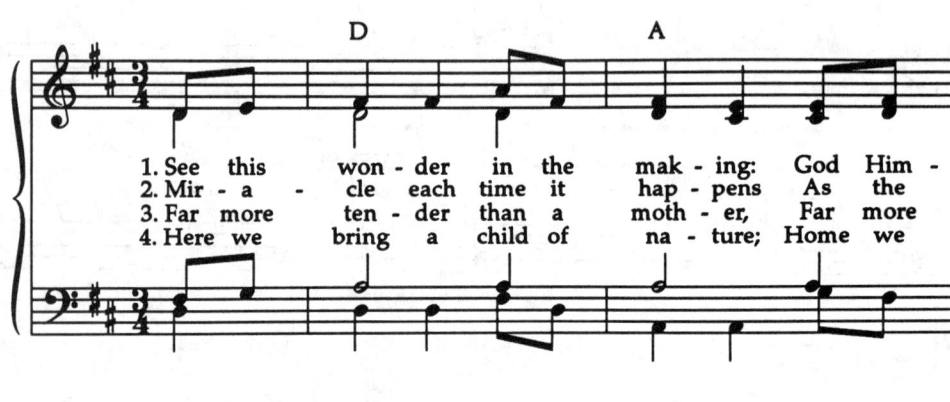

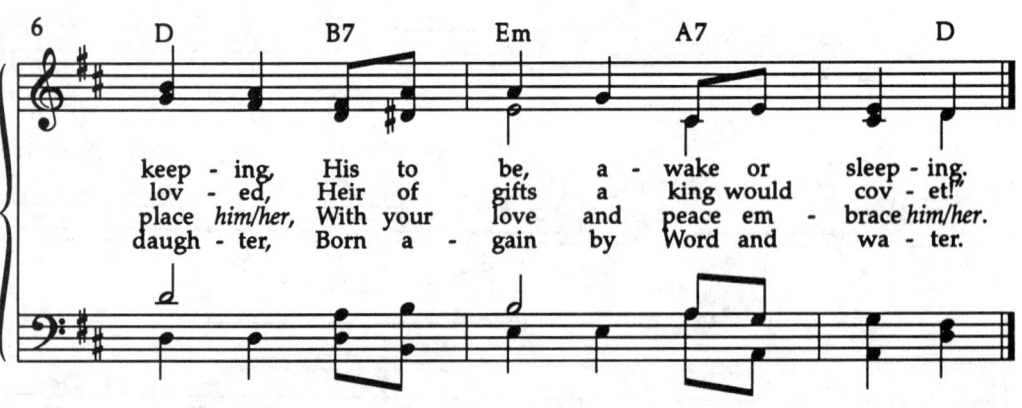

People will come from east and west and north and south, and will take their places at the feast in the Kingdom of God. (Luke 13:29)

197 Shout to the North

Martin Smith

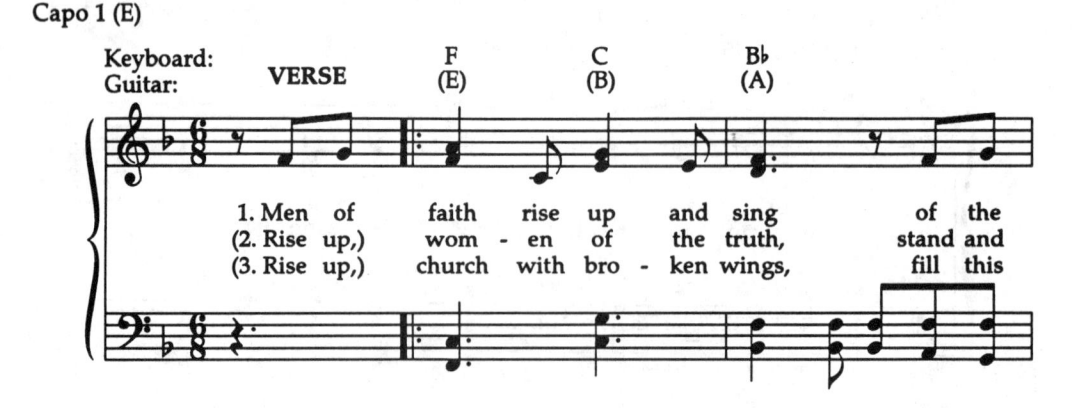

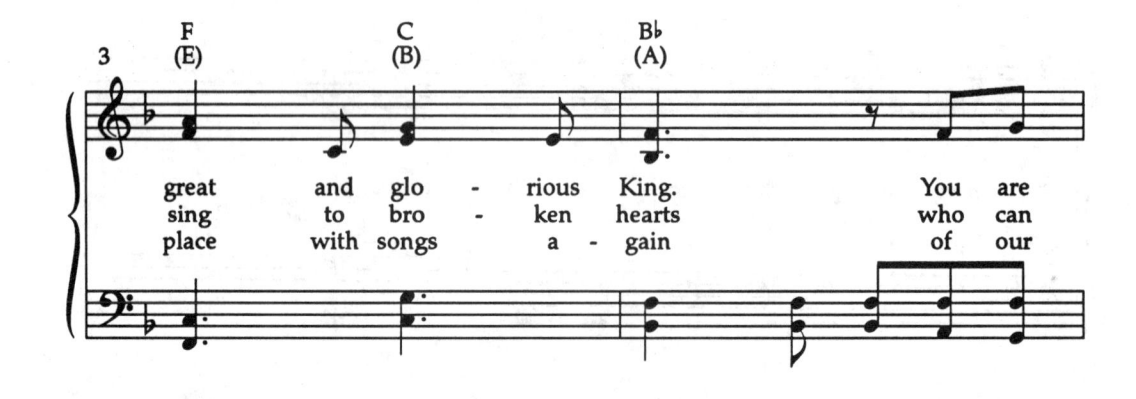

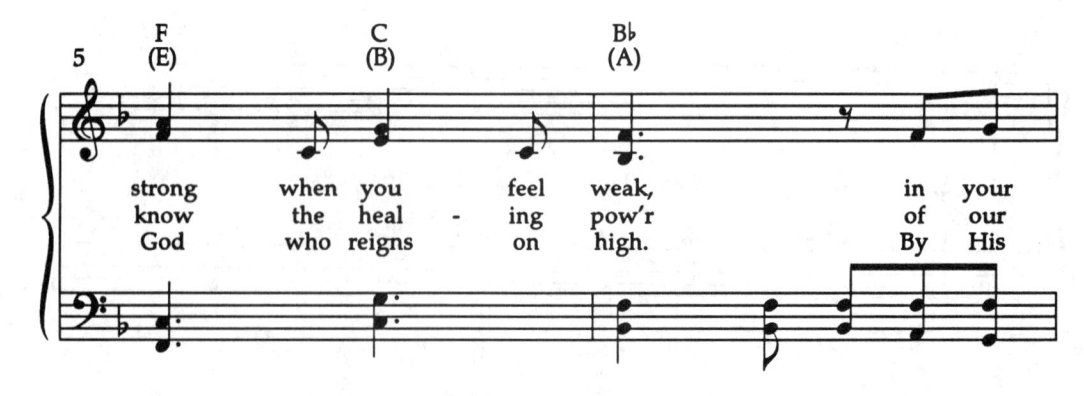

Capo 1 (E)

1. Men of faith rise up and sing of the great and glorious King. You are strong when you feel weak,
(2. Rise up,) women of the truth, stand and sing to broken hearts who can know the healing pow'r
(3. Rise up,) church with broken wings, fill this place with songs again of our God who reigns on high. By His

© Copyright 1995 Curious? Music U.K./Administered in North America by EMI Christian Music Publishing, P.O. Box 5085, Brentwood, TN 37024/5085. All Rights Reserved. Used by Permission.

7
F (E) C (B) B♭ (A)
bro - ken - ness com - plete.
glo - rious King of love.
grace a - gain we'll fly.
CHORUS
10
F (E) B♭ (A) C (B) F (E)
Shout to the north and the south; sing to the
13
B♭ (A) C (B) F (E) B♭ (A) C (B)
east and the west Je - sus is Sav - ior to all,
16
B♭ (A) C (B) F (E)
Last time to Coda
1.3.
2.
Lord of heav-en and earth.
2. Rise up,
3. Rise up,
BRIDGE
20
Dm (C♯m) B♭ (A) Dm (C♯m)
We've been through fire, we've been through rain; we've been re-fined by the
23
B♭ (A) Dm (C♯m) B♭ (A)
pow'r of His name. We've fall - en deep - er in love with You.
26
B♭ (A) F/A (E/G♯) Csus (Bsus) C (B)
D.S. al CODA
You've burned the truth on our lips.
CODA
29
B♭ (A) C (B) F (E) B♭ (A) C (B)
Lord of heav-en and earth, Lord of heav-en and
32
F (E) B♭ (A) C (B) F (E)
earth, Lord of heav-en and earth.

Shout for joy to the Lord all the earth, burst into jubilant song with music. (Psalm 98:4)

198   Shout to the Lord

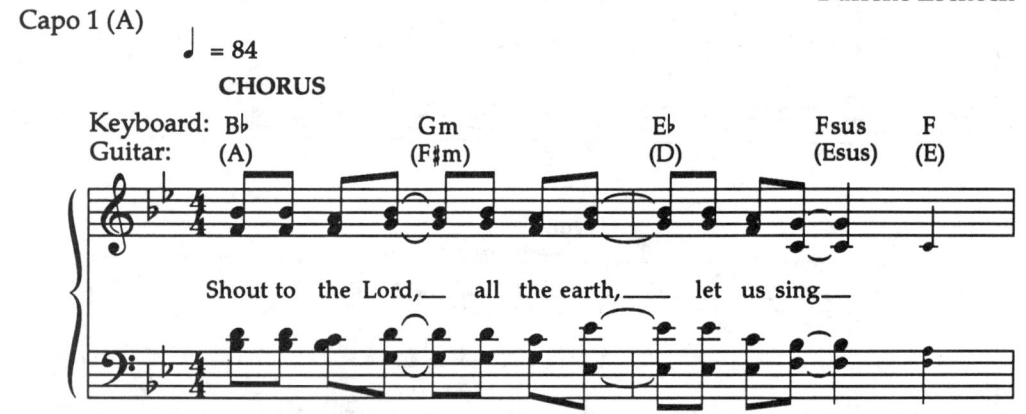

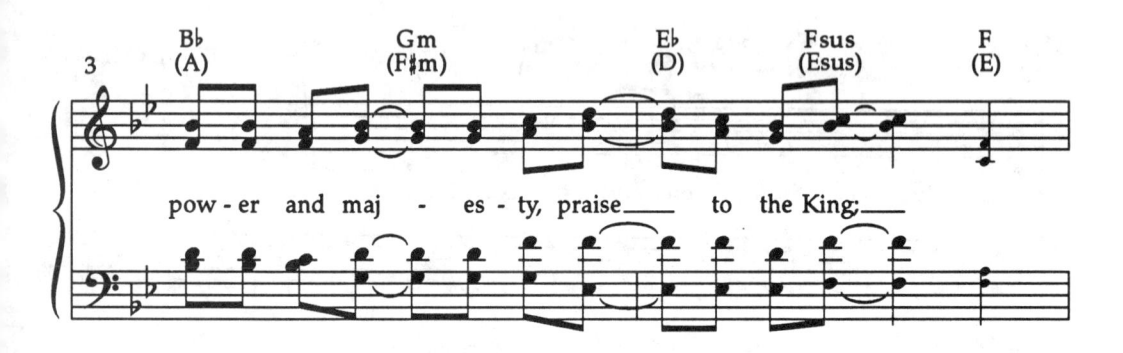

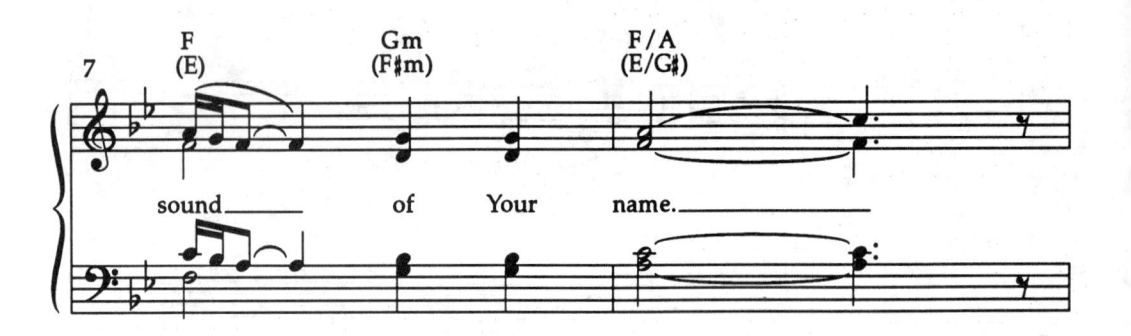

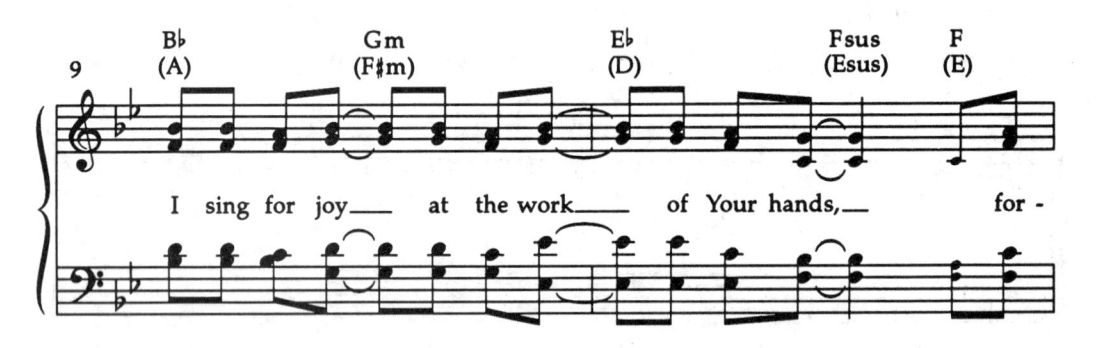

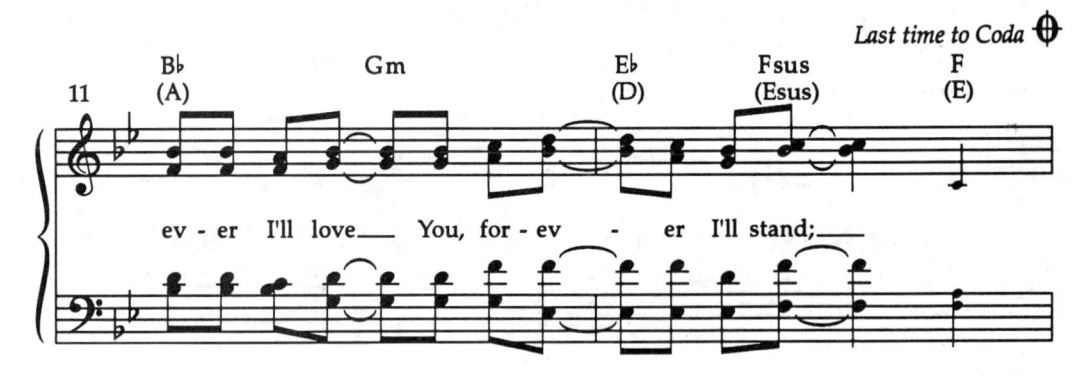

Darlene Zschech

Capo 1 (A)

♩ = 84

CHORUS

Shout to the Lord, all the earth, let us sing

pow-er and maj-es-ty, praise to the King;

Moun-tains bow down and the seas will roar at the

sound of Your name.

I sing for joy at the work of Your hands, for-

Last time to Coda

ev-er I'll love You, for-ev-er I'll stand;

Noth-ing com-pares to the prom-ise I have in You.

© Copyright 1993 Darlene Zschech/Hillsongs Australia (admin. in U.S. and Canada by Integrity's Hosanna! Music),
c/o Integrity Music, Inc., 1000 Cody Road, Mobile, AL 36695-3425.
All Rights Reserved. International Copyright Secured. Used by Permission.

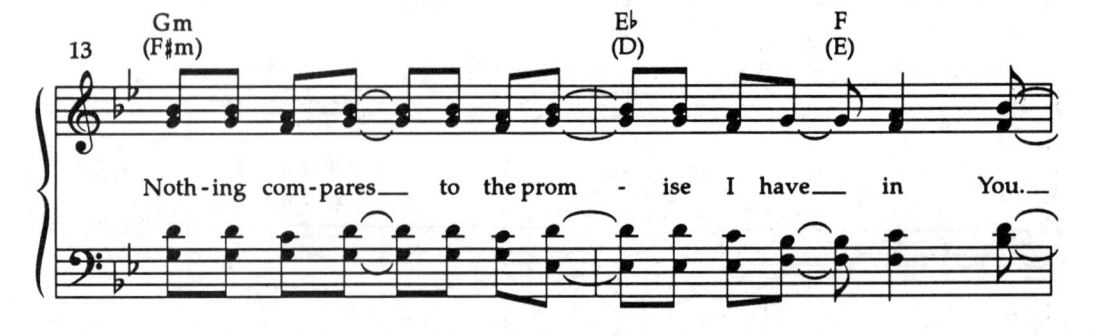

VERSE
D.C. al CODA
CODA
15 Bb (A) F (E) Bb (A) F (E)
My Jesus, my Savior,
19 Gm (F#m) F (E) Eb (D)
Lord, there is none like You, all of my days
21 Bb/D (A/C#) Eb (D) Bb/F (A/E) Gm (F#m)
I want to praise the wonders of Your
23 Ab (G) Eb/G (D/F#) Fsus (Esus) F (E) Bb (A) F (E)
mighty love: My Comfort, my Shelter,
27 Gm (F#m) F (E) Eb (D)
Tower of refuge and strength; Let ev'ry breath,
29 Bb/D (A/C#) Eb (D) Bb/F (A/E) Gm (F#m) Ab (G) Eb/G (D/F#) Fsus (Esus) F (E)
all that I am, never cease to worship You.
33 Gm (F#m) Eb (D) F (E)
Nothing compares to the promise I have in You.
35 Bb (A)

If anyone is thirsty let him come to me and drink. Whoever believes in me...streams of living water will flow from within him. By this he meant the Spirit. (John 7:37-39)

199 Someone Else Living in You

Michael Zehnder

With drive ♩ = 144

VERSE

1. Drink, drink, drink of His Spir - it; drink, drink, drink of His Word. Hold, hold, hold to His teach - ing, and show that you real - ly have heard.
2. Drink, drink, drink of His Spir - it; drink, drink, drink of His Word. Hold, hold, hold to His teach - ing, and show that you real - ly have heard.
3. Drink, drink, drink of His Spir - it; drink, drink, drink of His Word. Hold, hold, hold to His teach - ing, and show that you real - ly have heard.

Keep, keep, keep His com - mand - ments; live, live, live in His grace.
Thank, thank, thank Him for dai - ly bread; thank, thank, thank Him for love.
Sing, sing, sing with your heart on fire; sing, sing, sing with your mind.

Love, love, love as He first loved you, and run for the prize in the race. 1.3. For there is
Praise, praise, praise Him for Je - sus' blood; sal - va - tion's a gift from a - bove. 2. And there's a
Pray, pray, pray in the Spir - it, and love Him with heart, soul and mind.

© Copyright 2000 Michael Zehnder, P.O. Box 51510, Phoenix, AZ 85076.
All Rights Reserved. Used by Permission.

CHORUS
17 B♭ F Dm C
Some-one else___ liv-ing in you.___ For there is
new___ day___ wait-ing for you.___ And there's a
19 B♭ F Dm C
Some-one else___ dwell-ing in you.___ For there is
new___ day___ of heal-ing for you.___ And there's a
21 B♭maj7 Am7 Dm7 C F
Last time to Coda
Some-one else___ build-ing His king - dom in you,___
new___ day;___ Je - sus will come___ back for you,___
23 B♭/C
yes, in you.___ For there is
yes, for you.___ And there's a
25 B♭ F Dm C
Some-one else___ liv-ing in you.___ For there is
new___ day___ wait-ing for you.___ And there's a
27 B♭ F Dm C
Some-one else___ dwell-ing in you.___ For there is
new___ day___ of heal-ing for you.___ And there's a
29 B♭maj7 Am7 Dm7 C F
Some-one else___ build-ing His king - dom in you.___
new___ day;___ Je - sus will come___ back for you.___
31 1.2.
33 3.
D.S. al CODA
For there is
CODA
35 Dm7 C F
build-ing His king - dom in you.___

How great is the love the Father lavished on us, that we should be called children of God! And that is what we are! (1 John 3:1)

200 Someone Special

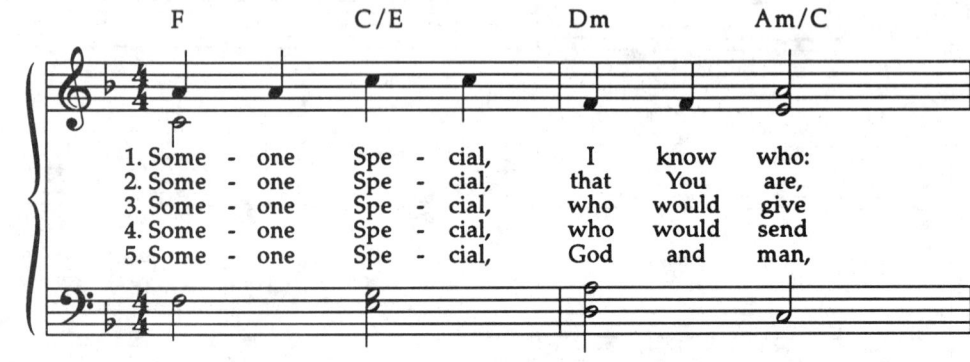

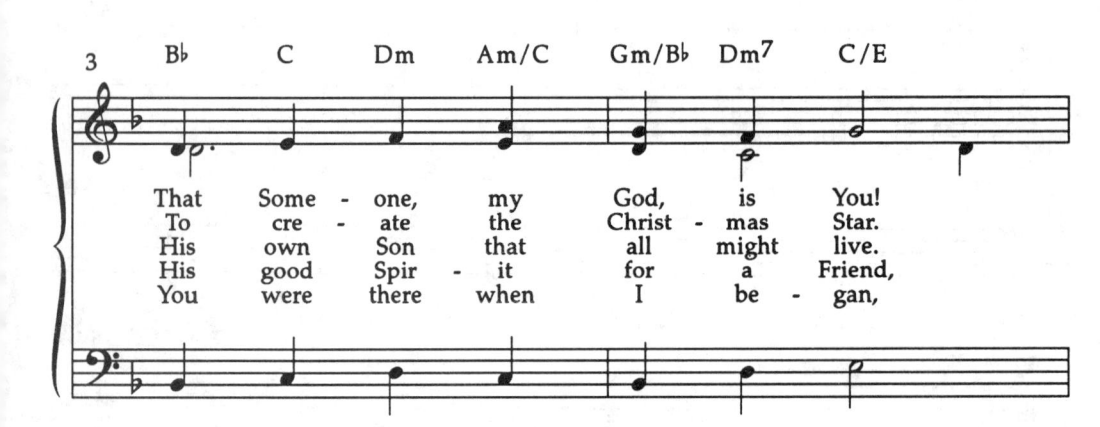

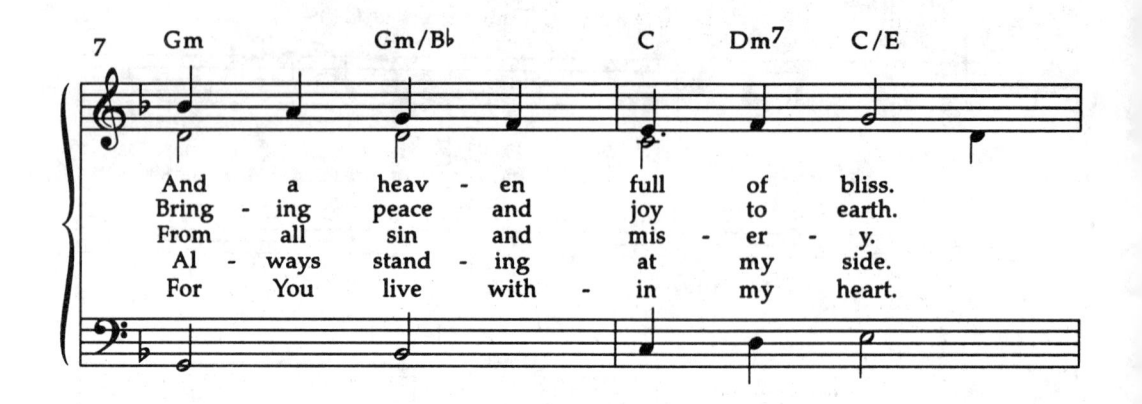

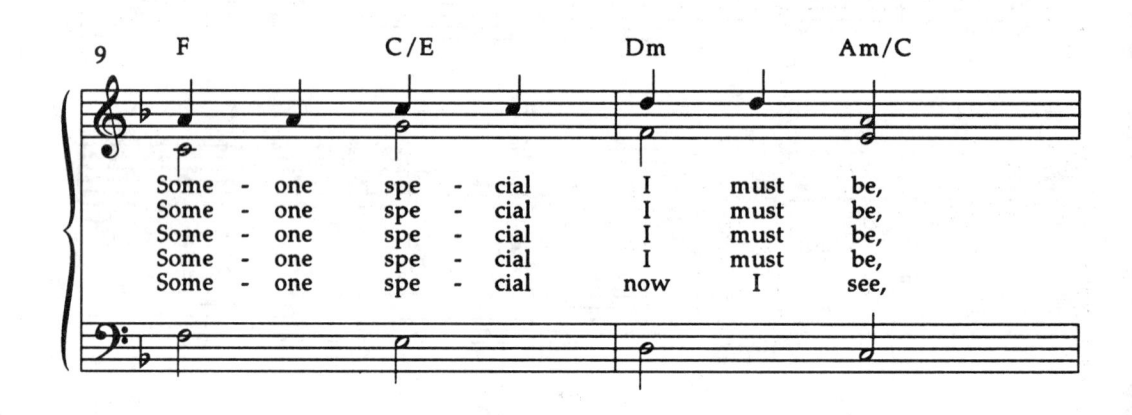

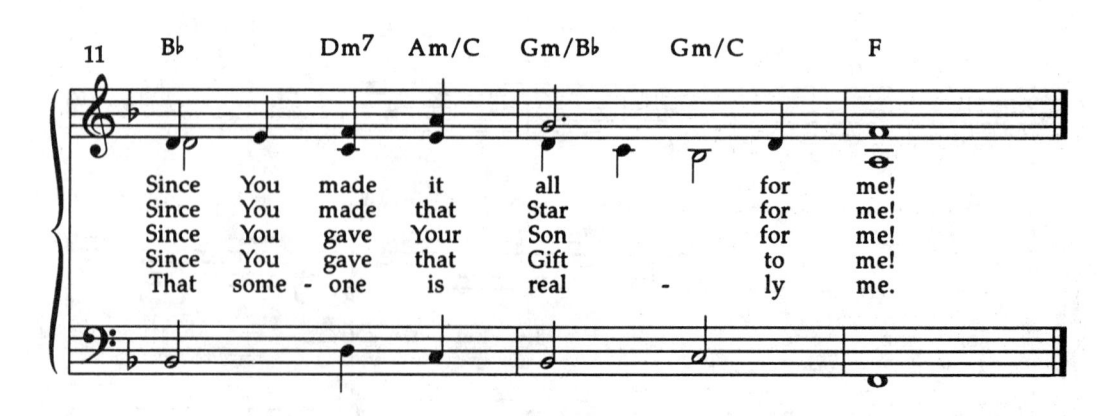

Jaroslav J. Vajda

Carl Schalk

1. Some-one Spe-cial, I know who:
2. Some-one Spe-cial, that You are,
3. Some-one Spe-cial, who would give
4. Some-one Spe-cial, who would send
5. Some-one Spe-cial, God and man,

That Some-one, my God, is You!
To cre-ate the Christ-mas Star.
His own Son that all might live.
His good Spir-it for a Friend,
You were there when I be-gan,

Who could make a world like this
Her-ald-ing the Sav-ior's birth,
And by Him would set us free
Faith Cre-a-tor, Light and Guide,
You'll be there when I de-part,

And a heav-en full of bliss.
Bring-ing peace and joy to earth.
From all sin and mis-er-y.
Al-ways stand-ing at my side.
For You live with-in my heart.

Some-one spe-cial I must be,
Some-one spe-cial I must be,
Some-one spe-cial I must be,
Some-one spe-cial I must be,
Some-one spe-cial now I see,

Since You made it all for me!
Since You made that Star for me!
Since You gave Your Son for me!
Since You gave that Gift to me!
That some-one is real-ly me.

Music and setting: © Copyright 1970 GIA Publications.
Text: © Copyright 1978 Jaroslav J. Vajda, 3534 Brookstone South Drive, St. Louis, MO 63129-2900.
All Rights Reserved. Used by Permission. This song is NOT covered by CCLI.
For permission to reprint, please contact the author as listed above or GIA Publications for the tune.

You show that you are a letter from Christ...written not with ink but with the Spirit of the living God. (2 Cor. 3:3)

201 Spirit of the Living God

Daniel Iverson

© Copyright 19__ Birdwing Music.
All Rights Reserved. Used by Permission.

And the peace of God, which transcends all understanding, will guard your hearts and your minds in Christ Jesus. (Philippians 4:7)

202 Spirit Song

John Wimber

Sweetly ♩ = 108

VERSE

1. O let the Son of God enfold you with His Spirit and His love, let Him fill your life and satisfy your soul.
2. O come and sing this song with gladness as your hearts are filled with joy, lift your hands in sweet surrender to His name.

O let Him have the things that hold you, and His Spirit, like a dove, will descend upon your life and make you whole.
O give Him all your tears and sadness, give Him all your years of pain, and you'll enter into life in Jesus' name.

CHORUS

Je-

© Copyright 1979 and this arr. © 1997 Mercy/Vineyard (ASCAP), Admin. By Music Services.
All Rights Reserved. International Copyright Secured. Used by Permission.

> "Be **filled** with the **Spirit**.
>
> Speak to one another with psalms, hymns and spiritual songs. Sing and make music in your heart to the Lord, always giving thanks to God the Father for everything, in the name of our Lord Jesus Christ."
>
> Ephesians 5:18-20

203 Spirit, Touch Your Church

After they prayed, the place where they were meeting was shaken. And they were all filled with the Holy Spirit and spoke the word of God boldly. (Acts 4:31)

Kim Bollinger

♩ = 84

VERSE 1: Lord, we need Your grace and mer-cy, we need to pray like nev-er be-fore; We need the pow-er of Your Ho-ly Spir-it to o-pen Heav-en's door. Spir-it,

CHORUS: touch Your Church, stir the hearts of men, re-vive us, Lord with Your pas-sion once a-gain. I want to care for oth-ers like Je-sus cares for me, let Your rain fall up-on me, let Your rain fall up-on me.

VERSE 2: Lord, we hum-bly come be-

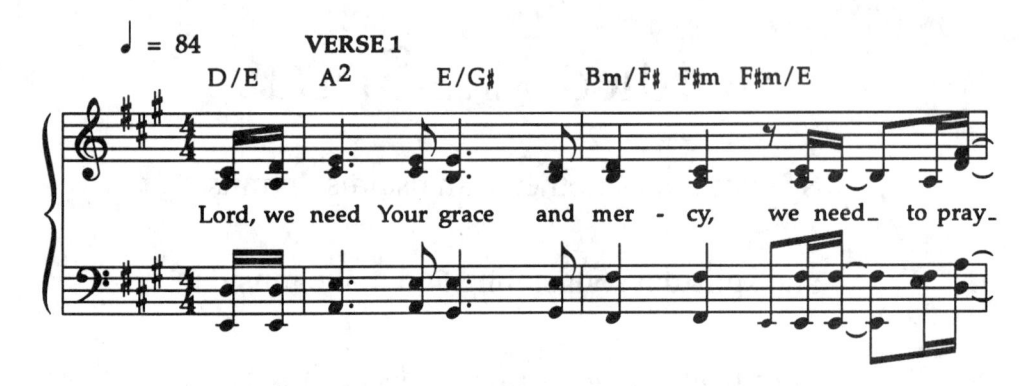

© Copyright 1990 Integrity's Hosanna! Music, c/o Integrity Music, Inc., 1000 Cody Road, Mobile, AL 36695-3425.
All Rights Reserved. International Copyright Secured. Used by Permission.

"Now, Lord, consider their threats and enable your servants to speak your word with **great** boldness. Stretch out your hand to heal and perform miraculous signs and wonders through the name of your holy servant Jesus." After they prayed, the place where they were meeting was shaken. And they were all *filled* with the Holy Spirit and spoke the word of God boldly.

All the believers were one in heart and mind. No one claimed that any of his possessions was his own, but they shared everything they had. With *great power* the apostles continued to testify to the resurrection of the Lord Jesus, and *much grace* was upon them all."

Acts 4:29-33

204 Shine, Jesus Shine
(Lord, the Light of Your Love)

You shine like stars in the universe as you hold out the word of life. (Philippians 2:15-16)

Graham Kendrick

VERSE

1. Lord, the light of Your love is shin-ing, In the midst of the dark-ness shin-ing; Je-sus, Light of the world, shine up-on us, Set us free by the truth You now bring us; Shine on me, Shine on me.

2. Lord, I come to Your awe-some pres-ence, From the shad-ows in-to Your ra-diance; By the blood I may en-ter Your bright-ness; Search me, try me, con-sume all my dark-ness; Shine on me, Shine on me.

CHORUS

Shine, Je-sus shine, fill this land with the Fa-ther's glo-ry. Blaze, Spir-it blaze; set our hearts on fire. Flow, riv-er flow, flood the na-tions with grace and mer-cy. Send forth Your Word, Lord, and let there be light.

© Copyright 1987 Make Way Music (admin. by Music Services in the Western Hemisphere) (ASCAP).
All Rights Reserved. Used by Permission.

Not by might, nor by power, but by my Spirit, says the Lord Almighty. (Zechariah 4:6)

205 The Battle Belongs to the Lord

Jamie Owens-Collins

1. In heav-en-ly ar-mor we'll en-ter the land,— The
2. When the pow-er of dark-ness comes in like a flood,— The
3. When your en-e-my press-es in hard,— do not fear,— The

bat-tle be-longs to the Lord.— No
bat-tle be-longs to the Lord.— He's
bat-tle be-longs to the Lord.— Take

weap-on that's fash-ioned a-gainst us will stand,—
raised up a stand-ard, the pow'r of His blood,—
cour-age, my friend, your re-demp-tion is near,— } The

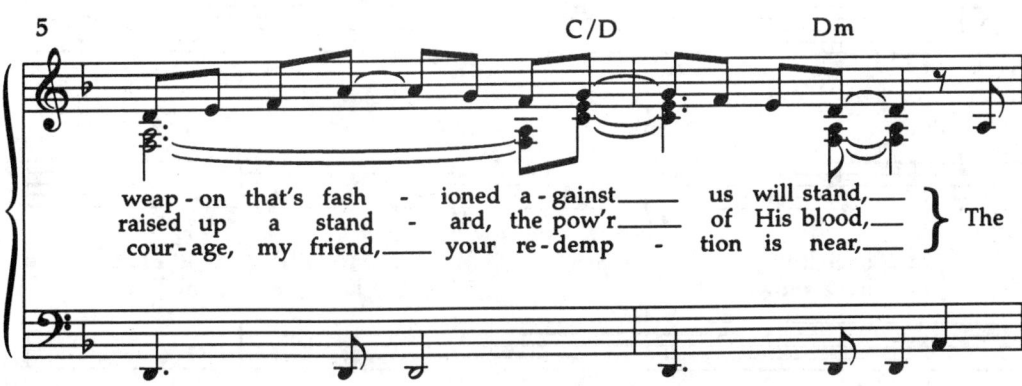

bat-tle be-longs to the Lord.— We sing

glo - ry, hon - or,

pow-er and strength to the Lord.— We sing

glo - ry, hon - or,

pow-er and strength to the Lord.—

© Copyright 1984 and this arr. © 1997 Fairhill Music, ASCAP.
All Rights Reserved. International Copyright Secured. Used by Permission.

Offer your bodies as living sacrifices, holy and pleasing to God — this is your spiritual act of worship. (Romans 12:1)

206 Take My Life, and Let It Be

Frances R. Havergal　　　　　　　　　　　　Henri A. César Malan

1. Take my life and let it be Con-se-crat-ed, Lord, to Thee; Take my hands and let them move At the im-pulse of Thy love, At the im-pulse of Thy love.
2. Take my feet and let them be Swift and beau-ti-ful for Thee; Take my voice and let me sing Al-ways, on-ly for my King, Al-ways, on-ly for my King.
3. Take my lips and let them be Filled with mes-sag-es for Thee; Take my sil-ver and my gold, Not a mite would I with-hold, Not a mite would I with-hold.
4. Take my love, my God, I pour At Thy feet its treas-ure store; Take my-self and I will be Ev-er, on-ly, all for Thee, Ev-er, on-ly, all for Thee.

Public Domain.

You are a chosen priesthood, a holy nation, a people belonging to God. (1 Peter 2:9)

207 Take Our Lives

Andy Park

♩ = 63-68

VERSE

1. You have called us chosen, a roy-al priest-hood, a ho-ly na-tion, and we be-long to You.
2. You have shown us mer-cy, You have re-deemed us, our hearts cry "Fa-ther we be-long to You."

You have called us chosen, a roy-al priest-hood,
You have shown us mer-cy, You have re-deemed us,

© Copyright 1991 Mercy/Vineyard Publishing (ASCAP).
All Rights Reserved. Used by Permission.

a ho - ly na - tion, and we be - long to You.
our hearts cry "Fa - ther, we be - long to You."
CHORUS
Take our lives as a sac - ri - fice
Shine in us Your ho - ly light.
Pu - ri - fy our hearts' de - sire,
3rd time to Coda
be to us a con - sum - ing
fire.
D.S. al CODA
fire.
CODA
fire.

208 Thank You, Lord!

Sing and make music in your heart to the Lord, always giving thanks to God the Father for everything, in the name of our Lord Jesus Christ. (Ephesians 5:19-20)

Dennis L. Jernigan

♩ = 120-128

For all that You've done, I will thank You, For all that You're going to do. For all that You've promised, and all that You are is all that has carried me through, Jesus, I thank You! And I thank You, thank You, thank You, thank You, Lord.

© Copyright 1991 Shepherd's Heart Music, Inc. (Admin. by Dayspring Music, Inc.) (BMI), 65 Music Square West, Nashville, TN 37203.
All Rights Reserved. Made in the U.S.A. International Copyright Secured. Used by Permission.

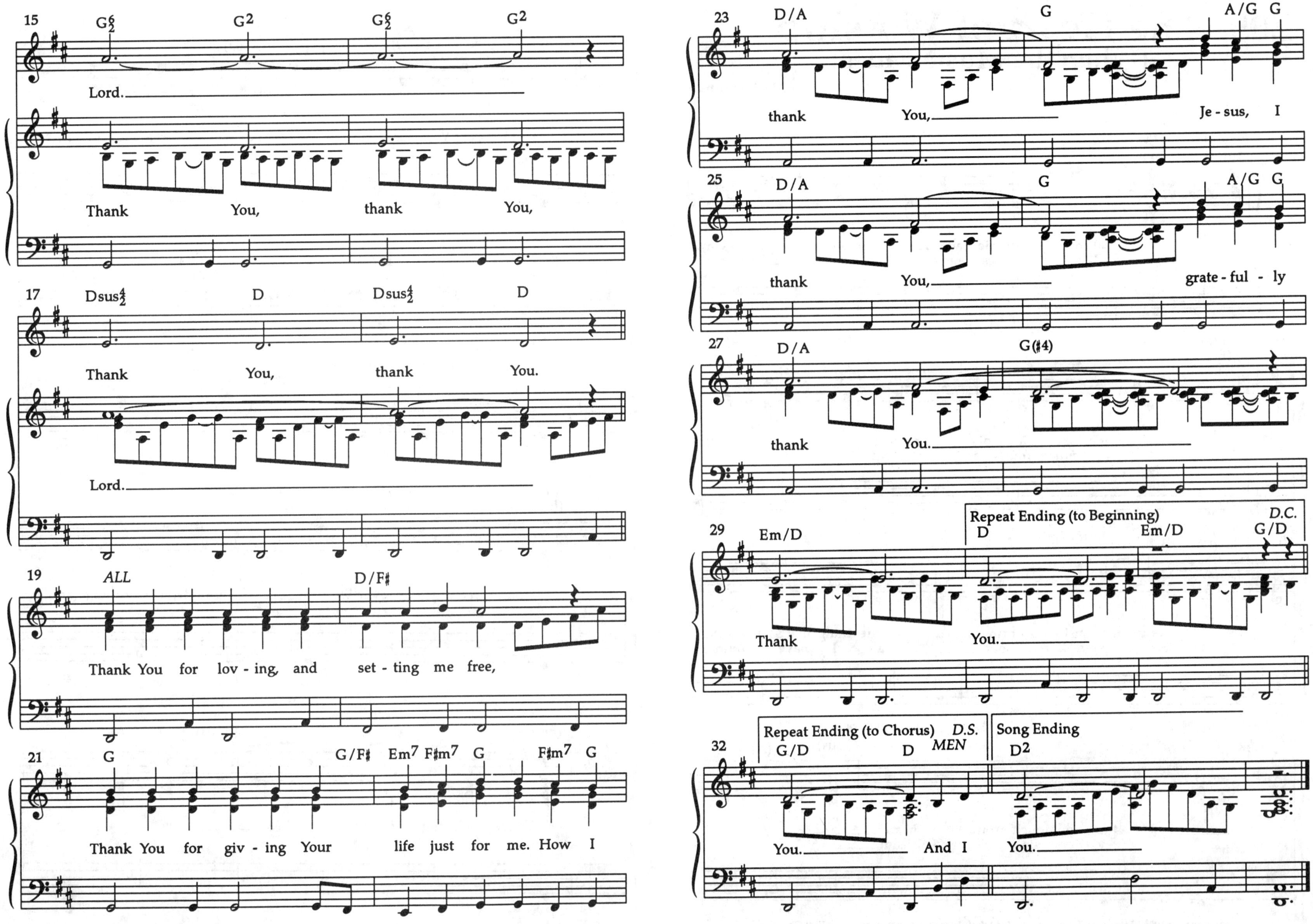
15
G6/2 G2 G6/2 G2
Lord.
Thank You, thank You,
17
Dsus4/2 D Dsus4/2 D
Thank You, thank You.
Lord.
19
ALL
D/F♯
Thank You for lov - ing, and set - ting me free,
21
G G/F♯ Em7 F♯m7 G F♯m7 G
Thank You for giv - ing Your life just for me. How I
23
D/A G A/G G
thank You, Jesus, I
25
D/A G A/G G
thank You, grate - ful - ly
27
D/A G(♯4)
thank You.
29
Em/D
Repeat Ending (to Beginning)
D.C.
D Em/D G/D
Thank You.
32
Repeat Ending (to Chorus)
D.S.
MEN
G/D D
You. And I
Song Ending
D2
You.

209 The Heart of Worship
(When the Music Fades)

True worshipers will worship the Father in spirit and truth, for they are the kind of worshipers the Father seeks. (John 4:23)

Matt Redman

Capo 1 (D)

Steadily ♩ = 80

Keyboard: E♭ (Guitar: D)

VERSE

1. When the music fades, all is stripped a-way, and I sim-ply come;
2. King of end-less worth, no one could ex-press how much You de-serve.

long-ing just to bring some-thing that's of worth that will touch Your heart.
Though I'm weak and poor, all I have is Yours, ev-'ry sin-gle breath.

I'll bring You more than a song, for a song in it-self is not what You have re-quired.
You search much deep-er with-in through the way things ap-pear; You're look-ing in-to my heart.

© Copyright 1999 Kingsway's Thankyou Music/Administered in North America by EMI Christian Music Publishing/P.O. Box 5085, Brentwood, TN 37024-5085
All Rights Reserved. International Copyright Secured. Used by Permission.

"[Jesus said], 'These people honor me with their lips, but their **hearts** are far from me. They worship me in vain...'"

Matthew 15:8-9

"A time is coming and has now come when the true worshipers will worship the Father in spirit and truth, for they are the kind of worshipers the Father seeks. God is spirit, and his worshipers must worship in **spirit** and in **truth**.'"

John 4:23-24

"The LORD does not look at the things man looks at. Man looks at the outward appearance, but the LORD **looks** at the **heart**."

1 Samuel 16:7

Worthy is the Lamb, who was slain, to receive power and wealth and wisdom and strength and honor and glory and praise. (Revelation 5:12)

210 The Lamb

Gerald Patrick Coleman

VERSE

1. The Lamb, the Lamb, O Father, where's the sacrifice? Faith sees, believes God will provide the Lamb of price!
2. The Lamb, the Lamb, One perfect final offering. The Lamb, the Lamb, Let earth join heaven His praise to sing.
3. The Lamb, the Lamb, As wayward sheep their shepherd kill. So still, His will on our behalf the Law to fill.
4. He sighs, He dies, He takes my sin and wretchedness. He lives, for gives, He gives me His own righteousness.
5. He rose, He rose, My heart with thanks now overflows. His song prolong 'Till ev'ry heart to Him belong.

CHORUS

Worthy is the Lamb whose death makes me His own! The Lamb is reigning on His throne! throne!

© Copyright 1987 Morning Star Music Publishers, St. Louis, MO.
All Rights Reserved. Used by Permission.

The Redeemer will come...My Spirit who is on you, and my words...will not depart...from this time on and forever. (Isaiah 59:20-21)

211 There Is a Redeemer

Melody Green

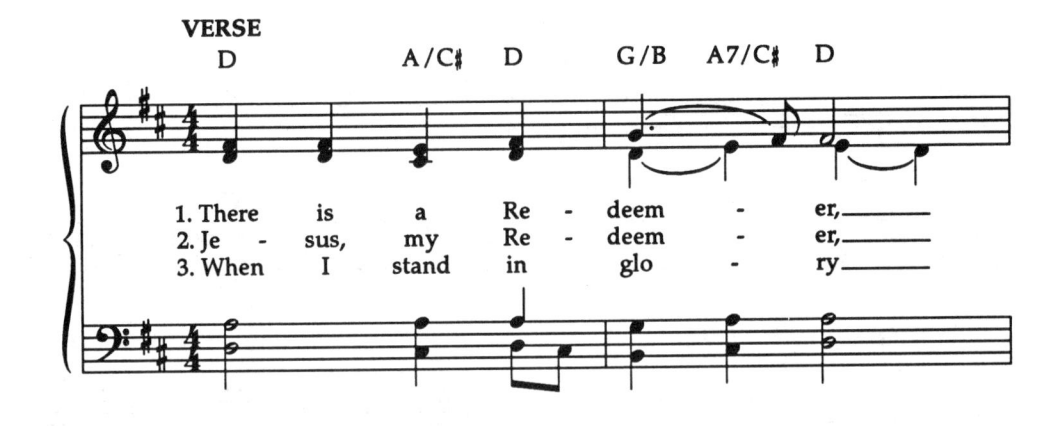

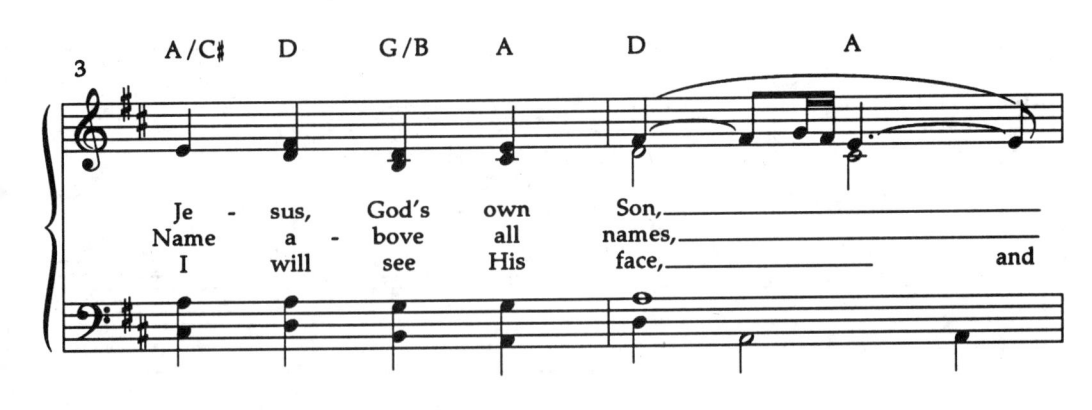

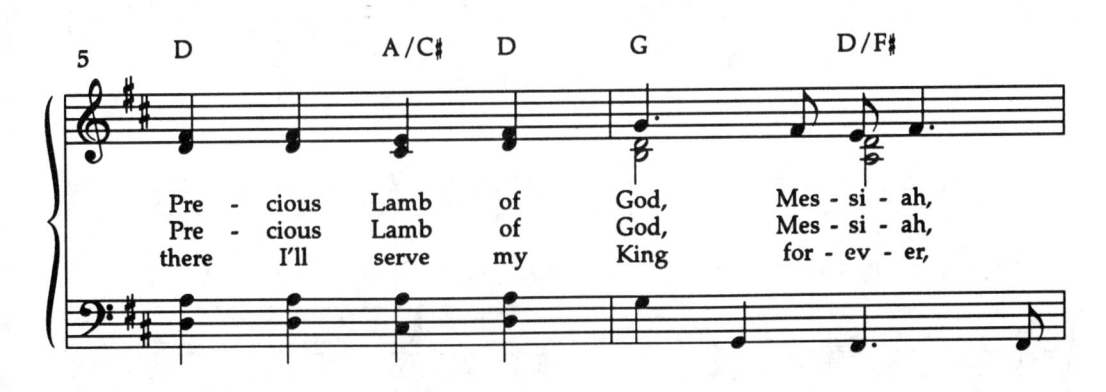

VERSE

1. There is a Redeemer, Jesus, God's own Son, Precious Lamb of God, Messiah, Holy One.
2. Jesus, my Redeemer, Name above all names, Precious Lamb of God, Messiah, hope for sinners slain.
3. When I stand in glory I will see His face, and there I'll serve my King forever, in that holy place.

CHORUS

Thank You, O my Father, for giving us Your Son; And leaving Your Spirit 'til the work on earth is done.

© Copyright 19__ Bud John Songs, Inc. (CL), Birdwing Music, Ears to Hear Music.
All Rights Reserved. Used by Permission.

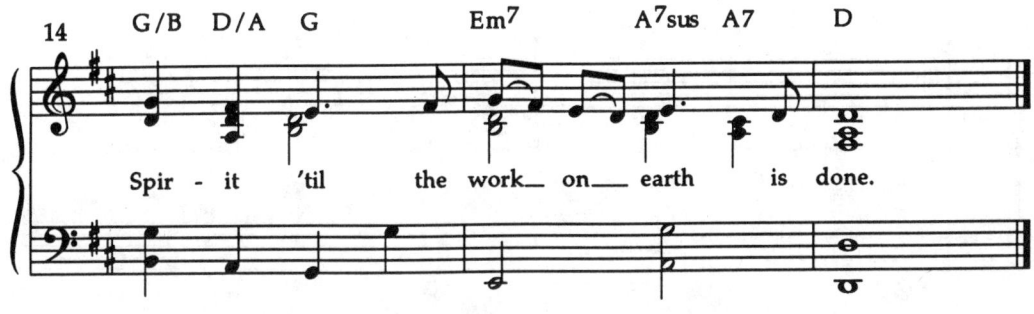

The name of the Lord is a strong tower, the righteous run to it and are safe. (Proverbs 18:10)

212 The Name of the Lord
(Blessed Be)

Clinton Utterbach

VERSE

1.4. Bless-ed be the name of the Lord,
2. Glo-ry to the name of the Lord,
3. Ho-ly is the name of the Lord,

Bless-ed be the name of the Lord,
Glo-ry to the name of the Lord,
Ho-ly is the name of the Lord,

Bless-ed be the name of the Lord most high.
Glo-ry to the name of the Lord most high.
Ho-ly is the name of the Lord most high.

Bless-ed be the name of the Lord,
Glo-ry to the name of the Lord,
Ho-ly is the name of the Lord,

Bless-ed be the name of the Lord,
Glo-ry to the name of the Lord,
Ho-ly is the name of the Lord,

4th time to Coda

Bless-ed be the name of the Lord most high.
Glo-ry to the name of the Lord most high.
Ho-ly is the name of the Lord most high.

most high. The name of the Lord

© Copyright 1989 Universal-Polygram International Publishing, Inc. and Utterbach Music, Inc.
All Rights for Utterbach Music, Inc. Controlled and Administered by Universal-Polygram International Publishing, Inc.
All Rights Reserved. Used by Permission.

"May his name endure forever; may it continue as long as the sun. All nations will be blessed through him, and they will call him blessed. Praise be to the LORD God, the God of Israel, who alone does marvelous deeds.

Praise be to his **glorious** name forever; may the whole earth be filled with his glory."

Amen and Amen.

Psalm 72:17-19

213 The Potter's Hand

...We are the clay, you are the potter; we are all the work of your hand. (Isaiah 64:8)

Darlene Zschech

♩ = 66

VERSE

Beau-ti-ful Lord,___ won-der-ful Sav - ior, I know for sure___ all of my days___ are held in Your hand,___ craft-ed in-to___ Your per - fect plan.___ You gent-ly call___ me in - to Your pres - ence, guid-ing me by___ Your Ho - ly Spir - it; teach me, dear Lord,___ to live all of my life___ through Your___ eyes.___ I'm cap-tured by___ Your ho - ly call - ing. Set me a - part;___ I know You're draw-ing me___

© Copyright 1997 Darlene Zschech/Hillsongs Australia (adm. in the U.S. and Canada by Integrity's Hosanna! Music)
c/o Integrity Music, Inc., 1000 Cody Road, Mobile, AL 36695-3425.
All Rights Reserved. International Copyright Secured. Used by Permission.

21
Em/A
A/C♯
to Your-self. Lead me, Lord, I
23
Dsus
D
pray.
25
G
CHORUS
D/F♯
Am7
Take me, mold me, use me,
28
Bm/E
Em
F
C/E
Am/E
Em7
Am
fill me; I give my life to the Pot - ter's hand.
31
Dsus
D/F♯
G
D/F♯
Call me, guide me,
34
Am7
Bm/E
Em
F
C/E
lead me, walk be - side me; I give my life to
37
Am/E
Em7
Am
1.
the Pot - ter's hand.
39
C/D
D
2.
Am
Dsus
D.S.
D/F♯
3.
Am
42
C/D
D
G
D/G
Em
D/E
Ooo Ooo
45
G/F
F
Dsus
D
G
Ooo

For God did not give us a spirit of timidity, but a spirit of power, of love and of self-discipline. (2 Timothy 1:7)

214 The Power of Your Love

Geoff Bullock

VERSE

1. Lord, I come to You, let my heart be changed, renewed, Flowing from the grace that I've found in You. And, Lord, I've come to know the weaknesses I see in me will be stripped away by the pow'r of Your love.

2. Lord, unveil my eyes, let me see You face to face, the knowledge of Your love as You live in me. Lord, renew my mind, as Your will unfolds in my life, in living ev'ry day in the pow'r of Your love.

CHORUS

Hold me close, let Your love surround me;

© 1992 Word Music, Inc. (ASCAP), 65 Music Square West, Nashville, TN 37203/
Maranatha! Music (Admin. by Word Music, Inc.) (ASCAP), 65 Music Square West, Nashville, TN 37203.
All Rights Reserved. International Copyright Secured. Used by Permission. www.maranathamusic.com

"Jesus, lover of my soul,

let me to thy mercy fly

While the nearer waters roll,

while the tempest still is high.

Hide me, O my Savior,

hide till the storm of life is past;

Safe into the haven guide.

Oh, receive my soul at last!"

Charles Wesley, 1707-1788

There is a river whose streams make glad the city of God. (Psalm 46:4)

215 The River Is Here

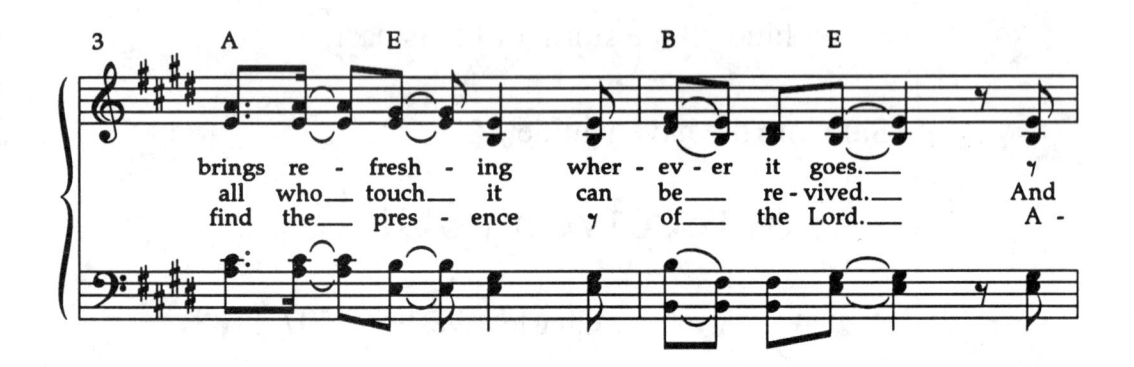

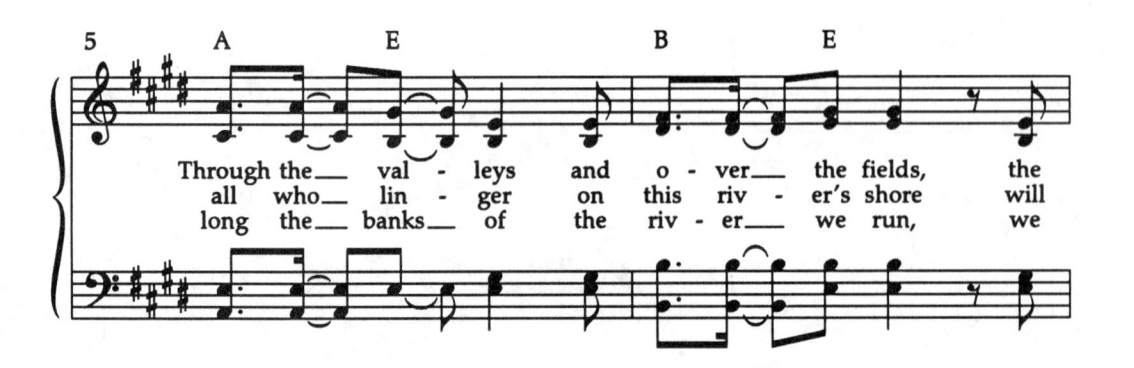

Andy Park

♩ = 117

VERSE

1. Down the mountain, the river flows and it brings refreshing wherever it goes. Through the valleys and over the fields, the river is rushing and the river is here. The
2. The river of God is teeming with life, and all who touch it can be revived. And all who linger on this river's shore will come back thirsting for more of the Lord. The
3. Up to the mountain we love to go, to find the presence of the Lord. Along the banks of the river we run, we dance with laughter, giving praise to the Son. The

CHORUS

river of God sets our feet to dancing, the river of God fills our hearts with cheer; The river of God fills our mouths with laughter and we rejoice for the river is here.

© Copyright 1994 Mercy/Vineyard Publishing (ASCAP), c/o Music Services, 209 Chapelwood Drive, Franklin, TN 37069.
All Rights Reserved. Used by Permission.

He lifted me out of the slimy pit, out of the mud and mire...He put a new song in my mouth, a hymn of praise to our God. (Psalm 40:2-3)

216 Then I Will Praise You, My Savior, Again

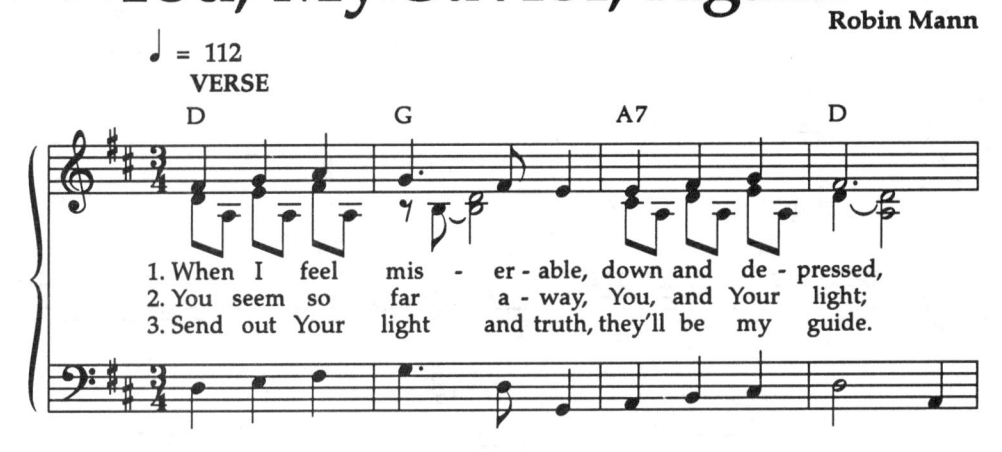

Robin Mann

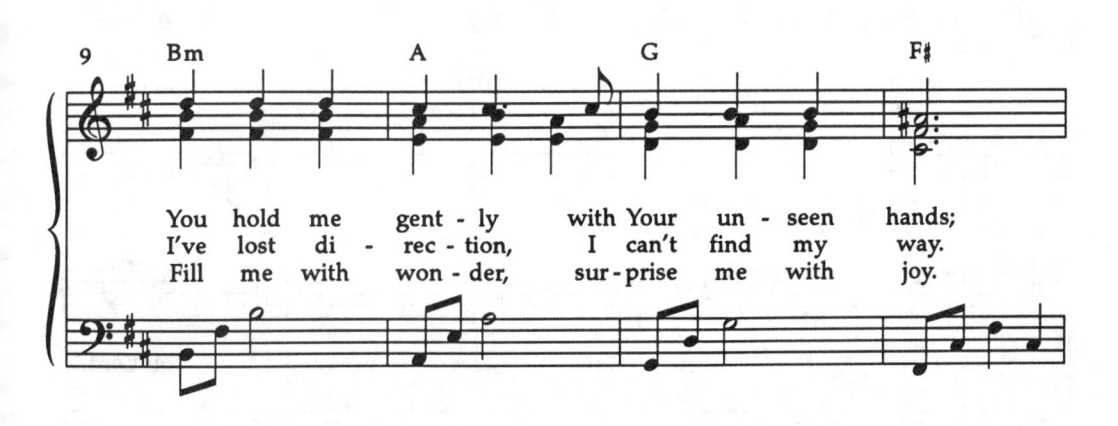

♩ = 112

VERSE

1. When I feel mis-er-a-ble, down and de-pressed, worth-less, I feel that I've nev-er been blessed, You hold me gent-ly, with Your un-seen hands; later I'll see You, my Friend.
2. You seem so far a-way, You, and Your light; dark-ness has cov-ered me, thick as the night; I've lost di-rec-tion, I can't find my way. God, bring this night to an end.
3. Send out Your light and truth, they'll be my guide. Where there's Your light and truth, trou-bles sub-side. Fill me with won-der, sur-prise me with joy. On-ly on You I de-pend.

CHORUS

Then I will praise You, God, I will praise You. Then I will praise You, my Sav-ior, a-gain.

© Copyright 1990 Robin Mann.
All Rights Reserved. International Copyright Secured. Used by Permission.

217 These Things Are True of You

Tommy Walker

The Son of God has come...so that we may know him who is true. And we are in him who is true. (1 John 5:20)

VERSE

1. Un-shak-a-ble, im-mov-a-ble, faith-ful and true; Full of wis-dom, strength and beau-ty: These things are true of You.

2. Pa-tient, com-pas-sion-ate, love flows thru You; You nev-er give up on the hope-less ones: These things are true of You.

Fear-less, cour-a-geous, right-eous-ness shines thru in all You do; Yet You're so hum-ble, You laid down Your life: These things are true of You.

Ho-ly and blame-less, You stand up for just-ice and truth; Yet You love mer-cy and for-give-ness: These things are true of You.

CHORUS

And as I turn my face to You, oh Lord,

© Copyright 1996 Doulos Publishing (Administered by The Copyright Company, Nashville, TN). All Rights Reserved. International Copyright Secured. Used by Permission.

"At that time his voice shook the earth, but now he has promised, 'Once more I will shake not only the earth but also the heavens.' The words 'once more' indicate the removing of what can be shaken—that is, created things—so that what cannot be shaken may remain. Therefore, since we are receiving a **kingdom** that cannot **be shaken,** let us be thankful, and so worship God acceptably with reverence and awe, for our 'God is a consuming fire.'"

Hebrews 12:26-29

O Lord, there is none like Thee, neither is there any God besides Thee. (1 Chronicles 17:20)

218 There Is None Like You

Lenny LeBlanc

♩ = 69
CHORUS

There is none like You,
no one else can touch my heart like You do;
I could search for all e-ter-ni-ty long and find
there is none like You.
Fine

Your mer-cy flows like a riv-er wide and
heal-ing comes from Your hands;
Suf-fer-ing chil-dren are safe in Your arms,
there is none like You.

D.C. al Fine

© Copyright 1991 Integrity's Hosanna! Music, c/o Integrity Music, Inc., 1000 Cody Road, Mobile, AL 36695-3425.
All Rights Reserved. International Copyright Secured. Used by Permission.

219 This Is the Day

Rejoice in the Lord always. I will say it again: Rejoice! (Philippians 4:4)

Rick Shelton

♩ = 156

VERSE 1

This is the day that the Lord has made, I will rejoice and be glad in it; Oh, this is the day that the Lord has made, I will rejoice and be glad in it.

CHORUS

Rejoice in the Lord, rejoice in the Lord.

VERSE 2

Celebrate the presence of the Lord, for He is worthy to be praised; Celebrate the presence of the Lord, for He is worthy to be praised. Re-

D.S. al CODA

CODA

Lord. Rejoice!

© Copyright 1990 Integrity's Hosanna! Music, c/o Integrity Music, Inc., 1000 Cody Road, Mobile, AL 36695-3425.
All Rights Reserved. International Copyright Secured. Used by Permission.

220 This Is the Day

This is the day the Lord has made, let us rejoice and be glad in it. (Psalm 118:24)

Bob Fitts

Capo 1 (E) ♩ = 132

CHORUS

This is the day that the Lord has made, I will rejoice and celebrate; This is the day that the Lord has made, I will rejoice, I will rejoice and celebrate.

1. He goes before...

© Copyright 1996 Integrity's Hosanna! Music, c/o Integrity Music, Inc., 1000 Cody Road, Mobile, AL 36695-3425.
All Rights Reserved. International Copyright Secured. Used by Permission.

VERSE
19
F (E) Bb/F (A/E) F (E) Bb (A)
He goes be-fore me,
me, He walks be-side
21
F (E) Bb/F (A/E) F (E) Bb (A)
He walks be-side me, He lives with-in
me,
23
F (E) Dm7 (C#m7) Gm7 (F#m7) F/C (E/B)
me, He's the Lov-er of my soul;
25
C (B) Csus (Bsus) C (B) Bb/C (A/B)
He's my de-fend-
27
F (E) Bb/F (A/E) F (E) Bb (A)
He's my de-fend-er,
er, He's my pro-vid-
29
F (E) Bb/F (A/E) F (E) Bb (A)
He's my pro-vid-er, His o-ver-flow-
er,
31
F (E) Dm7 (C#m7) Gm7 (F#m7) Bb/C (A/B) F (E) Bb/C (A/B)
-ing mer-cies are brand new ev-er-y day.
34
3.
F (E) Bb (A) C (B) F (E)

221 Thine the Amen, Thine the Praise

Then the angel said to me, 'Write: Blessed are those who are invited to the wedding supper of the Lamb!' And he added, 'These are the true words of God.' (Revelation 19:9)

Herbert F. Brokering
Carl F. Schalk

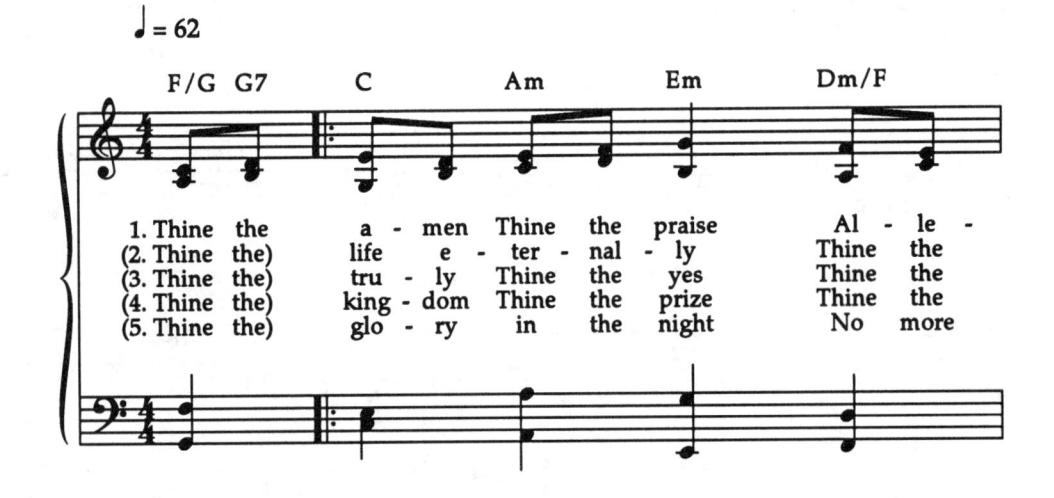

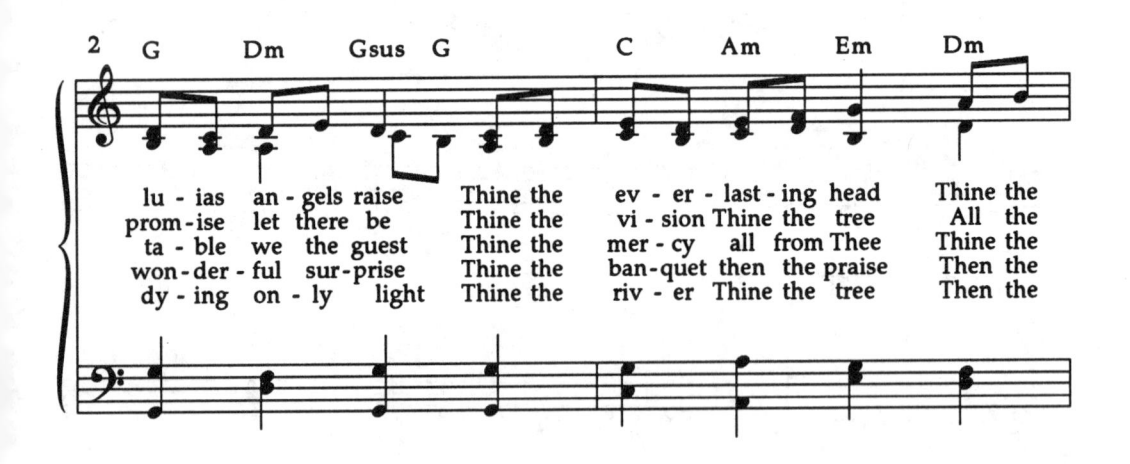

♩ = 62

1. Thine the a-men Thine the praise Al - le-lu - ias an - gels raise Thine the ev - er - last - ing head Thine the break-ing of the bread Thine the glo - ry Thine the sto - ry Thine the har - vest then the cup Thine the vine-yard then the cup is lift - ed up, lift - ed up.

2. Thine the life e - ter - nal - ly Thine the prom - ise let there be Thine the vi - sion Thine the tree All the earth on bend - ed knee Gone the nail - ing gone the rail - ing Gone the plead - ing gone the cry Gone the sigh - ing gone the dy - ing what was loss lift - ed high.

3. Thine the tru - ly Thine the yes Thine the ta - ble we the guest Thine the mer - cy all from Thee Thine the glo - ry yet to be Then the ring - ing and the sing - ing Then the end of all the war Thine the liv - ing Thine the lov - ing ev - er - more, ev - er - more.

4. Thine the king - dom Thine the prize Thine the won - der - ful sur - prise Thine the ban - quet then the praise Then the jus - tice of Thy ways Thine the glo - ry Thine the sto - ry Then the wel - come to the least Then the won - der all in - creas - ing at Thy feast, at Thy feast.

5. Thine the glo - ry in the night No more dy - ing on - ly light Thine the riv - er Thine the tree Then the Lamb e - ter - nal - ly Then the ho - ly, ho - ly, ho - ly Cel - e - bra - tion ju - bi - lee Thine the splen - dor Thine the bright - ness on - ly Thee, on - ly Thee.

© Copyright 1983 Augsburg Publishing House.
All Rights Reserved. Used by Permission.

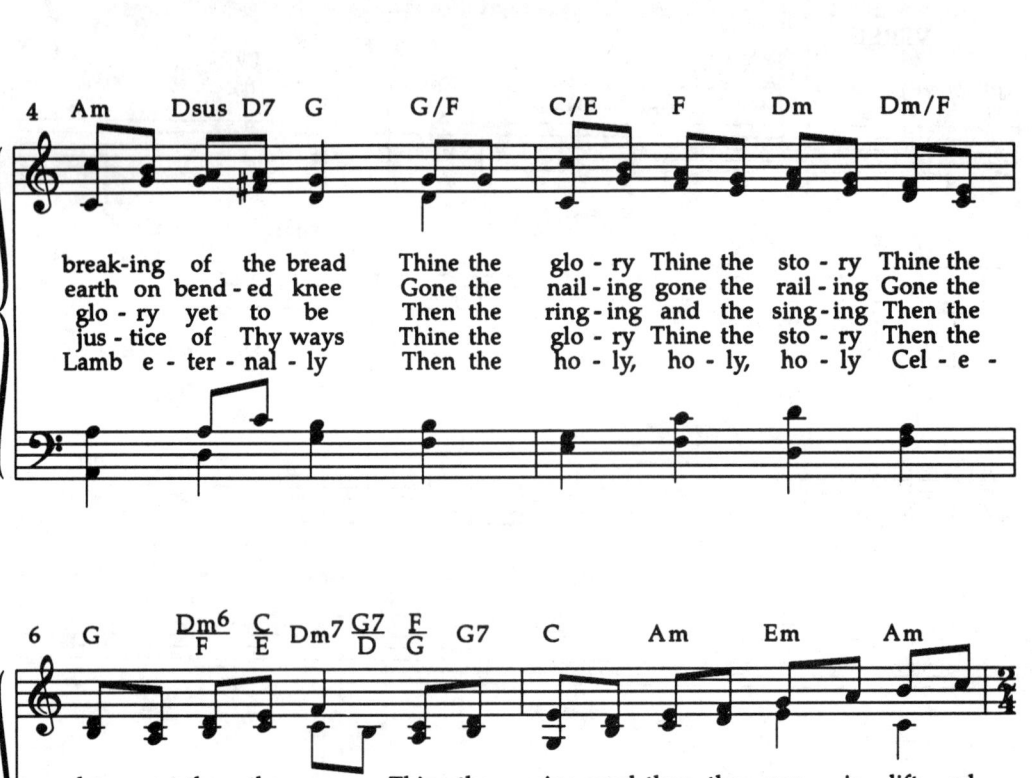

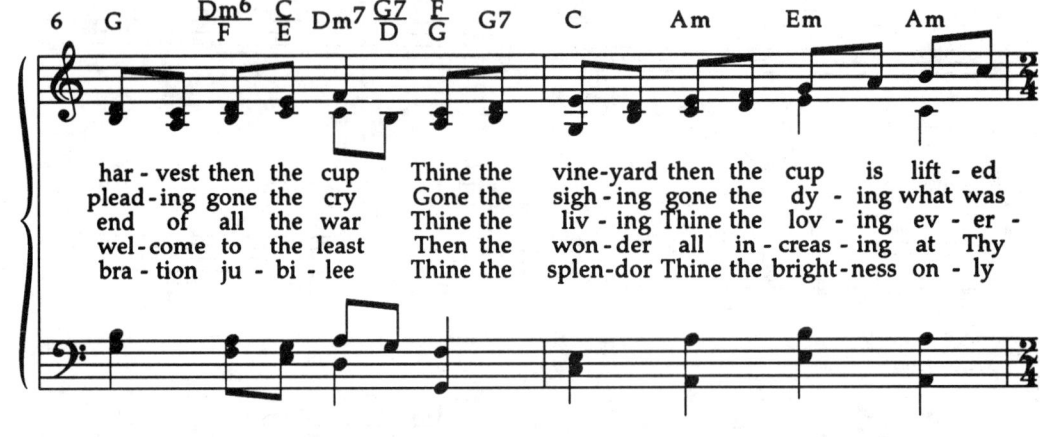

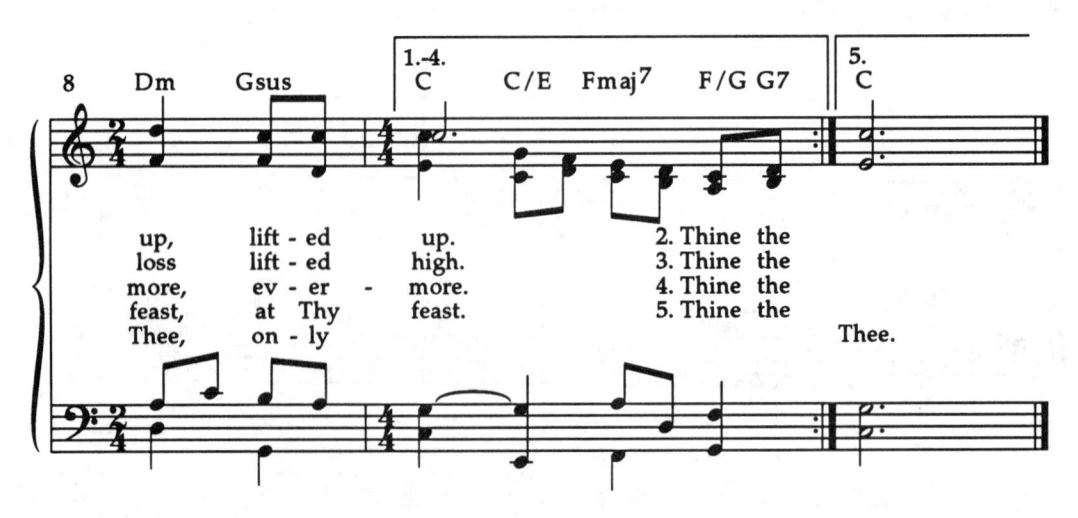

You are forgiving and good, O Lord, abounding in love to all who call on you. (Psalm 86:5)

222 Think about His Love

Walt Harrah

Think about His love,_____ think about His goodness,_____ Think about His grace that's brought us through. For as high as the heavens above_____ so great is the measure of our Father's love._____ Great is the measure of our Father's love._____

1. D.C.

2. TAG
Great is the measure of our Father's love.

© Copyright 1987, arr. © 1992 Integrity's Hosanna! Music,
c/o Integrity Music, Inc., 1000 Cody Road, Mobile, AL 36695-3425.
All Rights Reserved. International Copyright Secured. Used by Permission.

Now have come the salvation and the power and the Kingdom of God, and the authority of his Christ. (Revelation 12:10)

223 This Kingdom

Geoff Bullock

♩ = 86-92

VERSE

1. Jesus, God's righteousness revealed, the Son of Man, the Son of God, His kingdom comes; Jesus, redemption's sacrifice, now glorified, now justified, His kingdom comes.

2. Jesus, the expression of God's love, the grace of God, the Word of God, revealed to us; Jesus, God's holiness displayed, now glorified, now justified, His kingdom comes.

CHORUS

And this kingdom will know no end, and its glory shall know no bounds, for the majesty and power of this

© Copyright 1995 Word Music, Inc. (ASCAP), 65 Music Square West, Nashville, TN 37203,
Maranatha! Music (Admin. by Word Music, Inc.) 65 Music Square West, Nashville, TN 37203.
All Rights Reserved. Made in the U.S.A. International Copyright Secured. Used by Permission.
www.maranathamusic.com

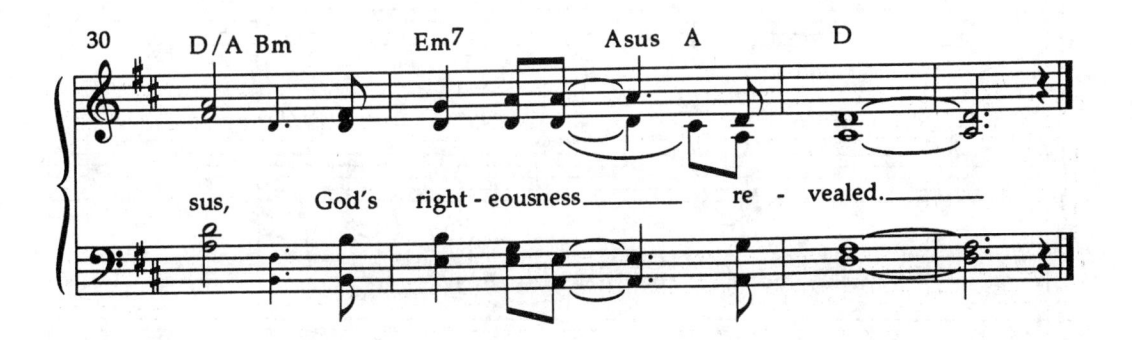

"Lo, he comes with clouds descending,

once for ev'ry sinner slain;

Thousand thousand saints attending

swell the triumph of his train:

Alleluia, alleluia!

Christ the Lord returns to reign.

Yea, amen, let all adore thee,

high on thine eternal throne;

Savior, take the *pow'r* and glory,

claim the *kingdom* for thine own.

Alleluia, alleluia!

Thou shalt reign, and thou alone!"

Charles Wesley, 1707-88

...I will turn their mourning into gladness; I will give them comfort and joy instead of sorrow. (Jeremiah 31:13)

224 Trading My Sorrows

Darrell Evans

CHORUS

I'm trad-ing my sor-rows;
I'm trad-ing my sick-ness;
I'm trad-ing my shame.
I'm trad-ing my pain.
I'm lay-ing them down for the joy of the
Lord.

Last time to Coda

Yes, Lord, yes, Lord, yes, yes, Lord. Yes, Lord, yes, Lord, yes, yes, Lord. Yes, Lord, yes, Lord, yes, yes, Lord. A-men.

VERSE *Opt.: LEADER*

I am pressed but not crushed, per-se-cut-ed, not a-ban-doned, struck down, but not de-stroyed. I am blessed.

© Copyright 1998 Integrity's Hosanna! Music, c/o Integrity Music, Inc., 1000 Cody Road, Mobile, AL 36695-3425.
All Rights Reserved. International Copyright Secured. Used by Permission.

21 A D F♯m E
— be-yond the curse, for His prom-ise will en-dure, that His
23 A D F♯m E
joy's gon-na be my strength. —
25 Opt.: ALL A/E E
Though the sor - row — may last for — the night, His joy —
27 G2 1. D 2. D.S. al CODA
— comes with the morn-ing. ing.
CODA
30 A D F♯m E
32 A D F♯m E
Lai,
34 A D F♯m E
lai, lai, — lai, lai, lai, — lai, lai, lai, — lai, lai. Lai,
36 A D F♯m E/G♯
lai, lai, — lai, lai, lai, — lai, lai, lai, — lai, lai. — Lai,
38 A D F♯m E/G♯
lai, lai, — lai, lai, lai, — lai, lai, lai, — lai, lai, lai, lai. —
40 A D F♯m E

225 'Tis So Sweet to Trust in Jesus

May the God of hope fill you with all joy and peace as you trust in him, so that you may overflow with hope by the power of the Holy Spirit. (Romans 15:13)

Louisa M. R. Stead

William J. Kirkpatrick

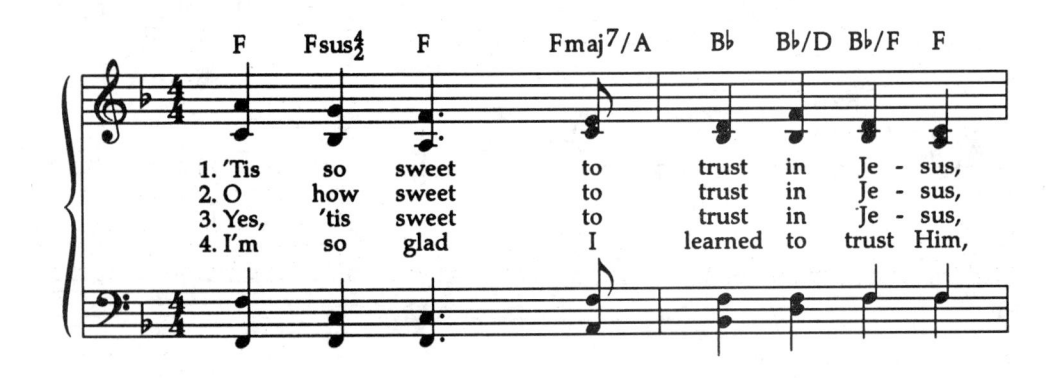

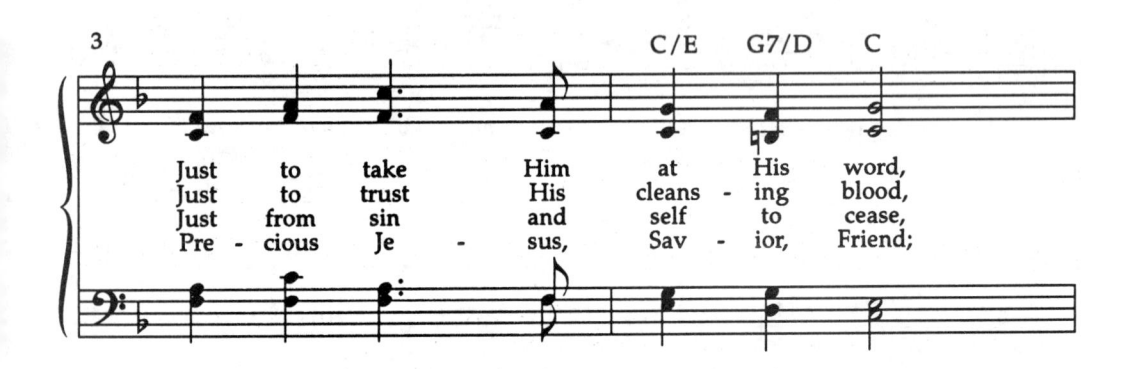

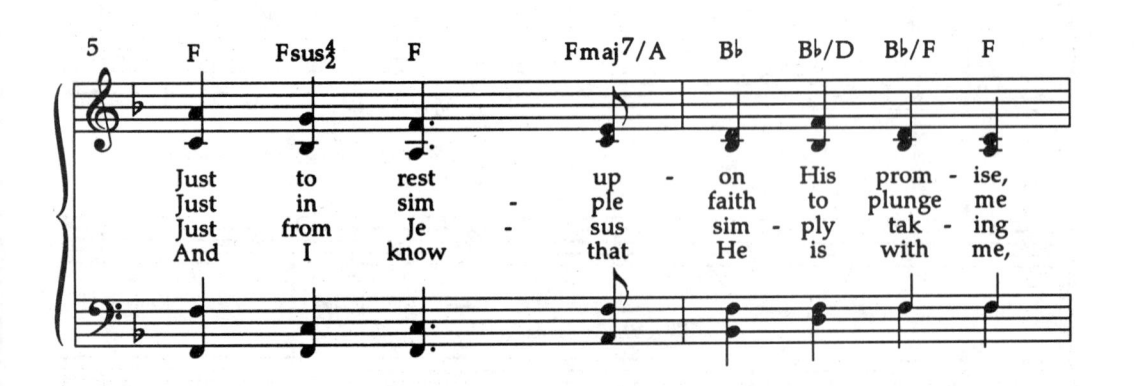

1. 'Tis so sweet to trust in Je-sus, Just to take Him at His word,
Just to rest upon His prom-ise, Just to know "Thus saith the Lord."

2. O how sweet to trust in Je-sus, Just to trust His cleans-ing blood,
Just in sim-ple faith to plunge me 'Neath the heal-ing, cleans-ing flood!

3. Yes, 'tis sweet to trust in Je-sus, Just from sin and self to cease,
Just from Je-sus sim-ply tak-ing Life and rest and joy and peace.

4. I'm so glad I learned to trust Him, Pre-cious Je-sus, Sav-ior, Friend;
And I know that He is with me, Will be with me to the end.

Je-sus, Je-sus, how I trust Him!
Proved He's faith-ful o'er and o'er!
Je-sus, Je-sus, pre-cious Je-sus!
O for grace to trust Him more!

Public Domain.

226 Victory Chant

How beautiful...are the feet of those who bring good news...who say to Zion, 'Your God reigns!' (Isaiah 52:7)

Joseph Vogels

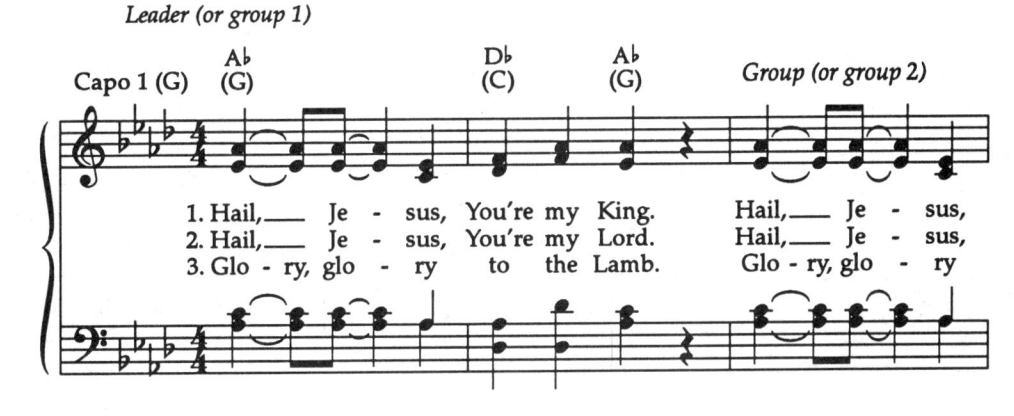

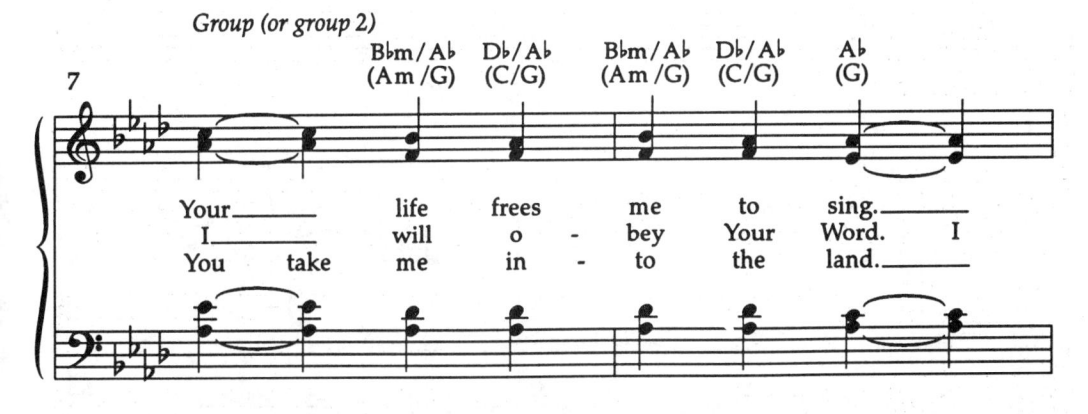

1. Hail, Jesus, You're my King. Hail, Jesus, You're my King. Your life frees me to sing. Your life frees me to sing. I will praise You all my days. I will praise You all my days. Perfect in all Your ways. Perfect in all Your ways. And proclaim that Jesus reigns, And proclaim that Jesus reigns.

2. Hail, Jesus, You're my Lord. Hail, Jesus, You're my Lord. I will obey Your Word. I will obey Your Word. I want to see Your kingdom come. I want to see Your kingdom come. Not my will, but Yours be done. Not my will, but Yours be done. And proclaim that Jesus reigns, And proclaim that Jesus reigns.

3. Glory, glory to the Lamb. Glory, glory to the Lamb. You take me into the land. You take me into the land. We will conquer in Your name, We will conquer in Your name, And proclaim that Jesus reigns, And proclaim that Jesus reigns. And proclaim that Jesus reigns, And proclaim that Jesus reigns.

© Copyright 1985 Scripture In Song (a div. of Integrity Music, Inc.)/ASCAP.
All Rights Reserved. Used by Permission.

227 Victory Song
(Through Our God)

Thanks be to God! He gives us the victory through our Lord Jesus Christ. (1 Cor. 15:57)

Dale Garratt

♩ = 130-138

Through our God we shall do val-iant-ly, It is He who shall tread down the en-e-my; We'll sing and shout the vic-to-ry:

Last time to Coda

Christ is King! For God has won the vic-to-ry and set His peo-ple free. His Word has slain the en-e-my. The

© Copyright 1979 Scripture In Song (admin. by Integrity's Hosanna! Music)
c/o Integrity Music, Inc., 1000 Cody Road, Mobile, AL 36695-3425.
All Rights Reserved. International Copyright Secured. Used by Permission.

"Everyone born of God overcomes the world. This is the **victory** that has **overcome** the world, even our faith. Who is it that overcomes the world? Only he who believes that Jesus is the Son of God."

1 John 5:4-5

"When the perishable has been clothed with the imperishable, and the mortal with immortality, then the saying that is written will come true:

'Death has been **swallowed up** in **victory**.'

'Where, O death, is your victory?

Where, O death, is your sting?'

The sting of death is sin, and the power of sin is the law. But thanks be to God! He gives us the victory through our Lord Jesus Christ."

1 Corinthians 15:54-57

228 Under the Blood

For the accuser of our brothers...has been hurled down...They overcame him by the blood of the Lamb and by the word of their testimony. (Revelation 12:10-11)

Martin J. Nystrom and Rhonda Gunter Scelsi

♩. = 60

VERSE

O the blood of the Pass-o-ver Lamb is ap-plied to the door of my life, no pow-er of dark-ness could ev-er with-stand the force of the blood sac-ri-fice; Though Sa-tan will bring ac-cu-sa-tions, I let him know right where I stand, for now there is no con-dem-na-tion. I'm un-der the blood of the Lamb. I'm

© Copyright 1991 Integrity's Hosanna! Music, c/o Integrity Music, Inc., 1000 Cody Road, Mobile, AL 36695-3425.
All Rights Reserved. International Copyright Secured. Used by Permission.

CHORUS
17
A A/C♯ D D/E E
under the blood of the Lamb that
19
A F♯m7 Bm7 Esus E
covers the guilt of my past,
21
F♯m C♯m D A/C♯
by the mercy of God,
23
Bm7 Bm/A Gmaj9 D/E E/G♯
holy and righteous I stand: I'm
25
A A/C♯ D D/E E
under the blood of the Lamb. I'm
27
A F♯m7 Bm7 Esus E
safe and secure from the enemy's plan,
29
F♯m C♯m D A/C♯
TAG
no weapon formed against me will stand, I'm
31
Bm7 D/E E A
under the blood of the Lamb.

229 Waterlife

This water symbolizes baptism that now saves you...by the resurrection of Jesus Christ. (1 Peter 3:21)

Handt Hanson

VERSE

1. Be-fore I can remember, the covenant was sealed with Father, Son, and Spirit, in water was revealed. The cleansing was for certain, with water and the Word; gentle words were spoken, in heaven they were heard.

2. A simple sweet beginning, a loving place to start: Christ began the singing that swells within my heart. His love became my calling, His life my ministry. His name is my adoption into His family.

3. My hope and expectation for true community begins with resurrection, His death and life in me. His Spirit fills the body; His church through water sees His promise for tomorrow, His waterlife in me.

CHORUS

They were singing waterlife, beginning life, waterlife, all my life, waterlife, Spirit life, waterlife.

© Copyright 1991 Prince of Peace Publishing, Changing Church, Inc.
All Rights Reserved. Used by Permission.

230 We'll Be Faithful

Forgetting what is behind and straining toward what is ahead, I press on toward the goal to win the prize for which God has called me heavenward in Christ Jesus. (Philippians 3:13-14)

Don Harris and Martin J. Nystrom

VERSE:
For-get-ting what lies be-hind, set-ting our hearts on the prize, al-ways keep-ing our eyes on our Lord Je-sus. We're run-ning the race to win, all the way to the end,

CHORUS:
lay-ing down ev-'ry sin that would seek to hin-der us. And we'll be faith-ful to our call-ing, for You are a-ble to keep us from fall-ing. For in Your prom-ise we will trust, You'll be faith-ful to fin-ish the work You be-gan in us.

© Copyright 1993 Integrity's Hosanna! Music, c/o Integrity Music, Inc., 1000 Cody Road, Mobile, AL 36695-3425.
All Rights Reserved. International Copyright Secured. Used by Permission.

231 We Are an Offering

Offer yourselves to God...and offer the parts of your body to him as instruments of righteousness. (Romans 6:13)

Dwight Liles

♩ = 58-63

VERSE

We lift our voic-es, we lift our hands, we lift our lives up to You, we are an of-fer-ing.

Lord, use our voic-es, Lord, use our hands, Lord, use our lives, they are Yours, we are an of-fer-ing.

CHORUS

All that we have, all that we are, all that we hope to be, we give to You, we give to You.

We lift our voic-es, we lift our hands, we lift our lives up to You, we are an of-fer-ing, we are an of-fer-ing.

© Copyright 1984 Word Music, Inc. (ASCAP) 65 Music Square West, Nashville, TN 37203.
All Rights Reserved. International Copyright Secured. Used by Permission.

232 We Are Marching in the Light of God
(Siyahamba)

Jehoshaphat appointed men to sing to the Lord and to praise him for the splendor of his holiness as they went out at the head of the army...As they began to sing and praise, the Lord set ambushes against the men who were invading Judah, and they were defeated. (2 Chronicles 20:21-22)

South African

We are march-ing in the light of God, we are
Si-ya-hamb' e-ku-kha-nyen' kwen-khos', si-ya-

march-ing in the light of God. We are
hamb' e-ku-kha-nyen' kwen-khos'. Si-ya-

march-ing in the light of God, we are
hamb' e-ku-kha-nyen' kwen-khos', si-ya-

march-ing in the light of God. We are
hamb' e-ku-kha-nyen' kwen-khos'. Si-ya-

march-ing in the light of, the light of God. We are
hamb' e-ku-kha-nyen' kwen -kha-nyen' kwen-khos'. Si-ya-

march-ing oo we are
ham-ba oo si-ya-

march-ing, march-ing, we are march-ing, march-ing, we are
ham-ba, ham-ba, si-ya-ham-ba, ham-ba, si-ya-

march-ing in the light of God. We are
hamb' e-ku-kha-nyen' kwen-khos'. Si-ya-

march-ing in the light of, the light of God. We are
hamb' e-ku-kha-nyen' kwen -kha-nyen' kwen-khos'. Si-ya-

march-ing oo
ham-ba oo

march-ing, march-ing, we are march-ing, march-ing, we are
ham-ba, ham-ba, si-ya-ham-ba, ham-ba, si-ya-

march-ing in the light of God.
hamb' e-ku-kha-nyen' kwen-khos'.

Additional stanzas ad lib:

We are singing...
We are dancing...
We are praying...

African Folksong. This arr. © Copyright 1984 by Utryck. All rights admin. by Walton Music Corp.
All Rights Reserved. International Copyright Secured. Used by Permission.

233 We Bow Down

Come, let us bow down in worship, let us kneel before the Lord our Maker. (Psalm 95:6)

Twila Paris

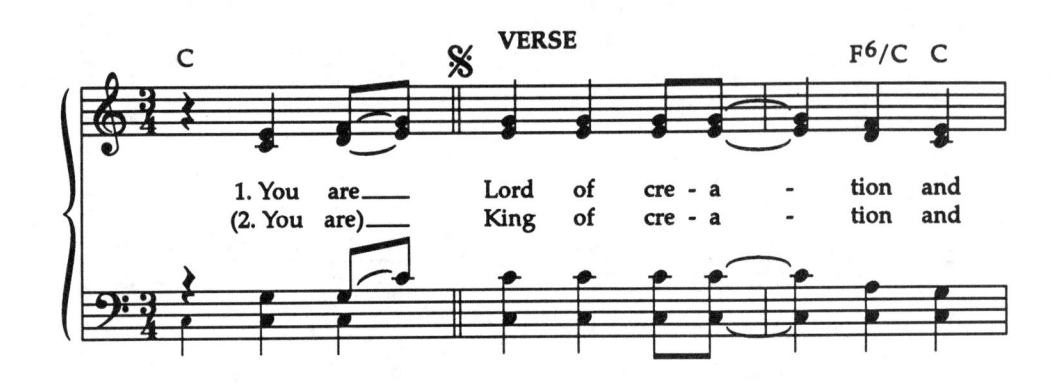

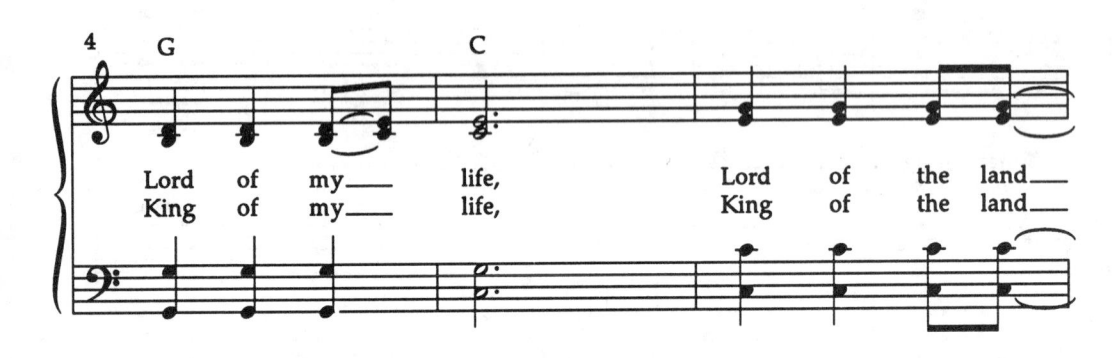

1. You are Lord of creation and Lord of my life, Lord of the land and the sea. You were Lord of the heavens before there was time. And Lord of all lords You will be!

2. You are King of creation and King of my life, King of the land and the sea. You were King of the heavens before there was time. And King of all kings You will be!

CHORUS:
(1.) We bow down (we bow down) and we worship You, Lord. We bow down (we bow down) and we worship You, Lord. We bow down and we worship You, Lord.

(2.) We bow down (we bow down) and we crown You the King. We bow down (we bow down) and we crown You the King. We bow down and we crown You the King.

(On repeat, sing same verse)

© Copyright 1984 by Singspiration Music, admin. by Brentwood-Benson Music Publishing, Inc. (ASCAP)
All Rights Reserved. Used by Permission.

"All hail the power of Jesus' Name!

Let angels prostrate fall;

Bring forth the royal diadem

and crown him Lord of all.

Oh, that with yonder sacred throng

we at his feet may fall!

We'll join the everlasting song

and crown him Lord of all."

vs.1, Edward Perronet, 1726-92;

vs. 2, John Rippon, 1787

234 We Bring the Sacrifice of Praise

He who sacrifices thank offerings honors me, and he prepares the way so that I may show him the salvation of God. (Psalm 50:23)

Kirk Dearman

Capo 1 (D)

We bring the sacrifice of praise into the house of the Lord; We bring the sacrifice of praise into the house of the Lord. And we offer up to You the sacrifices of thanksgiving; And we offer up to You the sacrifices of joy.

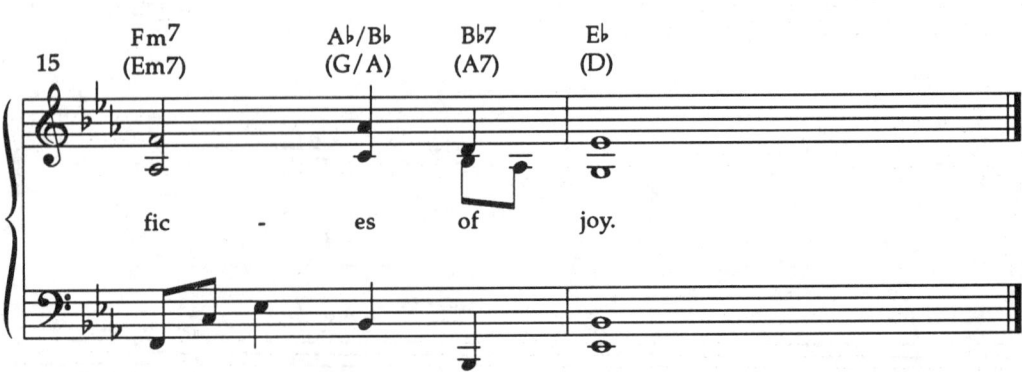

© Copyright 1984 John T. Benson Publishing Co., admin. by Brentwood-Benson Music Publishing, Inc. (ASCAP). All Rights Reserved. Used by Permission.

235 When I Survey the Wondrous Cross

For I resolved to know nothing while I was with you except Jesus Christ and him crucified. (1 Cor. 2:2)

Isaac Watts

Gregorian Chant
Arr. by Phil Kristianson

1. When I survey the wondrous cross
On which the Prince of Glory died,
My richest gain I count but loss,
And pour contempt on all my pride.

2. Forbid it, Lord, that I should boast,
Save in the death of Christ, my God.
All the vain things that charm me most,
I sacrifice them to His blood.

3. See, from His head, His hands, His feet,
Sorrow and love flow mingled down.
Did e'er such love and sorrow meet,
Or thorns compose so rich a crown?

4. Were the whole realm of nature mine,
That were an off'ring far too small.
Love so amazing, so divine,
Demands my soul, my life, my all!

"May I never boast except in the cross of our Lord Jesus Christ, through which the world has been crucified to me, and I to the world."

Galatians 6:14

© Copyright 1997 Maranatha! Music (Administered by The Copyright Company, Nashville, TN).
All Rights Reserved. International Copyright Secured. Used by Permission. www.maranathamusic.com

This cup is the new covenant in my blood; do this, whenever you drink it, in remembrance of me. (1 Cor. 11:25)

236   We Remember You

Rick Founds

VERSE

In broken bread and the cup that we share, we remember You.

In broken bread and the cup that we share, we remember You.

CHORUS

We remember You, Jesus. We remember Your love for us. We remember the blood You shed. We remember You.

© Copyright 1988 Maranatha! Music (Administered by The Copyright Company, Nashville, TN).
All Rights Reserved. International Copyright Secured. Used by Permission. www.maranathamusic.com

There is a friend who sticks closer than a brother. (Proverbs 18:24)

237 What a Friend I've Found

Martin Smith

Moderately slow

VERSE

1. What a Friend I've found, closer than a brother.
2. What a hope I've found, more faithful than a mother.

I have felt Your touch, more intimate than lovers.
It would break my heart to ever lose each other.

CHORUS

Jesus, Jesus, Jesus, Friend forever.

1. er.
2. er.

© Copyright 1993 Curious? Music UK.
All Rights Reserved. Used by Permission.

238 What a Friend We Have in Jesus

Do not be anxious about anything, but in everything, by prayer and petition, with thanksgiving, present your requests to God. (Philippians 4:6)

Joseph Scriven
Charles C. Converse

1. What a Friend we have in Jesus, all our sins and griefs to bear! What a privilege to carry ev'rything to God in prayer! O what peace we often forfeit, O what needless pain we bear, all because we do not carry ev'rything to God in prayer!

2. Have we trials and temptations, is there trouble anywhere? We should never be discouraged, take it to the Lord in prayer. Can we find a friend so faithful who will all our sorrows share? Jesus knows our every weakness, take it to the Lord in prayer.

3. Are we weak and heavy-laden, cumbered with a load of care? Precious Saviour, still our refuge, take it to the Lord in prayer. Do thy friends despise, forsake thee? Take it to the Lord in prayer; In His arms He'll take and shield thee, thou wilt find a solace there.

Public Domain.

*Is not the cup of thanksgiving for which we give thanks a participation in the blood of Christ?
And is not the bread that we break a participation in the body of Christ? (1 Cor. 10:16)*

239 What Is This Bread?

Frederic W. Baue

Jean Neuhauser Baue

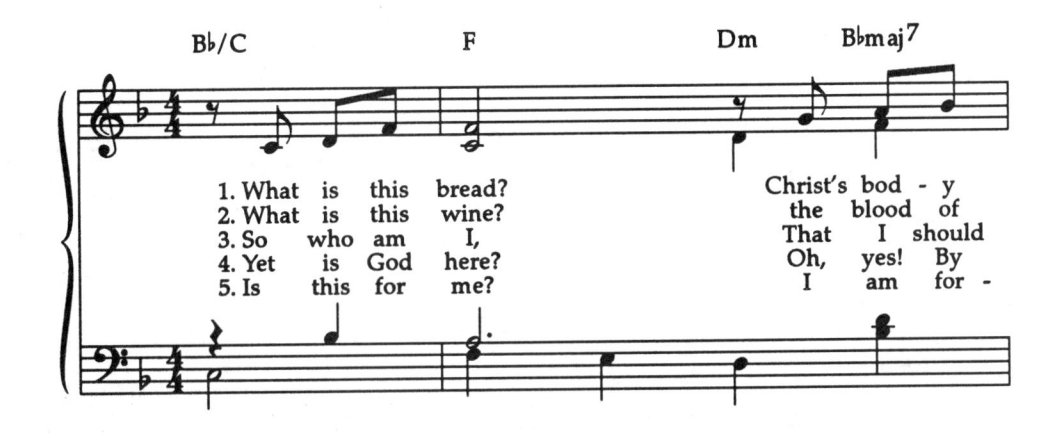

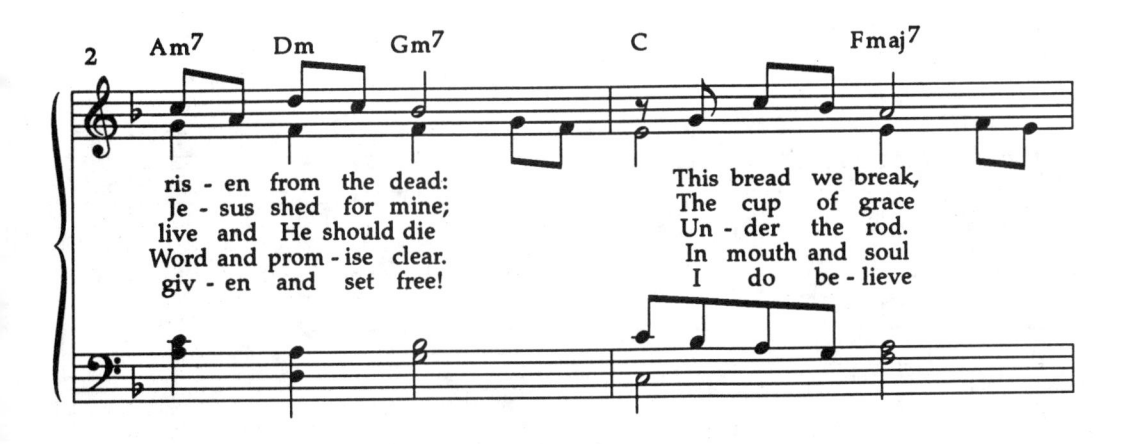

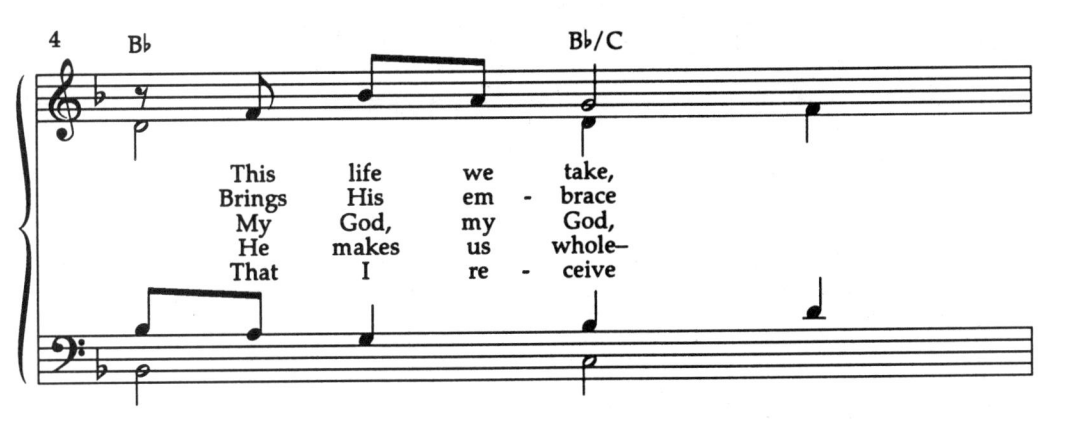

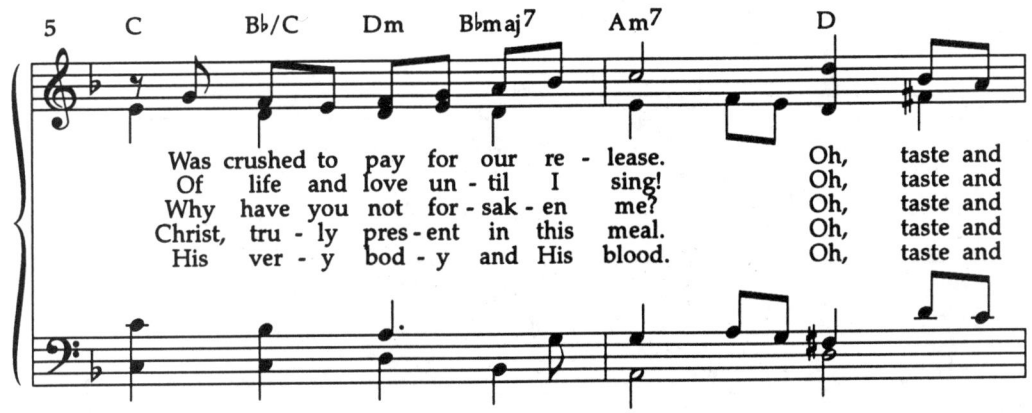

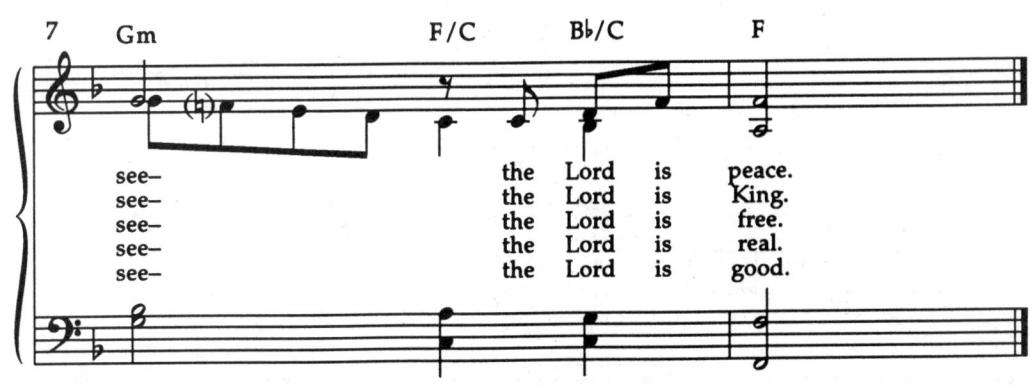

1. What is this bread? Christ's body risen from the dead: This bread we break, Was crushed to pay for our release. Oh, taste and see— the Lord is peace.
2. What is this wine? The blood of Jesus shed for mine; The cup of grace Of life and love until I sing! Oh, taste and see— the Lord is King.
3. So who am I, That I should live and He should die Under the rod. Why have you not forsaken me? Oh, taste and see— the Lord is free.
4. Yet is God here? Oh, yes! By Word and promise clear. In mouth and soul Christ, truly present in this meal. Oh, taste and see— the Lord is real.
5. Is this for me? I am forgiven and set free! I do believe This life we take, Brings His embrace, My God, my God, He makes us whole— That I receive His very body and His blood. Oh, taste and see— the Lord is good.

© Copyright 1991 and 1998 Fred and Jean Baue.
All Rights Reserved. Used by Permission.

240 When I Look into Your Holiness

One thing I ask of the Lord...that I may dwell in the house of the Lord all the days of my life, to gaze upon the beauty of the Lord. (Psalm 27:4)

Wayne and Cathy Perrin

♩ = 72-80

VERSE

When I look in-to Your hol-i-ness, When I gaze in-to Your love-li-ness, when all things that sur-round be-come shad-ows in the light of You, When I've found the joy of reach-ing Your heart, When my will be-comes en-thralled in Your love, When all things that sur-round be-come

© Copyright 1980, Arr. © 1992 Ingegrity's Hosanna! Music,
c/o Integrity Music, Inc., 1000 Cody Road, Mobile, AL 36695-3425.
All Rights Reserved. International Copyright Secured. Used by Permission.

19 F2 F Gsus Em/G F/G
shad - ows in the light of You,
CHORUS
21 Gsus G G9sus G Fmaj7
I wor - ship You;
23 G/F Fmaj7 G/F Em7
I wor - ship You.
25 Am7 Dm7 C/D Dm7
The rea - son I live
27 1. Gsus G F/G G7 Cmaj7 Dm7 G7/D
is to wor - ship You.
29 C2/E C/E C Dm7 Em7
I wor - ship
2. Gsus G F/G G7
is to wor - ship
31 C F2/G G13 G7
D.S.
You. When I
Song Ending
33 Gsus G F/G G7 C
is to wor - ship You.

241 White As Snow

Though your sins are like scarlet, they shall be white as snow. (Isaiah 1:18)

Leon Olguin

White as snow, white as snow, Though my sins were as scarlet, Lord, I know, Lord, I know That I'm clean and for-giv-en. Through the pow-er of Your blood, Through the won-der of Your love, Through faith in You I know that I can be white as snow.

© Copyright 1990 Sound Truth Publishing (Administered by Maranatha! Music c/o The Copyright Company, Nashville, TN)
Maranatha Praise, Inc. (Administered by The Copyright Company, Nashville, TN).
All Rights Reserved. International Copyright Secured. Used by Permission. www.maranathamusic.com

242 Worthy the Lamb That Was Slain

Worthy is the Lamb who was slain, to receive power and wealth and wisdom and strength and honor and glory and praise! (Revelation 5:12)

Don Moen

With a swing beat ♩ = 80-90

Lyrics:
Wor-thy, the Lamb that was slain.
Wor-thy, the Lamb that was slain, to re-ceive glo-ry and hon-or, wis-dom and pow-er.

TAG
Wor-thy, the Lamb that was slain.

© Copyright 1986 Integrity's Hosanna! Music, c/o Integrity Music, Inc., 1000 Cody Road, Mobile, AL 36695-3425.
All Rights Reserved. International Copyright Secured. Used by Permission.

Where your treasure is, there your heart will be also. (Matthew 6:21)

243 You Are My All in All

Dennis L. Jernigan

"I open my mouth and pant,

longing for **your** commands."

Psalm 119:131

"The kingdom of **heaven** is like

treasure hidden in a field. When a

man found it, he hid it again, and then in his joy

went and sold all he had and bought that field.

Again, the kingdom of heaven is like a merchant

looking for fine pearls. When he found one of

great value, he went away and sold everything

he had and bought it."

Matthew 13:44-46

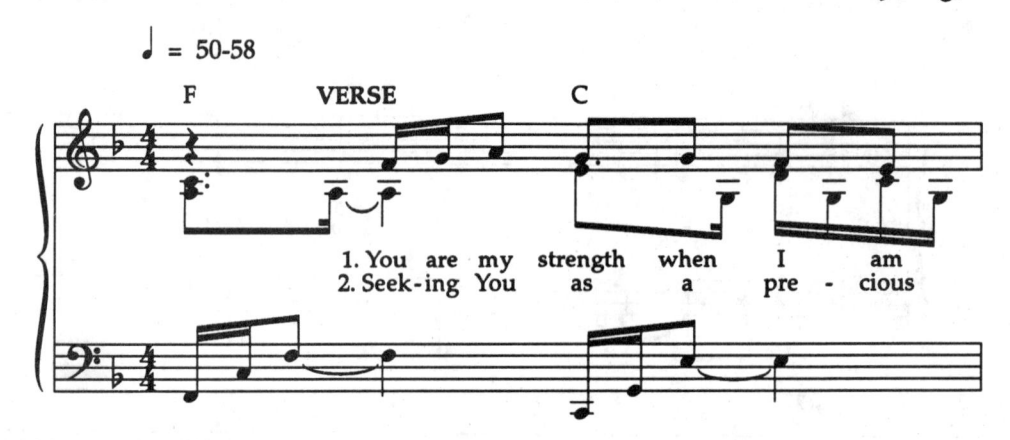

1. You are my strength when I am weak, You are the Treasure that I seek. You are my All in All.
2. Seeking You as a precious jewel, Lord, to give up I'd be a fool. You are my All in All!

© Copyright 1991 Shepherd's Heart Music, Inc. (Admin. by Dayspring Music, Inc.) (BMI),
65 Music Square West, Nashville, TN 37203.
All Rights Reserved. Made in the U.S.A. International Copyright Secured. Used by Permission.

PART I (May be sung as a 2-part round)
(opt. D.S.)
6
F CHORUS
C
Dm7
F2/A
Je - sus, Lamb of God,
8
B♭
F/C
C
F
C
Wor - thy is Your name.
10
F
C
Dm7
F2/A
Je - sus, Lamb of God,
12
B♭
F/C
C
B♭/F
F
B♭/C
Wor - thy is Your name.
PART II
14
F VERSE
C
Dm7
F2/A
Tak-ing my sin, my cross, my shame, ris-ing a-gain I bless Your
16
B♭
F/C
C
F
C
name. You are my All in All.
18
F
C
Dm
F2/A
When I fall down, You pick me up; When I am dry, You fill my
Repeat Ending
(Continue Round-Key of F)
D.S.
20
B♭
F/C
C
B♭/F
F
Gm7/F
cup. You are my All in All!

Song Ending (Key of F)
22
B♭/F F Gm7/F F
All!
Optional Modulation to Higher Key for Last Chorus
24
B♭/F F C/D
All!
CHORUS
25
(opt. D.S.)
G D
Je - sus,
26
Em7 Bm7 Am7 G/D D
Lamb of God, Wor - thy is Your
28
G D G D
name. Je - sus,
30
Em7 Bm7 Am7 G/D D
Lamb of God, Wor - thy is Your
32
G
name,
Repeat Ending (Key of G)
Am7 G/D D
Wor - thy is Your
34
C/G G C/D
name!
D.S. to 25
Song Ending (Key of G)
Am7 poco rit. G/D D
Wor - thy is Your
36
C/G G Am7/G G
name!

You are my hiding place; you will protect me from trouble and surround me with songs of deliverance. (Psalm 32:7)

244 You Are My Hiding Place

Michael Ledner

VERSE

You are my hiding place. You always fill my heart with songs of deliverance. Whenever I am afraid I will trust in

*CHORUS

You. I will trust in You. Let the weak say I am strong in the strength of the Lord. Lord. I will trust in You.

© Copyright 1981 Maranatha! Music (Administered by The Copyright Company, Nashville, TN). All Rights Reserved. International Copyright Secured. Used by Permission. www.maranathamusic.com

*May be sung as a round.

You Are My Own

You are heirs...of the covenant God made with your fathers. (Acts 3:25)

Gerald Patrick Coleman

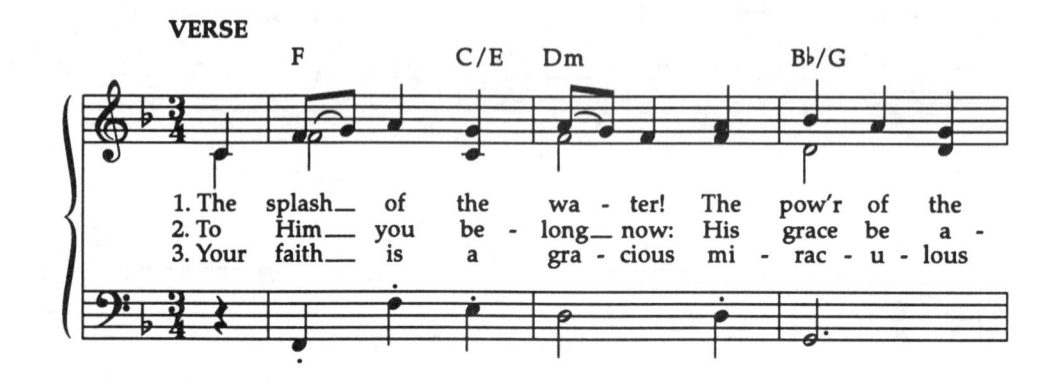

1. The splash of the water! The pow'r of the Word! The Spirit now binds you to Jesus your Lord! And wonder of wonders! Though by sin defiled The Father in heaven Now makes you His child!

2. To Him you belong now: His grace be adored! His grace which sustains as you grow in the Word! And grace of all graces! The vict'ry He won is your vict'ry now through your faith in the Son!

3. Your faith is a gracious miraculous gift: A miracle just like His rising from death. Both miracles yours now in Baptism's flood Secured by the covenant sealed with His blood.

CHORUS
A child of the promise His death has fulfilled! An heir of the covenant sure as His throne! His promise is "I shall be always with you." His covenant, "You are my own."

© Copyright 1989 Concordia Publishing House.
All Rights Reserved. Used by Permission.

My grace is sufficient for you, for power is perfected in weakness. (2 Corinthians 12:9)

246 Your Grace Is Sufficient

Martin J. Nystrom

♩ = 80

CHORUS

Your grace is suf-fi-cient for me, Your strength is made per-fect when I am weak. All that I cling to I lay at Your feet, Your grace is suf-fi-cient for me.

1. I'm
2. You

VERSE

1. no long-er striv-ing to mer-it Your love, I rest in Your prom-ise to me; That Your mer-cy is all that I need.
2. see me as right-eous be-cause of the blood that made the a-tone-ment for me; That Your mer-cy has tri-umphed where I should be judged, so now, by Your grace, I am free. Your

Fine

© Copyright 1991 Integrity's Hosanna! Music, c/o Integrity Music, Inc., 1000 Cody Road, Mobile, AL 36695-3425.
All Rights Reserved. International Copyright Secured. Used by Permission.

247 You Are Worthy of My Praise

Come, let us bow down in worship, let us kneel before the Lord our Maker. (Psalm 95:6)

David Ruis

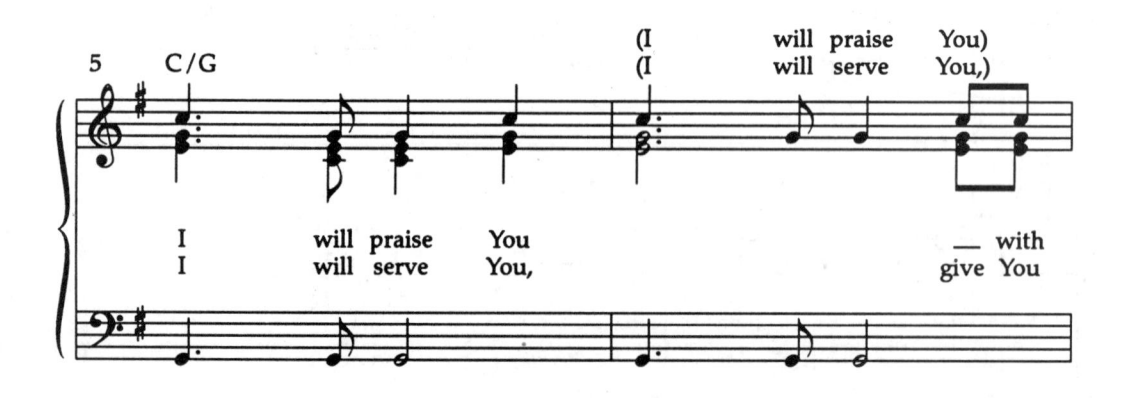

With Praise

VERSE

I will worship with all of my heart;
I will bow down, hail You as King;
I will praise You with all of my strength,
I will serve You, give You ev'rything.
I will seek You all of my days,
I will lift up my eyes to Your throne;
and I will follow, I will
I will trust You, follow, I will

> "Worthy is the Lamb, who was slain, to receive power and wealth and wisdom and strength and honor and glory and praise!"
>
> Revelation 5:12

For he has rescued us from the dominion of darkness and brought us into the kingdom of the Son he loves. (Colossians 1:13)

248   You Rescued Me

Geoff Bullock

Moderately ♩ = 80

You rescued me and picked me up, a living hope of grace revealed, a life transformed in righteousness; O Lord, You have rescued me. Forgiving me, You healed my heart and set me free from sin and death. You've brought me life; You've made me whole. O Lord, You have rescued me. And You loved me before I

© Copyright 1993 Word, Inc. (ASCAP), 65 Music Square West, Nashville, TN 37203 / Maranatha! Music (Admin. by Word Music, Inc.) (ASCAP), 65 Music Square West, Nashville, TN 37203. All Rights Reserved. Made in the U.S.A. International Copyright Reserved. Used by Permission.
www.maranathamusic.com

19
A/C♯ C♯m7 A E/G♯
knew You. And You knew me for all time.
21
Bsus B A/E E
I've been cre - at - ed in Your im -
23
A/C♯ C♯m7 B B2/A
- age, O Lord.
25
E2/G♯ E/G♯ F♯m7 A/E E
And You bought me and You sought
27
A/C♯ C♯m7 A E/G♯
me; Your blood poured out for me,
29
Bsus B A/E E E/G♯
a new cre - a - tion in Your im -
31
A E/G♯ Bsus B
- age, O Lord. You res - cued me.
34
F♯m7(4) B 1. E B/D♯
You res - cued me.
37
A/C♯ B7sus 2. E B/D♯ A/C♯
You res - cued me. You res - cued me.
40
F♯m7(4) A/B E
You res - cued me.

249 You Make Me Lie Down in Green Pastures

He makes me lie down in green pastures, he leads me beside quiet waters. (Psalm 23:2)

Kathy Zuziak

♩ = 94-108

CHORUS

You make me lie down in green pastures, You make me wanting for nothing. You fill my hunger with honey from Your sweet, sweet, Word; You let me worship before You so I will love and adore You.

TAG

You, You are my Shepherd, You are my Jesus, You are my Lord.

© Copyright 1985 Integrity's Hosanna! Music (Administered by Maranatha! Music c/o The Copyright Company, Nashville, TN)
Maranatha Praise, Inc. (Administered by The Copyright Company, Nashville, TN)
All Rights Reserved. International Copyright Secured. Used by Permission. www.maranathamusic.com

"I regard myself as the most wretched of all men, stinking and covered with sores, and as one who has committed all sorts of crimes against his King. Overcome by remorse, I confess all my wickedness to Him, ask His pardon and abandon myself entirely to Him to do with as He will. But this King, *filled with* **goodness** *and* **mercy,** far from chastising me, *lovingly* **embraces** me, makes me eat at His table, serves me with His own hands, gives me the keys of His treasures and treats me as His favorite. He talks with me and is delighted with me in a thousand and one ways; He forgives me and relieves me of my principal bad habits without talking about them; I beg Him to make me according to His heart and always the more weak and despicable I see myself to be, the more ***beloved*** I am of **God.**"

Brother Lawrence, 1605-1691

Where can I go from Thy Spirit? Or where can I flee from Thy presence? (Psalm 139:7)

250 Your Love

Don Moen and Martin J. Nystrom

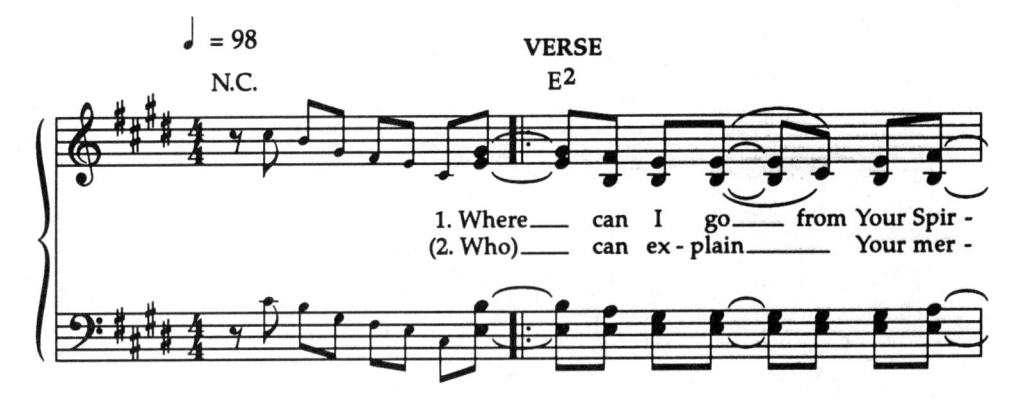

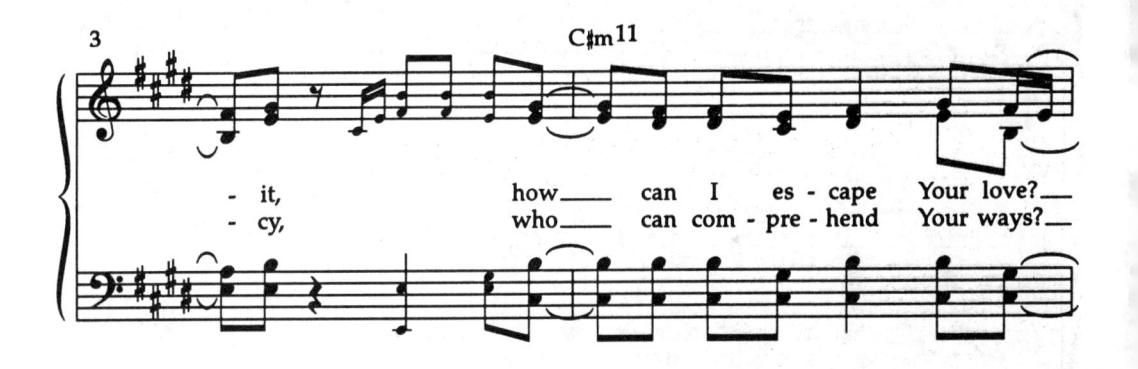

1. Where can I go from Your Spirit, how can I escape Your love?
(2.) Who can explain Your mercy, who can comprehend Your ways?

Your love for me is deep—
You showed me Your grace by tak—

© Copyright 1990 Integrity's Hosanna! Music, c/o Integrity Music, Inc., 1000 Cody Road, Mobile, AL 36695-3425.
All Rights Reserved. International Copyright Secured. Used by Permission.

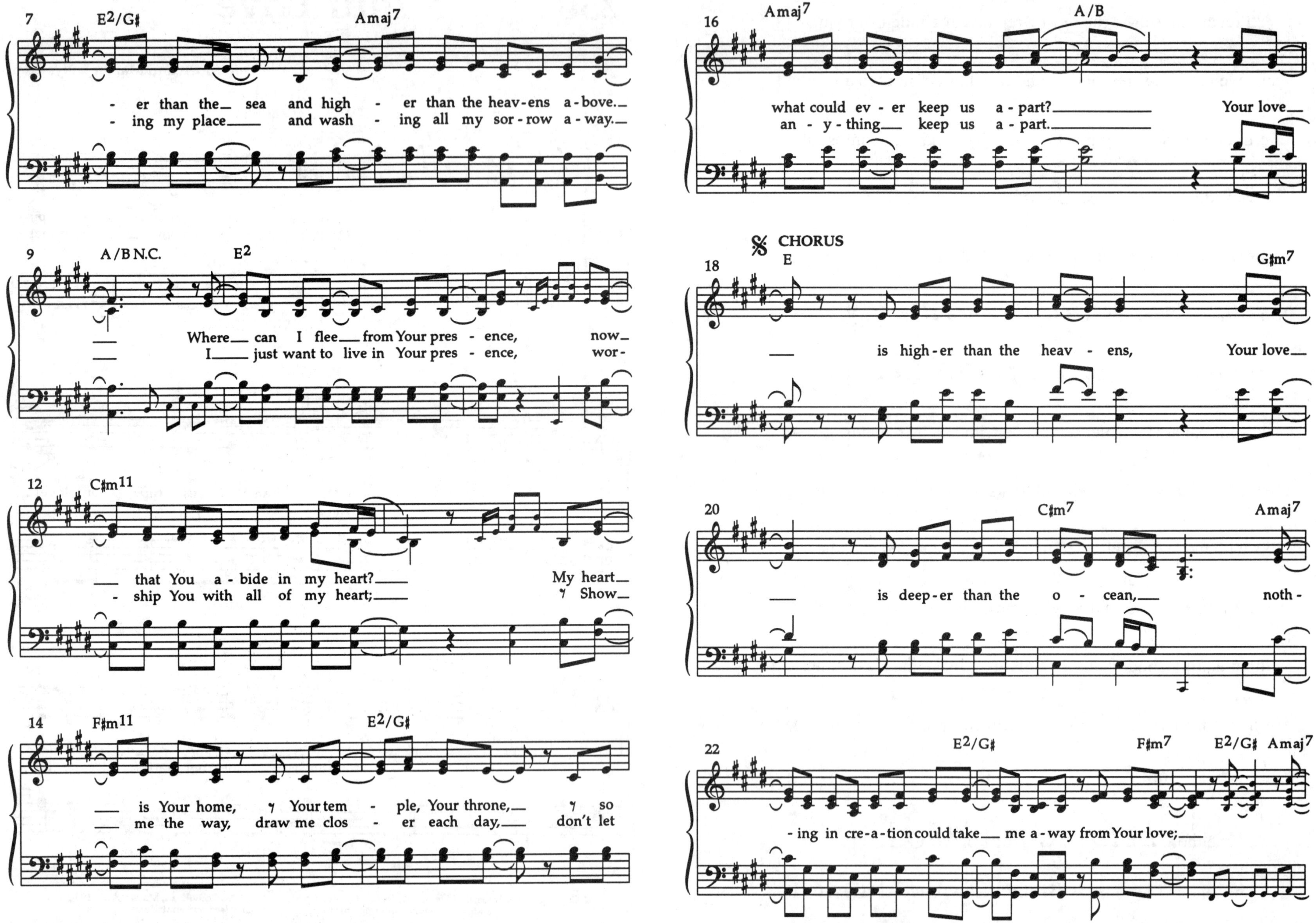

7 E2/G♯ Amaj7
- er than the sea and high - er than the heav-ens a-bove.
- ing my place and wash - ing all my sor-row a-way.
9 A/B N.C. E2
Where can I flee from Your pres - ence, now
I just want to live in Your pres - ence, wor-
12 C♯m11
that You a - bide in my heart? My heart
- ship You with all of my heart; Show
14 F♯m11 E2/G♯
is Your home, Your tem - ple, Your throne, so
me the way, draw me clos - er each day, don't let
16 Amaj7 A/B
what could ev - er keep us a - part? Your love
an - y - thing keep us a - part.
CHORUS
18 E G♯m7
is high-er than the heav - ens, Your love
20 C♯m7 Amaj7
is deep-er than the o - cean, noth-
22 E2/G♯ F♯m7 E2/G♯ Amaj7
- ing in cre-a-tion could take me a-way from Your love;

25
A/B E G♯m7
Your love, there is noth-ing great - er, Your love,
28
C♯m7 Amaj7
there is noth-ing strong - er. You
30
E2/G♯ F♯m7
came to me, gave Your life so I could be free.
32
1. A/B
2. A/B
2. Who I am per -
BRIDGE
35
Amaj9 B/A Amaj9
suad - ed that nei-ther death nor life can sep - a -
37
E2/G♯ G♯m7 E/G♯ C° C♯m9
rate us from the love of Christ; Noth -
39
E/F♯ F♯13
- ing in the pres-ent and noth - ing to come could take
41
F♯m9 B6/9 D.S. 𝄋
3.4. Amaj7 F♯m7/B D.S. 𝄋
me a-way from Your in - fi-nite love. Your love Your love
44
5. E2/G♯ Amaj7 A/B E
I can be free in Your love.

From everlasting to everlasting the Lord's love is with those who fear him. (Psalm 103.17)

251 Your Everlasting Love

Bill Batstone

1. Your ev-er-last-ing love is higher, higher, higher than the sky. Your ev-er-last-ing love is higher, higher than the sky, higher than the sky. Oh, the wonder of Your ev-er-last-ing love is higher than the sky.

(2.) -er-last-ing love is deeper, deeper, deeper than the sea. Your ev-er-last-ing love is deeper, deeper than the sea, deeper than the sea. Oh, the wonder of Your ev-er-last-ing love is deeper than the sea.

(3.) -er-last-ing love is reaching, reaching, reaching out to me. Your ev-er-last-ing love is reaching, reaching out to me, reaching out to me. Oh, the wonder of Your ev-er-last-ing love is reaching out to me.

© Copyright 1993 Maranatha Praise, Inc. (Administered by The Copyright Company, Nashville, TN). All Rights Reserved. International Copyright Secured. Used by Permission. www.maranathamusic.com

"I pray that you, being rooted and established in *love,* may have power, together with all the saints, to grasp how **wide** and **long** and **high** and **deep** is the **love** of Christ, and to know this love that surpasses knowledge— that you may be filled to the measure of all the fullness of God."

Ephesians 3:17-19

I pray that you...may have power...to know this love that surpasses knowledge...[He] is able to do immeasurably more than all we can ask or imagine, according to his power that is at work in us. (Ephesians 3:17-20)

252 Your Touch Is Loving

Dennis Haig

David Siebels

CHORUS

Your touch is lov-ing,— Your grip is strong, as You walk with— me all my life— long.— Your touch is lov-ing,— Your grip is strong, as You walk with— me all my life— long.— There is no

VERSE

peace that's deep-er— than Yours, Lord. There's no
love that's strong-er— than yours, Lord. There's no

joy I can cel-e-brate— more.
strength I can cel-e-brate— more.

Grant me,— I pray, Your grace— each day. There's no
Keep me— I pray, close to you each day. There's no

joy I can cel-e-brate— more. There is no
strength I can cel-e-brate

© Copyright 1997 Dave Siebels Productions.
All Rights Reserved. Used by Permission.

CHORUS
2.
18 B♭/F F B♭/C F
more. Your touch is lov - ing, Your grip is
20 C2/E C/E C F/B♭ C Dm
strong, as You walk with me all
22 C2/E C/E F B♭/C F
my life long. Your touch is lov - ing, Your grip is
24 C2/E C/E C F/B♭ C Dm
2nd time to Coda
strong, as You walk with me all
26 C2/E C/E F Gm/F F B♭/C
my life long. There is no
VERSE
28 F Em7(♭5) A7(♯5)
hope that's bright - er than mine, Lord. There's no
30 Dm Dm/C B♭ F/A Gm7
prom - ise I can cel - e - brate more. Heav - en
32 C/E A/C♯ Dm Dm/C
waits, You say, af - ter my fi - nal day. There's no
D.S. al CODA
34 B♭ F/A Gm C B♭/F F B♭/C
prom - ise I can cel - e - brate more. Your touch is
CODA
36 C2/E C/E B♭ F/A Gm7 C F
my life long.

Before I formed you in the womb I knew you, before you were born I set you apart. (Jeremiah 1:5)

253 God Knew Your Name

Jim Likens
Arr. by Chris Bergmann

"Before I formed you in the womb

I knew you,

before you were born

I set you apart…"

Jeremiah 1:5

♩ = 120

1. Be - fore the light of day shined on your lit - tle face, God knew your name. When no - one else could see
(2.) fore you walked a - round, be - fore you first fell down, God knew your name. Be - fore you rode your trike

© Copyright 1998 Story Tunes Publishing.
All Rights Reserved. Used by Permission. www.Godknewyourname.com

11
Fsus4/2
F
how precious you would be,
and then that first red bike,
13
B♭2
God knew your
God knew your
16
C7sus
C
F2
name.
name.
And He held you so
He was with you ev - 'ry
19
B♭2
close in His lov - ing hand,
day, right there by your side,
21
Gm
F/G
Gm
F/G
and He want - ed all to
e - ven when you made mis -
24
Csus
C
Fsus
F
see that be - fore the light of day
takes. And be - fore the light of day
27
Fsus
F
shined on your lit - tle face,
shined on your lit - tle face,
30
B♭2
Csus
C7
Fsus
God knew your name.
God knew your name.
33
1.
F
Fsus4/2
F
2. Be
36
2.
F
Gsus
G
3. Be -

39 Gsus4/2 G Gsus4/2 G
fore those wed-ding bells rang their sto-ry, well,
(4.) grace-ful-ly grew old, you know you had been told
42 C2 Gsus
God knew your name.
God knew your name.
46 G Gsus4/2 G
Be-fore that first new home and
And one day when you died, your
49 Gsus4/2 G C2
chil-dren of your own, God
friends and fam-'ly cried; God
52 D7sus D
knew your name. And through
knew your name. And my
55 G2 C2
all the times, both the good and
an-gels car-ried your soul to
58 Am G/A Am G/A
bad, He held you in His
me, and I said wel-come
61 Dsus D Gsus G
hand. And be-fore the light of day
home. You were one of mine.
64 Gsus G
shined on your lit-tle face,
I loved you for all time.
2nd time to Coda
67 C2 Dsus D7 Gsus G
God knew your name.
I knew your

[S.D.G. stands for *"Soli Deo Gloria,"* which means,

"To God alone be the glory!"

Bach wrote this at the end of all his musical scores and we follow his godly example here. We humbly acknowledge the riches and depth of a redeeming, gracious God, who through Jesus Christ created and continues to manage the universe, guides all human history and has bought us back into a relationship with Him through His precious blood. We dedicate this book to God the Father, God the Son and God the Holy Spirit and pray it will bring Him honor and praise. S.D.G. – ed.]

INTRODUCTION TO THE INDEXES AND LAYOUT

There are five sets of indexes: *Contents – Familiar Titles*, *Key and Tempo*, *Topical*, *Scripture References*, and *Copyright Holders*. The *Topical* and *Scripture Reference* tables are striking for a contemporary songbook because they are rather exhaustive. There are 59 pages (!) of song references to help you get the best out of *The Best of the Best*. Pastors, musicians, small groups Bible study leaders and individuals will find a wealth of material here to facilitate planning worship, group study or private devotion.

Let's say you're leading a Bible study or preaching on the little four-chapter book of Philippians. You'll find 56 songs listed in *Scripture References* that relate to the book of Philippians in some way! Likewise, the *Topical Indexes* aim to indicate the breadth of songs related to each subject. For instance, if you are teaching on the Bible verse, "Sing and make melody in your heart to the Lord" you'll find 27 songs listed under "Singing to God" that either are: (1) songs directly addressed to God or (2) songs that exhort worshippers to sing praise to the Lord.

Since you may use this book not just in large group worship, but also for personal and small group devotions, seminars and retreat settings, check out the topical section called "Intimacy with God." The list includes some lovely, heartfelt expressions of a deeply personal nature that will help draw you into personal, intimate, "Psalmist-like" worship.

A few subjects in the *Topical Index* one might expect to find only in a "hymnal." We hope this contribution will be especially helpful to churches that are trying to bridge stylistic boundaries in order to reach people with the timeless Gospel. Some of these "unusual" topics (for a contemporary songbook) include: Advent, Ascension, Confirmation, Funeral, Good Friday, Installation/Ordination, Lent, Marriage/Wedding, Palm Sunday, and Sanctification.

The *Contents – Familiar Titles* section obviously tells you "where to find it." However, there is another easy way to find songs. Though not always in alphabetical order, the "A's" are grouped together in the same section; then follow all the "B's" and so on, through the alphabet. There are only three exceptions to this letter grouping: *Emmanuel* comes before the "D's"; *Under the Blood* comes after the "V's" and *God Knew Your Name* is the final song in the book.

Every effort has been made to avoid page turns in both editions of the songbook. The four-page spread of the *Full Music Edition* was designed so instrumentalists would never have to "miss a beat." (Only four of 253 songs require page turns and these are still carefully placed.) Worship leaders will want to note that "verse" and "chorus" have been clearly indicated in nearly every song to assist your worship team and congregation in following familiar song patterns you may choose such as: verse-chorus-verse-chorus-chorus-tag.

Finally, an amusing insider's note. Because of the acronym formed by the first letters of "The Best of the Best," we affectionately refer to it as the "BOB" songbook.

So enjoy BOB! And may the Lord use this songbook to draw you close to His heart.

Mike Zehnder
Rev. Michael Zehnder, Compiler and Editor

Key and Tempo

A

Fast
- 62 For the Lord is Good
- 158 Mighty is Our God
- 191 Rock of Ages
- 224 Trading My Sorrows

Medium
- 5 All Heaven Declares
- 18 Be Exalted, O God
- 29 By Your Side
- 39 Come and Fill Me Up
- 51 Father Me, Again
- 75 God is the Strength of My Heart
- 123 I'm Forever Grateful
- 204 Shine, Jesus Shine
- 203 Spirit, Touch Your Church
- 228 Under the Blood

Slow
- 9 Above All
- 167 My Redeemer Lives (Willison)
- 242 Worthy the Lamb that Was Slain

A Flat

Medium
- 28 By Your Blood
- 38 Crown Him (King of Kings)
- 226 Victory Chant

Slow
- 100 I Am the Bread of Life (Toolan)

A Minor

Medium
- 182 Praise Adonai

Slow
- 244 You Are My Hiding Place

B Flat

Medium
- 7 All Over Again
- 47 Draw Me Close to You
- 198 Shout to the Lord

Slow
- 127 It's Your Blood

C

Fast
- 15 As High As the Heaven
- 78 Great and Mighty is He
- 230 We'll Be Faithful

Medium
- 16 As I Look Into Your Eyes
- 24 Blessed Assurance
- 33 Change My Heart, O God
- 45 Did You Feel the Mountains Tremble?
- 44 Emmanuel
- 49 Enter In
- 68 Glory to the Lamb
- 98 I Am Not My Own
- 105 I Live to Know You
- 115 I Want to Walk as a Child of the Light
- 124 In The Heart of God
- 141 Let It Be Said Of Us
- 152 Lord, You Love Me
- 157 Meekness and Majesty
- 170 No Other Name
- 181 Our Confidence is In the Lord
- 189 Renew Me
- 210 The Lamb
- 233 We Bow Down
- 246 Your Grace is Sufficient For Me

Slow
- 30 Cares Chorus
- 66 Glorify Thy Name
- 77 Grace Alone
- 79 He is Able
- 88 Here is Bread
- 92 Holy, Holy, Holy Is the Lord of Hosts
- 135 Jesus, Your Name
- 138 Knowing You
- 178 Only By Grace
- 221 Thine the Amen, Thine the Praise
- 231 We Are an Offering
- 236 We Remember You
- 237 What a Friend I've Found (...Friend Forever)
- 240 When I Look into Your Holiness

C Minor

Fast
- 227 Victory Song

Medium
- 193 Rock of My Salvation

Slow
- 113 I Want Jesus to Walk With Me

C to D

Medium
- 89 Holy Is Our God Medley

D

Fast
- 129 Jesus is Alive
- 172 O Magnify The Lord

Medium
- 10 Ancient of Days
- 27 Bring Forth the Kingdom
- 37 Come Thou Fount of Every Blessing
- 42 Cry of My Heart
- 54 Fear Not
- 55 Feed My Lambs
- 73 Great is Thy Faithfulness
- 94 Holy Lamb of God
- 97 How Shall I Call You?
- 118 In Moments Like These
- 145 Light One Candle
- 153 Love You So Much
- 164 My Dwelling Place
- 184 Purify My Heart
- 186 Raise Up an Army
- 190 Revival Fire, Fall
- 208 Thank You, Lord
- 216 Then I Will Praise You
- 211 There is A Redeemer
- 223 This Kingdom

Slow
- 2 A Shield About Me
- 11 Amazing Love
- 12 As the Deer
- 56 Fill Me
- 109 I Need You
- 112 I See the Lord (Falson)
- 122 I Will Glory in The Cross
- 119 I Will Praise Him
- 128 It's All About You (Jesus, Lover of My Soul)
- 139 Lamb of God
- 140 Lead Me to the Cross
- 162 My Faith Looks Up to Thee
- 176 On Eagle's Wings
- 187 Redeemer Savior Friend
- 196 See This Wonder
- 201 Spirit of the Living God
- 202 Spirit Song
- 222 Think About His Love

D Minor

Fast
- 195 Sing Unto the Lord

Medium
- 8 All Honor
- 205 The Battle Belongs to the Lord
- 249 You Make Me Lie Down In Green Pastures

Slow
- 84 Healer of My Heart

D to B Flat

Slow
- 82 Hear Me Say I Love You

E

Fast
- 32 Celebrate the Lord of Love
- 67 Glory
- 74 God is Good All the Time
- 144 Let the Walls Fall Down
- 166 My Redeemer Lives (Morgan)
- 215 The River is Here
- 219 This is the Day (Shelton)

Medium
- 23 Better is One Day
- 43 Comfort Comfort
- 81 He Will Come and Save You
- 85 Here Am I
- 101 I Believe in Jesus
- 111 I See the Lord (Baloche)
- 117 I Will Celebrate (Baloche)
- 143 Let the River Flow
- 150 Lord Most High
- 180 Open the Eyes of My Heart, Lord
- 248 You Rescued Me
- 250 Your Love

Slow
- 17 At the Cross
- 53 Feed Us Now
- 63 Friend of Sinners
- 93 Holy, Holy (...lift up his name)
- 217 These Things Are True of You

E Flat

Medium
- 20 Be Thou My Vision
- 22 Behold the Lamb
- 57 Find Us Faithful
- 110 I Want to Be More Like You
- 132 Jesus, Jesus
- 156 May the Feet of God Walk with You
- 209 The Heart of Worship
- 234 We Bring the Sacrifice of Praise

Slow
- 91 Hide Me in Your Holiness
- 174 Once Again

E Minor

Fast
- 120 I Will Celebrate (Duvall)

Slow
- 159 More Love, More Power

173 O The Deep, Deep Love of Jesus
207 Take Our Lives

F

Fast
31 Celebrate Jesus
106 I Love to Be in Your Presence
137 Joy and Thanksgiving
148 Living Stones
171 Nobody Fills My Heart Like Jesus
199 Someone Else Living in You
212 The Name of the Lord (Blessed Be)
220 This is the Day (Fitts)
251 Your Everlasting Love
252 Your Touch is Loving

Medium
1 A Broken Spirit
4 All Hail King Jesus
6 Almighty
19 Be My Home
36 Come and See
52 Father Welcomes
59 Firm Foundation
58 First Love
60 Flowing River
65 Give Thanks
70 Go, Make Disciples
103 I Could Sing of Your Love Forever
147 Lift Him Up
146 Light The Candle
149 Light the Fire Again
160 More of You
183 Peace Be Yours
188 Remember Me
192 Romans 16:19
197 Shout to the North
200 Someone Special
206 Take My Life and Let It Be
225 Tis So Sweet to Trust in Jesus
229 Waterlife
238 What a Friend we Have in Jesus
245 You Are My Own

Slow
21 Beautiful Savior (All My Days)
26 Blest Be The Tie That Binds
35 Come and Behold Him
40 Come to the Bread of Life
41 Come to the Table
61 Foolish Pride
72 Go, My Children with My Blessing
87 Here In This Place
102 I Exalt Thee
107 I Love You, Lord
108 I Offer My Life
131 Jesus, Draw Me Close
134 Jesus, Name Above All Names
155 Make Me a Servant
161 More Precious Than Silver
168 My Jesus, I Love Thee
169 Nothing But the Blood
175 Only By the Blood of the Lamb
239 What is This Bread?
241 White As Snow
243 You Are My All in All

F Minor

Fast
71 God is Good

F to G

Medium
253 God Knew Your Name

Slow
96 How Could You Love Me So Much?

G

Fast
13 All the Power You Need
69 Go Out As People of God
83 Heaven is in My Heart
95 Hosanna
136 Jesus, We Celebrate Your Victory
163 Mourning Into Dancing
165 My Life is In You, Lord
232 We Are Marching in the Light of God

Medium
3 A Simple Word of Grace
14 Arms of Love
25 Blessing and Honor
46 Do This In Remembrance of Me
48 Eagle's Wings
64 From My Heart to Yours
76 God Will Make a Way
80 He Who Began a Good Work in You
86 Here I Am Lord
104 I Give You My Heart
114 I Want to Be Where You Are
116 I Was There to Hear Your Borning Cry
121 I Will Change Your Name
125 In the Secret (I Want to Know You)
130 Jesus, Lover of My Soul
142 Let the Flame Burn Brighter
151 Lord, I Lift Your Name on High
154 Majesty
179 Only the Blood
177 Only You
185 Rest
214 The Power of Your Love
218 There is None Like You
247 You Are Worthy of My Praise

Slow
34 Christ Above Me
50 Faithful Father
90 Holy and Anointed One
99 I Am the Bread of Life (Talbot)
126 Isn't He?
133 Jesus, Lamb of God
194 Savior Again to Your Dear Name
213 The Potter's Hand
235 When I Survey the Wondrous Cross

Topical Index

Anniversary (of a Church)
see Installation, Confirmation

Advent
- 4 All Hail King Jesus
- 21 Beautiful Savior (All My Days)
- 35 Come and Behold Him
- 43 Comfort Comfort
- 38 Crown Him (King of Kings)
- 45 Did You Feel the Mountains Tremble?
- 44 Emmanuel
- 67 Glory
- 83 Heaven is in My Heart
- 95 Hosanna
- 126 Isn't He?
- 134 Jesus, Name Above All Names
- 145 Light One Candle
- 146 Light The Candle
- 200 Someone Special

Ascension
- 5 All Heaven Declares
- 40 Come to the Bread of Life
- 45 Did You Feel the Mountains Tremble?
- 90 Holy and Anointed One
- 151 Lord, I Lift Your Name on High

Assurance
- 1 A Broken Spirit
- 2 A Shield About Me
- 3 A Simple Word of Grace
- 13 All the Power You Need
- 6 Almighty
- 15 As High As the Heaven
- 17 At the Cross
- 19 Be My Home
- 20 Be Thou My Vision
- 24 Blessed Assurance
- 29 By Your Side
- 30 Cares Chorus
- 32 Celebrate the Lord of Love
- 34 Christ Above Me
- 41 Come to the Table
- 43 Comfort Comfort
- 47 Draw Me Close to You
- 48 Eagle's Wings
- 52 Father Welcomes
- 54 Fear Not
- 59 Firm Foundation
- 61 Foolish Pride
- 72 Go, My Children with My Blessing
- 71 God is Good
- 74 God is Good All the Time
- 75 God is the Strength of My Heart
- 253 God Knew Your Name
- 76 God Will Make a Way
- 73 Great is Thy Faithfulness
- 79 He is Able
- 80 He Who Began a Good Work in You
- 81 He Will Come and Save You
- 84 Healer of My Heart
- 113 I Want Jesus to Walk With Me
- 116 I Was There to Hear Your Borning Cry
- 121 I Will Change Your Name
- 124 In The Heart of God
- 156 May the Feet of God Walk with You
- 171 Nobody Fills My Heart Like Jesus
- 173 O The Deep, Deep Love of Jesus
- 176 On Eagle's Wings
- 178 Only By Grace
- 183 Peace Be Yours
- 185 Rest
- 193 Rock of My Salvation
- 199 Someone Else Living in You
- 205 The Battle Belongs to the Lord
- 216 Then I Will Praise You
- 224 Trading My Sorrows
- 228 Under the Blood
- 229 Waterlife
- 238 What a Friend we Have in Jesus
- 241 White As Snow
- 243 You Are My All in All
- 244 You Are My Hiding Place
- 245 You Are My Own
- 251 Your Everlasting Love

Baptism
- 39 Come and Fill Me Up
- 52 Father Welcomes
- 69 Go Out As People of God
- 70 Go, Make Disciples
- 72 Go, My Children with My Blessing
- 253 God Knew Your Name
- 80 He Who Began a Good Work in You
- 84 Healer of My Heart
- 116 I Was There to Hear Your Borning Cry
- 156 May the Feet of God Walk with You
- 196 See This Wonder
- 229 Waterlife
- 245 You Are My Own
- 246 Your Grace is Sufficient For Me

Belief
see Faith

Benediction/Close of Worship
- 26 Blest Be The Tie That Binds
- 27 Bring Forth the Kingdom
- 34 Christ Above Me
- 55 Feed My Lambs
- 56 Fill Me
- 57 Find Us Faithful
- 69 Go Out As People of God
- 70 Go, Make Disciples
- 72 Go, My Children with My Blessing
- 79 He is Able
- 80 He Who Began a Good Work in You
- 156 May the Feet of God Walk with You
- 183 Peace Be Yours
- 194 Savior Again to Your Dear Name

Blood of Christ
- 11 Amazing Love
- 17 At the Cross
- 21 Beautiful Savior (All My Days)
- 24 Blessed Assurance
- 28 By Your Blood
- 37 Come Thou Fount of Every Blessing
- 40 Come to the Bread of Life
- 41 Come to the Table
- 46 Do This In Remembrance of Me
- 49 Enter In
- 54 Fear Not
- 96 How Could You Love Me So Much?
- 98 I Am Not My Own
- 100 I Am the Bread of Life (Toolan)
- 122 I Will Glory in The Cross
- 119 I Will Praise Him
- 127 It's Your Blood
- 139 Lamb of God
- 140 Lead Me to the Cross
- 166 My Redeemer Lives (Morgan)
- 169 Nothing But the Blood
- 178 Only By Grace
- 175 Only By the Blood of the Lamb
- 179 Only the Blood
- 188 Remember Me
- 204 Shine, Jesus Shine
- 199 Someone Else Living in You
- 205 The Battle Belongs to the Lord
- 225 Tis So Sweet to Trust in Jesus
- 228 Under the Blood
- 236 We Remember You
- 239 What is This Bread?
- 235 When I Survey the Wondrous Cross
- 241 White As Snow
- 245 You Are My Own
- 248 You Rescued Me
- 246 Your Grace is Sufficient For Me

Body of Christ
- 26 Blest Be The Tie That Binds
- 27 Bring Forth the Kingdom
- 45 Did You Feel the Mountains Tremble?
- 57 Find Us Faithful
- 69 Go Out As People of God
- 88 Here is Bread
- 89 Holy Is Our God Medley
- 106 I Love to Be in Your Presence
- 141 Let It Be Said Of Us
- 142 Let the Flame Burn Brighter
- 144 Let the Walls Fall Down
- 148 Living Stones
- 186 Raise Up an Army
- 229 Waterlife

Christmas/Advent
- 4 All Hail King Jesus
- 38 Crown Him (King of Kings)
- 44 Emmanuel
- 126 Isn't He?
- 134 Jesus, Name Above All Names
- 145 Light One Candle
- 146 Light The Candle
- 156 May the Feet of God Walk with You
- 200 Someone Special

Church, The
- 26 Blest Be The Tie That Binds
- 27 Bring Forth the Kingdom
- 45 Did You Feel the Mountains Tremble?
- 52 Father Welcomes
- 55 Feed My Lambs
- 57 Find Us Faithful
- 69 Go Out As People of God
- 141 Let It Be Said Of Us
- 148 Living Stones
- 186 Raise Up an Army
- 197 Shout to the North
- 203 Spirit, Touch Your Church
- 229 Waterlife

Changelessness
see Faithfulness

Character
see Holiness or Character of God

Cleanse/Wash
- 11 Amazing Love
- 21 Beautiful Savior (All My Days)
- 39 Come and Fill Me Up
- 37 Come Thou Fount of Every Blessing
- 109 I Need You
- 119 I Will Praise Him
- 127 It's Your Blood
- 139 Lamb of God
- 164 My Dwelling Place
- 169 Nothing But the Blood
- 178 Only By Grace
- 179 Only the Blood
- 184 Purify My Heart
- 189 Renew Me
- 196 See This Wonder
- 207 Take Our Lives
- 225 Tis So Sweet to Trust in Jesus
- 229 Waterlife
- 241 White As Snow
- 246 Your Grace is Sufficient For Me
- 250 Your Love

Comfort

2 A Shield About Me
14 Arms of Love
15 As High As the Heaven
19 Be My Home
26 Blest Be The Tie That Binds
30 Cares Chorus
34 Christ Above Me
43 Comfort Comfort
47 Draw Me Close to You
51 Father Me, Again
54 Fear Not
72 Go, My Children with My Blessing
74 God is Good All the Time
76 God Will Make a Way
77 Grace Alone
81 He Will Come and Save You
84 Healer of My Heart
97 How Shall I Call You?
113 I Want Jesus to Walk With Me
121 I Will Change Your Name
124 In The Heart of God
156 May the Feet of God Walk with You
163 Mourning Into Dancing
162 My Faith Looks Up to Thee
176 On Eagle's Wings
183 Peace Be Yours
185 Rest
193 Rock of My Salvation
194 Savior Again to Your Dear Name
198 Shout to the Lord
202 Spirit Song
216 Then I Will Praise You
238 What a Friend we Have in Jesus
243 You Are My All in All
244 You Are My Hiding Place

Commitment/Consecration

1 A Broken Spirit
20 Be Thou My Vision
27 Bring Forth the Kingdom
33 Change My Heart, O God
37 Come Thou Fount of Every Blessing
42 Cry of My Heart
47 Draw Me Close to You
48 Eagle's Wings
51 Father Me, Again
52 Father Welcomes
55 Feed My Lambs
56 Fill Me
57 Find Us Faithful
58 First Love
60 Flowing River
63 Friend of Sinners
70 Go, Make Disciples
79 He is Able
80 He Who Began a Good Work in You

85 Here Am I
86 Here I Am Lord
104 I Give You My Heart
109 I Need You
108 I Offer My Life
110 I Want to Be More Like You
114 I Want to Be Where You Are
125 In the Secret (I Want to Know You)
130 Jesus, Lover of My Soul
142 Let the Flame Burn Brighter
149 Light the Fire Again
155 Make Me a Servant
159 More Love, More Power
162 My Faith Looks Up to Thee
174 Once Again
175 Only By the Blood of the Lamb
184 Purify My Heart
186 Raise Up an Army
187 Redeemer Savior Friend
190 Revival Fire Fall
192 Romans 16:19
199 Someone Else Living in You
201 Spirit of the Living God
202 Spirit Song
203 Spirit, Touch Your Church
206 Take My Life and Let It Be
207 Take Our Lives
209 The Heart of Worship
213 The Potter's Hand
214 The Power of Your Love
231 We Are an Offering
230 We'll Be Faithful
235 When I Survey the Wondrous Cross

Communion

11 Amazing Love
22 Behold the Lamb
28 By Your Blood
34 Christ Above Me
40 Come to the Bread of Life
41 Come to the Table
46 Do This In Remembrance of Me
53 Feed Us Now
65 Give Thanks
72 Go, My Children with My Blessing
84 Healer of My Heart
88 Here is Bread
99 I Am the Bread of Life (Talbot)
100 I Am the Bread of Life (Toolan)
127 It's Your Blood
140 Lead Me to the Cross
160 More of You
169 Nothing But the Blood
178 Only By Grace
175 Only By the Blood of the Lamb
179 Only the Blood
188 Remember Me
221 Thine the Amen, Thine the Praise

228 Under the Blood
236 We Remember You
239 What is This Bread?
241 White As Snow

Confession of Faith (Proclamation)

2 A Shield About Me
3 A Simple Word of Grace
9 Above All
8 All Honor
13 All the Power You Need
6 Almighty
11 Amazing Love
10 Ancient of Days
17 At the Cross
21 Beautiful Savior (All My Days)
24 Blessed Assurance
25 Blessing and Honor
28 By Your Blood
46 Do This In Remembrance of Me
62 For the Lord is Good
71 God is Good
74 God is Good All the Time
82 Hear Me Say I Love You
122 I Will Glory in The Cross
127 It's Your Blood
135 Jesus, Your Name
137 Joy and Thanksgiving
174 Once Again
186 Raise Up an Army
197 Shout to the North
206 Take My Life and Let It Be
226 Victory Chant
248 You Rescued Me

Confirmation

1 A Broken Spirit
21 Beautiful Savior (All My Days)
27 Bring Forth the Kingdom
29 By Your Side
33 Change My Heart, O God
34 Christ Above Me
51 Father Me, Again
52 Father Welcomes
55 Feed My Lambs
56 Fill Me
57 Find Us Faithful
58 First Love
63 Friend of Sinners
72 Go, My Children with My Blessing
79 He is Able
80 He Who Began a Good Work in You
108 I Offer My Life
115 I Want to Walk as a Child of the Light
116 I Was There to Hear Your Borning Cry
148 Living Stones
156 May the Feet of God Walk with You
207 Take Our Lives

231 We Are an Offering
237 What a Friend I've Found (...Friend Forever)
246 Your Grace is Sufficient For Me
252 Your Touch is Loving

Courage

2 A Shield About Me
13 All the Power You Need
30 Cares Chorus
32 Celebrate the Lord of Love
43 Comfort Comfort
51 Father Me, Again
54 Fear Not
59 Firm Foundation
69 Go Out As People of God
74 God is Good All the Time
75 God is the Strength of My Heart
76 God Will Make a Way
80 He Who Began a Good Work in You
81 He Will Come and Save You
84 Healer of My Heart
121 I Will Change Your Name
163 Mourning Into Dancing
176 On Eagle's Wings
181 Our Confidence is In the Lord
186 Raise Up an Army
193 Rock of My Salvation
205 The Battle Belongs to the Lord
216 Then I Will Praise You
232 We Are Marching in the Light of God
238 What a Friend we Have in Jesus
243 You Are My All in All
244 You Are My Hiding Place
see also Fear/Afraid

Creation

9 Above All
6 Almighty
18 Be Exalted, O God
32 Celebrate the Lord of Love
43 Comfort Comfort
67 Glory
69 Go Out As People of God
73 Great is Thy Faithfulness
82 Hear Me Say I Love You
89 Holy Is Our God Medley
97 How Shall I Call You?
116 I Was There to Hear Your Borning Cry
150 Lord Most High
158 Mighty is Our God
182 Praise Adonai
198 Shout to the Lord
200 Someone Special
233 We Bow Down

Cross, The

3 A Simple Word of Grace
9 Above All
11 Amazing Love

16 As I Look Into Your Eyes
17 At the Cross
21 Beautiful Savior (All My Days)
22 Behold the Lamb
24 Blessed Assurance
41 Come to the Table
96 How Could You Love Me So Much?
122 I Will Glory in The Cross
119 I Will Praise Him
123 I'm Forever Grateful
140 Lead Me to the Cross
141 Let It Be Said Of Us
151 Lord, I Lift Your Name on High
157 Meekness and Majesty
164 My Dwelling Place
168 My Jesus, I Love Thee
174 Once Again
235 When I Survey the Wondrous Cross
243 You Are My All in All
see also Lamb, Lent

Crucifixion
see Cross, The

Easter
5   All Heaven Declares
6   Almighty
21 Beautiful Savior (All My Days)
25 Blessing and Honor
28 By Your Blood
31 Celebrate Jesus
32 Celebrate the Lord of Love
45 Did You Feel the Mountains Tremble?
129 Jesus is Alive
136 Jesus, We Celebrate Your Victory
138 Knowing You
151 Lord, I Lift Your Name on High
166 My Redeemer Lives (Morgan)
167 My Redeemer Lives (Willison)
210 The Lamb
211 There is A Redeemer

Eternal Life
31 Celebrate Jesus
37 Come Thou Fount of Every Blessing
40 Come to the Bread of Life
54 Fear Not
83 Heaven is in My Heart
100 I Am the Bread of Life (Toolan)
128 It's All About You (Jesus, Lover of My Soul)
138 Knowing You
144 Let the Walls Fall Down
194 Savior Again to Your Dear Name
211 There is A Redeemer
221 Thine the Amen, Thine the Praise
223 This Kingdom
251 Your Everlasting Love
see also Heaven

Family of God
see Church, The

Faith
13 All the Power You Need
37 Come Thou Fount of Every Blessing
50 Faithful Father
52 Father Welcomes
74 God is Good All the Time
77 Grace Alone
81 He Will Come and Save You
100 I Am the Bread of Life (Toolan)
101 I Believe in Jesus
116 I Was There to Hear Your Borning Cry
138 Knowing You
162 My Faith Looks Up to Thee
166 My Redeemer Lives (Morgan)
167 My Redeemer Lives (Willison)
185 Rest
193 Rock of My Salvation
210 The Lamb
225 Tis So Sweet to Trust in Jesus
230 We'll Be Faithful
239 What is This Bread?
241 White As Snow
245 You Are My Own
246 Your Grace is Sufficient For Me

Faithfulness (God's)
13 All the Power You Need
6   Almighty
18 Be Exalted, O God
50 Faithful Father
54 Fear Not
59 Firm Foundation
62 For the Lord is Good
72 Go, My Children with My Blessing
74 God is Good All the Time
253 God Knew Your Name
73 Great is Thy Faithfulness
80 He Who Began a Good Work in You
97 How Shall I Call You?
116 I Was There to Hear Your Borning Cry
121 I Will Change Your Name
152 Lord, You Love Me
173 O The Deep, Deep Love of Jesus
176 On Eagle's Wings
191 Rock of Ages
193 Rock of My Salvation
200 Someone Special
216 Then I Will Praise You
217 These Things Are True of You
222 Think About His Love
238 What a Friend we Have in Jesus
251 Your Everlasting Love
252 Your Touch is Loving

Farewell
72 Go, My Children with My Blessing
156 May the Feet of God Walk with You
183 Peace Be Yours

Father, The
15 As High As the Heaven
16 As I Look Into Your Eyes
20 Be Thou My Vision
28 By Your Blood
50 Faithful Father
51 Father Me, Again
52 Father Welcomes
66 Glorify Thy Name
72 Go, My Children with My Blessing
71 God is Good
73 Great is Thy Faithfulness
82 Hear Me Say I Love You
85 Here Am I
97 How Shall I Call You?
99 I Am the Bread of Life (Talbot)
100 I Am the Bread of Life (Toolan)
115 I Want to Walk as a Child of the Light
196 See This Wonder
207 Take Our Lives
211 There is A Redeemer
245 You Are My Own

Father's Day
see Father, The

Fear/Afraid
26 Blest Be The Tie That Binds
30 Cares Chorus
74 God is Good All the Time
81 He Will Come and Save You
121 I Will Change Your Name
176 On Eagle's Wings
183 Peace Be Yours
205 The Battle Belongs to the Lord
216 Then I Will Praise You
244 You Are My Hiding Place
see also Courage

Forgiveness
13 All the Power You Need
11 Amazing Love
15 As High As the Heaven
17 At the Cross
21 Beautiful Savior (All My Days)
24 Blessed Assurance
28 By Your Blood
35 Come and Behold Him
39 Come and Fill Me Up
37 Come Thou Fount of Every Blessing
41 Come to the Table
43 Comfort Comfort
50 Faithful Father
61 Foolish Pride

69 Go Out As People of God
72 Go, My Children with My Blessing
73 Great is Thy Faithfulness
84 Healer of My Heart
91 Hide Me in Your Holiness
98 I Am Not My Own
109 I Need You
122 I Will Glory in The Cross
119 I Will Praise Him
129 Jesus is Alive
140 Lead Me to the Cross
141 Let It Be Said Of Us
168 My Jesus, I Love Thee
169 Nothing But the Blood
178 Only By Grace
210 The Lamb
217 These Things Are True of You
239 What is This Bread?
241 White As Snow
248 You Rescued Me

Funeral
20 Be Thou My Vision
21 Beautiful Savior (All My Days)
23 Better is One Day
26 Blest Be The Tie That Binds
37 Come Thou Fount of Every Blessing
43 Comfort Comfort
54 Fear Not
72 Go, My Children with My Blessing
253 God Knew Your Name
76 God Will Make a Way
115 I Want to Walk as a Child of the Light
116 I Was There to Hear Your Borning Cry
124 In The Heart of God
156 May the Feet of God Walk with You
163 Mourning Into Dancing
162 My Faith Looks Up to Thee
183 Peace Be Yours
194 Savior Again to Your Dear Name
216 Then I Will Praise You
238 What a Friend we Have in Jesus

Glory
see Majesty/Glory/Power of God

Good Friday
9   Above All
11 Amazing Love
16 As I Look Into Your Eyes
17 At the Cross
22 Behold the Lamb
28 By Your Blood
96 How Could You Love Me So Much?
127 It's Your Blood
139 Lamb of God
140 Lead Me to the Cross
157 Meekness and Majesty
168 My Jesus, I Love Thee

169 Nothing But the Blood
174 Once Again
175 Only By the Blood of the Lamb
187 Redeemer Savior Friend
188 Remember Me
210 The Lamb
235 When I Survey the Wondrous Cross

Gospel

3 A Simple Word of Grace
11 Amazing Love
17 At the Cross
21 Beautiful Savior (All My Days)
24 Blessed Assurance
25 Blessing and Honor
28 By Your Blood
40 Come to the Bread of Life
49 Enter In
50 Faithful Father
52 Father Welcomes
54 Fear Not
61 Foolish Pride
63 Friend of Sinners
65 Give Thanks
72 Go, My Children with My Blessing
71 God is Good
74 God is Good All the Time
77 Grace Alone
78 Great and Mighty is He
80 He Who Began a Good Work in You
84 Healer of My Heart
82 Hear Me Say I Love You
83 Heaven is in My Heart
86 Here I Am Lord
91 Hide Me in Your Holiness
89 Holy Is Our God Medley
96 How Could You Love Me So Much?
97 How Shall I Call You?
98 I Am Not My Own
99 I Am the Bread of Life (Talbot)
100 I Am the Bread of Life (Toolan)
101 I Believe in Jesus
116 I Was There to Hear Your Borning Cry
122 I Will Glory in The Cross
119 I Will Praise Him
123 I'm Forever Grateful
127 It's Your Blood
129 Jesus is Alive
136 Jesus, We Celebrate Your Victory
138 Knowing You
139 Lamb of God
140 Lead Me to the Cross
141 Let It Be Said Of Us
149 Light the Fire Again
151 Lord, I Lift Your Name on High
164 My Dwelling Place
166 My Redeemer Lives (Morgan)
167 My Redeemer Lives (Willison)

169 Nothing But the Blood
173 O The Deep, Deep Love of Jesus
174 Once Again
175 Only By the Blood of the Lamb
179 Only the Blood
187 Redeemer Savior Friend
188 Remember Me
189 Renew Me
185 Rest
196 See This Wonder
199 Someone Else Living in You
200 Someone Special
207 Take Our Lives
210 The Lamb
211 There is A Redeemer
217 These Things Are True of You
228 Under the Blood
229 Waterlife
243 You Are My All in All
248 You Rescued Me
see also Grace/Mercy

Grace/Mercy

3 A Simple Word of Grace
11 Amazing Love
15 As High As the Heaven
16 As I Look Into Your Eyes
17 At the Cross
21 Beautiful Savior (All My Days)
22 Behold the Lamb
24 Blessed Assurance
25 Blessing and Honor
39 Come and Fill Me Up
36 Come and See
37 Come Thou Fount of Every Blessing
40 Come to the Bread of Life
41 Come to the Table
49 Enter In
50 Faithful Father
52 Father Welcomes
54 Fear Not
55 Feed My Lambs
53 Feed Us Now
61 Foolish Pride
62 For the Lord is Good
63 Friend of Sinners
74 God is Good All the Time
77 Grace Alone
78 Great and Mighty is He
73 Great is Thy Faithfulness
84 Healer of My Heart
82 Hear Me Say I Love You
83 Heaven is in My Heart
88 Here is Bread
89 Holy Is Our God Medley
96 How Could You Love Me So Much?
98 I Am Not My Own
101 I Believe in Jesus

109 I Need You
122 I Will Glory in The Cross
127 It's Your Blood
132 Jesus, Jesus
138 Knowing You
140 Lead Me to the Cross
141 Let It Be Said Of Us
164 My Dwelling Place
162 My Faith Looks Up to Thee
174 Once Again
178 Only By Grace
175 Only By the Blood of the Lamb
179 Only the Blood
187 Redeemer Savior Friend
185 Rest
197 Shout to the North
199 Someone Else Living in You
203 Spirit, Touch Your Church
207 Take Our Lives
214 The Power of Your Love
218 There is None Like You
217 These Things Are True of You
221 Thine the Amen, Thine the Praise
222 Think About His Love
220 This is the Day (Fitts)
223 This Kingdom
228 Under the Blood
239 What is This Bread?
245 You Are My Own
248 You Rescued Me
246 Your Grace is Sufficient For Me
250 Your Love
252 Your Touch is Loving
see also Gospel

Gratitude

see Thanksgiving

Guidance

19 Be My Home
20 Be Thou My Vision
30 Cares Chorus
33 Change My Heart, O God
34 Christ Above Me
37 Come Thou Fount of Every Blessing
42 Cry of My Heart
51 Father Me, Again
55 Feed My Lambs
56 Fill Me
72 Go, My Children with My Blessing
74 God is Good All the Time
76 God Will Make a Way
73 Great is Thy Faithfulness
89 Holy Is Our God Medley
97 How Shall I Call You?
113 I Want Jesus to Walk With Me
115 I Want to Walk as a Child of the Light
116 I Was There to Hear Your Borning Cry

156 May the Feet of God Walk with You
199 Someone Else Living in You
200 Someone Special
213 The Potter's Hand
216 Then I Will Praise You
220 This is the Day (Fitts)
249 You Make Me Lie Down In Green Pastures
250 Your Love
252 Your Touch is Loving

Healing

13 All the Power You Need
34 Christ Above Me
43 Comfort Comfort
51 Father Me, Again
84 Healer of My Heart
88 Here is Bread
97 How Shall I Call You?
101 I Believe in Jesus
103 I Could Sing of Your Love Forever
132 Jesus, Jesus
135 Jesus, Your Name
143 Let the River Flow
163 Mourning Into Dancing
166 My Redeemer Lives (Morgan)
172 O Magnify The Lord
197 Shout to the North
199 Someone Else Living in You
216 Then I Will Praise You
218 There is None Like You
224 Trading My Sorrows
248 You Rescued Me

Heaven

4 All Hail King Jesus
10 Ancient of Days
18 Be Exalted, O God
20 Be Thou My Vision
21 Beautiful Savior (All My Days)
23 Better is One Day
37 Come Thou Fount of Every Blessing
50 Faithful Father
54 Fear Not
55 Feed My Lambs
67 Glory
253 God Knew Your Name
83 Heaven is in My Heart
100 I Am the Bread of Life (Toolan)
111 I See the Lord (Baloche)
112 I See the Lord (Falson)
115 I Want to Walk as a Child of the Light
116 I Was There to Hear Your Borning Cry
162 My Faith Looks Up to Thee
173 O The Deep, Deep Love of Jesus
182 Praise Adonai
199 Someone Else Living in You
211 There is A Redeemer
221 Thine the Amen, Thine the Praise

252 Your Touch is Loving
see also Eternal Life

Holiness or Character of God
6 Almighty
10 Ancient of Days
21 Beautiful Savior (All My Days)
28 By Your Blood
36 Come and See
42 Cry of My Heart
50 Faithful Father
62 For the Lord is Good
65 Give Thanks
67 Glory
68 Glory to the Lamb
73 Great is Thy Faithfulness
82 Hear Me Say I Love You
83 Heaven is in My Heart
91 Hide Me in Your Holiness
90 Holy and Anointed One
89 Holy Is Our God Medley
94 Holy Lamb of God
93 Holy, Holy (…lift up his name)
92 Holy, Holy, Holy Is the Lord of Hosts
111 I See the Lord (Baloche)
112 I See the Lord (Falson)
133 Jesus, Lamb of God
134 Jesus, Name Above All Names
135 Jesus, Your Name
139 Lamb of God
157 Meekness and Majesty
161 More Precious Than Silver
173 O The Deep, Deep Love of Jesus
179 Only the Blood
180 Open the Eyes of My Heart, Lord
181 Our Confidence is In the Lord
182 Praise Adonai
184 Purify My Heart
212 The Name of the Lord (Blessed Be)
211 There is A Redeemer
217 These Things Are True of You
223 This Kingdom
226 Victory Chant
240 When I Look into Your Holiness
see also Name(s) of God

Holy Spirit
8 All Honor
23 Better is One Day
39 Come and Fill Me Up
56 Fill Me
58 First Love
60 Flowing River
61 Foolish Pride
66 Glorify Thy Name
69 Go Out As People of God
72 Go, My Children with My Blessing
74 God is Good All the Time

82 Hear Me Say I Love You
88 Here is Bread
90 Holy and Anointed One
89 Holy Is Our God Medley
97 How Shall I Call You?
105 I Live to Know You
143 Let the River Flow
146 Light The Candle
190 Revival Fire Fall
204 Shine, Jesus Shine
199 Someone Else Living in You
200 Someone Special
201 Spirit of the Living God
202 Spirit Song
203 Spirit, Touch Your Church
213 The Potter's Hand
214 The Power of Your Love
211 There is A Redeemer
229 Waterlife
245 You Are My Own
250 Your Love

Hope
2 A Shield About Me
3 A Simple Word of Grace
13 All the Power You Need
6 Almighty
20 Be Thou My Vision
26 Blest Be The Tie That Binds
31 Celebrate Jesus
37 Come Thou Fount of Every Blessing
45 Did You Feel the Mountains Tremble?
48 Eagle's Wings
54 Fear Not
55 Feed My Lambs
59 Firm Foundation
69 Go Out As People of God
75 God is the Strength of My Heart
77 Grace Alone
73 Great is Thy Faithfulness
83 Heaven is in My Heart
108 I Offer My Life
142 Let the Flame Burn Brighter
145 Light One Candle
146 Light The Candle
163 Mourning Into Dancing
162 My Faith Looks Up to Thee
165 My Life is In You, Lord
167 My Redeemer Lives (Willison)
186 Raise Up an Army
193 Rock of My Salvation
202 Spirit Song
224 Trading My Sorrows
229 Waterlife
237 What a Friend I've Found (…Friend Forever)
248 You Rescued Me
252 Your Touch is Loving

Humility
1 A Broken Spirit
12 As the Deer
28 By Your Blood
33 Change My Heart, O God
36 Come and See
48 Eagle's Wings
49 Enter In
61 Foolish Pride
84 Healer of My Heart
87 Here In This Place
108 I Offer My Life
128 It's All About You (Jesus, Lover of My Soul)
141 Let It Be Said Of Us
144 Let the Walls Fall Down
149 Light the Fire Again
155 Make Me a Servant
157 Meekness and Majesty
169 Nothing But the Blood
174 Once Again
203 Spirit, Touch Your Church
217 These Things Are True of You
233 We Bow Down
235 When I Survey the Wondrous Cross
247 You Are Worthy of My Praise

Hunger for God
7 All Over Again
14 Arms of Love
12 As the Deer
20 Be Thou My Vision
23 Better is One Day
39 Come and Fill Me Up
42 Cry of My Heart
47 Draw Me Close to You
48 Eagle's Wings
53 Feed Us Now
56 Fill Me
61 Foolish Pride
64 From My Heart to Yours
75 God is the Strength of My Heart
90 Holy and Anointed One
104 I Give You My Heart
115 I Want to Walk as a Child of the Light
125 In the Secret (I Want to Know You)
132 Jesus, Jesus
133 Jesus, Lamb of God
130 Jesus, Lover of My Soul
138 Knowing You
149 Light the Fire Again
152 Lord, You Love Me
153 Love You So Much
159 More Love, More Power
160 More of You
161 More Precious Than Silver
177 Only You
180 Open the Eyes of My Heart, Lord

190 Revival Fire Fall
204 Shine, Jesus Shine
202 Spirit Song
214 The Power of Your Love
247 You Are Worthy of My Praise

Hymn of Praise
see Praise and Worship

Incarnation (Word made flesh)
44 Emmanuel
123 I'm Forever Grateful
126 Isn't He?
134 Jesus, Name Above All Names
151 Lord, I Lift Your Name on High
157 Meekness and Majesty
185 Rest

Installation
13 All the Power You Need
19 Be My Home
26 Blest Be The Tie That Binds
27 Bring Forth the Kingdom
34 Christ Above Me
42 Cry of My Heart
48 Eagle's Wings
51 Father Me, Again
55 Feed My Lambs
56 Fill Me
57 Find Us Faithful
70 Go, Make Disciples
253 God Knew Your Name
86 Here I Am Lord
104 I Give You My Heart
108 I Offer My Life
110 I Want to Be More Like You
116 I Was There to Hear Your Borning Cry
141 Let It Be Said Of Us
148 Living Stones
155 Make Me a Servant
156 May the Feet of God Walk with You
203 Spirit, Touch Your Church
206 Take My Life and Let It Be
213 The Potter's Hand
231 We Are an Offering
252 Your Touch is Loving
see also Commitment, Confirmation

Intercession for the Nation
85 Here Am I
142 Let the Flame Burn Brighter
204 Shine, Jesus Shine
203 Spirit, Touch Your Church

Intimacy with God
7 All Over Again
14 Arms of Love
16 As I Look Into Your Eyes
12 As the Deer
19 Be My Home

20	Be Thou My Vision
23	Better is One Day
24	Blessed Assurance
29	By Your Side
34	Christ Above Me
35	Come and Behold Him
39	Come and Fill Me Up
42	Cry of My Heart
46	Do This In Remembrance of Me
47	Draw Me Close to You
48	Eagle's Wings
44	Emmanuel
50	Faithful Father
51	Father Me, Again
55	Feed My Lambs
53	Feed Us Now
56	Fill Me
58	First Love
61	Foolish Pride
63	Friend of Sinners
64	From My Heart to Yours
72	Go, My Children with My Blessing
71	God is Good
75	God is the Strength of My Heart
82	Hear Me Say I Love You
90	Holy and Anointed One
104	I Give You My Heart
114	I Want to Be Where You Are
115	I Want to Walk as a Child of the Light
121	I Will Change Your Name
118	In Moments Like These
125	In the Secret (I Want to Know You)
131	Jesus, Draw Me Close
133	Jesus, Lamb of God
138	Knowing You
152	Lord, You Love Me
168	My Jesus, I Love Thee
171	Nobody Fills My Heart Like Jesus
177	Only You
201	Spirit of the Living God
202	Spirit Song
209	The Heart of Worship
214	The Power of Your Love
216	Then I Will Praise You
218	There is None Like You
237	What a Friend I've Found (...Friend Forever)
238	What a Friend we Have in Jesus
240	When I Look into Your Holiness
249	You Make Me Lie Down In Green Pastures
250	Your Love
252	Your Touch is Loving

Jesus Christ

11	Amazing Love
14	Arms of Love
17	At the Cross
21	Beautiful Savior (All My Days)
22	Behold the Lamb
24	Blessed Assurance
25	Blessing and Honor
28	By Your Blood
29	By Your Side
31	Celebrate Jesus
34	Christ Above Me
40	Come to the Bread of Life
38	Crown Him (King of Kings)
45	Did You Feel the Mountains Tremble?
46	Do This In Remembrance of Me
44	Emmanuel
54	Fear Not
55	Feed My Lambs
59	Firm Foundation
58	First Love
63	Friend of Sinners
65	Give Thanks
66	Glorify Thy Name
67	Glory
68	Glory to the Lamb
72	Go, My Children with My Blessing
77	Grace Alone
82	Hear Me Say I Love You
83	Heaven is in My Heart
88	Here is Bread
90	Holy and Anointed One
89	Holy Is Our God Medley
115	I Want to Walk as a Child of the Light
122	I Will Glory in The Cross
129	Jesus is Alive
132	Jesus, Jesus
133	Jesus, Lamb of God
130	Jesus, Lover of My Soul
134	Jesus, Name Above All Names
135	Jesus, Your Name
148	Living Stones
154	Majesty
157	Meekness and Majesty
171	Nobody Fills My Heart Like Jesus
174	Once Again
204	Shine, Jesus Shine
198	Shout to the Lord
211	There is A Redeemer
225	Tis So Sweet to Trust in Jesus
237	What a Friend I've Found (...Friend Forever)
243	You Are My All in All

Joy

14	Arms of Love
15	As High As the Heaven
12	As the Deer
21	Beautiful Savior (All My Days)
24	Blessed Assurance
31	Celebrate Jesus
32	Celebrate the Lord of Love
37	Come Thou Fount of Every Blessing
45	Did You Feel the Mountains Tremble?
55	Feed My Lambs
71	God is Good
83	Heaven is in My Heart
97	How Shall I Call You?
106	I Love to Be in Your Presence
115	I Want to Walk as a Child of the Light
117	I Will Celebrate (Baloche)
120	I Will Celebrate (Duvall)
121	I Will Change Your Name
136	Jesus, We Celebrate Your Victory
137	Joy and Thanksgiving
138	Knowing You
140	Lead Me to the Cross
145	Light One Candle
151	Lord, I Lift Your Name on High
163	Mourning Into Dancing
166	My Redeemer Lives (Morgan)
171	Nobody Fills My Heart Like Jesus
177	Only You
186	Raise Up an Army
189	Renew Me
198	Shout to the Lord
200	Someone Special
202	Spirit Song
215	The River is Here
216	Then I Will Praise You
220	This is the Day (Fitts)
219	This is the Day (Shelton)
225	Tis So Sweet to Trust in Jesus
224	Trading My Sorrows
234	We Bring the Sacrifice of Praise
240	When I Look into Your Holiness
252	Your Touch is Loving

Kingdom of God

10	Ancient of Days
25	Blessing and Honor
27	Bring Forth the Kingdom
32	Celebrate the Lord of Love
83	Heaven is in My Heart
105	I Live to Know You
133	Jesus, Lamb of God
166	My Redeemer Lives (Morgan)
182	Praise Adonai
186	Raise Up an Army
190	Revival Fire Fall
199	Someone Else Living in You
221	Thine the Amen, Thine the Praise
223	This Kingdom
226	Victory Chant

see also Lordship

Lamb of God

5	All Heaven Declares
22	Behold the Lamb
25	Blessing and Honor
28	By Your Blood
36	Come and See
41	Come to the Table
68	Glory to the Lamb
98	I Am Not My Own
119	I Will Praise Him
127	It's Your Blood
129	Jesus is Alive
133	Jesus, Lamb of God
139	Lamb of God
164	My Dwelling Place
162	My Faith Looks Up to Thee
178	Only By Grace
175	Only By the Blood of the Lamb
210	The Lamb
211	There is A Redeemer
228	Under the Blood
242	Worthy the Lamb that Was Slain

see also Cross, Lent

Lent

3	A Simple Word of Grace
9	Above All
11	Amazing Love
16	As I Look Into Your Eyes
17	At the Cross
22	Behold the Lamb
25	Blessing and Honor
28	By Your Blood
35	Come and Behold Him
36	Come and See
49	Enter In
96	How Could You Love Me So Much?
122	I Will Glory in The Cross
123	I'm Forever Grateful
127	It's Your Blood
139	Lamb of God
140	Lead Me to the Cross
157	Meekness and Majesty
168	My Jesus, I Love Thee
169	Nothing But the Blood
174	Once Again
178	Only By Grace
175	Only By the Blood of the Lamb
179	Only the Blood
187	Redeemer Savior Friend
210	The Lamb
211	There is A Redeemer
228	Under the Blood
235	When I Survey the Wondrous Cross
243	You Are My All in All
248	You Rescued Me
246	Your Grace is Sufficient For Me

Lordship/Rule of Christ

9	Above All
4	All Hail King Jesus
5	All Heaven Declares
8	All Honor
10	Ancient of Days
18	Be Exalted, O God

20	Be Thou My Vision
21	Beautiful Savior (All My Days)
23	Better is One Day
25	Blessing and Honor
27	Bring Forth the Kingdom
32	Celebrate the Lord of Love
33	Change My Heart, O God
34	Christ Above Me
36	Come and See
38	Crown Him (King of Kings)
45	Did You Feel the Mountains Tremble?
56	Fill Me
57	Find Us Faithful
61	Foolish Pride
67	Glory
68	Glory to the Lamb
74	God is Good All the Time
78	Great and Mighty is He
81	He Will Come and Save You
82	Hear Me Say I Love You
95	Hosanna
97	How Shall I Call You?
101	I Believe in Jesus
102	I Exalt Thee
105	I Live to Know You
115	I Want to Walk as a Child of the Light
133	Jesus, Lamb of God
137	Joy and Thanksgiving
142	Let the Flame Burn Brighter
150	Lord Most High
154	Majesty
158	Mighty is Our God
167	My Redeemer Lives (Willison)
170	No Other Name
174	Once Again
182	Praise Adonai
189	Renew Me
198	Shout to the Lord
197	Shout to the North
211	There is A Redeemer
223	This Kingdom
226	Victory Chant
227	Victory Song
233	We Bow Down
247	You Are Worthy of My Praise
249	You Make Me Lie Down In Green Pastures

Love (God's Love for Us)

3	A Simple Word of Grace
11	Amazing Love
14	Arms of Love
15	As High As the Heaven
16	As I Look Into Your Eyes
28	By Your Blood
29	By Your Side
34	Christ Above Me
35	Come and Behold Him
39	Come and Fill Me Up

49	Enter In
50	Faithful Father
51	Father Me, Again
52	Father Welcomes
54	Fear Not
55	Feed My Lambs
53	Feed Us Now
56	Fill Me
61	Foolish Pride
62	For the Lord is Good
72	Go, My Children with My Blessing
71	God is Good
253	God Knew Your Name
73	Great is Thy Faithfulness
82	Hear Me Say I Love You
89	Holy Is Our God Medley
96	How Could You Love Me So Much?
97	How Shall I Call You?
99	I Am the Bread of Life (Talbot)
100	I Am the Bread of Life (Toolan)
103	I Could Sing of Your Love Forever
128	It's All About You (Jesus, Lover of My Soul)
130	Jesus, Lover of My Soul
140	Lead Me to the Cross
152	Lord, You Love Me
156	May the Feet of God Walk with You
163	Mourning Into Dancing
171	Nobody Fills My Heart Like Jesus
173	O The Deep, Deep Love of Jesus
187	Redeemer Savior Friend
188	Remember Me
189	Renew Me
190	Revival Fire Fall
193	Rock of My Salvation
196	See This Wonder
197	Shout to the North
199	Someone Else Living in You
200	Someone Special
202	Spirit Song
208	Thank You, Lord
214	The Power of Your Love
217	These Things Are True of You
222	Think About His Love
220	This is the Day (Fitts)
223	This Kingdom
229	Waterlife
236	We Remember You
240	When I Look into Your Holiness
235	When I Survey the Wondrous Cross
241	White As Snow
248	You Rescued Me
251	Your Everlasting Love
250	Your Love
252	Your Touch is Loving

Love (Our Love for Each Other)

| 26 | Blest Be The Tie That Binds |
| 60 | Flowing River |

— p. 18 —

141	Let It Be Said Of Us
155	Make Me a Servant
203	Spirit, Touch Your Church

Love (Our Love for God)

7	All Over Again
14	Arms of Love
12	As the Deer
29	By Your Side
34	Christ Above Me
39	Come and Fill Me Up
56	Fill Me
58	First Love
60	Flowing River
63	Friend of Sinners
64	From My Heart to Yours
66	Glorify Thy Name
82	Hear Me Say I Love You
90	Holy and Anointed One
96	How Could You Love Me So Much?
104	I Give You My Heart
105	I Live to Know You
107	I Love You, Lord
118	In Moments Like These
130	Jesus, Lover of My Soul
138	Knowing You
139	Lamb of God
144	Let the Walls Fall Down
152	Lord, You Love Me
153	Love You So Much
164	My Dwelling Place
162	My Faith Looks Up to Thee
168	My Jesus, I Love Thee
177	Only You
198	Shout to the Lord
197	Shout to the North
199	Someone Else Living in You
206	Take My Life and Let It Be
237	What a Friend I've Found (...Friend Forever)
249	You Make Me Lie Down In Green Pastures

Majesty/Glory/Power of God

9	Above All
4	All Hail King Jesus
5	All Heaven Declares
8	All Honor
13	All the Power You Need
6	Almighty
10	Ancient of Days
18	Be Exalted, O God
21	Beautiful Savior (All My Days)
23	Better is One Day
25	Blessing and Honor
28	By Your Blood
36	Come and See
45	Did You Feel the Mountains Tremble?
67	Glory
68	Glory to the Lamb

78	Great and Mighty is He
73	Great is Thy Faithfulness
82	Hear Me Say I Love You
83	Heaven is in My Heart
87	Here In This Place
93	Holy, Holy (...lift up his name)
92	Holy, Holy, Holy Is the Lord of Hosts
95	Hosanna
102	I Exalt Thee
111	I See the Lord (Baloche)
112	I See the Lord (Falson)
135	Jesus, Your Name
143	Let the River Flow
153	Love You So Much
154	Majesty
157	Meekness and Majesty
158	Mighty is Our God
170	No Other Name
172	O Magnify The Lord
182	Praise Adonai
204	Shine, Jesus Shine
198	Shout to the Lord
195	Sing Unto the Lord
205	The Battle Belongs to the Lord
212	The Name of the Lord (Blessed Be)
221	Thine the Amen, Thine the Praise
223	This Kingdom
226	Victory Chant
242	Worthy the Lamb that Was Slain

Marriage/Wedding

20	Be Thou My Vision
26	Blest Be The Tie That Binds
72	Go, My Children with My Blessing
253	God Knew Your Name
116	I Was There to Hear Your Borning Cry
156	May the Feet of God Walk with You
183	Peace Be Yours

Mercy

see Grace/Mercy

Mission

27	Bring Forth the Kingdom
55	Feed My Lambs
57	Find Us Faithful
69	Go Out As People of God
70	Go, Make Disciples
77	Grace Alone
85	Here Am I
86	Here I Am Lord
110	I Want to Be More Like You
137	Joy and Thanksgiving
142	Let the Flame Burn Brighter
186	Raise Up an Army
204	Shine, Jesus Shine
197	Shout to the North
203	Spirit, Touch Your Church
205	The Battle Belongs to the Lord

— p. 19 —

226 Victory Chant
232 We Are Marching in the Light of God

Name(s) of God
63 Friend of Sinners
66 Glorify Thy Name
78 Great and Mighty is He
81 He Will Come and Save You
89 Holy Is Our God Medley
94 Holy Lamb of God
105 I Live to Know You
134 Jesus, Name Above All Names
135 Jesus, Your Name
137 Joy and Thanksgiving
147 Lift Him Up
154 Majesty
158 Mighty is Our God
170 No Other Name
187 Redeemer Savior Friend
191 Rock of Ages
194 Savior Again to Your Dear Name
197 Shout to the North
212 The Name of the Lord (Blessed Be)
211 There is A Redeemer
229 Waterlife
243 You Are My All in All

Obedience
27 Bring Forth the Kingdom
33 Change My Heart, O God
42 Cry of My Heart
55 Feed My Lambs
56 Fill Me
57 Find Us Faithful
69 Go Out As People of God
70 Go, Make Disciples
79 He is Able
80 He Who Began a Good Work in You
85 Here Am I
86 Here I Am Lord
105 I Live to Know You
109 I Need You
110 I Want to Be More Like You
115 I Want to Walk as a Child of the Light
125 In the Secret (I Want to Know You)
128 It's All About You (Jesus, Lover of My Soul)
131 Jesus, Draw Me Close
149 Light the Fire Again
171 Nobody Fills My Heart Like Jesus
186 Raise Up an Army
189 Renew Me
192 Romans 16:19
199 Someone Else Living in You
206 Take My Life and Let It Be
207 Take Our Lives
213 The Potter's Hand
214 The Power of Your Love
226 Victory Chant

230 We'll Be Faithful
247 You Are Worthy of My Praise

Offertory
27 Bring Forth the Kingdom
29 By Your Side
56 Fill Me
79 He is Able
108 I Offer My Life
115 I Want to Walk as a Child of the Light
117 I Will Celebrate (Baloche)
120 I Will Celebrate (Duvall)
184 Purify My Heart
189 Renew Me
231 We Are an Offering
234 We Bring the Sacrifice of Praise

Ordination
see Installation, Commitment

Palm Sunday
25 Blessing and Honor
95 Hosanna
212 The Name of the Lord (Blessed Be)

Peace
3 A Simple Word of Grace
24 Blessed Assurance
34 Christ Above Me
52 Father Welcomes
53 Feed Us Now
72 Go, My Children with My Blessing
77 Grace Alone
73 Great is Thy Faithfulness
88 Here is Bread
140 Lead Me to the Cross
141 Let It Be Said Of Us
145 Light One Candle
146 Light The Candle
183 Peace Be Yours
194 Savior Again to Your Dear Name
200 Someone Special
225 Tis So Sweet to Trust in Jesus
238 What a Friend we Have in Jesus
249 You Make Me Lie Down In Green Pastures
252 Your Touch is Loving

Pentecost
see Holy Spirit

People of God
see Body of Christ

Power
see Majesty/Glory/Power of God

Praise and Worship
3 A Simple Word of Grace
4 All Hail King Jesus
8 All Honor
7 All Over Again
6 Almighty

10 Ancient of Days
18 Be Exalted, O God
22 Behold the Lamb
24 Blessed Assurance
31 Celebrate Jesus
32 Celebrate the Lord of Love
36 Come and See
37 Come Thou Fount of Every Blessing
38 Crown Him (King of Kings)
45 Did You Feel the Mountains Tremble?
49 Enter In
50 Faithful Father
59 Firm Foundation
62 For the Lord is Good
64 From My Heart to Yours
65 Give Thanks
66 Glorify Thy Name
67 Glory
68 Glory to the Lamb
71 God is Good
74 God is Good All the Time
78 Great and Mighty is He
73 Great is Thy Faithfulness
82 Hear Me Say I Love You
83 Heaven is in My Heart
87 Here In This Place
89 Holy Is Our God Medley
94 Holy Lamb of God
93 Holy, Holy (...lift up his name)
92 Holy, Holy, Holy Is the Lord of Hosts
95 Hosanna
96 How Could You Love Me So Much?
103 I Could Sing of Your Love Forever
102 I Exalt Thee
104 I Give You My Heart
105 I Live to Know You
106 I Love to Be in Your Presence
107 I Love You, Lord
117 I Will Celebrate (Baloche)
120 I Will Celebrate (Duvall)
119 I Will Praise Him
118 In Moments Like These
126 Isn't He?
131 Jesus, Draw Me Close
133 Jesus, Lamb of God
130 Jesus, Lover of My Soul
137 Joy and Thanksgiving
147 Lift Him Up
150 Lord Most High
151 Lord, I Lift Your Name on High
153 Love You So Much
154 Majesty
159 More Love, More Power
161 More Precious Than Silver
165 My Life is In You, Lord
170 No Other Name
172 O Magnify The Lord

173 O The Deep, Deep Love of Jesus
182 Praise Adonai
191 Rock of Ages
198 Shout to the Lord
195 Sing Unto the Lord
208 Thank You, Lord
210 The Lamb
212 The Name of the Lord (Blessed Be)
215 The River is Here
216 Then I Will Praise You
221 Thine the Amen, Thine the Praise
220 This is the Day (Fitts)
219 This is the Day (Shelton)
226 Victory Chant
233 We Bow Down
234 We Bring the Sacrifice of Praise
240 When I Look into Your Holiness
235 When I Survey the Wondrous Cross
242 Worthy the Lamb that Was Slain
243 You Are My All in All
247 You Are Worthy of My Praise
250 Your Love

Prayer
26 Blest Be The Tie That Binds
30 Cares Chorus
48 Eagle's Wings
56 Fill Me
81 He Will Come and Save You
85 Here Am I
142 Let the Flame Burn Brighter
162 My Faith Looks Up to Thee
172 O Magnify The Lord
185 Rest
199 Someone Else Living in You
203 Spirit, Touch Your Church
213 The Potter's Hand
216 Then I Will Praise You
217 These Things Are True of You
232 We Are Marching in the Light of God
238 What a Friend we Have in Jesus

Presence of God
2 A Shield About Me
7 All Over Again
14 Arms of Love
19 Be My Home
20 Be Thou My Vision
23 Better is One Day
28 By Your Blood
29 By Your Side
34 Christ Above Me
35 Come and Behold Him
39 Come and Fill Me Up
47 Draw Me Close to You
48 Eagle's Wings
44 Emmanuel
49 Enter In

50 Faithful Father
51 Father Me, Again
54 Fear Not
55 Feed My Lambs
53 Feed Us Now
60 Flowing River
70 Go, Make Disciples
72 Go, My Children with My Blessing
74 God is Good All the Time
253 God Knew Your Name
76 God Will Make a Way
73 Great is Thy Faithfulness
81 He Will Come and Save You
82 Hear Me Say I Love You
83 Heaven is in My Heart
88 Here is Bread
101 I Believe in Jesus
105 I Live to Know You
106 I Love to Be in Your Presence
113 I Want Jesus to Walk With Me
114 I Want to Be Where You Are
116 I Was There to Hear Your Borning Cry
131 Jesus, Draw Me Close
132 Jesus, Jesus
134 Jesus, Name Above All Names
147 Lift Him Up
146 Light The Candle
153 Love You So Much
156 May the Feet of God Walk with You
160 More of You
164 My Dwelling Place
178 Only By Grace
177 Only You
180 Open the Eyes of My Heart, Lord
183 Peace Be Yours
185 Rest
190 Revival Fire Fall
204 Shine, Jesus Shine
200 Someone Special
213 The Potter's Hand
214 The Power of Your Love
215 The River is Here
216 Then I Will Praise You
220 This is the Day (Fitts)
219 This is the Day (Shelton)
225 Tis So Sweet to Trust in Jesus
239 What is This Bread?
245 You Are My Own
250 Your Love
252 Your Touch is Loving

Protection/Strength
2 A Shield About Me
14 Arms of Love
12 As the Deer
19 Be My Home
23 Better is One Day
29 By Your Side

30 Cares Chorus
34 Christ Above Me
51 Father Me, Again
59 Firm Foundation
65 Give Thanks
72 Go, My Children with My Blessing
74 God is Good All the Time
75 God is the Strength of My Heart
253 God Knew Your Name
76 God Will Make a Way
77 Grace Alone
73 Great is Thy Faithfulness
79 He is Able
81 He Will Come and Save You
97 How Shall I Call You?
113 I Want Jesus to Walk With Me
124 In The Heart of God
130 Jesus, Lover of My Soul
135 Jesus, Your Name
153 Love You So Much
171 Nobody Fills My Heart Like Jesus
176 On Eagle's Wings
181 Our Confidence is In the Lord
183 Peace Be Yours
189 Renew Me
185 Rest
191 Rock of Ages
193 Rock of My Salvation
198 Shout to the Lord
199 Someone Else Living in You
205 The Battle Belongs to the Lord
212 The Name of the Lord (Blessed Be)
216 Then I Will Praise You
218 There is None Like You
217 These Things Are True of You
220 This is the Day (Fitts)
224 Trading My Sorrows
228 Under the Blood
238 What a Friend we Have in Jesus
243 You Are My All in All
244 You Are My Hiding Place
252 Your Touch is Loving

Provision
73 Great is Thy Faithfulness
172 O Magnify The Lord
208 Thank You, Lord
220 This is the Day (Fitts)
249 You Make Me Lie Down In Green Pastures

Reconciliation (with each other)
5 All Heaven Declares
26 Blest Be The Tie That Binds
45 Did You Feel the Mountains Tremble?
141 Let It Be Said Of Us
144 Let the Walls Fall Down

Redemption
see Gospel, Grace/Mercy

Refuge
see Protection/Strength

Renewal/Revival
8 All Honor
39 Come and Fill Me Up
45 Did You Feel the Mountains Tremble?
48 Eagle's Wings
56 Fill Me
61 Foolish Pride
69 Go Out As People of God
115 I Want to Walk as a Child of the Light
132 Jesus, Jesus
133 Jesus, Lamb of God
142 Let the Flame Burn Brighter
143 Let the River Flow
149 Light the Fire Again
162 My Faith Looks Up to Thee
177 Only You
180 Open the Eyes of My Heart, Lord
184 Purify My Heart
186 Raise Up an Army
189 Renew Me
190 Revival Fire Fall
204 Shine, Jesus Shine
197 Shout to the North
199 Someone Else Living in You
201 Spirit of the Living God
203 Spirit, Touch Your Church
214 The Power of Your Love
215 The River is Here
243 You Are My All in All

Repentance
1 A Broken Spirit
33 Change My Heart, O God
52 Father Welcomes
61 Foolish Pride
84 Healer of My Heart
91 Hide Me in Your Holiness
128 It's All About You (Jesus, Lover of My Soul)
187 Redeemer Savior Friend
209 The Heart of Worship
235 When I Survey the Wondrous Cross
241 White As Snow

Rest/Weary
81 He Will Come and Save You
84 Healer of My Heart
99 I Am the Bread of Life (Talbot)
113 I Want Jesus to Walk With Me
124 In The Heart of God
185 Rest
216 Then I Will Praise You
224 Trading My Sorrows
238 What a Friend we Have in Jesus
249 You Make Me Lie Down In Green Pastures

Resurrection
5 All Heaven Declares
25 Blessing and Honor
31 Celebrate Jesus
54 Fear Not
90 Holy and Anointed One
100 I Am the Bread of Life (Toolan)
101 I Believe in Jesus
129 Jesus is Alive
151 Lord, I Lift Your Name on High
185 Rest
229 Waterlife

Righteousness
115 I Want to Walk as a Child of the Light
138 Knowing You
140 Lead Me to the Cross
147 Lift Him Up
149 Light the Fire Again
189 Renew Me
196 See This Wonder
210 The Lamb
217 These Things Are True of You
223 This Kingdom
228 Under the Blood
248 You Rescued Me
246 Your Grace is Sufficient For Me

Sacrifice (of God)
11 Amazing Love
16 As I Look Into Your Eyes
17 At the Cross
22 Behold the Lamb
24 Blessed Assurance
25 Blessing and Honor
40 Come to the Bread of Life
89 Holy Is Our God Medley
96 How Could You Love Me So Much?
98 I Am Not My Own
127 It's Your Blood
139 Lamb of God
157 Meekness and Majesty
174 Once Again
175 Only By the Blood of the Lamb
187 Redeemer Savior Friend
188 Remember Me
200 Someone Special
208 Thank You, Lord
210 The Lamb
211 There is A Redeemer
221 Thine the Amen, Thine the Praise
223 This Kingdom
228 Under the Blood
236 We Remember You
239 What is This Bread?
235 When I Survey the Wondrous Cross
242 Worthy the Lamb that Was Slain
248 You Rescued Me
see also Cross, Gospel, Lamb, Lent

– p. 22 –

– p. 23 –

Safety
see Protection/Strength

Salvation
see Gospel, Grace/Mercy

Sanctification/Character
- 1   A Broken Spirit
- 20   Be Thou My Vision
- 27   Bring Forth the Kingdom
- 29   By Your Side
- 33   Change My Heart, O God
- 37   Come Thou Fount of Every Blessing
- 42   Cry of My Heart
- 55   Feed My Lambs
- 56   Fill Me
- 57   Find Us Faithful
- 58   First Love
- 60   Flowing River
- 61   Foolish Pride
- 77   Grace Alone
- 79   He is Able
- 80   He Who Began a Good Work in You
- 84   Healer of My Heart
- 104   I Give You My Heart
- 105   I Live to Know You
- 110   I Want to Be More Like You
- 115   I Want to Walk as a Child of the Light
- 116   I Was There to Hear Your Borning Cry
- 141   Let It Be Said Of Us
- 149   Light the Fire Again
- 148   Living Stones
- 155   Make Me a Servant
- 179   Only the Blood
- 184   Purify My Heart
- 186   Raise Up an Army
- 187   Redeemer Savior Friend
- 189   Renew Me
- 190   Revival Fire Fall
- 192   Romans 16:19
- 194   Savior Again to Your Dear Name
- 204   Shine, Jesus Shine
- 199   Someone Else Living in You
- 201   Spirit of the Living God
- 206   Take My Life and Let It Be
- 207   Take Our Lives
- 213   The Potter's Hand
- 217   These Things Are True of You
- 229   Waterlife
- 231   We Are an Offering
- 230   We'll Be Faithful
- 245   You Are My Own
- 248   You Rescued Me

Sanctity of Life
- 253   God Knew Your Name

Second Coming
- 83   Heaven is in My Heart
- 100   I Am the Bread of Life (Toolan)
- 116   I Was There to Hear Your Borning Cry
- 167   My Redeemer Lives (Willison)
- 199   Someone Else Living in You

Servanthood
- 27   Bring Forth the Kingdom
- 42   Cry of My Heart
- 70   Go, Make Disciples
- 77   Grace Alone
- 79   He is Able
- 80   He Who Began a Good Work in You
- 105   I Live to Know You
- 108   I Offer My Life
- 110   I Want to Be More Like You
- 155   Make Me a Servant

Singing to God
- 23   Better is One Day
- 82   Hear Me Say I Love You
- 93   Holy, Holy (…lift up his name)
- 106   I Love to Be in Your Presence
- 107   I Love You, Lord
- 118   In Moments Like These
- 133   Jesus, Lamb of God
- 147   Lift Him Up
- 150   Lord Most High
- 151   Lord, I Lift Your Name on High
- 153   Love You So Much
- 164   My Dwelling Place
- 182   Praise Adonai
- 198   Shout to the Lord
- 197   Shout to the North
- 195   Sing Unto the Lord
- 199   Someone Else Living in You
- 206   Take My Life and Let It Be
- 205   The Battle Belongs to the Lord
- 209   The Heart of Worship
- 210   The Lamb
- 226   Victory Chant
- 232   We Are Marching in the Light of God
- 243   You Are My All in All
- 247   You Are Worthy of My Praise
- 249   You Make Me Lie Down In Green Pastures
- 248   You Rescued Me

see also Praise and Worship

Stewardship
- 27   Bring Forth the Kingdom
- 29   By Your Side
- 109   I Need You
- 108   I Offer My Life
- 186   Raise Up an Army
- 201   Spirit of the Living God
- 206   Take My Life and Let It Be
- 209   The Heart of Worship
- 213   The Potter's Hand
- 231   We Are an Offering
- 247   You Are Worthy of My Praise

Strength
see Protection/Strength

Surrender/Submission
- 1   A Broken Spirit
- 12   As the Deer
- 29   By Your Side
- 30   Cares Chorus
- 33   Change My Heart, O God
- 34   Christ Above Me
- 42   Cry of My Heart
- 47   Draw Me Close to You
- 48   Eagle's Wings
- 51   Father Me, Again
- 58   First Love
- 61   Foolish Pride
- 84   Healer of My Heart
- 85   Here Am I
- 104   I Give You My Heart
- 109   I Need You
- 108   I Offer My Life
- 110   I Want to Be More Like You
- 128   It's All About You (Jesus, Lover of My Soul)
- 149   Light the Fire Again
- 159   More Love, More Power
- 168   My Jesus, I Love Thee
- 184   Purify My Heart
- 189   Renew Me
- 201   Spirit of the Living God
- 202   Spirit Song
- 206   Take My Life and Let It Be
- 207   Take Our Lives
- 213   The Potter's Hand
- 226   Victory Chant
- 231   We Are an Offering
- 246   Your Grace is Sufficient For Me

Testimony
see Confession of Faith

Thanksgiving
- 14   Arms of Love
- 18   Be Exalted, O God
- 36   Come and See
- 61   Foolish Pride
- 65   Give Thanks
- 96   How Could You Love Me So Much?
- 106   I Love to Be in Your Presence
- 117   I Will Celebrate (Baloche)
- 120   I Will Celebrate (Duvall)
- 123   I'm Forever Grateful
- 137   Joy and Thanksgiving
- 153   Love You So Much
- 171   Nobody Fills My Heart Like Jesus
- 172   O Magnify The Lord
- 187   Redeemer Savior Friend
- 188   Remember Me
- 199   Someone Else Living in You
- 208   Thank You, Lord
- 210   The Lamb
- 211   There is A Redeemer
- 234   We Bring the Sacrifice of Praise

Trinity
- 8   All Honor
- 66   Glorify Thy Name
- 82   Hear Me Say I Love You
- 89   Holy Is Our God Medley
- 97   How Shall I Call You?
- 229   Waterlife

Trust
- 13   All the Power You Need
- 21   Beautiful Savior (All My Days)
- 24   Blessed Assurance
- 30   Cares Chorus
- 34   Christ Above Me
- 37   Come Thou Fount of Every Blessing
- 43   Comfort Comfort
- 51   Father Me, Again
- 54   Fear Not
- 59   Firm Foundation
- 75   God is the Strength of My Heart
- 76   God Will Make a Way
- 79   He is Able
- 148   Living Stones
- 164   My Dwelling Place
- 176   On Eagle's Wings
- 181   Our Confidence is In the Lord
- 185   Rest
- 213   The Potter's Hand
- 216   Then I Will Praise You
- 225   Tis So Sweet to Trust in Jesus
- 230   We'll Be Faithful
- 243   You Are My All in All
- 244   You Are My Hiding Place
- 247   You Are Worthy of My Praise

Unity
- 45   Did You Feel the Mountains Tremble?
- 88   Here is Bread
- 89   Holy Is Our God Medley
- 141   Let It Be Said Of Us
- 142   Let the Flame Burn Brighter
- 144   Let the Walls Fall Down
- 148   Living Stones
- 186   Raise Up an Army
- 229   Waterlife

Victory
- 13   All the Power You Need
- 6   Almighty
- 20   Be Thou My Vision
- 24   Blessed Assurance
- 25   Blessing and Honor
- 32   Celebrate the Lord of Love
- 43   Comfort Comfort

38	Crown Him (King of Kings)
54	Fear Not
59	Firm Foundation
61	Foolish Pride
65	Give Thanks
68	Glory to the Lamb
76	God Will Make a Way
81	He Will Come and Save You
129	Jesus is Alive
136	Jesus, We Celebrate Your Victory
163	Mourning Into Dancing
183	Peace Be Yours
189	Renew Me
192	Romans 16:19
205	The Battle Belongs to the Lord
221	Thine the Amen, Thine the Praise
224	Trading My Sorrows
226	Victory Chant
227	Victory Song
232	We Are Marching in the Light of God
245	You Are My Own
248	You Rescued Me
246	Your Grace is Sufficient For Me

Word (of God)

27	Bring Forth the Kingdom
34	Christ Above Me
35	Come and Behold Him
52	Father Welcomes
59	Firm Foundation
58	First Love
61	Foolish Pride
74	God is Good All the Time
76	God Will Make a Way
86	Here I Am Lord
90	Holy and Anointed One
116	I Was There to Hear Your Borning Cry
134	Jesus, Name Above All Names
183	Peace Be Yours
199	Someone Else Living in You
223	This Kingdom
226	Victory Chant
227	Victory Song
229	Waterlife
245	You Are My Own
249	You Make Me Lie Down In Green Pastures

Scripture References

Genesis
1:26-27	69	Go Out As People of God
1:26-27	89	Holy Is Our God Medley
3:15	166	My Redeemer Lives (Morgan)
9:6	69	Go Out As People of God
15:1	2	A Shield About Me
22:7-8	210	The Lamb
28:14	197	Shout to the North
28:15	54	Fear Not

Exodus
3:14	49	Enter In
12:13, 22	228	Under the Blood
15:1-3	244	You Are My Hiding Place
15:2	171	Nobody Fills My Heart Like Jesus
15:11	6	Almighty
15:11	218	There is None Like You
17:7	172	O Magnify The Lord
18:11	218	There is None Like You
19:4	48	Eagle's Wings
19:4	176	On Eagle's Wings
19:5	231	We Are an Offering
19:5-6	72	Go, My Children with My Blessing
24:17	128	It's All About You (Jesus, Lover of My Soul)
33:12, 17	253	God Knew Your Name
33:13	42	Cry of My Heart
33:14	185	Rest
34:6-7	50	Faithful Father
34:6-7	73	Great is Thy Faithfulness

Leviticus
11:44	206	Take My Life and Let It Be
25:10-52	45	Did You Feel the Mountains Tremble?
26:12	113	I Want Jesus to Walk With Me
27:17-24	45	Did You Feel the Mountains Tremble?

Numbers
6:24-26	72	Go, My Children with My Blessing
6:24-26	183	Peace Be Yours
12:7	57	Find Us Faithful

Deuteronomy
3:24	191	Rock of Ages
3:24	218	There is None Like You
4:24	128	It's All About You (Jesus, Lover of My Soul)
4:29	159	More Love, More Power
6:4-5	159	More Love, More Power
6:5	29	By Your Side
6:5	58	First Love
6:5	64	From My Heart to Yours
6:5	104	I Give You My Heart
6:5	153	Love You So Much
6:5	165	My Life is In You, Lord
6:5	199	Someone Else Living in You
6:5	247	You Are Worthy of My Praise
6:5-9	55	Feed My Lambs
7:6	72	Go, My Children with My Blessing
10:12	29	By Your Side
10:12	58	First Love
10:12	64	From My Heart to Yours
10:14	231	We Are an Offering
10:20	199	Someone Else Living in You
11:1, 13, 22	64	From My Heart to Yours
11:13, 22	199	Someone Else Living in You
11:24	142	Let the Flame Burn Brighter
13:3	64	From My Heart to Yours
13:4	199	Someone Else Living in You
14:2	72	Go, My Children with My Blessing
19:9	64	From My Heart to Yours
20:1	54	Fear Not
26:18-19	72	Go, My Children with My Blessing
30:6	58	First Love
30:6, 16, 20	64	From My Heart to Yours
30:20	199	Someone Else Living in You
31:6-8	74	God is Good All the Time
31:8	220	This is the Day (Fitts)
32:4	226	Victory Chant
32:10	96	How Could You Love Me So Much?
32:31, 39	191	Rock of Ages
33:27	14	Arms of Love
33:27	29	By Your Side
33:29	2	A Shield About Me

Joshua
1:3	142	Let the Flame Burn Brighter
1:5	47	Draw Me Close to You
1:5-7, 9	81	He Will Come and Save You
1:6-9	54	Fear Not
6:5, 20	144	Let the Walls Fall Down
6:13	232	We Are Marching in the Light of God
14:9	142	Let the Flame Burn Brighter
21:44	185	Rest
21:45	198	Shout to the Lord
22:5	64	From My Heart to Yours

Ref	#	Title
22:5	199	Someone Else Living in You
23:11	64	From My Heart to Yours
23:11	153	Love You So Much
23:14	198	Shout to the Lord

Judges

Ref	#	Title
5:1	244	You Are My Hiding Place
5:2-3	87	Here In This Place

Ruth

Ref	#	Title
1:16-17	155	Make Me a Servant

1 Samuel

Ref	#	Title
2:2	191	Rock of Ages
2:2	193	Rock of My Salvation
2:8	243	You Are My All in All
3:4-10	86	Here I Am Lord
12:24	209	The Heart of Worship
16:7	209	The Heart of Worship
17:47	205	The Battle Belongs to the Lord

2 Samuel

Ref	#	Title
5:24-25	232	We Are Marching in the Light of God
6:14-16	32	Celebrate the Lord of Love
6:21	31	Celebrate Jesus
6:21	32	Celebrate the Lord of Love
22:1	244	You Are My Hiding Place
22:3	176	On Eagle's Wings
22:3	212	The Name of the Lord (Blessed Be)
22:3	252	Your Touch is Loving
22:4	68	Glory to the Lamb
22:31	226	Victory Chant
22:47	212	The Name of the Lord (Blessed Be)

1 Kings

Ref	#	Title
3:9-12	192	Romans 16:19
8:54	233	We Bow Down
8:56	198	Shout to the Lord
19:11	105	I Live to Know You
19:12-13	125	In the Secret (I Want to Know You)

2 Kings

Ref	#	Title
17:36	247	You Are Worthy of My Praise
23:25	159	More Love, More Power
23:25	247	You Are Worthy of My Praise

1 Chronicles

Ref	#	Title
14:15-16	232	We Are Marching in the Light of God
15:27-28	232	We Are Marching in the Light of God
16:8	208	Thank You, Lord
16:23-25	195	Sing Unto the Lord
16:25	16	As I Look Into Your Eyes
16:25	68	Glory to the Lamb
16:25	247	You Are Worthy of My Praise
16:28-29	8	All Honor
16:29	78	Great and Mighty is He
16:34, 41	251	Your Everlasting Love
16:36	182	Praise Adonai
17:20	218	There is None Like You
22:19	20	Be Thou My Vision
28:9	131	Jesus, Draw Me Close
28:20	54	Fear Not
28:20	81	He Will Come and Save You
29:11	25	Blessing and Honor
29:11	67	Glory
29:11	78	Great and Mighty is He
29:11	154	Majesty
29:11-16	231	We Are an Offering
29:14	108	I Offer My Life
29:17	209	The Heart of Worship
29:20	182	Praise Adonai

2 Chronicles

Ref	#	Title
6:40	87	Here In This Place
6:40	107	I Love You, Lord
7:15	87	Here In This Place
14:11	205	The Battle Belongs to the Lord
15:2	131	Jesus, Draw Me Close
20:15	205	The Battle Belongs to the Lord
20:15	227	Victory Song
20:21	103	I Could Sing of Your Love Forever
20:21	251	Your Everlasting Love
20:21-22	232	We Are Marching in the Light of God
32:7-8	205	The Battle Belongs to the Lord

Ezra

Ref	#	Title
3:11	153	Love You So Much
3:11	234	We Bring the Sacrifice of Praise

Nehemiah

Ref	#	Title
1:1, 6, 11	156	May the Feet of God Walk with You
8:10	224	Trading My Sorrows
9:5-6	182	Praise Adonai
9:5-6	212	The Name of the Lord (Blessed Be)

Esther

Ref	#	Title
9:22	163	Mourning Into Dancing
9:22	224	Trading My Sorrows

Job

Ref	#	Title
5:19	113	I Want Jesus to Walk With Me
7:17	200	Someone Special
11:17	74	God is Good All the Time
14:5	109	I Need You
19:25-27	166	My Redeemer Lives (Morgan)
19:25-27	167	My Redeemer Lives (Willison)
19:25-27	211	There is A Redeemer
32:18-19	143	Let the River Flow
33:4	48	Eagle's Wings
37:22	154	Majesty
40:10	78	Great and Mighty is He
41:11	231	We Are an Offering

Psalm

Ref	#	Title
2:9	85	Here Am I
3:3	2	A Shield About Me
3:3	132	Jesus, Jesus
3:6	244	You Are My Hiding Place
4:7	171	Nobody Fills My Heart Like Jesus
5:8	51	Father Me, Again
5:11	19	Be My Home
5:11	63	Friend of Sinners
5:11	103	I Could Sing of Your Love Forever
6:9	21	Beautiful Savior (All My Days)
8:1, 9	18	Be Exalted, O God
8:4	200	Someone Special
9:1	153	Love You So Much
9:7	5	All Heaven Declares
9:9	244	You Are My Hiding Place
16:2	161	More Precious Than Silver
16:8-11	106	I Love to Be in Your Presence
16:11	56	Fill Me
16:11	83	Heaven is in My Heart
16:11	105	I Live to Know You
16:11	114	I Want to Be Where You Are
17:8	91	Hide Me in Your Holiness
17:8	96	How Could You Love Me So Much?
17:15	23	Better is One Day
17:15	105	I Live to Know You
17:15	114	I Want to Be Where You Are
17:15	166	My Redeemer Lives (Morgan)
17:15	167	My Redeemer Lives (Willison)
18:1	64	From My Heart to Yours
18:1	82	Hear Me Say I Love You
18:1	107	I Love You, Lord
18:1	118	In Moments Like These
18:1	153	Love You So Much
18:1	168	My Jesus, I Love Thee
18:1-2	165	My Life is In You, Lord
18:1-2	193	Rock of My Salvation
18:2	2	A Shield About Me
18:2	191	Rock of Ages
18:2	212	The Name of the Lord (Blessed Be)
18:2	252	Your Touch is Loving
18:3	16	As I Look Into Your Eyes
18:3	68	Glory to the Lamb
18:3	247	You Are Worthy of My Praise
18:4-6	216	Then I Will Praise You
18:5-6	244	You Are My Hiding Place
18:7-15	45	Did You Feel the Mountains Tremble?
18:10	124	In The Heart of God
18:16	216	Then I Will Praise You
18:16-17	130	Jesus, Lover of My Soul
18:28	115	I Want to Walk as a Child of the Light
18:30	226	Victory Chant
18:49	18	Be Exalted, O God
19:13	189	Renew Me
20:7	205	The Battle Belongs to the Lord
22:1	239	What is This Bread?
22:3	65	Give Thanks
22:6	174	Once Again
22:27-29	150	Lord Most High
23:2	249	You Make Me Lie Down In Green Pastures
23:4	47	Draw Me Close to You
23:4	74	God is Good All the Time
23:4	244	You Are My Hiding Place
23:5	243	You Are My All in All
23:6	21	Beautiful Savior (All My Days)
23:6	114	I Want to Be Where You Are
24:1	231	We Are an Offering
24:4-5	184	Purify My Heart
24:8	78	Great and Mighty is He
24:8-10	235	When I Survey the Wondrous Cross
25:16-18	216	Then I Will Praise You
25:20	19	Be My Home
26:8	23	Better is One Day
26:8	240	When I Look into Your Holiness
26:9	177	Only You
27:1	19	Be My Home
27:1	252	Your Touch is Loving
27:1-2	54	Fear Not
27:1-2	59	Firm Foundation
27:1-3	244	You Are My Hiding Place
27:4	21	Beautiful Savior (All My Days)
27:4	23	Better is One Day
27:4	35	Come and Behold Him
27:4	47	Draw Me Close to You

Ref	#	Title
27:4	240	When I Look into Your Holiness
27:4	247	You Are Worthy of My Praise
27:5	14	Arms of Love
27:5	48	Eagle's Wings
27:5	124	In The Heart of God
27:5	130	Jesus, Lover of My Soul
27:5	244	You Are My Hiding Place
27:6	232	We Are Marching in the Light of God
27:10	237	What a Friend I've Found (...Friend Forever)
27:11	42	Cry of My Heart
27:11	51	Father Me, Again
28:1	193	Rock of My Salvation
28:6-7	21	Beautiful Savior (All My Days)
28:7	2	A Shield About Me
28:7	137	Joy and Thanksgiving
28:7	165	My Life is In You, Lord
28:7-8	224	Trading My Sorrows
28:8	59	Firm Foundation
29:1-2	8	All Honor
29:2	78	Great and Mighty is He
29:2	135	Jesus, Your Name
29:2	158	Mighty is Our God
29:11	252	Your Touch is Loving
30:1	216	Then I Will Praise You
30:5	15	As High As the Heaven
30:5	163	Mourning Into Dancing
30:5, 11	224	Trading My Sorrows
30:11-12	163	Mourning Into Dancing
30:12	123	I'm Forever Grateful
31:1-2	19	Be My Home
31:3	193	Rock of My Salvation
31:19	198	Shout to the Lord
31:22	21	Beautiful Savior (All My Days)
31:33	64	From My Heart to Yours
32:5	109	I Need You
32:7	244	You Are My Hiding Place
32:8	42	Cry of My Heart
32:11	219	This is the Day (Shelton)
33:1	195	Sing Unto the Lord
33:2-3	182	Praise Adonai
33:4	217	These Things Are True of You
34:1	208	Thank You, Lord
34:1-2	31	Celebrate Jesus
34:1-6, 15-20	172	O Magnify The Lord
34:5	240	When I Look into Your Holiness
34:8	239	What is This Bread?
34:15-19	113	I Want Jesus to Walk With Me
34:18	1	A Broken Spirit
35:8-9	84	Healer of My Heart
35:9	107	I Love You, Lord
35:27	107	I Love You, Lord
36:5	15	As High As the Heaven
36:5	50	Faithful Father
36:5	73	Great is Thy Faithfulness
36:5	173	O The Deep, Deep Love of Jesus
36:7	14	Arms of Love
36:7-9	37	Come Thou Fount of Every Blessing
36:8-9	199	Someone Else Living in You
36:8-9	215	The River is Here
36:9	19	Be My Home
36:9	21	Beautiful Savior (All My Days)
37:3, 5, 7	30	Cares Chorus
37:4	47	Draw Me Close to You
37:4	171	Nobody Fills My Heart Like Jesus
40:1-3	21	Beautiful Savior (All My Days)
40:2	130	Jesus, Lover of My Soul
40:2-3	216	Then I Will Praise You
40:3	244	You Are My Hiding Place
40:8	190	Revival Fire, Fall
40:8	226	Victory Chant
40:10	62	For the Lord is Good
40:16	64	From My Heart to Yours
41:4, 10	109	I Need You
42:1	160	More of You
42:1-2	12	As the Deer
42:1-2	39	Come and Fill Me Up
42:1-2	47	Draw Me Close to You
42:1-2	75	God is the Strength of My Heart
42:1-2	104	I Give You My Heart
42:1-4	177	Only You
42:2	199	Someone Else Living in You
42:4	137	Joy and Thanksgiving
42:7-8	177	Only You
42:8	118	In Moments Like These
43:3	19	Be My Home
43:3-4	154	Majesty
43:3-4	171	Nobody Fills My Heart Like Jesus
43:4	78	Great and Mighty is He
45:3-4	14	Arms of Love
46:1	165	My Life is In You, Lord
46:1-3	130	Jesus, Lover of My Soul
46:1-3, 11	244	You Are My Hiding Place
46:4	60	Flowing River
46:4	103	I Could Sing of Your Love Forever
46:4	215	The River is Here
46:7	47	Draw Me Close to You
46:7, 11	44	Emmanuel
46:7, 11	134	Jesus, Name Above All Names
46:7-11	54	Fear Not
46:10	102	I Exalt Thee
47:1	198	Shout to the Lord
47:7-8	232	We Are Marching in the Light of God
48:1	16	As I Look Into Your Eyes
48:1	68	Glory to the Lamb
48:1	78	Great and Mighty is He
48:1	247	You Are Worthy of My Praise
48:10	150	Lord Most High
50:2	35	Come and Behold Him
50:12	231	We Are an Offering
50:14	87	Here In This Place
50:14, 23	234	We Bring the Sacrifice of Praise
50:23	172	O Magnify The Lord
51:1	222	Think About His Love
51:1-3, 7	109	I Need You
51:2	246	Your Grace is Sufficient For Me
51:6, 10	209	The Heart of Worship
51:6-7	207	Take Our Lives
51:7	179	Only the Blood
51:7	241	White As Snow
51:10	33	Change My Heart, O God
51:10-12	56	Fill Me
51:10-12	189	Renew Me
51:12	203	Spirit, Touch Your Church
51:17	1	A Broken Spirit
55:12-13	238	What a Friend we Have in Jesus
55:22	30	Cares Chorus
56:13	19	Be My Home
57:5, 9-11	18	Be Exalted, O God
57:7	199	Someone Else Living in You
57:10	15	As High As the Heaven
57:10	173	O The Deep, Deep Love of Jesus
59:16	103	I Could Sing of Your Love Forever
59:16	224	Trading My Sorrows
60:12	227	Victory Song
61:2	51	Father Me, Again
61:2	130	Jesus, Lover of My Soul
61:4	124	In The Heart of God
62:1-2	181	Our Confidence is In the Lord
62:2, 5-7	193	Rock of My Salvation
62:7	176	On Eagle's Wings
63:1	84	Healer of My Heart
63:1	160	More of You
63:1	177	Only You
63:1	199	Someone Else Living in You
63:1-5	12	As the Deer
63:1-5	39	Come and Fill Me Up
63:1-8	47	Draw Me Close to You
63:2	35	Come and Behold Him
63:2-5	23	Better is One Day
63:2-5	171	Nobody Fills My Heart Like Jesus
63:4	117	I Will Celebrate (Baloche)
63:4	120	I Will Celebrate (Duvall)
63:4	147	Lift Him Up
65:4	105	I Live to Know You
65:13	32	Celebrate the Lord of Love
66:1-4	198	Shout to the Lord
66:5, 16	36	Come and See
66:9	243	You Are My All in All
68:34	8	All Honor
69:1-2, 13-18	130	Jesus, Lover of My Soul
69:1-2, 14-18	216	Then I Will Praise You
69:30-31	234	We Bring the Sacrifice of Praise
69:36	63	Friend of Sinners
71:1-3	19	Be My Home
71:3	193	Rock of My Salvation
71:3, 19	191	Rock of Ages
71:5-6	253	God Knew Your Name
71:8	147	Lift Him Up
71:17-19	186	Raise Up an Army
71:22	65	Give Thanks
71:23	151	Lord, I Lift Your Name on High
72:17-19	212	The Name of the Lord (Blessed Be)
72:18-19	25	Blessing and Honor
72:18-19	67	Glory
73:1	71	God is Good
73:1	74	God is Good All the Time
73:25	47	Draw Me Close to You
73:25	104	I Give You My Heart
73:25	159	More Love, More Power
73:25	160	More of You
73:25	161	More Precious Than Silver
73:25-26	75	God is the Strength of My Heart
73:28	19	Be My Home
73:28	71	God is Good
73:28	74	God is Good All the Time
78:11	172	O Magnify The Lord
79:9	179	Only the Blood
79:13	69	Go Out As People of God

Reference	#	Title
80:18-19	190	Revival Fire, Fall
81:16	86	Here I Am Lord
83:18	9	Above All
83:18	102	I Exalt Thee
83:18	150	Lord Most High
84:1	164	My Dwelling Place
84:1-2, 10	23	Better is One Day
84:2	12	As the Deer
84:2	39	Come and Fill Me Up
84:2	42	Cry of My Heart
84:2	47	Draw Me Close to You
84:2	177	Only You
84:2	201	Spirit of the Living God
84:10	240	When I Look into Your Holiness
84:11	71	God is Good
84:11	74	God is Good All the Time
85:6	189	Renew Me
85:6	190	Revival Fire, Fall
85:8	194	Savior Again to Your Dear Name
86:1	184	Purify My Heart
86:4	177	Only You
86:5	62	For the Lord is Good
86:5, 15	222	Think About His Love
86:6	156	May the Feet of God Walk with You
86:8	191	Rock of Ages
86:8	218	There is None Like You
86:11	42	Cry of My Heart
86:12	66	Glorify Thy Name
86:12	153	Love You So Much
86:13	130	Jesus, Lover of My Soul
89:1	62	For the Lord is Good
89:1-2	18	Be Exalted, O God
89:1-2	73	Great is Thy Faithfulness
89:1-2, 5, 8	50	Faithful Father
89:1-7	78	Great and Mighty is He
89:6, 8	191	Rock of Ages
89:8	158	Mighty is Our God
89:11	231	We Are an Offering
89:27	134	Jesus, Name Above All Names
90:1	164	My Dwelling Place
90:4	103	I Could Sing of Your Love Forever
90:12	109	I Need You
90:14	21	Beautiful Savior (All My Days)
90:14	177	Only You
91:1-10	176	On Eagle's Wings
91:1-2	14	Arms of Love
91:1-2	124	In The Heart of God
91:2	193	Rock of My Salvation
91:2	252	Your Touch is Loving
91:4	19	Be My Home
91:4	48	Eagle's Wings
91:11	72	Go, My Children with My Blessing
91:11-12	253	God Knew Your Name
91:14	212	The Name of the Lord (Blessed Be)
91:15	172	O Magnify The Lord
92:1	154	Majesty
92:1	182	Praise Adonai
93:1	78	Great and Mighty is He
93:4	158	Mighty is Our God
95:1	198	Shout to the Lord
95:1-7	150	Lord Most High
95:2	232	We Are Marching in the Light of God
95:3	102	I Exalt Thee
95:6	247	You Are Worthy of My Praise
95:6-7	233	We Bow Down
95:7	69	Go Out As People of God
96:1	64	From My Heart to Yours
96:1	117	I Will Celebrate (Baloche)
96:1	120	I Will Celebrate (Duvall)
96:1, 4	195	Sing Unto the Lord
96:1-9	150	Lord Most High
96:4	16	As I Look Into Your Eyes
96:4	68	Glory to the Lamb
96:4-9	78	Great and Mighty is He
96:7-8	8	All Honor
96:11-13	32	Celebrate the Lord of Love
97:9	9	Above All
97:9	18	Be Exalted, O God
97:9	102	I Exalt Thee
97:9	150	Lord Most High
97:12	219	This is the Day (Shelton)
98:1	117	I Will Celebrate (Baloche)
98:1	120	I Will Celebrate (Duvall)
98:1-9	198	Shout to the Lord
98:7-9	32	Celebrate the Lord of Love
100:1-2	198	Shout to the Lord
100:3	69	Go Out As People of God
100:4	49	Enter In
100:4	65	Give Thanks
100:5	62	For the Lord is Good
101:1	64	From My Heart to Yours
101:2	192	Romans 16:19
102:12	5	All Heaven Declares
103:1	153	Love You So Much
103:1-2	182	Praise Adonai
103:1-4	178	Only By Grace
103:5	48	Eagle's Wings
103:5	176	On Eagle's Wings
103:8	222	Think About His Love
103:11, 17	173	O The Deep, Deep Love of Jesus
103:11-12	15	As High As the Heaven
103:12	28	By Your Blood
103:17	251	Your Everlasting Love
103:20-22	182	Praise Adonai
104:1	154	Majesty
104:1	182	Praise Adonai
104:32-33	45	Did You Feel the Mountains Tremble?
104:33	117	I Will Celebrate (Baloche)
104:33	120	I Will Celebrate (Duvall)
104:35	182	Praise Adonai
105:2	186	Raise Up an Army
106:1	62	For the Lord is Good
106:1-2	182	Praise Adonai
106:13	172	O Magnify The Lord
107:1, 8	62	For the Lord is Good
107:9	39	Come and Fill Me Up
107:15, 22	62	For the Lord is Good
107:21-22	234	We Bring the Sacrifice of Praise
107:22	65	Give Thanks
107:22	234	We Bring the Sacrifice of Praise
108:1	199	Someone Else Living in You
108:3-5	18	Be Exalted, O God
108:4	62	For the Lord is Good
108:13	227	Victory Song
110:1-2	10	Ancient of Days
111:1	153	Love You So Much
112:6-8	181	Our Confidence is In the Lord
116:1	64	From My Heart to Yours
116:1	82	Hear Me Say I Love You
116:1	107	I Love You, Lord
116:1-2	21	Beautiful Savior (All My Days)
116:1-6	168	My Jesus, I Love Thee
116:3-9	216	Then I Will Praise You
116:6	49	Enter In
116:7	185	Rest
116:13	243	You Are My All in All
116:17	65	Give Thanks
116:17-19	234	We Bring the Sacrifice of Praise
117:1	182	Praise Adonai
117:2	62	For the Lord is Good
118:6-7	244	You Are My Hiding Place
118:14	171	Nobody Fills My Heart Like Jesus
118:18	180	Open the Eyes of My Heart, Lord
118:19	49	Enter In
118:19-23	45	Did You Feel the Mountains Tremble?
118:22	148	Living Stones
118:24	220	This is the Day (Fitts)
118:24	219	This is the Day (Shelton)
118:25-26	95	Hosanna
118:26	212	The Name of the Lord (Blessed Be)
119:17-20	42	Cry of My Heart
119:18	213	The Potter's Hand
119:20	12	As the Deer
119:20	160	More of You
119:31	199	Someone Else Living in You
119:35-37	20	Be Thou My Vision
119:40	160	More of You
119:48	39	Come and Fill Me Up
119:57	75	God is the Strength of My Heart
119:68	62	For the Lord is Good
119:72	161	More Precious Than Silver
119:81	39	Come and Fill Me Up
119:103-105	90	Holy and Anointed One
119:105	19	Be My Home
119:105	51	Father Me, Again
119:105	56	Fill Me
119:114	2	A Shield About Me
119:114	124	In The Heart of God
119:114	244	You Are My Hiding Place
119:127	159	More Love, More Power
119:127, 131	12	As the Deer
119:131	243	You Are My All in All
119:132	63	Friend of Sinners
119:133	189	Renew Me
121:2	97	How Shall I Call You?
121:4-8	72	Go, My Children with My Blessing
123:3	109	I Need You
124:8	97	How Shall I Call You?
125:1	30	Cares Chorus
125:1-2	217	These Things Are True of You
126:1-2	163	Mourning Into Dancing
126:5-6	15	As High As the Heaven
130:1-2	21	Beautiful Savior (All My Days)
130:1-2, 5-6	216	Then I Will Praise You
130:2	156	May the Feet of God Walk with You
130:3-4	178	Only By Grace
130:5-6	125	In the Secret (I Want to Know You)
133:1	26	Blest Be The Tie That Binds
134:1	182	Praise Adonai
134:2	118	In Moments Like These
135:1-3, 19-21	182	Praise Adonai

Ref	No.	Title
136:1	251	Your Everlasting Love
138:1	153	Love You So Much
138:6	61	Foolish Pride
138:7	244	You Are My Hiding Place
138:8	80	He Who Began a Good Work in You
139:1-16	116	I Was There to Hear Your Borning Cry
139:1-4	34	Christ Above Me
139:3	109	I Need You
139:7	250	Your Love
139:13-16	50	Faithful Father
142:5	75	God is the Strength of My Heart
143:6	39	Come and Fill Me Up
143:6	75	God is the Strength of My Heart
143:6	177	Only You
143:6-7	12	As the Deer
143:6-8	47	Draw Me Close to You
143:6-8	104	I Give You My Heart
143:9	244	You Are My Hiding Place
143:10	51	Father Me, Again
144:3	200	Someone Special
144:5-6	45	Did You Feel the Mountains Tremble?
145:1-2	147	Lift Him Up
145:2	123	I'm Forever Grateful
145:3	16	As I Look Into Your Eyes
145:3	68	Glory to the Lamb
145:3	78	Great and Mighty is He
145:3	247	You Are Worthy of My Praise
145:3-7	6	Almighty
145:13	198	Shout to the Lord
145:16	160	More of You
145:18	131	Jesus, Draw Me Close
145:18-20	172	O Magnify The Lord
145:21	147	Lift Him Up
146:1-2	182	Praise Adonai
146:2	117	I Will Celebrate (Baloche)
146:2	120	I Will Celebrate (Duvall)
146:6	50	Faithful Father
146:7-9	6	Almighty
147:1	153	Love You So Much
147:5	78	Great and Mighty is He
147:11	107	I Love You, Lord
147:14	86	Here I Am Lord
148:1-14	182	Praise Adonai
149:1	195	Sing Unto the Lord
149:4	107	I Love You, Lord
150:1-6	182	Praise Adonai
150:3-6	137	Joy and Thanksgiving

Proverbs

Ref	No.	Title
2:1-22	20	Be Thou My Vision
3:5	30	Cares Chorus
3:5	124	In The Heart of God
3:5-6	185	Rest
3:15	161	More Precious Than Silver
3:34	61	Foolish Pride
8:11	161	More Precious Than Silver
15:33	61	Foolish Pride
17:3	184	Purify My Heart
18:10	212	The Name of the Lord (Blessed Be)
18:10	252	Your Touch is Loving
18:24	237	What a Friend I've Found (...Friend Forever)
18:24	238	What a Friend we Have in Jesus
20:9	189	Renew Me
21:31	227	Victory Song
27:21	20	Be Thou My Vision

Ecclesiastes

Ref	No.	Title
8:15	21	Beautiful Savior (All My Days)

Song of Songs

Ref	No.	Title
2:16	118	In Moments Like These
2:16	168	My Jesus, I Love Thee

Isaiah

Ref	No.	Title
1:18	179	Only the Blood
1:18	228	Under the Blood
1:18	241	White As Snow
1:25	184	Purify My Heart
6:1, 3	111	I See the Lord (Baloche)
6:1, 3	112	I See the Lord (Falson)
6:1-3	180	Open the Eyes of My Heart, Lord
6:2-3	89	Holy Is Our God Medley
6:3	6	Almighty
6:3	93	Holy, Holy (...lift up his name)
6:3	92	Holy, Holy, Holy Is the Lord of Hosts
6:3	133	Jesus, Lamb of God
6:8	85	Here Am I
6:8	86	Here I Am Lord
7:14	4	All Hail King Jesus
7:14	38	Crown Him (King of Kings)
7:14	44	Emmanuel
7:14	67	Glory
7:14	146	Light The Candle
8:8-10	44	Emmanuel
8:17	125	In the Secret (I Want to Know You)
9:2	145	Light One Candle
9:2, 6	146	Light The Candle
9:6	21	Beautiful Savior (All My Days)
9:6	38	Crown Him (King of Kings)
9:6	44	Emmanuel
9:6	67	Glory
9:6	126	Isn't He?
9:6	134	Jesus, Name Above All Names
11:6-9	26	Blest Be The Tie That Binds
12:2	30	Cares Chorus
12:2	165	My Life is In You, Lord
12:2	171	Nobody Fills My Heart Like Jesus
12:3	37	Come Thou Fount of Every Blessing
12:3	84	Healer of My Heart
12:3	199	Someone Else Living in You
12:6	65	Give Thanks
12:6	198	Shout to the Lord
20:24	86	Here I Am Lord
24:14	154	Majesty
24:16	150	Lord Most High
25:1	50	Faithful Father
25:8	163	Mourning Into Dancing
26:2	45	Did You Feel the Mountains Tremble?
26:3	252	Your Touch is Loving
26:3-4	30	Cares Chorus
26:8-9	47	Draw Me Close to You
26:8-9	104	I Give You My Heart
26:8-9	160	More of You
26:9	12	As the Deer
26:12	108	I Offer My Life
26:12	231	We Are an Offering
28:12	185	Rest
28:16	59	Firm Foundation
28:16	81	He Will Come and Save You
28:16	148	Living Stones
29:13	209	The Heart of Worship
29:16	213	The Potter's Hand
29:19	65	Give Thanks
30:23	249	You Make Me Lie Down In Green Pastures
30:27, 30	128	It's All About You (Jesus, Lover of My Soul)
33:2	73	Great is Thy Faithfulness
34:4	76	God Will Make a Way
35:3-4	43	Comfort Comfort
35:3-4	81	He Will Come and Save You
35:6-10	76	God Will Make a Way
35:10	224	Trading My Sorrows
40:1-2	81	He Will Come and Save You
40:1-4	43	Comfort Comfort
40:3-4	76	God Will Make a Way
40:3-5	45	Did You Feel the Mountains Tremble?
40:6-8	76	God Will Make a Way
40:11	14	Arms of Love
40:11	29	By Your Side
40:11	55	Feed My Lambs
40:18	191	Rock of Ages
40:28-31	48	Eagle's Wings
40:29-31	13	All the Power You Need
40:31	214	The Power of Your Love
41:8	237	What a Friend I've Found (...Friend Forever)
41:8	238	What a Friend we Have in Jesus
41:10	47	Draw Me Close to You
41:10	54	Fear Not
41:10	81	He Will Come and Save You
41:10	244	You Are My Hiding Place
41:10-14	81	He Will Come and Save You
41:10-14, 27	43	Comfort Comfort
41:13	51	Father Me, Again
41:17-18	84	Healer of My Heart
41:18	76	God Will Make a Way
41:18	215	The River is Here
42:1	90	Holy and Anointed One
42:6	51	Father Me, Again
42:6	72	Go, My Children with My Blessing
42:6	145	Light One Candle
42:6-7	146	Light The Candle
42:10	117	I Will Celebrate (Baloche)
42:10	120	I Will Celebrate (Duvall)
42:10-12	150	Lord Most High
42:11	137	Joy and Thanksgiving
43:1-3	72	Go, My Children with My Blessing
43:1-5	54	Fear Not
43:1-6	81	He Will Come and Save You
43:5-7	197	Shout to the North
43:19	76	God Will Make a Way
44:2	81	He Will Come and Save You
44:3	143	Let the River Flow
44:3	199	Someone Else Living in You
44:3-4	60	Flowing River
44:22	241	White As Snow
44:23	32	Celebrate the Lord of Love
44:23	198	Shout to the Lord
45:9	213	The Potter's Hand
45:22	162	My Faith Looks Up to Thee
47:4	187	Redeemer Savior Friend
49:1, 5	253	God Knew Your Name
49:6	145	Light One Candle
49:6	146	Light The Candle
49:6	186	Raise Up an Army
49:9-10	249	You Make Me Lie Down In Green Pastures

Ref	#	Title
49:13	32	Celebrate the Lord of Love
49:15	237	What a Friend I've Found (...Friend Forever)
50:5	42	Cry of My Heart
50:10	56	Fill Me
50:10	115	I Want to Walk as a Child of the Light
51:1	193	Rock of My Salvation
51:3	137	Joy and Thanksgiving
51:3, 11	224	Trading My Sorrows
51:3, 12	43	Comfort Comfort
51:6	76	God Will Make a Way
51:9	186	Raise Up an Army
52:7	206	Take My Life and Let It Be
52:7	226	Victory Chant
52:10	186	Raise Up an Army
52:13	157	Meekness and Majesty
53:3	11	Amazing Love
53:4	239	What is This Bread?
53:5	122	I Will Glory in The Cross
53:6	187	Redeemer Savior Friend
53:6	210	The Lamb
53:7	210	The Lamb
53:9	151	Lord, I Lift Your Name on High
54:4-5	81	He Will Come and Save You
54:5	166	My Redeemer Lives (Morgan)
54:5	167	My Redeemer Lives (Willison)
54:10	76	God Will Make a Way
54:17	205	The Battle Belongs to the Lord
54:17	228	Under the Blood
55:1	39	Come and Fill Me Up
55:1	84	Healer of My Heart
55:1	199	Someone Else Living in You
55:1-2	37	Come Thou Fount of Every Blessing
55:1-2	41	Come to the Table
55:6-7	131	Jesus, Draw Me Close
55:8-9	128	It's All About You (Jesus, Lover of My Soul)
55:9	74	God is Good All the Time
55:11	76	God Will Make a Way
55:12	32	Celebrate the Lord of Love
56:6	63	Friend of Sinners
57:15	1	A Broken Spirit
57:15	61	Foolish Pride
57:18-19	194	Savior Again to Your Dear Name
58:6	45	Did You Feel the Mountains Tremble?
58:8-10	74	God is Good All the Time
59:20	187	Redeemer Savior Friend
59:20-21	211	There is A Redeemer
59:21	60	Flowing River
59:21	199	Someone Else Living in You
60:1-3	145	Light One Candle
60:1-3	146	Light The Candle
60:1-3	204	Shine, Jesus Shine
60:2	216	Then I Will Praise You
60:19	132	Jesus, Jesus
61:1	90	Holy and Anointed One
61:1-2	186	Raise Up an Army
61:1-3	6	Almighty
61:1-3	43	Comfort Comfort
61:2	45	Did You Feel the Mountains Tremble?
61:3	224	Trading My Sorrows
62:2, 4	121	I Will Change Your Name
62:10	45	Did You Feel the Mountains Tremble?
63:7	71	God is Good
63:7	74	God is Good All the Time
64:1-3	45	Did You Feel the Mountains Tremble?
64:8	33	Change My Heart, O God
64:8	82	Hear Me Say I Love You
64:8	213	The Potter's Hand
65:1	85	Here Am I
65:1	86	Here I Am Lord
65:8	33	Change My Heart, O God
65:14	232	We Are Marching in the Light of God
65:15	121	I Will Change Your Name
66:2	1	A Broken Spirit
66:2	61	Foolish Pride
66:2	209	The Heart of Worship
66:18	36	Come and See
66:18-19	186	Raise Up an Army

Jeremiah

Ref	#	Title
1:5	253	God Knew Your Name
1:5	116	I Was There to Hear Your Borning Cry
1:7-8	54	Fear Not
6:16	185	Rest
10:6	191	Rock of Ages
10:6	218	There is None Like You
10:23-24	189	Renew Me
13:27	189	Renew Me
15:19-20	81	He Will Come and Save You
16:19	193	Rock of My Salvation
17:7-8	30	Cares Chorus
23:5	38	Crown Him (King of Kings)
29:11	74	God is Good All the Time
31:10-14	43	Comfort Comfort
31:33	224	Trading My Sorrows
31:35-36	76	God Will Make a Way
32:17, 27	79	He is Able
33:11	62	For the Lord is Good
33:11	137	Joy and Thanksgiving
33:11	198	Shout to the Lord
42:11	81	He Will Come and Save You

Lamentations

Ref	#	Title
2:19	42	Cry of My Heart
3:22-23	50	Faithful Father
3:22-23	62	For the Lord is Good
3:22-23	73	Great is Thy Faithfulness
3:22-24	185	Rest
3:23	220	This is the Day (Fitts)
3:24	75	God is the Strength of My Heart
3:41	83	Heaven is in My Heart
3:53-57	130	Jesus, Lover of My Soul
5:19	21	Beautiful Savior (All My Days)

Ezekiel

Ref	#	Title
3:12	164	My Dwelling Place
11:19	86	Here I Am Lord
16:8	72	Go, My Children with My Blessing
18:31	189	Renew Me
18:31	207	Take Our Lives
22:30	203	Spirit, Touch Your Church
34:13-14	249	You Make Me Lie Down In Green Pastures
34:30-31	69	Go Out As People of God
36:25-27	189	Renew Me
36:26	86	Here I Am Lord
36:27	199	Someone Else Living in You
37:9	48	Eagle's Wings
38:20	45	Did You Feel the Mountains Tremble?
39:29	60	Flowing River
47:8-12	215	The River is Here

Daniel

Ref	#	Title
2:37	67	Glory
2:37	233	We Bow Down
2:44	217	These Things Are True of You
2:44	223	This Kingdom
2:47	38	Crown Him (King of Kings)
3:28	231	We Are an Offering
4:37	67	Glory
7:9, 13-14, 22	10	Ancient of Days
7:13-14	133	Jesus, Lamb of God
7:14, 27	217	These Things Are True of You
7:18, 27	223	This Kingdom

Hosea

Ref	#	Title
1:7	205	The Battle Belongs to the Lord
2:8	231	We Are an Offering
6:1-2	131	Jesus, Draw Me Close
6:2-3	190	Revival Fire, Fall
13:14	187	Redeemer Savior Friend

Joel

Ref	#	Title
2:28	199	Someone Else Living in You
2:28-29	60	Flowing River
2:32	63	Friend of Sinners

Amos

Ref	#	Title
4:13	9	Above All
4:13	97	How Shall I Call You?

Obadiah

Ref	#	Title
1:3-4	61	Foolish Pride

Jonah

Ref	#	Title
2:2-4	216	Then I Will Praise You
2:2-9	51	Father Me, Again
2:9	65	Give Thanks
2:9	171	Nobody Fills My Heart Like Jesus

Micah

Ref	#	Title
3:8	203	Spirit, Touch Your Church
7:18-19	241	White As Snow

Nahum

Ref	#	Title
1:5	45	Did You Feel the Mountains Tremble?

Habakkuk

Ref	#	Title
3:3, 6	45	Did You Feel the Mountains Tremble?

Zephaniah

Ref	#	Title
2:3	247	You Are Worthy of My Praise
3:5	73	Great is Thy Faithfulness
3:14	198	Shout to the Lord
3:14	199	Someone Else Living in You
3:16-17	81	He Will Come and Save You
3:17	107	I Love You, Lord

Haggai

Ref	#	Title
2:2-5	205	The Battle Belongs to the Lord
2:4	81	He Will Come and Save You
2:9	194	Savior Again to Your Dear Name

Zechariah

Ref	#	Title
1:3	131	Jesus, Draw Me Close
3:3	228	Under the Blood
4:6	205	The Battle Belongs to the Lord
8:3	45	Did You Feel the Mountains Tremble?
8:20-23	45	Did You Feel the Mountains Tremble?
9:9	35	Come and Behold Him
13:1	179	Only the Blood
13:1	228	Under the Blood
13:7	210	The Lamb
13:9	72	Go, My Children with My Blessing

13:9	184	Purify My Heart	6:33	247	You Are Worthy of My Praise	24:35	76	God Will Make a Way	28:20	245	You Are My Own
13:9	190	Revival Fire, Fall	7:11	51	Father Me, Again	25:10	40	Come to the Bread of Life	**Mark**		
14:8	215	The River is Here	7:25	59	Firm Foundation	25:21, 33	57	Find Us Faithful	1:3	45	Did You Feel the Mountains Tremble?
Malachi			9:2, 5	84	Healer of My Heart	25:31	133	Jesus, Lamb of God			
3:1	45	Did You Feel the Mountains Tremble?	9:10-11	63	Friend of Sinners	25:34	198	Shout to the Lord	2:5, 9	84	Healer of My Heart
			9:20-22	132	Jesus, Jesus	25:40	55	Feed My Lambs	3:10	132	Jesus, Jesus
3:2-3	184	Purify My Heart	9:20-22	252	Your Touch is Loving	26:26-28	40	Come to the Bread of Life	5:27-34	252	Your Touch is Loving
3:2-3	190	Revival Fire, Fall	10:16	192	Romans 16:19	26:26-28	41	Come to the Table	6:41	199	Someone Else Living in You
3:3	179	Only the Blood	10:29-31	185	Rest	26:26-28	46	Do This In Remembrance of Me	6:56	252	Your Touch is Loving
3:6	73	Great is Thy Faithfulness	10:37	7	All Over Again				8:6	199	Someone Else Living in You
3:7	131	Jesus, Draw Me Close	10:37	75	God is the Strength of My Heart	26:26-28	88	Here is Bread	8:22	132	Jesus, Jesus
3:16-17	107	I Love You, Lord				26:26-28	188	Remember Me	8:29	100	I Am the Bread of Life (Toolan)
3:17	72	Go, My Children with My Blessing	10:37	104	I Give You My Heart	26:26-28	236	We Remember You			
			11:19	63	Friend of Sinners	26:26-28	239	What is This Bread?	9:36-37	52	Father Welcomes
Matthew			11:28-29	185	Rest	26:28	127	It's Your Blood	9:50	27	Bring Forth the Kingdom
1:23	44	Emmanuel	13:15	180	Open the Eyes of My Heart, Lord	26:28	210	The Lamb	9:50	70	Go, Make Disciples
1:23	67	Glory				26:31	210	The Lamb	10:13-16	52	Father Welcomes
1:23	134	Jesus, Name Above All Names	13:44	91	Hide Me in Your Holiness	26:39, 42	24	Blessed Assurance	10:13-16	252	Your Touch is Loving
			13:44-46	161	More Precious Than Silver	26:64	133	Jesus, Lamb of God	10:16	14	Arms of Love
3:3	45	Did You Feel the Mountains Tremble?	13:44-46	243	You Are My All in All	27:30-31	139	Lamb of God	10:16	29	By Your Side
			14:19	199	Someone Else Living in You	27:37	159	More Love, More Power	10:28	42	Cry of My Heart
3:11	201	Spirit of the Living God	14:28-30	51	Father Me, Again	27:39	139	Lamb of God	10:43-45	155	Make Me a Servant
4:4	48	Eagle's Wings	14:36	132	Jesus, Jesus	27:46	239	What is This Bread?	10:45	123	I'm Forever Grateful
4:16	145	Light One Candle	15:6-11	209	The Heart of Worship	27:60	151	Lord, I Lift Your Name on High	10:45	157	Meekness and Majesty
4:16	146	Light The Candle	15:36	199	Someone Else Living in You				11:9	95	Hosanna
4:16	171	Nobody Fills My Heart Like Jesus	16:16	100	I Am the Bread of Life (Toolan)	28:6-7	31	Celebrate Jesus	11:9	212	The Name of the Lord (Blessed Be)
						28:6-7	129	Jesus is Alive			
4:19	85	Here Am I	18:2-5	52	Father Welcomes	28:19	55	Feed My Lambs	12:10-11	148	Living Stones
4:20-22	86	Here I Am Lord	19:13-14	52	Father Welcomes	28:19	69	Go Out As People of God	12:29-30, 33	58	First Love
5:3	1	A Broken Spirit	19:27	42	Cry of My Heart	28:19	84	Healer of My Heart	12:30	64	From My Heart to Yours
5:3	149	Light the Fire Again	20:26-28	155	Make Me a Servant	28:19	85	Here Am I	12:30	117	I Will Celebrate (Baloche)
5:4	15	As High As the Heaven	20:28	96	How Could You Love Me So Much?	28:19	145	Light One Candle	12:30	153	Love You So Much
5:8	189	Renew Me				28:19	186	Raise Up an Army	12:30	199	Someone Else Living in You
5:13-14	70	Go, Make Disciples	20:28	123	I'm Forever Grateful	28:19	229	Waterlife	12:30, 33	29	By Your Side
5:13-16	27	Bring Forth the Kingdom	20:28	157	Meekness and Majesty	28:19-20	70	Go, Make Disciples	12:30, 33	104	I Give You My Heart
5:14-16	86	Here I Am Lord	21:9	95	Hosanna	28:19-20	203	Spirit, Touch Your Church	12:30, 33	247	You Are Worthy of My Praise
5:14-16	142	Let the Flame Burn Brighter	21:9	212	The Name of the Lord (Blessed Be)	28:20	47	Draw Me Close to You	12:30-33	159	More Love, More Power
5:14-16	204	Shine, Jesus Shine				28:20	44	Emmanuel	12:42-44	206	Take My Life and Let It Be
5:16	55	Feed My Lambs	21:42	148	Living Stones	28:20	54	Fear Not	14:22-24	40	Come to the Bread of Life
5:18	76	God Will Make a Way	22:8-9	40	Come to the Bread of Life	28:20	72	Go, My Children with My Blessing	14:22-24	46	Do This In Remembrance of Me
6:6-9	51	Father Me, Again	22:37	29	By Your Side						
6:9	82	Hear Me Say I Love You	22:37	58	First Love	28:20	74	God is Good All the Time	14:22-24	88	Here is Bread
6:10	133	Jesus, Lamb of God	22:37	64	From My Heart to Yours	28:20	253	God Knew Your Name	14:22-24	188	Remember Me
6:10	190	Revival Fire, Fall	22:37	104	I Give You My Heart	28:20	101	I Believe in Jesus	14:22-24	236	We Remember You
6:10	223	This Kingdom	22:37	117	I Will Celebrate (Baloche)	28:20	113	I Want Jesus to Walk With Me	14:22-24	239	What is This Bread?
6:10	226	Victory Chant	22:37	153	Love You So Much				14:27	210	The Lamb
6:11	199	Someone Else Living in You	22:37	199	Someone Else Living in You	28:20	116	I Was There to Hear Your Borning Cry	14:62	133	Jesus, Lamb of God
6:13	67	Glory	23:37	86	Here I Am Lord				15:16-17	70	Go, Make Disciples
6:13	97	How Shall I Call You?	23:39	95	Hosanna	28:20	134	Jesus, Name Above All Names	15:34	239	What is This Bread?
6:19-21	20	Be Thou My Vision	23:39	212	The Name of the Lord (Blessed Be)				15:46	151	Lord, I Lift Your Name on High
6:21	243	You Are My All in All				28:20	156	May the Feet of God Walk with You			
6:33	20	Be Thou My Vision	24:12	149	Light the Fire Again				16:6	129	Jesus is Alive
6:33	160	More of You	24:13	199	Someone Else Living in You	28:20	183	Peace Be Yours	16:15-16	186	Raise Up an Army
			24:31	253	God Knew Your Name	28:20	185	Rest	16:16	52	Father Welcomes

Luke

Ref	Pg	Song
1:33	25	Blessing and Honor
1:35	38	Crown Him (King of Kings)
1:49	78	Great and Mighty is He
1:50	251	Your Everlasting Love
1:51	61	Foolish Pride
1:68	25	Blessing and Honor
2:11	38	Crown Him (King of Kings)
2:14	126	Isn't He?
2:14	183	Peace Be Yours
2:15, 20	36	Come and See
2:32	132	Jesus, Jesus
2:32	145	Light One Candle
2:32	146	Light The Candle
3:4	45	Did You Feel the Mountains Tremble?
3:4-5	76	God Will Make a Way
3:16	184	Purify My Heart
3:16	190	Revival Fire, Fall
3:16	199	Someone Else Living in You
3:16	201	Spirit of the Living God
3:22	90	Holy and Anointed One
4:18	90	Holy and Anointed One
4:18-19	6	Almighty
4:18-19	45	Did You Feel the Mountains Tremble?
4:18-19	186	Raise Up an Army
5:20, 23	84	Healer of My Heart
5:34	31	Celebrate Jesus
6:19	132	Jesus, Jesus
6:19	252	Your Touch is Loving
6:48	59	Firm Foundation
7:22	186	Raise Up an Army
7:34	63	Friend of Sinners
7:48	84	Healer of My Heart
8:43-49	252	Your Touch is Loving
9:1	135	Jesus, Your Name
9:16	199	Someone Else Living in You
9:47-48	52	Father Welcomes
9:57	42	Cry of My Heart
10:5	183	Peace Be Yours
10:9-11	223	This Kingdom
10:27	29	By Your Side
10:27	58	First Love
10:27	64	From My Heart to Yours
10:27	104	I Give You My Heart
10:27	117	I Will Celebrate (Baloche)
10:27	153	Love You So Much
10:27	159	More Love, More Power
10:27	199	Someone Else Living in You
10:27	247	You Are Worthy of My Praise
10:41-42	202	Spirit Song
11:2	82	Hear Me Say I Love You
11:2	223	This Kingdom
11:2	226	Victory Chant
11:3	199	Someone Else Living in You
11:12	133	Jesus, Lamb of God
12:22-31	20	Be Thou My Vision
12:32	51	Father Me, Again
12:34	243	You Are My All in All
12:42-43	57	Find Us Faithful
13:10-16	171	Nobody Fills My Heart Like Jesus
13:29	197	Shout to the North
13:34	86	Here I Am Lord
13:35	212	The Name of the Lord (Blessed Be)
14:25-27, 33	42	Cry of My Heart
14:26	237	What a Friend I've Found (...Friend Forever)
14:34	27	Bring Forth the Kingdom
15:1-2	63	Friend of Sinners
15:20	14	Arms of Love
15:20	97	How Shall I Call You?
15:22-24	71	God is Good
15:24, 32	171	Nobody Fills My Heart Like Jesus
16:10-12	57	Find Us Faithful
16:22	253	God Knew Your Name
17:11-19	172	O Magnify The Lord
17:16-18	65	Give Thanks
17:21	83	Heaven is in My Heart
18:13	109	I Need You
18:15-17	52	Father Welcomes
18:15-17	252	Your Touch is Loving
18:28	42	Cry of My Heart
19:7	63	Friend of Sinners
19:10	123	I'm Forever Grateful
19:16	231	We Are an Offering
19:37-38	95	Hosanna
19:37-38	186	Raise Up an Army
19:38	212	The Name of the Lord (Blessed Be)
19:40	6	Almighty
20:17	148	Living Stones
21:2-4	206	Take My Life and Let It Be
21:27-28	133	Jesus, Lamb of God
22:19-20	40	Come to the Bread of Life
22:19-20	46	Do This In Remembrance of Me
22:19-20	88	Here is Bread
22:19-20	188	Remember Me
22:19-20	236	We Remember You
22:19-20	239	What is This Bread?
22:27	157	Meekness and Majesty
22:33-34	42	Cry of My Heart
22:42	226	Victory Chant
23:53	151	Lord, I Lift Your Name on High
24:6, 34	31	Celebrate Jesus
24:6-7	129	Jesus is Alive
24:30	199	Someone Else Living in You
24:34	129	Jesus is Alive
24:45	180	Open the Eyes of My Heart, Lord
24:47-48	70	Go, Make Disciples
24:47-48	186	Raise Up an Army

John

Ref	Pg	Song
1:1-2, 14	44	Emmanuel
1:9	204	Shine, Jesus Shine
1:12	51	Father Me, Again
1:12	245	You Are My Own
1:12-13	52	Father Welcomes
1:13	116	I Was There to Hear Your Borning Cry
1:14	67	Glory
1:14	123	I'm Forever Grateful
1:14	157	Meekness and Majesty
1:14	185	Rest
1:29	119	I Will Praise Him
1:29	127	It's Your Blood
1:29	133	Jesus, Lamb of God
1:29	210	The Lamb
1:29	211	There is A Redeemer
1:29	243	You Are My All in All
1:29, 36	22	Behold the Lamb
1:29, 36	35	Come and Behold Him
1:29, 36	139	Lamb of God
1:46	36	Come and See
2:19-22	129	Jesus is Alive
3:3-6	196	See This Wonder
3:3-6	245	You Are My Own
3:3-7	52	Father Welcomes
3:3-7	116	I Was There to Hear Your Borning Cry
3:15-18, 36	52	Father Welcomes
3:16	11	Amazing Love
3:16	89	Holy Is Our God Medley
3:16	96	How Could You Love Me So Much?
3:16	130	Jesus, Lover of My Soul
3:16	152	Lord, You Love Me
3:16	198	Shout to the Lord
3:16	200	Someone Special
3:16	211	There is A Redeemer
3:16-17	77	Grace Alone
3:30	240	When I Look into Your Holiness
3:35	10	Ancient of Days
4:7-11	215	The River is Here
4:9-15	39	Come and Fill Me Up
4:10	84	Healer of My Heart
4:10, 14	37	Come Thou Fount of Every Blessing
4:10, 14	199	Someone Else Living in You
4:10-11, 14	82	Hear Me Say I Love You
4:14	99	I Am the Bread of Life (Talbot)
4:14	143	Let the River Flow
4:14	202	Spirit Song
4:23-24	199	Someone Else Living in You
4:23-24	209	The Heart of Worship
4:23-24	232	We Are Marching in the Light of God
4:29	36	Come and See
4:34	226	Victory Chant
5:14	84	Healer of My Heart
5:24-25	166	My Redeemer Lives (Morgan)
5:24-25	167	My Redeemer Lives (Willison)
6:11	199	Someone Else Living in You
6:27	20	Be Thou My Vision
6:32-58	53	Feed Us Now
6:35	39	Come and Fill Me Up
6:35	40	Come to the Bread of Life
6:35	135	Jesus, Your Name
6:35	199	Someone Else Living in You
6:37	213	The Potter's Hand
6:38	226	Victory Chant
6:44	99	I Am the Bread of Life (Talbot)
6:44	100	I Am the Bread of Life (Toolan)
6:44, 65	213	The Potter's Hand
6:48-50	40	Come to the Bread of Life
6:51-58	99	I Am the Bread of Life (Talbot)
6:51-58	100	I Am the Bread of Life (Toolan)
6:53-56	40	Come to the Bread of Life
6:53-56	88	Here is Bread
6:53-56	188	Remember Me
6:53-56	236	We Remember You
6:53-56	239	What is This Bread?
6:53-58	41	Come to the Table
6:56	34	Christ Above Me
6:69	101	I Believe in Jesus
7:37	39	Come and Fill Me Up
7:37	84	Healer of My Heart
7:37	37	Come Thou Fount of Every Blessing
7:37-39	199	Someone Else Living in You
7:38	143	Let the River Flow
7:38-39	215	The River is Here
8:11	84	Healer of My Heart

Verse	#	Song
8:12	19	Be My Home
8:12	115	I Want to Walk as a Child of the Light
8:12	135	Jesus, Your Name
8:12	171	Nobody Fills My Heart Like Jesus
8:12	204	Shine, Jesus Shine
8:31	199	Someone Else Living in You
8:32	136	Jesus, We Celebrate Your Victory
8:32	200	Someone Special
8:46	171	Nobody Fills My Heart Like Jesus
9:5	19	Be My Home
9:25	171	Nobody Fills My Heart Like Jesus
9:40-41	149	Light the Fire Again
10:11, 15	16	As I Look Into Your Eyes
10:11, 15	187	Redeemer Savior Friend
10:14-16	69	Go Out As People of God
10:16	144	Let the Walls Fall Down
10:26-28	69	Go Out As People of God
10:28-30	152	Lord, You Love Me
11:4	66	Glorify Thy Name
11:5	186	Raise Up an Army
11:24-25	167	My Redeemer Lives (Willison)
11:25	135	Jesus, Your Name
11:25-26	166	My Redeemer Lives (Morgan)
11:25-27	100	I Am the Bread of Life (Toolan)
11:52	144	Let the Walls Fall Down
12:13	95	Hosanna
12:13	212	The Name of the Lord (Blessed Be)
12:23, 28	66	Glorify Thy Name
12:28	67	Glory
12:36	19	Be My Home
12:41	111	I See the Lord (Baloche)
12:41	112	I See the Lord (Falson)
13:3	135	Jesus, Your Name
13:12-17	97	How Shall I Call You?
13:13-16	157	Meekness and Majesty
13:14-16	155	Make Me a Servant
13:15	110	I Want to Be More Like You
13:31-32	66	Glorify Thy Name
13:34-35	26	Blest Be The Tie That Binds
13:36-38	42	Cry of My Heart
14:1, 27	225	Tis So Sweet to Trust in Jesus
14:1-3	54	Fear Not
14:3	199	Someone Else Living in You
14:6	19	Be My Home
14:6	21	Beautiful Savior (All My Days)
14:6	56	Fill Me
14:6	135	Jesus, Your Name
14:6	170	No Other Name
14:7	138	Knowing You
14:15, 26	200	Someone Special
14:15-19	211	There is A Redeemer
14:16-17	199	Someone Else Living in You
14:16-17, 23	34	Christ Above Me
14:16-18	54	Fear Not
14:16-18, 26	82	Hear Me Say I Love You
14:18-23	47	Draw Me Close to You
14:23	19	Be My Home
14:23	48	Eagle's Wings
14:23	199	Someone Else Living in You
14:27	183	Peace Be Yours
14:27	194	Savior Again to Your Dear Name
14:27	252	Your Touch is Loving
14:28	199	Someone Else Living in You
15:4	48	Eagle's Wings
15:4-10	199	Someone Else Living in You
15:5	121	I Will Change Your Name
15:5, 13	200	Someone Special
15:13	11	Amazing Love
15:13	16	As I Look Into Your Eyes
15:13-15	47	Draw Me Close to You
15:13-15	187	Redeemer Savior Friend
15:13-15	237	What a Friend I've Found (...Friend Forever)
15:13-15	238	What a Friend we Have in Jesus
15:15	63	Friend of Sinners
15:15	97	How Shall I Call You?
15:26	82	Hear Me Say I Love You
16:13	201	Spirit of the Living God
16:13	213	The Potter's Hand
16:13-15	82	Hear Me Say I Love You
16:14	66	Glorify Thy Name
16:20	163	Mourning Into Dancing
16:20-22	15	As High As the Heaven
16:22	224	Trading My Sorrows
16:24-26	170	No Other Name
16:33	124	In The Heart of God
16:33	136	Jesus, We Celebrate Your Victory
16:33	183	Peace Be Yours
16:33	252	Your Touch is Loving
17:1-5	66	Glorify Thy Name
17:3	135	Jesus, Your Name
17:3	138	Knowing You
17:11	72	Go, My Children with My Blessing
17:11, 21	26	Blest Be The Tie That Binds
17:11-12	170	No Other Name
19:37	235	When I Survey the Wondrous Cross
19:40-41	151	Lord, I Lift Your Name on High
20:19, 21, 26	183	Peace Be Yours
20:21	70	Go, Make Disciples
20:22	48	Eagle's Wings
20:31	135	Jesus, Your Name
20:31	170	No Other Name
21:15	118	In Moments Like These
21:15	159	More Love, More Power
21:15	168	My Jesus, I Love Thee
21:15	202	Spirit Song
21:15-17	7	All Over Again
21:15-17	64	From My Heart to Yours
21:15-17	82	Hear Me Say I Love You
21:15-19	55	Feed My Lambs

Acts

Verse	#	Song
1:5	199	Someone Else Living in You
1:8	56	Fill Me
1:8	70	Go, Make Disciples
1:8	186	Raise Up an Army
1:9	151	Lord, I Lift Your Name on High
1:11	133	Jesus, Lamb of God
1:11	199	Someone Else Living in You
2:3-4, 17-19	190	Revival Fire, Fall
2:17-18	60	Flowing River
2:21	63	Friend of Sinners
2:21	170	No Other Name
2:23-24	17	At the Cross
2:24	25	Blessing and Honor
2:28	56	Fill Me
2:28	83	Heaven is in My Heart
2:28	106	I Love to Be in Your Presence
2:33, 39	60	Flowing River
2:36	66	Glorify Thy Name
2:36	166	My Redeemer Lives (Morgan)
2:36	167	My Redeemer Lives (Willison)
2:38	245	You Are My Own
2:38-39	52	Father Welcomes
2:38-39	196	See This Wonder
3:13	66	Glorify Thy Name
3:25	245	You Are My Own
4:11-12	148	Living Stones
4:12	63	Friend of Sinners
4:12	170	No Other Name
4:29-31	203	Spirit, Touch Your Church
7:55-56	133	Jesus, Lamb of God
8:32	210	The Lamb
8:32-35	139	Lamb of God
8:33	24	Blessed Assurance
10:38	90	Holy and Anointed One
10:38	135	Jesus, Your Name
10:39	235	When I Survey the Wondrous Cross
10:43	170	No Other Name
10:44	201	Spirit of the Living God
11:15-16	201	Spirit of the Living God
11:23	199	Someone Else Living in You
13:46-47	186	Raise Up an Army
13:47	70	Go, Make Disciples
13:47	145	Light One Candle
13:47	146	Light The Candle
13:47	204	Shine, Jesus Shine
13:48	229	Waterlife
15:9	184	Purify My Heart
15:9	189	Renew Me
15:9	207	Take Our Lives
16:14	180	Open the Eyes of My Heart, Lord
17:27	183	Peace Be Yours
17:28	243	You Are My All in All
18:9-10	54	Fear Not
19:8	203	Spirit, Touch Your Church
20:24	85	Here Am I
22:16	246	Your Grace is Sufficient For Me
26:17-18	171	Nobody Fills My Heart Like Jesus
26:18	180	Open the Eyes of My Heart, Lord
26:23	145	Light One Candle
26:23	146	Light The Candle
27:35	199	Someone Else Living in You
28:28	70	Go, Make Disciples
28:31	203	Spirit, Touch Your Church

Romans

Verse	#	Song
1:4	135	Jesus, Your Name
1:16	141	Let It Be Said Of Us
2:4-5	86	Here I Am Lord
3:5	61	Foolish Pride
3:20, 27-28	24	Blessed Assurance
3:21-26	77	Grace Alone
3:25	246	Your Grace is Sufficient For Me
4:2	24	Blessed Assurance
4:16	77	Grace Alone
4:21	79	He is Able
4:25	151	Lord, I Lift Your Name on High
5:1-2	49	Enter In
5:1-2	77	Grace Alone
5:2	28	By Your Blood
5:2	162	My Faith Looks Up to Thee
5:5	34	Christ Above Me

Ref	#	Title
5:5	202	Spirit Song
5:6-8	16	As I Look Into Your Eyes
5:6-8	187	Redeemer Savior Friend
5:8	11	Amazing Love
5:8	61	Foolish Pride
5:8	74	God is Good All the Time
5:8	152	Lord, You Love Me
5:9	122	I Will Glory in The Cross
5:20	61	Foolish Pride
6:4-10	166	My Redeemer Lives (Morgan)
6:4-10	167	My Redeemer Lives (Willison)
6:5	229	Waterlife
6:6	52	Father Welcomes
6:13, 16, 19	108	I Offer My Life
6:13, 16, 19	206	Take My Life and Let It Be
6:13, 16, 19	231	We Are an Offering
6:18	136	Jesus, We Celebrate Your Victory
6:18, 22	96	How Could You Love Me So Much?
6:18-23	248	You Rescued Me
6:22	136	Jesus, We Celebrate Your Victory
7:24	149	Light the Fire Again
7:24	248	You Rescued Me
8:1	228	Under the Blood
8:2	136	Jesus, We Celebrate Your Victory
8:2	135	Jesus, Your Name
8:2	248	You Rescued Me
8:6	189	Renew Me
8:9, 11, 14	199	Someone Else Living in You
8:9-11	34	Christ Above Me
8:10	199	Someone Else Living in You
8:11	245	You Are My Own
8:14-16	51	Father Me, Again
8:15	136	Jesus, We Celebrate Your Victory
8:15-16	82	Hear Me Say I Love You
8:15-17	52	Father Welcomes
8:18	198	Shout to the Lord
8:23, 26-27	51	Father Me, Again
8:26	209	The Heart of Worship
8:26-27	51	Father Me, Again
8:28	80	He Who Began a Good Work in You
8:28	198	Shout to the Lord
8:28, 30, 33	229	Waterlife
8:28-33	248	You Rescued Me
8:29	51	Father Me, Again
8:29	253	God Knew Your Name
8:29	110	I Want to Be More Like You
8:31	81	He Will Come and Save You
8:32	96	How Could You Love Me So Much?
8:35-39	124	In The Heart of God
8:35-39	250	Your Love
8:37	24	Blessed Assurance
8:37-39	136	Jesus, We Celebrate Your Victory
8:38-39	152	Lord, You Love Me
9:5	44	Emmanuel
9:11, 16	24	Blessed Assurance
9:20-21	213	The Potter's Hand
9:21	33	Change My Heart, O God
9:33	243	You Are My All in All
10:9	101	I Believe in Jesus
10:11	243	You Are My All in All
10:13	63	Friend of Sinners
10:13	170	No Other Name
10:15	206	Take My Life and Let It Be
10:18	70	Go, Make Disciples
10:18	186	Raise Up an Army
11:5	229	Waterlife
11:6	24	Blessed Assurance
11:6	77	Grace Alone
11:33-36	128	It's All About You (Jesus, Lover of My Soul)
11:33-36	157	Meekness and Majesty
12:1	108	I Offer My Life
12:1	206	Take My Life and Let It Be
12:1	231	We Are an Offering
12:1-2	199	Someone Else Living in You
12:1-2	207	Take Our Lives
12:2	33	Change My Heart, O God
12:2	56	Fill Me
12:2	189	Renew Me
12:2	190	Revival Fire, Fall
12:6	77	Grace Alone
12:16	61	Foolish Pride
14:9	166	My Redeemer Lives (Morgan)
14:9	167	My Redeemer Lives (Willison)
14:17	27	Bring Forth the Kingdom
14:17	83	Heaven is in My Heart
14:17	225	Tis So Sweet to Trust in Jesus
15:6-9	66	Glorify Thy Name
15:11	182	Praise Adonai
15:13	56	Fill Me
15:13	160	More of You
15:13	225	Tis So Sweet to Trust in Jesus
15:13	252	Your Touch is Loving
16:19-20	192	Romans 16:19
16:25	79	He is Able
16:27	24	Blessed Assurance

1 Corinthians

Ref	#	Title
1:10	26	Blest Be The Tie That Binds
1:17-18, 23	17	At the Cross
1:18	140	Lead Me to the Cross
1:18	235	When I Survey the Wondrous Cross
1:18, 23	122	I Will Glory in The Cross
1:23	88	Here is Bread
1:23	141	Let It Be Said Of Us
1:23	235	When I Survey the Wondrous Cross
1:23-24	140	Lead Me to the Cross
1:29-31	24	Blessed Assurance
2:2	88	Here is Bread
2:2	122	I Will Glory in The Cross
2:2	138	Knowing You
2:2	140	Lead Me to the Cross
2:2	141	Let It Be Said Of Us
2:2	235	When I Survey the Wondrous Cross
2:4-5	205	The Battle Belongs to the Lord
2:9	198	Shout to the Lord
2:14	180	Open the Eyes of My Heart, Lord
2:14	201	Spirit of the Living God
3:10-11	59	Firm Foundation
3:11	170	No Other Name
3:16	199	Someone Else Living in You
4:2, 16-17	57	Find Us Faithful
4:20	223	This Kingdom
5:2	61	Foolish Pride
5:7	139	Lamb of God
5:7	210	The Lamb
6:11	119	I Will Praise Him
6:11	164	My Dwelling Place
6:11	179	Only the Blood
6:11	196	See This Wonder
6:11	228	Under the Blood
6:11	245	You Are My Own
6:13-20	108	I Offer My Life
6:13-20	231	We Are an Offering
6:19	199	Someone Else Living in You
6:19-20	206	Take My Life and Let It Be
6:20	98	I Am Not My Own
6:20	231	We Are an Offering
7:23	98	I Am Not My Own
9:24-27	125	In the Secret (I Want to Know You)
10:3	188	Remember Me
10:3-4	40	Come to the Bread of Life
10:3-4	88	Here is Bread
10:3-4	236	We Remember You
10:3-4	239	What is This Bread?
10:4, 21	199	Someone Else Living in You
10:13	113	I Want Jesus to Walk With Me
10:16	53	Feed Us Now
10:16-17	40	Come to the Bread of Life
10:16-17	46	Do This In Remembrance of Me
10:16-17	88	Here is Bread
10:16-17	188	Remember Me
10:16-17	236	We Remember You
10:16-17	239	What is This Bread?
10:26	231	We Are an Offering
10:31	66	Glorify Thy Name
11:1	57	Find Us Faithful
11:1	110	I Want to Be More Like You
11:2	199	Someone Else Living in You
11:23-26	40	Come to the Bread of Life
11:23-26	46	Do This In Remembrance of Me
11:23-26	53	Feed Us Now
11:23-26	88	Here is Bread
11:23-26	188	Remember Me
11:23-26	236	We Remember You
11:23-26	239	What is This Bread?
11:32	149	Light the Fire Again
12:12-13	144	Let the Walls Fall Down
12:13	199	Someone Else Living in You
13:4	61	Foolish Pride
13:12	67	Glory
14:15, 19	199	Someone Else Living in You
14:20	192	Romans 16:19
15:3-4	101	I Believe in Jesus
15:3-4	151	Lord, I Lift Your Name on High
15:3-7	129	Jesus is Alive
15:10	108	I Offer My Life
15:10	246	Your Grace is Sufficient For Me
15:34	84	Healer of My Heart
15:54-57	24	Blessed Assurance
15:54-57	227	Victory Song
15:55-57	6	Almighty
15:57	136	Jesus, We Celebrate Your Victory
15:57	208	Thank You, Lord
15:58	56	Fill Me
16:22	7	All Over Again

2 Corinthians

Ref	#	Title
1:4	43	Comfort Comfort
1:21-22	69	Go Out As People of God
1:22	201	Spirit of the Living God
2:14	208	Thank You, Lord
3:4-5	13	All the Power You Need
3:4-5	181	Our Confidence is In the Lord
3:5	20	Be Thou My Vision

Ref	#	Title
3:5	108	I Offer My Life
3:18	35	Come and Behold Him
3:18	67	Glory
4:4-6	66	Glorify Thy Name
4:6	171	Nobody Fills My Heart Like Jesus
4:6	180	Open the Eyes of My Heart, Lord
4:6	204	Shine, Jesus Shine
4:7	33	Change My Heart, O God
4:7	201	Spirit of the Living God
4:7	213	The Potter's Hand
4:7	243	You Are My All in All
4:8-9	224	Trading My Sorrows
4:15	65	Give Thanks
4:17-18	230	We'll Be Faithful
5:7	74	God is Good All the Time
5:17	33	Change My Heart, O God
5:17	56	Fill Me
5:17	84	Healer of My Heart
5:17	189	Renew Me
5:17	248	You Rescued Me
5:20	206	Take My Life and Let It Be
5:21	223	This Kingdom
5:21	243	You Are My All in All
6:13	45	Did You Feel the Mountains Tremble?
6:16	201	Spirit of the Living God
6:18	51	Father Me, Again
7:1	60	Flowing River
7:1	184	Purify My Heart
8:5	231	We Are an Offering
8:9	65	Give Thanks
8:9	96	How Could You Love Me So Much?
8:9	174	Once Again
9:11, 15	65	Give Thanks
9:15	208	Thank You, Lord
10:4-5	205	The Battle Belongs to the Lord
10:5	34	Christ Above Me
12:9-10	13	All the Power You Need
12:9-10	65	Give Thanks
12:9-10	243	You Are My All in All
12:9-10	246	Your Grace is Sufficient For Me
12:10	171	Nobody Fills My Heart Like Jesus
12:10	197	Shout to the North
12:10	244	You Are My Hiding Place
13:4	166	My Redeemer Lives (Morgan)
13:4	167	My Redeemer Lives (Willison)
13:5	199	Someone Else Living in You

Galatians

Ref	#	Title
1:4	248	You Rescued Me
1:15	253	God Knew Your Name
2:20	34	Christ Above Me
2:21	77	Grace Alone
3:1	235	When I Survey the Wondrous Cross
3:13	151	Lord, I Lift Your Name on High
3:13-14	25	Blessing and Honor
3:13-14	129	Jesus is Alive
3:18	77	Grace Alone
3:26	51	Father Me, Again
3:28	26	Blest Be The Tie That Binds
3:28	144	Let the Walls Fall Down
3:29	245	You Are My Own
4:4-5	157	Meekness and Majesty
4:5	25	Blessing and Honor
4:6	199	Someone Else Living in You
4:6	209	The Heart of Worship
4:6-7	51	Father Me, Again
4:6-7	52	Father Welcomes
4:6-7	82	Hear Me Say I Love You
5:1	136	Jesus, We Celebrate Your Victory
5:1	200	Someone Special
5:16	201	Spirit of the Living God
5:22-25	217	These Things Are True of You
6:14	122	I Will Glory in The Cross
6:14	140	Lead Me to the Cross
6:14	141	Let It Be Said Of Us
6:14	235	When I Survey the Wondrous Cross
6:15	84	Healer of My Heart
6:15	116	I Was There to Hear Your Borning Cry
6:15	248	You Rescued Me

Ephesians

Ref	#	Title
1:4	229	Waterlife
1:4	248	You Rescued Me
1:5	51	Father Me, Again
1:5	82	Hear Me Say I Love You
1:6-8	11	Amazing Love
1:6-8	241	White As Snow
1:7	119	I Will Praise Him
1:7	127	It's Your Blood
1:7	166	My Redeemer Lives (Morgan)
1:7	167	My Redeemer Lives (Willison)
1:7	169	Nothing But the Blood
1:7	179	Only the Blood
1:7-8	210	The Lamb
1:13-14	69	Go Out As People of God
1:17-18	138	Knowing You
1:18	180	Open the Eyes of My Heart, Lord
1:18-20	56	Fill Me
1:18-23	79	He is Able
1:18-23	214	The Power of Your Love
1:19	78	Great and Mighty is He
1:20-21	102	I Exalt Thee
1:20-23	134	Jesus, Name Above All Names
1:20-23	170	No Other Name
1:21	9	Above All
1:21	150	Lord Most High
2:4-5, 7	222	Think About His Love
2:4-7	15	As High As the Heaven
2:4-7	173	O The Deep, Deep Love of Jesus
2:5, 8-9	77	Grace Alone
2:7	61	Foolish Pride
2:8-9	24	Blessed Assurance
2:8-9	178	Only By Grace
2:8-9	199	Someone Else Living in You
2:8-9	245	You Are My Own
2:8-9	246	Your Grace is Sufficient For Me
2:10	56	Fill Me
2:10	108	I Offer My Life
2:10	189	Renew Me
2:14	144	Let the Walls Fall Down
2:14-17	183	Peace Be Yours
2:18	28	By Your Blood
2:20	59	Firm Foundation
2:20	148	Living Stones
2:22	199	Someone Else Living in You
3:12	24	Blessed Assurance
3:12	49	Enter In
3:12	162	My Faith Looks Up to Thee
3:12	181	Our Confidence is In the Lord
3:14-15	233	We Bow Down
3:16	13	All the Power You Need
3:16-19	202	Spirit Song
3:17-19	34	Christ Above Me
3:17-19	138	Knowing You
3:17-19	173	O The Deep, Deep Love of Jesus
3:17-19	214	The Power of Your Love
3:17-19	222	Think About His Love
3:17-19	251	Your Everlasting Love
3:17-19	250	Your Love
3:17-20	252	Your Touch is Loving
3:20	79	He is Able
3:21	25	Blessing and Honor
3:21	67	Glory
4:3-6	26	Blest Be The Tie That Binds
4:8-10	151	Lord, I Lift Your Name on High
4:16	144	Let the Walls Fall Down
4:22-24	33	Change My Heart, O God
4:22-24	52	Father Welcomes
4:22-24	56	Fill Me
4:22-24	189	Renew Me
4:24	69	Go Out As People of God
4:24	89	Holy Is Our God Medley
4:24	248	You Rescued Me
5:1-2	110	I Want to Be More Like You
5:1-2	189	Renew Me
5:2	155	Make Me a Servant
5:2	187	Redeemer Savior Friend
5:2, 8-10, 14	204	Shine, Jesus Shine
5:4	208	Thank You, Lord
5:8	171	Nobody Fills My Heart Like Jesus
5:8	204	Shine, Jesus Shine
5:8-14	142	Let the Flame Burn Brighter
5:17	192	Romans 16:19
5:18-20	199	Someone Else Living in You
5:18-20	202	Spirit Song
5:19	194	Savior Again to Your Dear Name
5:19	232	We Are Marching in the Light of God
5:19-20	55	Feed My Lambs
5:19-20	208	Thank You, Lord
5:19-20	234	We Bring the Sacrifice of Praise
5:20	65	Give Thanks
5:26	196	See This Wonder
5:26	245	You Are My Own
5:26-27	184	Purify My Heart
5:26-27	228	Under the Blood
6:10	13	All the Power You Need
6:10	81	He Will Come and Save You
6:10	252	Your Touch is Loving
6:10-18	205	The Battle Belongs to the Lord
6:17	58	First Love
6:18	199	Someone Else Living in You
6:18-20	203	Spirit, Touch Your Church
6:23-24	64	From My Heart to Yours
6:24	7	All Over Again
6:24	153	Love You So Much

Philippians

Ref	#	Title
1:6	80	He Who Began a Good Work in You
1:9	159	More Love, More Power
1:20	206	Take My Life and Let It Be
1:21	165	My Life is In You, Lord
1:23	114	I Want to Be Where You Are

Ref	#	Title
2:2-5	26	Blest Be The Tie That Binds
2:5	110	I Want to Be More Like You
2:5-7	155	Make Me a Servant
2:6-11	174	Once Again
2:6-8	24	Blessed Assurance
2:6-8	96	How Could You Love Me So Much?
2:6-8	157	Meekness and Majesty
2:7-8	123	I'm Forever Grateful
2:8	217	These Things Are True of You
2:9	134	Jesus, Name Above All Names
2:9	211	There is A Redeemer
2:9-11	9	Above All
2:9-11	10	Ancient of Days
2:9-11	36	Come and See
2:9-11	38	Crown Him (King of Kings)
2:9-11	66	Glorify Thy Name
2:9-11	90	Holy and Anointed One
2:9-11	97	How Shall I Call You?
2:9-11	102	I Exalt Thee
2:9-11	158	Mighty is Our God
2:9-11	170	No Other Name
2:10-11	233	We Bow Down
2:13	80	He Who Began a Good Work in You
2:13	108	I Offer My Life
2:15-16	142	Let the Flame Burn Brighter
2:15-16	204	Shine, Jesus Shine
3:1	31	Celebrate Jesus
3:3-4	181	Our Confidence is In the Lord
3:7	20	Be Thou My Vision
3:7-11	138	Knowing You
3:7-8	75	God is the Strength of My Heart
3:8	47	Draw Me Close to You
3:8-10	48	Eagle's Wings
3:8-11	105	I Live to Know You
3:8-14	125	In the Secret (I Want to Know You)
3:8-9	235	When I Survey the Wondrous Cross
3:10	128	It's All About You (Jesus, Lover of My Soul)
3:13	230	We'll Be Faithful
3:17	57	Find Us Faithful
4:4	31	Celebrate Jesus
4:4	219	This is the Day (Shelton)
4:6	30	Cares Chorus
4:6	54	Fear Not
4:6	65	Give Thanks
4:6	208	Thank You, Lord
4:6	238	What a Friend we Have in Jesus
4:6-7	202	Spirit Song
4:7	72	Go, My Children with My Blessing
4:7	183	Peace Be Yours
4:7	252	Your Touch is Loving
4:13	13	All the Power You Need

Colossians

Ref	#	Title
1:10-14	208	Thank You, Lord
1:11	13	All the Power You Need
1:12	65	Give Thanks
1:13	248	You Rescued Me
1:15-18	170	No Other Name
1:17	243	You Are My All in All
1:18	134	Jesus, Name Above All Names
1:20	17	At the Cross
1:27	34	Christ Above Me
1:27	165	My Life is In You, Lord
1:27	199	Someone Else Living in You
1:29	79	He is Able
2:7	65	Give Thanks
2:9	157	Meekness and Majesty
2:13-15	17	At the Cross
3:1-3	91	Hide Me in Your Holiness
3:1-4	19	Be My Home
3:1-4	20	Be Thou My Vision
3:3-4	165	My Life is In You, Lord
3:9-10	52	Father Welcomes
3:10	56	Fill Me
3:10	69	Go Out As People of God
3:10	189	Renew Me
3:10	214	The Power of Your Love
3:11	144	Let the Walls Fall Down
3:11	243	You Are My All in All
3:15	183	Peace Be Yours
3:15-17	65	Give Thanks
3:16	55	Feed My Lambs
3:16	118	In Moments Like These
3:16	199	Someone Else Living in You
3:16	234	We Bring the Sacrifice of Praise
3:17	170	No Other Name
3:17	208	Thank You, Lord
4:3	70	Go, Make Disciples
4:6	27	Bring Forth the Kingdom

1 Thessalonians

Ref	#	Title
1:10	248	You Rescued Me
3:12	159	More Love, More Power
4:9-10	159	More Love, More Power
4:13, 17	72	Go, My Children with My Blessing
4:16-17	199	Someone Else Living in You

– p. 48 –

Ref	#	Title
5:10	72	Go, My Children with My Blessing
5:10	164	My Dwelling Place
5:12-13	55	Feed My Lambs
5:16-18	31	Celebrate Jesus
5:18	65	Give Thanks
5:18	208	Thank You, Lord
5:19	142	Let the Flame Burn Brighter
5:23	72	Go, My Children with My Blessing
5:23	84	Healer of My Heart
5:23-24	80	He Who Began a Good Work in You
5:24	80	He Who Began a Good Work in You

2 Thessalonians

Ref	#	Title
1:11	80	He Who Began a Good Work in You
1:11	230	We'll Be Faithful
2:13	229	Waterlife
2:13-14	248	You Rescued Me
2:15	199	Someone Else Living in You
3:9	57	Find Us Faithful
3:16	183	Peace Be Yours

1 Timothy

Ref	#	Title
1:9-10	229	Waterlife
1:12	57	Find Us Faithful
1:14	3	A Simple Word of Grace
1:14	214	The Power of Your Love
1:16	61	Foolish Pride
1:17	24	Blessed Assurance
2:1	65	Give Thanks
2:5-6	170	No Other Name
3:16	44	Emmanuel
3:16	157	Meekness and Majesty
4:16	199	Someone Else Living in You
6:12	141	Let It Be Said Of Us
6:12	230	We'll Be Faithful
6:15	67	Glory
6:15	82	Hear Me Say I Love You
6:15	95	Hosanna
6:15-16	38	Crown Him (King of Kings)
6:16	111	I See the Lord (Baloche)

2 Timothy

Ref	#	Title
1:6	142	Let the Flame Burn Brighter
1:7	214	The Power of Your Love
1:7	217	These Things Are True of You
1:7	252	Your Touch is Loving
1:9	24	Blessed Assurance
1:9	77	Grace Alone
1:10	135	Jesus, Your Name
1:12	124	In The Heart of God
1:14	199	Someone Else Living in You
2:8	236	We Remember You
2:19	59	Firm Foundation
2:19	72	Go, My Children with My Blessing
2:19	253	God Knew Your Name
2:20-21	33	Change My Heart, O God
2:20-21	201	Spirit of the Living God
3:14	199	Someone Else Living in You
4:7	141	Let It Be Said Of Us
4:7-8	230	We'll Be Faithful
4:17	54	Fear Not
4:22	44	Emmanuel

Titus

Ref	#	Title
1:2	50	Faithful Father
2:11-14	60	Flowing River
2:13-14	187	Redeemer Savior Friend
2:14	184	Purify My Heart
3:3-5	77	Grace Alone
3:4-7	24	Blessed Assurance
3:5	56	Fill Me
3:5	116	I Was There to Hear Your Borning Cry
3:5	189	Renew Me
3:5	196	See This Wonder
3:5-6	60	Flowing River

Philemon

Ref	#	Title
2:9-11	150	Lord Most High
2:15	192	Romans 16:19
3:8	104	I Give You My Heart

Hebrews

Ref	#	Title
1:3	133	Jesus, Lamb of God
1:3	154	Majesty
1:4	170	No Other Name
1:8	25	Blessing and Honor
1:12	73	Great is Thy Faithfulness
2:4	13	All the Power You Need
2:6	200	Someone Special
2:9	154	Majesty
2:14	123	I'm Forever Grateful
3:5	57	Find Us Faithful
3:8	73	Great is Thy Faithfulness
3:14	181	Our Confidence is In the Lord
4:8-9	185	Rest
4:12-13	58	First Love
4:13	109	I Need You
4:14-16	51	Father Me, Again
4:14-16	162	My Faith Looks Up to Thee
4:16	49	Enter In
4:16	77	Grace Alone
4:16	178	Only By Grace
4:16	181	Our Confidence is In the Lord
4:16	246	Your Grace is Sufficient For Me

– p. 49 –

Verse	#	Song		Verse	#	Song
5:5-9	66	Glorify Thy Name		13:12	228	Under the Blood
5:7	216	Then I Will Praise You		13:15	65	Give Thanks
5:8-9	24	Blessed Assurance		13:15	87	Here In This Place
7:25	79	He is Able		13:15	153	Love You So Much
8:10	72	Go, My Children with My Blessing		13:15	234	We Bring the Sacrifice of Praise
9:11-14, 25	49	Enter In		13:15-16	108	I Offer My Life
9:12	98	I Am Not My Own		13:20	245	You Are My Own
9:12, 23-25	28	By Your Blood		13:20-21	80	He Who Began a Good Work in You
9:12-14	127	It's Your Blood				
9:12-14	178	Only By Grace		**James**		
9:12-14	210	The Lamb		1:2-3	113	I Want Jesus to Walk With Me
9:14	21	Beautiful Savior (All My Days)		1:6	24	Blessed Assurance
9:14	179	Only the Blood		1:12	198	Shout to the Lord
9:15	96	How Could You Love Me So Much?		1:17	73	Great is Thy Faithfulness
				1:18	116	I Was There to Hear Your Borning Cry
9:15	136	Jesus, We Celebrate Your Victory		2:5	65	Give Thanks
9:22	127	It's Your Blood		2:23	63	Friend of Sinners
9:22	169	Nothing But the Blood		2:23	237	What a Friend I've Found (...Friend Forever)
9:24-28	178	Only By Grace		2:23	238	What a Friend we Have in Jesus
9:28	199	Someone Else Living in You		3:13-18	192	Romans 16:19
10:7	226	Victory Chant		4:6	61	Foolish Pride
10:19	28	By Your Blood		4:6	197	Shout to the North
10:19	181	Our Confidence is In the Lord		4:8	60	Flowing River
10:19-22	24	Blessed Assurance		4:8	131	Jesus, Draw Me Close
10:19-22	49	Enter In		4:8	207	Take Our Lives
10:19-22	162	My Faith Looks Up to Thee		5:13	24	Blessed Assurance
10:19-23	178	Only By Grace				
10:22	21	Beautiful Savior (All My Days)		**1 Peter**		
10:22	131	Jesus, Draw Me Close		1:2	229	Waterlife
10:22	246	Your Grace is Sufficient For Me		1:3	116	I Was There to Hear Your Borning Cry
11:10	59	Firm Foundation		1:3	229	Waterlife
11:19	79	He is Able		1:3-5	248	You Rescued Me
12:1-2	230	We'll Be Faithful		1:6-9	149	Light the Fire Again
12:2	80	He Who Began a Good Work in You		1:7	184	Purify My Heart
12:2	96	How Could You Love Me So Much?		1:8	7	All Over Again
				1:8	137	Joy and Thanksgiving
12:2	133	Jesus, Lamb of God		1:8	171	Nobody Fills My Heart Like Jesus
12:2	174	Once Again		1:13-15	189	Renew Me
12:2	187	Redeemer Savior Friend		1:18-19	49	Enter In
12:2	243	You Are My All in All		1:18-19	83	Heaven is in My Heart
12:5-13	149	Light the Fire Again		1:18-19	98	I Am Not My Own
12:12	81	He Will Come and Save You		1:18-19	119	I Will Praise Him
12:27-28	217	These Things Are True of You		1:18-19	127	It's Your Blood
12:29	128	It's All About You (Jesus, Lover of My Soul)		1:18-19	139	Lamb of God
				1:18-19	161	More Precious Than Silver
13:1	26	Blest Be The Tie That Binds		1:18-19	169	Nothing But the Blood
13:6	181	Our Confidence is In the Lord		1:18-19	175	Only By the Blood of the Lamb
13:7	57	Find Us Faithful				

– p. 50 –

Verse	#	Song		Verse	#	Song
1:18-19	210	The Lamb		2:9	113	I Want Jesus to Walk With Me
1:18-19	228	Under the Blood				
1:19	94	Holy Lamb of God		3:7-12	76	God Will Make a Way
1:19	179	Only the Blood		3:14	184	Purify My Heart
1:19-20	22	Behold the Lamb		3:18	67	Glory
1:22	60	Flowing River				
1:22	207	Take Our Lives		**1 John**		
1:23	116	I Was There to Hear Your Borning Cry		1:5-8	115	I Want to Walk as a Child of the Light
1:25	76	God Will Make a Way		1:7	119	I Will Praise Him
2:2	160	More of You		1:7	127	It's Your Blood
2:2-3	239	What is This Bread?		1:7	169	Nothing But the Blood
2:4-10	148	Living Stones		1:7	179	Only the Blood
2:4-7	83	Heaven is in My Heart		1:7	184	Purify My Heart
2:5	108	I Offer My Life		2:1-2	28	By Your Blood
2:6	243	You Are My All in All		2:2	22	Behold the Lamb
2:7	161	More Precious Than Silver		2:2	119	I Will Praise Him
2:9	69	Go Out As People of God		2:2	127	It's Your Blood
2:9	72	Go, My Children with My Blessing		2:2	179	Only the Blood
				2:3, 5	125	In the Secret (I Want to Know You)
2:9	171	Nobody Fills My Heart Like Jesus		2:6	115	I Want to Walk as a Child of the Light
2:9	207	Take Our Lives		2:15	20	Be Thou My Vision
2:9	229	Waterlife		2:24, 27	199	Someone Else Living in You
2:21	110	I Want to Be More Like You		3:1	200	Someone Special
2:24	122	I Will Glory in The Cross		3:1-2	51	Father Me, Again
2:24	151	Lord, I Lift Your Name on High		3:1-3	245	You Are My Own
2:25	210	The Lamb		3:2-3	91	Hide Me in Your Holiness
3:8-9	26	Blest Be The Tie That Binds		3:3	184	Purify My Heart
3:18	151	Lord, I Lift Your Name on High		3:9	84	Healer of My Heart
				3:14-19	26	Blest Be The Tie That Binds
3:18	187	Redeemer Savior Friend		3:16	11	Amazing Love
3:21	196	See This Wonder		3:16	55	Feed My Lambs
3:21	229	Waterlife		3:16	110	I Want to Be More Like You
3:21	245	You Are My Own		3:16	187	Redeemer Savior Friend
4:11	66	Glorify Thy Name		3:19-21	24	Blessed Assurance
4:11	67	Glory		3:21	181	Our Confidence is In the Lord
4:14-16	170	No Other Name		3:24	199	Someone Else Living in You
5:3	57	Find Us Faithful		4:4	34	Christ Above Me
5:5	61	Foolish Pride		4:4	199	Someone Else Living in You
5:5	197	Shout to the North		4:7-10	187	Redeemer Savior Friend
5:7	30	Cares Chorus		4:9-10	11	Amazing Love
5:7	202	Spirit Song		4:9-10	152	Lord, You Love Me
5:10-11	67	Glory		4:12-13	199	Someone Else Living in You
5:11	25	Blessing and Honor		4:17	181	Our Confidence is In the Lord
				4:19	7	All Over Again
2 Peter				4:19	82	Hear Me Say I Love You
1:2	3	A Simple Word of Grace		4:19	118	In Moments Like These
1:16-19	112	I See the Lord (Falson)		4:19	152	Lord, You Love Me
1:17	154	Majesty		4:19	168	My Jesus, I Love Thee
1:19	21	Beautiful Savior (All My Days)		4:19	199	Someone Else Living in You
1:19	56	Fill Me		5:1	116	I Was There to Hear Your Borning Cry
				5:2-3	199	Someone Else Living in You

– p. 51 –

Ref	#	Title
5:2-5	58	First Love
5:4-5	136	Jesus, We Celebrate Your Victory
5:4-5	227	Victory Song
5:6, 8	179	Only the Blood
5:14	181	Our Confidence is In the Lord
5:20	217	These Things Are True of You

2 John

Ref	#	Title
1:6	115	I Want to Walk as a Child of the Light

3 John

Ref	#	Title
1:4	115	I Want to Walk as a Child of the Light

Jude

Ref	#	Title
1:20	199	Someone Else Living in You
1:24	72	Go, My Children with My Blessing
1:24	79	He is Able
1:25	25	Blessing and Honor
1:25	67	Glory
1:25	197	Shout to the North

Revelation

Ref	#	Title
1:5, 9	127	It's Your Blood
1:5-6	25	Blessing and Honor
1:6	67	Glory
1:7-8	133	Jesus, Lamb of God
1:8	93	Holy, Holy (…lift up his name)
1:8	128	It's All About You (Jesus, Lover of My Soul)
1:8	129	Jesus is Alive
1:13	112	I See the Lord (Falson)
1:13-14, 16	111	I See the Lord (Baloche)
1:18	25	Blessing and Honor
1:18	31	Celebrate Jesus
2:4	149	Light the Fire Again
2:10	57	Find Us Faithful
2:10	81	He Will Come and Save You
2:17	91	Hide Me in Your Holiness
2:17	121	I Will Change Your Name
3:12	121	I Will Change Your Name
3:14	217	These Things Are True of You
3:15-18	149	Light the Fire Again
3:17-18	210	The Lamb
3:20	34	Christ Above Me
4:8	6	Almighty
4:8	89	Holy Is Our God Medley
4:8	93	Holy, Holy (…lift up his name)
4:8	92	Holy, Holy, Holy Is the Lord of Hosts
4:8	123	I'm Forever Grateful
4:8	180	Open the Eyes of My Heart, Lord
4:8-11	111	I See the Lord (Baloche)
4:9-11	67	Glory
4:11	8	All Honor
4:11	36	Come and See
4:11	94	Holy Lamb of God
4:11	210	The Lamb
4:11	242	Worthy the Lamb that Was Slain
5:3	16	As I Look Into Your Eyes
5:6	139	Lamb of God
5:6	210	The Lamb
5:6, 12-13	22	Behold the Lamb
5:9	94	Holy Lamb of God
5:9	98	I Am Not My Own
5:9	195	Sing Unto the Lord
5:9	228	Under the Blood
5:9	242	Worthy the Lamb that Was Slain
5:9, 12	210	The Lamb
5:9-14	66	Glorify Thy Name
5:12	36	Come and See
5:12	94	Holy Lamb of God
5:12	243	You Are My All in All
5:12	247	You Are Worthy of My Praise
5:12-13	25	Blessing and Honor
5:12-13	68	Glory to the Lamb
5:12-13	226	Victory Chant
5:12-13	242	Worthy the Lamb that Was Slain
5:13	5	All Heaven Declares
5:13	154	Majesty
5:13-14	67	Glory
7:9-10	197	Shout to the North
7:9-10, 17	68	Glory to the Lamb
7:10	5	All Heaven Declares
7:10	244	You Are My Hiding Place
7:10-14	28	By Your Blood
7:10-14	175	Only By the Blood of the Lamb
7:12	65	Give Thanks
7:12	205	The Battle Belongs to the Lord
7:12	242	Worthy the Lamb that Was Slain
7:14	119	I Will Praise Him
7:14	139	Lamb of God
7:14	164	My Dwelling Place
7:14	179	Only the Blood
7:14	210	The Lamb
7:14	228	Under the Blood
7:14	241	White As Snow
7:16	99	I Am the Bread of Life (Talbot)
7:17	43	Comfort Comfort
7:17	82	Hear Me Say I Love You
7:17	202	Spirit Song
7:17	215	The River is Here
7:17	249	You Make Me Lie Down In Green Pastures
10:1	111	I See the Lord (Baloche)
10:1	112	I See the Lord (Falson)
10:9-10	90	Holy and Anointed One
11:15	10	Ancient of Days
11:15	25	Blessing and Honor
11:15	38	Crown Him (King of Kings)
11:15	223	This Kingdom
11:17	21	Beautiful Savior (All My Days)
11:17	93	Holy, Holy (…lift up his name)
12:10	223	This Kingdom
12:10-11	228	Under the Blood
12:11	28	By Your Blood
12:11	175	Only By the Blood of the Lamb
12:11	228	Under the Blood
13:8	22	Behold the Lamb
14:1	210	The Lamb
14:3	195	Sing Unto the Lord
14:7	8	All Honor
14:12	57	Find Us Faithful
14:12	230	We'll Be Faithful
14:13	185	Rest
15:2-3	244	You Are My Hiding Place
15:3	6	Almighty
15:3-4	18	Be Exalted, O God
15:3-4	78	Great and Mighty is He
15:3-4	89	Holy Is Our God Medley
15:3-4	92	Holy, Holy, Holy Is the Lord of Hosts
17:14	22	Behold the Lamb
17:14	38	Crown Him (King of Kings)
17:14	82	Hear Me Say I Love You
17:14	95	Hosanna
17:14	233	We Bow Down
19:1-9	221	Thine the Amen, Thine the Praise
19:6-7	95	Hosanna
19:7	68	Glory to the Lamb
19:7	226	Victory Chant
19:7-9	40	Come to the Bread of Life
19:11	217	These Things Are True of You
19:12	111	I See the Lord (Baloche)
19:16	4	All Hail King Jesus
19:16	38	Crown Him (King of Kings)
19:16	67	Glory
19:16	82	Hear Me Say I Love You
19:16	95	Hosanna
19:16	233	We Bow Down
20:6	4	All Hail King Jesus
20:6	229	Waterlife
21:1-7	221	Thine the Amen, Thine the Praise
21:4	43	Comfort Comfort
21:4	84	Healer of My Heart
21:4	163	Mourning Into Dancing
21:4	202	Spirit Song
21:6	39	Come and Fill Me Up
21:6	37	Come Thou Fount of Every Blessing
21:6	84	Healer of My Heart
21:6	82	Hear Me Say I Love You
21:6	128	It's All About You (Jesus, Lover of My Soul)
21:6	129	Jesus is Alive
21:6	199	Someone Else Living in You
21:6	215	The River is Here
21:23	68	Glory to the Lamb
21:23	132	Jesus, Jesus
21:23-24	115	I Want to Walk as a Child of the Light
21:24	45	Did You Feel the Mountains Tremble?
22:1, 17	199	Someone Else Living in You
22:1-2	82	Hear Me Say I Love You
22:1-2	132	Jesus, Jesus
22:1-2	143	Let the River Flow
22:1-2	215	The River is Here
22:1-6	221	Thine the Amen, Thine the Praise
22:3	5	All Heaven Declares
22:3	68	Glory to the Lamb
22:3	129	Jesus is Alive
22:13	128	It's All About You (Jesus, Lover of My Soul)
22:13	129	Jesus is Alive
22:16	4	All Hail King Jesus
22:16	21	Beautiful Savior (All My Days)
22:17	39	Come and Fill Me Up
22:17	37	Come Thou Fount of Every Blessing
22:17	84	Healer of My Heart
22:17	83	Heaven is in My Heart
22:17	146	Light The Candle
22:17	201	Spirit of the Living God
22:17	221	Thine the Amen, Thine the Praise
22:20	7	All Over Again
22:20	115	I Want to Walk as a Child of the Light
22:20	190	Revival Fire, Fall

Copyright Holders and Administrators

* indicates CCLI listings as of this printing

A'HEARN, REV. BLAIR
1221 Roland Drive
Normal, IL 61761
(309) 827-6121
ahearnblair@hotmail.com

AUGSBURG FORTRESS PRESS
P.O. Box 1209
Minneapolis, MN 55440-1209
(800) 421-0239 or (612) 330-3300
(612) 330-3252 FAX
copyright@augsburgfortress.org

BAUE, REV. FRED AND JEAN
908 Brownell Avenue
St. Louis, MO 63122
(314) 268-1258
Jbaue751@cs.com

BILLY CHRISTOPHER*
P.O. Box 11704
Glendale, AZ 85318-1704
(623) 581-8191
(480) 838-9187 FAX
BillyChristopher@Juno.com

BLS MINISTRIES*
C/o Bobby and Julie Schroeder
15808 Manchester Road
Ellisville, MO 63011
(314) 394-4100, x707
(314) 394-9853
BLSWWJD@aol.com

BRENTWOOD-BENSON MUSIC PUB INC.*
741 Cool Springs Blvd.
Franklin, TN 37067
(615) 742-6800
(615) 261-3386 FAX

CHANGING CHURCH, INC.*
(Prince of Peace Publishing)
200 East Nicollet Blvd.
Burnsville, MN 55337-4521
(952) 435-8102
(952) 898-9371 FAX
www.changingchurch.org

CONCORDIA PUBLISHING HOUSE
3558 South Jefferson Avenue
St. Louis, MO 63118-3968
(314) 268-1000
(314) 268-1329 FAX
copyrights@cph.org

COPYRIGHT CO, THE*
40 Music Square East
Nashville, TN 37203
(615) 244-5588
(615) 244-5591 FAX
thecpyrtco@cs.com

DAVID SIEBELS PRODUCTIONS
3619 W. Magnolia Blvd., S-327
Burbank, CA 91505
(818) 842-8011
(818) 249-9964 FAX
djsmusic@earthlink.net

EMI CHRISTIAN MUSIC PUBLISHING*
P.O. Box 5085
Brentwood, TN 37024-5085
(615) 371-4400
(615) 371-6897 FAX

FAIRHILL MUSIC COMPANY*
P.O. Box 4467
Oceanside, CA 92052-4467
760-806-3672
760-806-3673 FAX
dgraffx@earthlink.net

GABRIEL MUSIC*
P.O. Box 840999
Houston, TX 77284-0999
(281) 463-7785
(281) 855-4466 FAX

GIA PUBLICATIONS, INC.
7404 South Mason Avenue
Chicago, IL 60638
(800) 442-1358
(708) 496-3828 FAX
www.giamusic.com

GIBBONS, LANA
3014 North Deerpass
Marengo, IL 60152
(815) 568-7835
Lanasong@email.com

GLORIA PUBLISHING
1604 Southeast 9th Street
Willmar, MN 56201
(320) 235-2508
(320) 235-2543 FAX
cti@willmar.com

GRINDAL, GRACIA
c/o Luther Seminary
2481 Como Avenue
St. Paul, MN 55108-1496
(651) 641-3230 or (615) 641-3456
(651) 523-1609 FAX

HAL LEONARD (FOR WALTON MUSIC)
P.O. Box 13819
7777 W. Bluemound Road
Milwaukee, WI 53213
414-774-3630; 414-774-3259 FAX
hlcopyright@halleonard.com

HINSHAW MUSIC, INC.
P.O. Box 470
Chapel Hill, NC 27514
(919) 933-1691
(919) 967-3399 FAX
www.hinshawmusic.com

HOPE PUBLISHING COMPANY*
380 South Main Place
Carol Stream, IL 60188
(800) 323-1049
(630) 665-2552 FAX
www.hopepublishing.com

INTEGRITY MUSIC, INC.*
1000 Cody Road
Mobile, AL 36695-3425
(334) 633-9000
(334) 633-5202 FAX
CPRIGHT@INTEGINC.COM

JANZEN, JANET L.
1147 Perry
Wichita, KS 67203
(316) 267-9280
janzej@friends.edu

KEVIN MAYHEW LTD.*
Buxhall, Stowmarket
Suffolk IP14 3BW U.K.
01449 737978
01449 737834 FAX
info@kevinmayhewltd.com

LORENZ CORPORATION, THE
P. O. Box 802
Dayton, OH 45401-0802
(800) 444-1144
(937) 223-2042 FAX
Info@Lorenz.com

MANN, ROBIN
54 Currawong Crescent
Modbury Heights
South Australia 5092 Australia
Phone/Fax 011-61-8-8396-5019
robinman@dove.net.au

MARANATHA! MUSIC*
See COPYRIGHT CO., THE*

MARK ZEHNDER PUBLISHING
14909 Dorcas Circle
Omaha, NE 68144
(402) 333-6464
(402) 697-5128 FAX
Mark@kingofkingsomaha.org

MORNING STAR MUSIC PUBLISHERS
1727 Larkin Williams Road
Fenton, MO 63026
(636) 305-0100
(636) 305-0121 FAX
MorningStar@MorningStarMusic.com

MUSIC SERVICES*
209 Chapelwood Drive
Franklin, TN 37069
(615) 794-9018
(615) 704-0793 FAX
www.musicservices.org

NEW DAWN MUSIC
C/o Oregon Catholic Press
5536 NE Hassalo
Portland, OR 97213-3638
(800) 548-8749 or (503) 281-1191
(503) 282-3486 FAX

OUTREACH MUSIC/WHOLEHEART MUSIC*
Attn: Rev. Richard Oddie
13 Coolaman Court
Mt. Cotton-Brisbane, QLD, 4165 Australia
011-61-7-3829-9508
011-61-7-3209-9840 FAX

PODLICH, REV. AUBREY
2 Matthew Street
Boonah, Queensland 4310 Australia
011-61-7-5463-1194

ROCKSMITH/MANDINA MUSIC*
C/o Trust Music Mgt. Inc.
P.O. Box 22274
Carmel, CA 93922-0274
(831) 626-1030
(831) 626-1026 FAX
ROCKSMITH2@aol.com

ROM ADMINISTRATION*
P.O. Box 1252
Fairhope, AL 36533
334-929-2411
334-929-2404 FAX
romadm@aol.com

SCHMID, MICHAEL A.
1701 Monarch Drive
Napa, CA 94538
(707) 255-0119
(707) 255-3041 FAX
pstrmike@fcs.net

STORYTUNES PUBLISHING*
5250 A Neosho
St. Louis, MO 63109
314-481-7603
314-481-4403 FAX
Jim@godknewyourname.com

SUN DAY PUBLICATIONS
W266 S3867 Donald Drive
Waukesha, WI 53189
(262) 547-8518; (262) 547-8100 FAX

SWANSONG MUSIC, INC.*
3517 South 163rd Street
Omaha, NE 68130-2118
(402) 333-3194
(402) 333-6505 FAX
swansong@radiks.net

TREBLE C MUSIC*
P.O. Box 1754
Glen Burnie, MD 21061
410-553-6351
TrebleCMus@aol.com

VAJDA, REV. JAROSLAV
3534 Brookstone Drive
St. Louis, MO 63129
(314) 892-9473

UNIVERSAL-POLYGRAM INTERNATIONAL
PUBLISHING, INC.
c/o Warner Bros. Publications U.S., Inc.
15800 N.W. 48th Avenue
Miami, FL 33014
(305) 521-1689
(305) 625-3480 FAX

WALTON MUSIC
See Hal Leonard

WINGS OF GRACE, INC. *
Community of Grace Church
15405 Adams Street
Omaha, NE 68137
(402) 896-0808
(402) 896-5444 FAX
HisGrace4U@aol.com

WORD MUSIC, INC.*
C/o Acuff-Rose Music Publishing, Inc.
65 Music Square West
Nashville, TN 37203
(615) 321-5000
(615) 327-0560 FAX

YLVISAKER, JOHN
New Generation Publishers, Inc
P. O. Box 321
Waverly, IA 50677-0321
(319) 352-0765

ZEHNDER, REV. MICHAEL*
Fellowship Ministries
P.O. Box 51510
Phoenix, AZ 85076
(480) 838-8500
(480) 838-9187 FAX
www.thefellowship.com

ZION SONG MUSIC*
P.O. Box 574044
Orlando, FL 32857
(407) 851-7377
(407) 851-7872 FAX
www.zionsong.com

– p. 56 –

Contents - Familiar Titles

#	Title	#	Title
1	A Broken Spirit	48	Eagle's Wings
2	A Shield About Me	44	Emmanuel
3	A Simple Word of Grace	49	Enter In
9	Above All	50	Faithful Father
4	All Hail King Jesus	51	Father Me, Again
5	All Heaven Declares	52	Father Welcomes
8	All Honor	54	Fear Not
7	All Over Again	55	Feed My Lambs
13	All the Power You Need	53	Feed Us Now
6	Almighty	56	Fill Me
11	Amazing Love	57	Find Us Faithful
10	Ancient of Days	59	Firm Foundation
14	Arms of Love	58	First Love
15	As High As the Heaven	60	Flowing River
16	As I Look Into Your Eyes	61	Foolish Pride
12	As the Deer	62	For the Lord is Good
17	At the Cross	63	Friend of Sinners
18	Be Exalted, O God	64	From My Heart to Yours
19	Be My Home	65	Give Thanks
20	Be Thou My Vision	66	Glorify Thy Name
21	Beautiful Savior (All My Days)	67	Glory
22	Behold the Lamb	68	Glory to the Lamb
23	Better is One Day	69	Go Out As People of God
24	Blessed Assurance	70	Go, Make Disciples
25	Blessing and Honor	72	Go, My Children with My Blessing
26	Blest Be The Tie That Binds	71	God is Good
27	Bring Forth the Kingdom	74	God is Good All the Time
28	By Your Blood	75	God is the Strength of My Heart
29	By Your Side	253	God Knew Your Name
30	Cares Chorus	76	God Will Make a Way
31	Celebrate Jesus	77	Grace Alone
32	Celebrate the Lord of Love	78	Great and Mighty is He
33	Change My Heart, O God	73	Great is Thy Faithfulness
34	Christ Above Me	79	He is Able
35	Come and Behold Him	80	He Who Began a Good Work in You
39	Come and Fill Me Up	81	He Will Come and Save You
36	Come and See	84	Healer of My Heart
37	Come Thou Fount of Every Blessing	82	Hear Me Say I Love You
40	Come to the Bread of Life	83	Heaven is in My Heart
41	Come to the Table	85	Here Am I
43	Comfort Comfort	86	Here I Am Lord
38	Crown Him (King of Kings)	87	Here In This Place
42	Cry of My Heart	88	Here is Bread
45	Did You Feel the Mountains Tremble?	91	Hide Me in Your Holiness
		90	Holy and Anointed One
46	Do This In Remembrance of Me	89	Holy Is Our God Medley
47	Draw Me Close to You	94	Holy Lamb of God

– p. 57 –

#	Title
93	Holy, Holy (...lift up his name)
92	Holy, Holy, Holy Is the Lord of Hosts
95	Hosanna
96	How Could You Love Me So Much?
97	How Shall I Call You?
98	I Am Not My Own
99	I Am the Bread of Life (Talbot)
100	I Am the Bread of Life (Toolan)
101	I Believe in Jesus
103	I Could Sing of Your Love Forever
102	I Exalt Thee
104	I Give You My Heart
105	I Live to Know You
106	I Love to Be in Your Presence
107	I Love You, Lord
109	I Need You
108	I Offer My Life
111	I See the Lord (Baloche)
112	I See the Lord (Falson)
113	I Want Jesus to Walk With Me
110	I Want to Be More Like You
114	I Want to Be Where You Are
115	I Want to Walk as a Child of the Light
116	I Was There to Hear Your Borning Cry
117	I Will Celebrate (Baloche)
120	I Will Celebrate (Duvall)
121	I Will Change Your Name
122	I Will Glory in The Cross
119	I Will Praise Him
123	I'm Forever Grateful
118	In Moments Like These
124	In The Heart of God
125	In the Secret (I Want to Know You)
126	Isn't He?
128	It's All About You (Jesus, Lover of My Soul)
127	It's Your Blood
129	Jesus is Alive
131	Jesus, Draw Me Close
132	Jesus, Jesus
133	Jesus, Lamb of God
130	Jesus, Lover of My Soul
134	Jesus, Name Above All Names
136	Jesus, We Celebrate Your Victory
135	Jesus, Your Name
137	Joy and Thanksgiving
138	Knowing You
139	Lamb of God
140	Lead Me to the Cross
141	Let It Be Said Of Us
142	Let the Flame Burn Brighter
143	Let the River Flow
144	Let the Walls Fall Down
147	Lift Him Up
145	Light One Candle
146	Light The Candle
149	Light the Fire Again
148	Living Stones
150	Lord Most High
151	Lord, I Lift Your Name on High
152	Lord, You Love Me
153	Love You So Much
154	Majesty
155	Make Me a Servant
156	May the Feet of God Walk with You
157	Meekness and Majesty
158	Mighty is Our God
159	More Love, More Power
160	More of You
161	More Precious Than Silver
163	Mourning Into Dancing
164	My Dwelling Place
162	My Faith Looks Up to Thee
168	My Jesus, I Love Thee
165	My Life is In You, Lord
166	My Redeemer Lives (Morgan)
167	My Redeemer Lives (Willison)
170	No Other Name
171	Nobody Fills My Heart Like Jesus
169	Nothing But the Blood
172	O Magnify The Lord
173	O The Deep, Deep Love of Jesus
176	On Eagle's Wings
174	Once Again
178	Only By Grace
175	Only By the Blood of the Lamb
179	Only the Blood
177	Only You
180	Open the Eyes of My Heart, Lord
181	Our Confidence is In the Lord
183	Peace Be Yours
182	Praise Adonai
184	Purify My Heart
186	Raise Up an Army
187	Redeemer Savior Friend
188	Remember Me
189	Renew Me
185	Rest
190	Revival Fire, Fall
191	Rock of Ages
193	Rock of My Salvation
192	Romans 16:19
194	Savior Again to Your Dear Name
196	See This Wonder
204	Shine, Jesus Shine
198	Shout to the Lord
197	Shout to the North
195	Sing Unto the Lord
199	Someone Else Living in You
200	Someone Special
201	Spirit of the Living God
202	Spirit Song
203	Spirit, Touch Your Church
206	Take My Life and Let It Be
207	Take Our Lives
208	Thank You, Lord
205	The Battle Belongs to the Lord
209	The Heart of Worship
210	The Lamb
212	The Name of the Lord (Blessed Be)
213	The Potter's Hand
214	The Power of Your Love
215	The River is Here
216	Then I Will Praise You
211	There is A Redeemer
218	There is None Like You
217	These Things Are True of You
221	Thine the Amen, Thine the Praise
222	Think About His Love
220	This is the Day (Fitts)
219	This is the Day (Shelton)
223	This Kingdom
225	Tis So Sweet to Trust in Jesus
224	Trading My Sorrows
228	Under the Blood
226	Victory Chant
227	Victory Song
229	Waterlife
231	We Are an Offering
232	We Are Marching in the Light of God
233	We Bow Down
234	We Bring the Sacrifice of Praise
236	We Remember You
230	We'll Be Faithful
237	What a Friend I've Found (...Friend Forever)
238	What a Friend we Have in Jesus
239	What is This Bread?
240	When I Look into Your Holiness
235	When I Survey the Wondrous Cross
241	White As Snow
242	Worthy the Lamb that Was Slain
243	You Are My All in All
244	You Are My Hiding Place
245	You Are My Own
247	You Are Worthy of My Praise
249	You Make Me Lie Down In Green Pastures
248	You Rescued Me
251	Your Everlasting Love
246	Your Grace is Sufficient For Me
250	Your Love
252	Your Touch is Loving

INDEXES

Introduction to the Indexes and Layout	1
Key and Tempo Index	2-5
Topical Index	6-26
Scripture References Index	27-53
Copyright Holders/Administrators	54-56
Contents – Familiar Titles	57-59

The NIV Worship Bible
from Maranatha! Publishing™ and Zondervan Publishing House

Saint Ambrose said, "As in Paradise, God walks in the Holy Scriptures, seeking man." This profound insight leads us to the question: When God finds me in the Holy Scriptures, what will I say to Him?

The NIV Worship Bible will help you express your personal worship response to your encounters with God in Scripture.

The unique aspect of this Bible is that the notes do not interact with you, the reader. Instead, they interact with God through prayer. On every page of Scripture you will find prayers that will become launching points for your own personal worship.

The special features of The NIV Worship Bible include:

- *Hear My Prayer*: 1800 meditative prayers written in response to specific passages of Scripture provide a model for your own expression of worship.
- *Quotations*: 1000 thought-provoking quotes from history's great worshipers and church leaders, from Saint Augustine to Philip Yancey, to inspire your worship.
- *Song Lyrics*: 800 familiar hymns and contemporary worship songs that correspond to the Scripture text and the *Hear My Prayer* features.
- *My Beloved™*: 36 full-page "personal letters" from God. These are paraphrased collections of Scripture designed to help you discover God's heart toward you.
- *Book Introductions*: The book introductions prepare you for your encounter with God by pointing out how God uniquely reveals Himself in each book. They also give direction to your worship experience by highlighting key worship passages.

Pastors, worship leaders and small group leaders will find the prayers, quotes and song texts to be helpful materials in planning meaningful worship services.

BINIVWORBL	Burgundy, bonded leather	$52.99
BINIVWORHC	Hard Cover	$32.99
BIBIVWORSC	Soft Cover	$24.99

TO PLACE YOUR ORDER: www.maranathamusic.com 800-245-SONG

Fellowship Ministries

Over 25 years of serving the church with vital resources for the advancement of the Gospel through Worship, Music, & Evangelism

Your Partner In Worship Ministry!

Check out our web site for the most current list of conferences and products to help you in your Worship Ministry!
www.thefellowship.com

Created to Praise Conferences and Workshops

Worship Leaders, Musicians, Pastors, Technicians, Choral Directors, Praise Bands, Drama Teams, Spiritual Growth Seekers--these conferences are for you! *Created to Praise Conferences* are now in their eighth year. Thousands have attended these 2 to 4 day conferences, experiencing hands-on training, in-depth workshops, resource networking and personal spiritual growth.

Past speakers/leaders/musicians have included: *Marty Nystrom, Paul Baloche, Bob Fitts, Gerrit Gustafson, Randy Rothwell, Steve Bowersox, Kent Hunter, Custer & Hoose, Robert Webber, Steve Green, Leith Anderson, Larnelle Harris...and many more!*

Worship ALIVE!

Need help in worship planning? *Worship ALIVE!* is a weekly contemporary worship service planning tool for churches that plan topic-based or lectionary-based worship services. Each setting gives you choices between traditional and cutting edge music--such as the songs in this songbook, drama, responsive readings, sermon ideas and illustrations, children's worship ideas, multimedia resources and more! Now in it's 9th year, *Worship ALIVE!* is flexible, seeker-sensitive, and cross-generational. Available in hard copy or computer diskette.

ChapelTime Videos

Is someone you love in a nursing home, or in hospice care, or a shut-in? Here's a meaningful ministry product especially made for our older adults. Try the new *ChapelTime Devotional Video Series!* It's a collection of **9** devotionals on **3-set video**, recorded live at the Good Shepherd Retirement Center in Sun City, AZ. Each 15-minute segment weaves three familiar hymns and gospel songs with a devotional based on the Psalms. It is sure to delight and minister to your seniors and give them the assurance of God's presence and love for them.

And a variety of more Worship & Music products!

Fellowship Ministries has CD's, cassettes, songbooks, and other materials to help you plan your worship! Check out *The Other Songbook, Volume One* and the *Just For Kids Songbook* and its companion products which include split-track CD or cassette and musician's large-print book!

To contact *Fellowship Ministries*
Call: 480-838-8500 • Fax: 480-838-9187 • www.thefellowship.com
P.O. Box 51510 • Phoenix, AZ 85076